Conversations
with
Nostradamus
His Prophecies Explained

*(Revised with
Addendum: 1996)*

Volume 1

BY

DOLORES CANNON

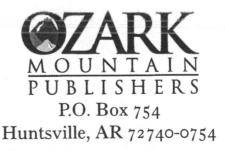

OZARK
MOUNTAIN
PUBLISHERS
P.O. Box 754
Huntsville, AR 72740-0754

For permission, or serialization, condensation, adaptations, or for our catalog of other publications, write to Ozark Mountain Publishing, Inc., P.O. Box 754, Huntsville, AR 72740 Attn: Permission Department.

Library of Congress Cataloging-in-publication Data
Cannon, Dolores, 1931-2014
Conversations with Nostradamus by Dolores Cannon
    Communication from Nostradamus via several mediums through hypnosis, supervised by Dolores Cannon. Includes the Prophecies of Nostradamus, in Middle French with English translation. Includes Index.
1. Nostradamus, 1503-1566. 2. Prophecies. 3. Hypnosis 4. Reincarnation therapy. 5. Astrology.
I. Cannon, Dolores, 1931-2014 ll. Nostradamus, 1503-1566, Prophecies English & French. III. Title

Library of Congress Catalog Card Number: 96-092695
ISBN: 1-886940-00-2
First Edition printed by American West Publishers, 1989.
Revised Edition published, 1992; Second printing, 1994.
New Edition with Addendum, 1997; Second printing, 2001
Cover Design: Joe Alexander. Computer enhancement: Jenelle Johannes.
Book set in: Old Style 7, San Marco & Eurostile typefaces.
Book Design: Kris Kleeberg
Published by.

P.O. Box 754
Huntsville AR 72740
WWW.OZARKMT.COM
Printed in the United States of America

Dedication

To Elena, Brenda and John,
who helped me discover the portal of time
and pulled me through to the incredible dimension
where Nostradamus is still living.

Drawing of Nostradamus, as seen by Elena in trance.

Table of Contents

Foreword

THE NAME DOLORES CANNON may not be familiar to many readers, yet she has been working in the field of hypnotic regression for many years. Dolores is not a scholar, yet she has a scholar's devotion to detail, precision, and the truth. She is tireless in her pursuit of knowledge as her readers will come to know when they have followed her relentless path through the labyrinth of the human mind and spirit. It's not surprising that she has gained a wide following among the *cognoscenti,* her investigative peers in the paranormal. In Dolores' house, as you will see, there are many mansions.

I met Dolores a couple of years ago, and she told me of the work she was doing. She didn't claim to understand the full import of the material she gleaned from her subjects while they were under hypnosis. She didn't profess to know all the answers, yet with singular open-mindedness, she believed that those spirits who claimed to be speaking to her through the mouths of living people could possibly be real entities, outside our time perhaps, existing on a different plane than ours.

As one familiar with hypnosis, I was most interested in hearing what Ms. Cannon had to say. I had learned hypnotic technique many years ago from a famous doctor in Florida. Later, I had the privilege to work with one of the foremost pioneers in clinical hypnosis, William S. Kroger, M.D. of Beverly Hills.

I questioned Dolores closely on her techniques and was convinced she was not leading her subjects while they were under her guidance, nor furnishing any of the material that came to light under hypnosis. I listened to several tapes very carefully, looking for any missteps or questionable methodology. I found she was extremely careful not to guide the subjects nor to prompt them. If anything, she was most diligent in standing to the side and letting the material come through untainted by her questions. She did not offer answers, theories, probabilities or suppositions. Rather, she let the subject lead her through the sessions with those other voices in other rooms.

Dolores Cannon is a serious practitioner of the hypnotic art, and is especially skilled in the techniques of regression. I asked to read some portion of one of her manuscripts. She sent it to me and I was impressed with the material she had discovered. It seemed to me she was somewhat amazed by both the material and the way it had come to light. Her material was fascinating, to say the least, and very well organized.

There were good reasons for her being startled by what her subjects had to say while under hypnosis. I questioned her about these subjects. Many were rural housewives, born of farming families, with very little education. These were people one would not consider intellectuals. Thus, the material seemed more impressive than if it had emerged from someone who was familiar with studies of the paranormal.

Dolores knew that she had some exciting material. She is a very good writer. She writes clearly and cleanly of extraordinary matters. I believe her work gains an even greater stature when you consider what she has done to verify the undocumented source material. Unlike other hypnotists who discover some startling fact or body of knowledge during hypnotic sessions, she did not rush into print with her findings. Nor did she make premature judgments regarding her discoveries. Rather, she crosschecked the material she dredged up from the subconscious, attempting, as much as possible, to substantiate verifiable facts obtained from her subjects. She did this in two ways.

When a "spirit" spoke from another time, such as the witness to the holocaust of Hiroshima, Dolores researched the facts through published sources. This gave her valuable insight into her evaluation of the material. But, with a stroke of brilliance, she went even further. She began to explore the same timespan and past-life experiences (or knowledge) with other subjects; none of whom knew one another, were aware of the other material, and did not even live in the same town or region as the prime source subject.

Her subjects, it must be noted, come from all walks of life. Some are more educated than others, college students as well as blue collar. Some are wealthy, and some are living on the margin of the poverty level. I am sure that someday her public will want to know more about these people who are anonymous, of course, and must remain so. Dolores, however, has fully documented all of her sessions, taken notes, preserved her private comments, and archived her tapes.

More than that, Dolores has delved into histories, poured over maps, and retrieved material that seems to bolster the dialogues of people who lived many years ago and are now speaking to us through subjects who have no knowledge of those ages or the peoples who lived in those ancient times.

This brings us to Nostradamus.

As far as I know, Dolores Cannon had never read a quatrain of Nostradamus and knew virtually nothing about the man or his prophecies prior to discovering him while regressing a subject to a previous life. When the material began coming through her subjects, although the temptation was great, she did not do any research about the man and his writing until the project was completed. In her books, which deal with this fascinating historical figure's prophecies, Dolores is careful to delineate the matters that came out through the hypnotic regression of her subjects and what she has learned through her outside research.

Nostradamus has intrigued scholars and curious people for centuries. His quatrains, though arcane, seem to invite deeper investigation, for he claimed to be a man who could see into the future. Over the years scholars have attempted to explain his obscure poems of prophecy, written in archaic French, Latin and other languages, his allusions to events that have occurred since his lifetime and will occur in the future, even beyond the 20th century.

Briefly, the man we call Nostradamus was a physician and an astrologer. He was French, born in Saint Remi, Provence, in 1503. He studied at both Avignon and Montpellier, and became quite a skilled physician. His real name was Michel de Notredame, but as his interest in astrology grew, he Latinized his name and became known, thereafter, as Nostradamus.

He achieved widespread renown for his treatment of plague victims, particularly in southern France. He worked tirelessly in Aix and Lyons in 1545 when the plague attained epidemic proportions in those cities.

It was during this time of death that Nostradamus began to attract attention as a seer, a man who claimed he could predict the future. Ten years later, in 1555, he published a collection of his prophecies in rhymed quatrains. He called the book *Centuries.*

His talent as an astrologer was widely known and in demand among the upper classes. None other than Catherine de' Medici, Queen of France, invited him to her court. There, he cast the horoscopes of her sons.

When Charles IX accessed the throne, he appointed Nostradamus as court physician. The man who came to be known as Nostradamus died in 1566, when he was 63 years old. Remarkably, he lived longer than many of his countrymen, and he achieved a kind of immortality through the publication of his prophetic quatrains. He was a mysterious man in his own time and remains so to this day.

Dolores Cannon, however, has shed considerable light on the man and his prophecies through her work and the books now being published as a result of that work.

We do not understand time. Time is one of the great mysteries of this universe. Einstein said time was curved, and the universe itself was curved. Yet the universe is also infinite, without beginning or end. How can this be? Perhaps, as Dolores' findings reveal, Nostradamus is not dead, but, as he seems to be, alive and well in his own linear time. Gone perhaps from our time, but existing still, eternally, in that never-ending, never-the-same river we call time. If you step into this river, it flows on, and further down the mountain it becomes another river and is different, yet the same. The water changes, yet it is still water, and the water we stepped in that has gone on, still exists in a dimension beyond our vision.

Perhaps Nostradamus was able to penetrate the immutable and unfathomable fabric of time and the universe. Perhaps he was able to see through cracks in the warp of eternity and predict the future.

Dolores' revelations are astonishing. During Nostradamus's time, he tells her through a go-between in trance, he had to shroud his quatrains in obscure allusion because of political ramifications. That is, he feared for his life if he wrote too clearly of the events he "saw." He seems, as Dolores' books relate, to have been able to see clearly those crumbling empires, defeats in battle, holocausts, invasions, revolutions, diseases, and other horrors that would inflict man for centuries. It must have been a terrible cross for a sensitive man to bear. Now, it seems, there is an even greater urgency that his prophecies be understood. We are faced with the dire prospect of a nuclear winter, and the HIV virus, AIDS, has raised its hideous head, not unlike the plagues that Nostradamus fought so honorably and bravely in his own time.

It is my pleasure to introduce the works of Dolores Cannon to you. Whether you believe in her discoveries or not, you will be impressed with her ability to gather complex material from a number of ordinary subjects and present it with illuminating clarity.

I believe we must continue to forge ahead with our investigations of man and his universe if we are to survive, if our planet is to survive. Dolores Cannon may well be one of the important keys to our understanding of those areas science is too fearful to explore, at least out in the open.

She does not claim to have any special gifts. I believe that she does, however. Dolores Cannon has an enquiring mind and considerable skill as a hypnotist. Beyond that, she is sincere and compassionate, mindful of her subjects' right to privacy and sensitivity.

Ultimately, Dolores Cannon's works, I hope, will lead to further scientific investigation into seemingly inexplicable phenomena such as she uncovers and reveals in her books. We know there is more to life than we can see with our mortal eyes. We know that not only is the universe more complicated than we imagine, it is more profound and complex than we can imagine.

If nothing else, Dolores Cannon has opened up still another door to this vast and mysterious universe. Walk right in. I think you will learn something that might be important to you. In this house of hers, there are indeed, many mansions.

Jory Sherman, Author
Cedarcreek, Missouri
1989

Preface

Nostradamus has broken through the barriers of time and space and spoken to our present day. This book and its sequels contain two remarkable stories. The first is the adventure of how the contact with the great psychic was made. The second is the legacy he wanted to reveal to our world. In retrospect it all seems impossible. But since it has occurred and cannot be denied, then we must try to analyze what we have been shown and try to learn from it. Through time immortal man has been curious about his future. In all the histories of the world there have always been oracles, magicians, shamans, and seers, using innumerable methods to warn the various civilizations of events to come. Why does man have this preoccupation with knowing the future? When a prediction is made, do we accept it with a resigned sense of doom and gloom, thinking it is set and therefore unchangeable? That would be a very morbid reason for wanting to know our destinies. Or do we want to know in the hope that this knowledge can allow us to change what is predicted? Without hope and free will, man is nothing but a puppet, with no control over his life. Nostradamus believed, as I do, in the theory of probable futures, of nexus on the lines of time with many possible courses branching off in all directions. He believed that if man had knowledge he could see which time line his future was headed down and reverse it before it was too late. He believed that without this knowledge man was nothing more than a piece of driftwood being tossed about at the whim of the waves. Many of the prophecies that Nostradamus revealed to us are filled with depressing horror and paint a very bleak picture of our future. But he said, "If I show you the most horrible things you can do to yourself, will you do something to change it?" These books are intended for the open-minded who can think about the events coming to pass and have a different way of looking at them. To be able to see that time is malleable, the future is not set, that the paths are many and it is our choice which one we choose to travel upon.

I believe Nostradamus did not want his prophecies to come true. He did not have the ego of wanting to be proven right. He wanted us to negate the horror he saw, and to prove him wrong. This is the greatest reward any psychic can have, that his disastrous prophecies do not come true.

Dolores Cannon

Section One

The Contact

Chapter 1

Message from a Guide

NOSTRADAMUS. Even his very name carries with it the aura of mystery. Who was he, really? The greatest prophet that ever lived or the greatest charlatan? Could he really foresee the future or did he just write in unintelligible form in order to confuse and keep man guessing? Perhaps he was all of these things, but one thing for certain, he was the greatest author of enigmatic puzzles that ever lived. To keep mankind interested and trying to solve his riddles for over four hundred years was no easy task. But maybe if he had not written in riddles his work would not have survived. If he had written his prophecies in simple, unmistakable language, he might have been declared a madman in league with the Devil, and been burned at the stake and his work along with him. If he truly was a great prophet he deliberately made his work obscure so that man's inquisitive nature would continue to attempt to decipher his meanings until the event came to pass. Hindsight is wonderful. Translators of his work can usually see what he was trying to predict *after* the event has occurred.

Nostradamus lived in France in the 1500s. He wrote his prophecies in quatrains which are four-lined poems. There are almost a thousand of them. Each quatrain was supposed to pertain to a specific event, but they were made difficult because of his inserting Latin and other obscure words into the Old French of his time. He also loved to use symbolism, anagrams and play-on-words. An anagram is a word that becomes another word by changing the order of the letters and even adding or omitting letters. It is quite popular with puzzle fans and it is generally agreed that Nostradamus used anagrams liberally in his predictions, especially when referring to proper names.

There are also experts that claim that many of his quatrains are nonsense and impossible to solve. They say that any resemblance to events that did occur were merely coincidences. They claim that the man merely played a gigantic hoax that has continued to perplex man all these years and that Nostradamus should be enjoying a good laugh that he has succeeded in fooling people for such a long time. Prophet or charlatan, he has continued to spark interest and will continue to do so as long as man loves a challenge and a mystery.

When my adventure began I probably knew only as much about this man as anyone else. Because I have been interested in psychic phenomenon for many years, I have read about him and I have seen the TV special, *The Man Who Saw Tomorrow*, narrated by Orson Wells. Nostradamus was primarily a doctor and was an enigma in his own time because of his ability to provide cures that the other doctors could not begin to accomplish. I had never studied his quatrains. Who would want to? They are too complicated. From the limited amount that I knew of him, I was inclined to think that he was ahead of his own time and probably could foresee events in the future. I believe that he could not understand what he saw and thus used symbolism, as is used in the Bible (especially in the prophetic vision in Revelation) to describe his visions.

Although I have always admired the man, I never in my wildest dreams could have conceived the idea of meeting him or of working as an instrument in the translation of his mysterious prophecies. As a regressionist I have had some exciting adventures in time and space through hypnotism by reliving history through the past lives of my subjects. But the idea of working with Nostradamus or even finding anything out about him had never even once entered my mind.

The adventure began with deceptive innocence and simplicity. I routinely attend meetings of people who are interested in psychic phenomenon and metaphysical topics. I go to several of these each month and I feel that being around others of kindred spirit recharges my battery. It is always good to be with others who share similar interests. The freedom to speak on such strange topics without fear of recrimination is wonderful.

It was at one of these meetings in 1985 that I first met Elena, a very attractive dark-haired woman in her forties. I can still remember the first night that she and her daughter entered the room looking like two lost sheep. This group was engaged in studying the Seth material which can become quite complicated. Elena had sat quietly with wide eyes listening to everything that was said and obviously understanding nothing. She said later that she had come solely out of curiosity and felt like she had just stepped out of kindergarten into college. She could not even understand the simplest metaphysical terms that we used. But instead of being discouraged she continued to attend. She enjoyed the friendliness and openness of the others and wanted to learn more about these things.

At the time, all I knew about her was that she was helping to run a restaurant in the nearby resort town, and was a portrait-artist in her spare time. I was later to learn that she was the mother of ten children, most of whom were grown and on their own. She married at such an early age that she did not complete high school. One of her daughters was a deaf-mute and Elena had learned sign language in order to communicate with her. Elena was raised as a Catholic but in later years did not feel that religion held the answers she was seeking. At that time she began searching the dogmas of different Protestant sects looking for one that felt comfortable to her. She said the Mormon religion came the closest to what she could believe would happen to a person after death. Traveling extensively and living in many places, she and her family had only recently moved to our area from Alaska. She possessed a delightfully warm and loving personality. Elena worked long and hard at the restaurant and caring for her family, and she often seemed very tired when she attended the meeting. I believed her interest must have been genuine or she would have gone straight home to rest. She also had an avid curiosity and felt no shyness as she asked many questions trying to understand this newfound interest, psychic phenomenon. The group encouraged her and wanted to help her learn.

In time we learned that although Elena was not familiar with the technicalities of psychic phenomenon, she was really no stranger to it. In the late sixties she had experienced a *NDE* (Near Death Experience). She had a tubular pregnancy that ruptured filling her abdomen with internal bleeding.

She described the experience, "I remember going into the operating room, and I was thinking, 'Oh, my God, I'm still awake!' I could hear the voices of the doctors and nurses on either side of me. Then I felt a *tremendous* pain, and I rose above the voices. I heard everything that was going on but I didn't feel bad anymore. Then off in the distance I saw this white light and I started to go toward it. At that moment it was just like a huge hand reached out and pulled me back into my body. It was the most horrible feeling, I mean, the *pain* of being pulled back in. And more pain as I got closer into the body."

When she was awake and able to communicate, she startled the doctor by saying, "You know, that was a terrible thing for the nurse to say, 'I don't think she's going to make it,' and there I was wide awake."

The confused doctor asked her how she knew that. Had someone told her what the nurse had said? Elena replied emphatically that she had heard the nurse say it in the operating room. The doctor shook his head and said, "There's no way you could have heard her, you were completely out. You weren't even conscious when we brought you into the emergency room."

She had truly been very close to death because her husband told her the doctor had said he didn't think she would make it. This experience must have shaken the doctor's belief system because he was aggravated and tried for days afterward to disprove Elena's story. He even brought in the nurse and confronted her. He tried to convince her that it was impossible for her to have heard what she claimed. But Elena would not be swayed. She did not understand what had happened but no one could convince her that it had not happened.

The medical personnel were amazed at the speed of her recovery, but they believed she would never be able to have another child. Such news did not discourage Elena. She and her husband applied to adopt another deaf child to raise with her own handicapped daughter. Before the papers could go through she found that her own private miracle had occurred. She was pregnant with her tenth and last child.

NDEs did not become common knowledge until the 1970s when Dr. Elisabeth Kubler-Ross and Dr. Raymond Moody did their research into this phenomenon and wrote the book *Life After Life*. During that time Elena read about some of these cases in a tabloid. She was excited to find that hers was not a unique experience. She remembered waving the paper and shouting to her family, "Lookit, this has actually happened to somebody else." She had needed no verification during all those years, but the fact that others had experienced strange events opened the door to the possibility of psychic phenomenon.

At this time there were several people in the group that wanted to experience hypnotic regression into past lives and I scheduled appointments. I always felt that a good subject might come from this group but up to this time they had only experienced normal, average trance states. This group's interest in metaphysics did not increase the odds or change the patterns I have observed so many times in the past.

I never know what I am looking for until I find it. I was working with several good subjects and receiving much information but I am always on the lookout for another somnambulist. This is the type of subject that is the most useful for my research work because of their ability to go into such a deep trance that they transform completely into the other personality. They are hard to find, but I believe my odds have been greater because I work with so many people. Little did I know that the one who would emerge from the group and plunge me headlong into this new adventure would be the mature, quiet, and inquisitive Elena.

I know that the story I shall tell of my association with Nostradamus will sound so unbelievable that many skeptics will say fraud is the only explanation. But I know that with all the demands on her time as a busy wife, mother, and wage earner, there was no inclination for Elena to try to invent an elaborate hoax. Meeting with the group became one of the rare diversions in her busy schedule, but her family always seemed to come first.

When she saw that the others were making appointments for regression sessions, she asked if she could try it too. Her motive was purely curiosity; she just wanted to see what it would feel like to be hypnotized. Up until she joined the group her reading had consisted entirely of horror fiction, Stephen King-type books. She was now anxious to learn about psychic phenomenon but knew very little about reincarnation. She said she certainly had never entertained the idea of having lived before.

In her first session I was surprised at the ease with which she entered a deep somnambulistic trance. She completely dispelled the theory that subjects will play it safe and only report a life in an area that they are familiar with. She came into a scene with such strange surroundings that I had no idea where she was. I can usually identify the locale through questioning about buildings, clothes, living conditions, and surroundings, but the buildings were of a type that I had never heard of. She described the life of a merchant in a strange land where the bodies of dead monks lined the walls of the Buddhist temple. The man died when a suspended rope bridge collapsed into a ravine. Later when she awakened she drew a sketch of the buildings since this first view was the only thing she remembered from the entire regression. They appeared Oriental but did not suggest Japan or China.

Elena proved during this first session to be an excellent somnambulist subject, so I conditioned her with a keyword to eliminate the time-consuming induction if we were ever to work together again. I have had keywords work successfully even as long as a year after they have been given. The subconscious accepts them as easily as if they had been given yesterday.

Up until this first session Elena had had no experience with any type of altered state, and she was very excited about the results of the regression.

Since I am always looking for successful somnambulists, I wanted to work further with her in addition to the others I was obtaining information from. She was willing if she could arrange it into her busy schedule. In the months that followed, this turned out to be the biggest problem. Because her family was very important to her, she often cancelled sessions at the last minute due to things going on in her personal life. This under-scored the fact that the metaphysics group and the hypnotic regressions were not a compulsive, consuming part of her life. On the contrary, they were almost incidental. She felt she had found a new important belief system but it did not take priority in her life. Her family and her job took up most of her time.

On the day of our second appointment, I arrived at the restaurant around closing time. Since she did not drive, I intended to take her to her house after work for a session before her husband and children would arrive and require her attention. The restaurant was still full of people. She explained that a sudden influx of tourists meant they would have to remain open for another hour or so and by that time it would be too late for a session. Since I am never at a loss to find people to regress, I intended to leave and call some of the others who were on the waiting list.

But she firmly grabbed my arm and led me to a booth. "Please stay for a while," she begged. "Something very strange has happened. I've got to talk about it. Just wait till I get some of these people served." The expression on her face and her tone of voice seemed so serious that I agreed. For about a half an hour I sat sipping a coke and watching as she bustled busily back and forth from the kitchen, occasionally flashing me a smile to assure me that it was important.

Finally there was a lull and hastily she wiped her hands on her apron and sat down across from me. Grasping my hand in both of hers, she said with great excitement, "I'm glad you waited. I can't hold this in any longer. I've had such a strange experience. Nothing like it has ever happened before in my life."

She explained that the incident had occurred a few nights before as she was going to sleep. She knew she was still awake when she became aware of the figure of a man standing beside her bed. A situation that would normally cause fright, but instead she felt a serene calmness. The figure identified himself as Andy, her guide.

"You've got to understand," she said, "that nothing like this has ever happened to me before. I don't even know what a guide is and I sure don't know anyone named Andy."

I patiently explained that from my work I have found that everyone has a guide and sometimes more than one assigned to them before their birth. These are sometimes called "guardian angels," and their purpose is to help us on our journey through life. She could accept that because it was a reasonable explanation, especially since it harmonized with her Catholic upbringing. But what confused her even more was what he told her.

"He said it was most important that I keep working with you. Then he gave me a message for you." For me? That was certainly a surprise. "It doesn't make sense to me, but he said that you would understand. He said that your books must be published, that you must not give up. He said that there were also others on that side who were concerned that you might be losing hope and getting discouraged. They want you to know that the books are extremely important."

This was an odd experience because I did not know Elena very well at that time and I had not discussed my writing with her. She knew nothing about my books, what they were about or the problems I was having getting them into the hands of publishers. She also did not know about a recent set of discouraging developments that was causing me to despair of ever getting them published. I knew I would not give up, but at this point I felt so alone and had been hoping for at least one little sign of encouragement that my work would not be in vain. Maybe this was that sign. It had to be valid because Elena was only conveying a message she did not understand. That was what confused her, because she did not really know the meaning of the message but felt compelled to pass it along to me. If it had been for anyone else she would have been hesitant about telling them for fear of ridicule.

She sighed with relief as I told her I understood. "I realize that the books are important and I want them to be published, but *I* am not the problem. The problem is finding a publisher and I seem to have reached a dead-end on that."

She had no answer to that because the solution was not part of the message. It was only meant as one of hope and encouragement. This was my first experience with something of this type. Maybe the first hypnotic session had opened her psychic awareness more than we had thought. She said she seriously wanted to expand her psychic abilities and had been practicing meditation which she had never done before. Maybe she had a natural receptivity that was beginning to come forth. Whatever caused the strange experience, I was glad that it had not frightened her. If that had happened, she might have immediately shut off any more excursions into the unknown and our adventure would most certainly never have materialized.

IT WAS SEVERAL WEEKS before Elena was finally able to find time in her busy schedule for a hypnotic regression. The session was held at her home with one of her teen-age daughters present. I used the keyword and watched as she quickly and effortlessly entered into a deep trance. Then I directed her to go to a lifetime that was important to her. I often do this when the subject has no specific desire to find out about the source of phobias, problems or karmic relationships with others in their life. Instead of waiting for something to come through at random, I direct them to open the file on a life that has some importance in relation to this life they are presently living. Often some amazing insights are discovered this way.

When I finished counting Elena found herself as a man looking at a large fieldstone wall which enclosed a big city. She was then walking down a street within the city. By her facial expressions I could tell that she was disturbed by something. I asked if anything was bothering her and she answered, "I have to go see the teacher." When I asked for more information, she became more disturbed and hesitated to talk about it. A silent battle seemed to be raging within her. Knowing this was something she couldn't talk about, yet desiring to share it with me. There were long pauses. Her answers were short and sprinkled with a sense of uneasy suspicion as though she was unsure if she should even be speaking about this at all.

I tried to reassure her. I have run into this type of situation before. It usually happens when there is some kind of secrecy involved. Either the person belongs to a private or mysterious organization, they are involved in something esoteric or it is something they simply cannot talk about. Quite often, as in my work with the Essene teacher in my book, *Jesus and the Essenes,* and my work with ancient Druids, they have been sworn to secrecy and cannot reveal these things to anyone, often under pain of death. No matter how much they want to answer my questions, in a case like this I am asking them to go against their basic moral structure of that lifetime. Often I can get around it by tactful questioning or trying to inspire trust. But there have been times when nothing could penetrate this type of shell. I suspected this was such a case by Elena's eye movements, facial expressions, and hesitant answers.

When I asked about the teacher, all she would say was that he was a very learned man who had to teach in secret. The tone of her voice told me that she considered even revealing this much was a betrayal. I tried to reassure her that I understood her reasons for being careful and attempted to get more information. There was a long pause when I asked if he would be in danger if she talked about him. She was trying to decide whether or not to answer. This procedure was very tedious for me. Although she was definitely in a somnambulistic state, her answers were coming very slowly with carefully measured caution. Her voice was very soft-spoken and relaxed. This made what happened next even more unexpected.

There was a pause after my last question, then a confident, booming voice abruptly burst forth addressing me by name. "Dolores! This is Andy. I am Elena's guide. She's not ready for this yet!" I was so startled that I almost dropped the microphone.

To say I was surprised is putting it mildly. I am used to the unexpected when I work, but this took me completely off guard. I remembered Elena had said that the apparition that had appeared by her bed to deliver the message to me had called himself Andy. Whether I was dealing here with her real guide, guardian or with her subconscious, the tone of voice was so authoritative that I thought it best not to argue with it. This personality was speaking at a normal rate and was very confident. Even if it was her subconscious, it obviously had her welfare at heart so I was sure no danger would be done by conversing with "it." I assured it that if Elena was not yet ready, we could back off quite easily, even though I had not seen anything in what we were discussing that I considered a problem.

He continued, "She's confused. And while this life with Nostradamus has happened for her, she's not quite ready to look at it yet."

Nostradamus? What did he mean? Had Elena experienced a lifetime with the great psychic?

A glance at her daughter showed that she was even more confused than I was to hear such strange things coming out of her mother. All I could do was shrug my shoulders. After all, I was supposed to be controlling the session even though I had no idea what was happening. I always use the white light of protection, but I wanted to make sure this entity was only trying to help her.

D: *I want you to realize that her welfare is my main concern. It's very important to me that she be guarded and taken care of.*

E: Oh, yes! I know that. We are very pleased with the way you treat your subjects. This is why we like to work with you, you are so protective. I have tried to do this before. She's stubborn, but she's ... she's going to be good. *(The voice sounded like a mother reprimanding a child.)*

D: *Maybe later, when she's ready for it, we could examine this life that she started into.*

There wasn't time to ponder any of this as I was being instructed to take her elsewhere for the time being. This was the first time something like this had ever happened to me while conducting a regression. But when I agreed, the entity was delighted that I would cooperate.

D. *Do you want to take her to something that she can look at comfortably?*
E: I would rather you do this. I think one of her more recent past lives is going to be comfortable for her. *(Pause)* The 19th century.

I was preparing to direct her to go to that life, but the voice prevented me. Apparently he was not through speaking to me yet. Again I was startled. None of this was common procedure for regressions.

E: She did tell you how I felt? That I want you to continue with what you're doing? We all do.
D. *Yes, but you're probably aware of the difficulties I've been facing.*
E: Yes, but they will pass. You're being tested.
D. *Sometimes I feel I'm being tested too much.*
E: Don't feel that way and don't be discouraged. What you're doing is very important. You know, all of us are watching and some of us get very frustrated because we're not able to speak.
D: *Do you know my guide?*
E: No. None of us are aware of each other, individually or personally, as we're all on different levels. And some are on higher levels than I am. But we're ... you'll have to forgive me, I'm using the words she knows. There is something there that we're aware of. It's just like you're aware of the air but you can't see it. A common ground for us will be found. Even a guide can get anxious that the path is being taken the right way. You'll all be on the right path, it's just that some roads get a little more curvy than others. Just hang in there; it's going to be very good for the people who have a chance to read your books. There are negative forces also that work against this. It's ... oh, the simplest way to explain it is, I call them "little kids." They don't want to see progression that can be made amongst people without having to go through so many different lifetimes. And we have come to a point in time where an enlightenment of all *can* happen. And this is being fought against or repressed, I should say. Of course, sometimes repression occurs amongst the uninformed, but right now this is also happening at different levels. Public reaction will be favorable. You're going to get public awareness that this is the truth and there will also be this small group that will defy it and be against it. But what you do is very important. You must not be sidetracked. I can sense, as well as others, that you're becoming very discouraged. And this is why it's important to let you know that you have to hang in there.

The entity then proceeded to give me advice on where to send the manuscripts and the time elements involved, all of which have surprisingly happened since that day. He also advised strongly against allowing anyone to cut up the Jesus material, which, unknown to Elena, had been suggested by two companies. He then gave a message for Elena telling her how to meditate and be more receptive when he tried to communicate and advise her. He said the life she had glimpsed at the beginning of this session was important and we would be allowed to see it later. He then again asked me to take her to the 1800s where she would find a lifetime that she could more comfortably handle.

After bidding this amazing entity farewell, I directed her to go to the time period he had specified. She went immediately into a mundane life involving a woman who was married to a hard-working wheat farmer in Kansas in the 1800s. After the unexpected direction this regression had just taken, it was very boring to listen to her recall of that life. The details are unimportant, but this shows the adjustment period her subconscious went through.

Whether it was truly her guide or her subconscious that had come through to speak and give guidance, it only reinforced my belief that normally, in the beginning of my work with new subjects, they will not be shown a life they cannot handle. This is why they usually recall a dull, ordinary one. This is always the pattern I have found. What made this session so unusual was that I had never before had direct intervention from anything, let alone something that identified itself as a separate personality. This was a very unusual experience, but I have to keep reminding myself that in this line of work, the unusual should be expected. Her daughter was as surprised as I was by the sudden intrusion of Elena's guide. Even more so when I told her this was the first time this had ever happened.

Upon awakening, Elena was delighted with the regression of the woman farmer even though I found it very dull. She was surprised when I told her Andy had interrupted the session. She had no memory of it. But she did remember feeling uncomfortable during the beginning of the session.

"I don't remember much about what happened, but I felt uncomfortable, as though I had somehow invaded a confidence. I feel very strongly that it was a life that really happened. It was something about a teacher, and his teachings were very private at the time. I felt very uneasy even talking about it. I was getting real emotional inside, as though I was violating some kind of a rule or something. Do you understand what I mean?"

I asked her if she knew anything about the 16th century psychic, Nostradamus. She had never heard of him and couldn't even pronounce his name.

Maybe this was the reason her guide had intervened; he could sense the turmoil going on inside of her. All I could see was that she was disturbed. Normally the subject can become objective or jump out of a scene to something else if anything bothers them. They can also wake themselves up if the experience becomes too objectionable. Apparently Elena needed the intervention of her guide. Who knows? I was unsure what do think about this. I am the last one who would know what really happened or why it happened. The whole thing confused Elena too, and I knew she was in a deep enough trance that she had no conscious control over what happened. Her guide also spoke about things that Elena had no knowledge of. Whatever was going on, I felt comfortable with it. My curiosity was aroused, and I thought the lifetime she had glimpsed might be worth pursuing if Andy would allow it.

Chapter 2

I Meet Dyonisus

TWO MONTHS WERE TO PASS before Elena and I were able to meet for another session. The tourist season was in full swing in that resort town and the restaurant had been swamped. Elena was also busy with portraits she had been commissioned to do. She tried to set aside a little time each day to practice meditation as she felt that it calmed her mind and helped her to relax. A few times she was certain her guide, Andy, had come to her and given her encouragement and advice about problems. I had been busy with several other subjects on various projects and only saw her at the group meetings. Finally we were able to meet for a session on her day off.

After giving her the keyword, she lapsed into a deep trance, and I began the session by asking her to go back to a time that was important to her. I was hoping we might again tap into the lifetime with the teacher, but it would all depend upon her protective subconscious. I really had no idea where we would end up, but I knew that wherever it was it would be important to Elena, if not to me.

When she entered the scene, she was again a man walking on a road going to the teacher who had a home on the outskirts of the city. It would seem we had again contacted the same life. However, this time her answers were much more spontaneous. She did not seem disturbed, although at times she was hesitant to reply. I gave her reassurance to try to bypass the secrecy that had been present at the earlier session. Although she felt more at ease about talking to me, she was still cautious. She said she was one of six students who were studying with this teacher. They would occasionally all meet with him as a group, but he also gave them private lessons. She said in a voice filled with awe, "He's teaching me the study of life. How to heal the body. How to heal the mind. How to see the future. He knows more than any man on earth."

D: *To me those are wonderful things. Why does this have to be kept secret?*

E: Because the people are superstitious. The people of the church ... the Catholic church.

D: *Does this man have to hide because of his beliefs?*

E: No. He's a good doctor. But he's also a doctor of *all* things. Some of the things he believes in, he keeps secret.

I was trying to find out who this teacher was without putting any suggestions into her mind. She could not think of the name of the city or the year we were in, but this is not uncommon. Scientific studies have shown that during my type of work, the subject is utilizing primarily the right side of the brain where imagery and visualization are located. I have discovered that names and dates are located in the left half of the brain or the analytical, logical part. Experts also say that the subconscious does not understand numbers or time. After working with a subject on a specific lifetime over a long period, all the details of that life eventually become readily available. But in the beginning, it's as though we are merely grazing the surface, and mistakes with names and dates are common and can be overlooked. The story and the emotions are the important thing, and I can usually determine where we are by questioning. Like a detective looking for clues, these answers can be utilized to pinpoint the locale and time frame. She described what she was wearing. "I have on leggings. Footwear. A shirt with pantaloons. My cloak has a hood." She was a middle-aged man named Dyonisus. Since that was such a strange, foreign-sounding name I knew I would have trouble pronouncing it.

I decided to move him ahead to when he was at the teacher's house and he was studying with him. She went there immediately and began to describe the scene.

E: The room is big. I see the table, books. The steps leading up to the entrance of the house, the main part of the house.

D: *Then you are in the lower part?*

E: Yes. The fireplace is against the wall. There's a raised hearth in front of us, and we're sitting on cushions looking into the fire. The teacher says with this we can clear our minds.

D: *Is there someone else there besides you and the teacher?*

E: There are two others.

D: *Men or women?*

E: They're men. No women!

D: *Is there a reason why no women are allowed?*

E: It's the culture of our times. Only men are allowed to learn. I understand the need for women to learn. But society has not allowed this with the classes.

D: *Do you mean you have different classes in your society?*

E: Yes. There is the wealthy and the working class which would consist of the doctors, merchants, tradespeople, and the poor that work at the most menial tasks. The men that have families in a trade would learn to read and write and the necessary things to be able to perform that trade well. I have been very lucky in that my family had money enough where I could continue learning beyond what was necessary for my family's trade.

Dyonisus was about 30 years old at this time and had never married.

D: *Then your only desire is to learn from the master?*
E: Yes, it seems that there is so much to learn.
D: *How much longer will you have to go to the university to become a physician?*
E: The time I have spent is sufficient, but to learn more I feel it is necessary to continue. I prefer working with Nostradamus as I feel he has the information I need, not only to help the people as a physician but to help myself within also.

When he mentioned Nostradamus I was elated. I had suspected he was the teacher because of what Andy, the guide, had said. But now I was puzzled as to what questions to ask about him. I was trying to remember what I had read about the man, and I was wondering just how much one of his students would really know about him.

D: *Do you have an idea how long you will study with him?*
E: I hope never to stop.
D: *That would be good if you could do both, practice your medicine and still work with him. Are all the other students studying under him of the same level of learning?*
E: No, there are three that came to him approximately the same time, and two that have started at a later date. I started with the other three.
D: *Does he teach you all together or does he have separate classes?*
E: Regarding the healing of the body, we work together. Regarding the teachings of the mind, we work separate.

I asked for a description of Nostradamus. He said he had long brown hair, a beard, and large eyes. He was not old at this time and had been a doctor for about 10 years. Dyonisus said that he worked with him every day like an apprentice, helping him and learning from him.

D: *What has he taught you that has been especially helpful?*
E: To see. To open the mind. To hear.
D: *These are very important. Didn't Nostradamus write things down?*
E: Yes. He says there will be people that will learn from him many years ahead.
D: *I've also heard that he writes in rhyme or in mystery or in puzzles that*

are difficult to understand. Is that true?
E: He does this. Those that will understand, there will be no difficulty. Those who aren't able or ready to understand will not comprehend.
D: *Wouldn't it be easier to write things down in normal language?*
E: For those who are not ready it would be frightening. They don't comprehend or understand.
D: *Has he ever told you how he receives this information that he writes about?* (He answered with an emphatic: Yes!) *Can you share it with me?*
E: There's so much to say.
D: *We have to begin somewhere.*

He seemed to be confused as to where to start or how to explain it to me. Faltering, he began.

E: The fire ... opens the way.
D: *Do you mean by staring at the fire?*
E: *(Emphatically)* Yes! The mind's eye sees the fire. The voices come to you, to help and guide you. You get inside ... within yourself. It has to be prepared. The calming of your body, of your mind. The using of the elements to help guide you. The four elements.
D: Has he given you an exercise or something that helps with the calming?
E: Your voices tell you the exercise that is best for you. Our teacher helps you use it to its fullest purpose. Looking into the fire helps you control the wandering of the mind.

This sounded like basic meditation. To be effective, there should be something to concentrate on. Sometimes an object can be used as a focus instead of a fire.

D: *Does it have to be the fire or could it be anything?*
E: The fire is a symbol of the light. He uses many ways. The fire is one of the ways he teaches the students.

I wanted to find out about the other methods, but she became confused and disturbed again.

E: I hear ... I hear many voices right now.

I asked her if she could tell me what they were saying, but they seemed to be a jumble and she was afraid she was losing my voice among the others. I gave suggestions that she would always be able to hear me clearly and distinctly and that my voice would override the others, but she was still confused.

E: They're not ... they're part of the voices ... They are trying to tell me things I'm not understanding.

He was obviously in a meditative state and was concentrating on something besides my voice. It would be useless to try to question him under such distracting circumstances, so I moved him out of that scene. I asked him to go to where he lived, where he ate and slept and carried on his daily life. When I finished counting, the distractions were obviously gone. He said he did not live with his family but shared this place with another one of Nostradamus' students, named Tellvini (phonetic). I asked for a description of the house. He said, "It is nice, but I have no need for material things."

The two students had a housekeeper who lived with them and did the cooking. Dyonisus liked to eat fish and the breads that the woman prepared. The cooking was done in an area near the outer wall where there were tables and a fireplace for cooking. I wondered how he could afford these things, and he replied that the money came from his family. This was obviously why he didn't have to work.

While I was speaking to him he was sitting at a table reading. This would not have been so unusual except that he said he was reading "The Lost Books ... of the Book of God." Apparently he meant the Bible.

D: *Yes, I've heard there are some books that were lost. No one knows what they have in them.*
E: There are those within the church that are trying to separate and remove parts.

The book was written in French but he also knew Latin, so he apparently was highly educated.

D: *How did you find these books?*
E: Through my teacher. He said it's important to know *all* the things.
D: *I agree. What part of the lost books are you reading?*
E: The childhood of Christ.

I was naturally interested in this because at the time I was involved in the rewriting of my book, *Jesus and the Essenes*, which dealt with the life of Christ. It was so uppermost in my mind that it was difficult for me to work with other subjects on other projects. I had trouble thinking of questions dealing with any other time period. This was part of the reason I had difficulty formulating questions about Nostradamus. I knew this would be a tremendous opportunity to find out about the famous psychic, but I could not get my mind off the Jesus project. Thus, when Dyonisus mentioned he was reading about the childhood of Jesus from the lost books of the Bible, I leapt on it as a chance to get more information to add to the other book. I asked him to share with me what he was reading.

E: That when he was very young he had the powers he did as a man. But
    he did not have the compassion he did as a man, and sometimes used
    his gifts willfully and mischievously. That he had a playmate fall
    down dead because he was angry with him. And he brought him back
    to life because he was sorry for him. These are the things they are
    taking out. People want to know only the good.

D: *I suppose they don't want people to know that He was capable of
    human emotions. Does that part you are reading have a name or is it
    all in one book?*

E: There are many different times ... passages, but it's in one book.

D: *I thought the book might have sections or something that had
    someone's name that wrote them.* (Similar to our present Bible.)

E: *(Pause)* I don't have that information.

D: *What else does it say about the life of Christ that they are taking out?*

E: The family that he had. Brothers. Sisters. The foolishness. He was
    a normal child growing up. And they don't believe that he should
    have been.

He said the book didn't tell how large a family he had. It just told of
some of the events of his life such as the incident with the playmate.

E: It seems like there are excerpts from different things, as if parts that
    were in the first book have been deleted.

D: *Was there anything about the early times, like on his birth, that have
    been taken out and put into this book?*

E: Yes, but I can't recall.

I thought I would attempt an experiment. You never know what will
bring results in work such as this. It's all hit-and-miss; there are no guide-
lines. I asked if he would look at that part in the book and read it to me.
He was perfectly willing to do it. He said the book was arranged in order
so it would be easy to find. Then another confusing thing happened. He
apparently found the part and was silently reading it, but for some reason
he couldn't repeat it to me.

E: I'm sorry, I can't. I don't know why. *(She seemed uncomfortable.)* I
    feel like I have a weight on my chest

I didn't understand what she meant but I didn't want her to be
uncomfortable. I assumed that her subconscious still felt bound by some
code of secrecy and was not totally ready to let everything be revealed.

D: *Is it something you shouldn't talk about?*

E: It seems like it hasn't been ... known yet.

D: *But you're allowed to read it, aren't you?*

E: I know. But the voices are telling me ... *(Surprised)* It's not to come
    through me! You are going to receive it from another source.

I couldn't imagine what she meant, but I had to go along with it. "I thought maybe they didn't trust me."

E: *(Emphatic)* No! That's not it.

Any other questions about the lost books were met by stony silence, so I knew I would have to change the subject. I wondered if Nostradamus lived near him.

E: He has more than one home. Sometimes he stays with others. Sometimes he stays with his family.

D: *You said that Nostradamus was a medical doctor. Does he have a hospital, or do you know that word?*

E: He treats the people in their homes.

D: *Did he study a long time to do this?*

E: To be a doctor? He did not study very long. He was able to understand everything the first time he was taught.

D: *What about the other training he had, the one with the mind. Did he study that somewhere?*

E: Through several different wise men that taught him.

D: *Was he taught these things at the same time he was learning the medicine?*

E: Part of it was during that time, more of it came later.

D: *You said he had other methods of healing besides the conventional methods he's teaching you. Can you speak of that?*

E: *(She paused and seemed confused again.)* Not this time. *(The voice changed. It was more confident. Was it Andy?)* There is a lot that you are to know from this life. But what I don't understand is ... they just block some of it.

D: *It's all right if they want me to wait. I have lots of patience. I want you to become very secure with me and to feel that you can trust me.*

E: They trust you. But they say that part of something else that you will learn will come together with the telling of this life. And to learn only part of it now would not make sense. You are to learn something from a different source that will blend in with the telling of this life.

I didn't understand what they meant, but I felt obliged to go along with it. Maybe it would fall into place later.

D: *Then they want me to do that first before I work with you or what?*

E: It will happen before and you will know it.

D: *And then I will put the two together?*

E: Yes. It will be clear for you. You can ... we are to talk again.

D: *Yes, I look forward to speaking again, for I am always searching for knowledge. I am very glad that they have allowed you to speak with me. Last time they didn't want you to talk about it. This is an encouragement if they feel you should know of this life. Is there anything particular that they wish you to know about it that you can speak of?*

E: *(A long pause.)* Not at this time.

D: *I suppose that's why these feelings are being reawakened. What you learn is never taken away. It's always there.*

E: That's part of the reason. There'll be much learning for you from this life. And something that will tie in with it will occur before you come back.

I realized I had been a little muddled about what to ask because of my preoccupation with the Jesus material.

E: When you come back, you will know the questions to ask. It will occur to you.

Since they would not let us have any more information, there was nothing to do but take her out of that life and bring her forward to full consciousness. I was a little relieved, because, as I have said, I was too preoccupied to devote my full attention and energy to this project at that time. Apparently they sensed this. I kept thinking it would be interesting to find out something about Nostradamus. But what kind of information could I obtain from a student? How much had he been taught? Had Nostradamus told him anything about the real meaning of his quatrains and would he be able to understand them even if he had? I thought at the time I might be able to find out something about his life during the time that Dyonisus knew him and maybe discover some of his healing methods, but surely nothing intimate about Nostradamus' inner thoughts and visions. Under the circumstances I thought maybe I would be able to get enough information for a chapter in a future book of miscellaneous stories, surely nothing more. But I believed Dyonisus was right, by the time I came back I would be better prepared for asking questions.

SOMETHING STRANGE did happen before I came back. Dyonisus would not give me the information about Jesus because he said it would not come through Elena but through someone else. Katie Harris [pseudoynm], the subject that had given me the material for *A Soul Remembers Hiroshima* and *Jesus and the Essenes* had moved away and I was finishing the rewriting of that book on the life of Christ. I still felt there were a few gaps that I would like to have filled. At the time I was working with Elena, I was also working with a young college student named Brenda who was majoring in music at the local university. She was also an excellent subject, and I had already received a great deal of important information from her which will be transformed into future books. None of these three women knew each other and they all lived in different cities.

The strange incident happened while I was working with Brenda a few weeks after this session with Elena. She was in a deep trance when a strange voice suddenly announced that it had information that should be included in the Jesus material. For a hour it supplied the answers I had been seeking to fill the few gaps in the book. Later, when I inserted them in the proper places they meshed so perfectly it was as if they had always been there. Ninety-nine percent of that book came from Katie and only a small one percent from Brenda, but I now knew that book was complete. It was as though somehow "they" (whoever "they" are) knew I needed the additional pieces and also knew I couldn't get it from Katie, so they very cleverly found another method to get it to me. But Elena was correct, the information was not to come from her. Her story would concentrate on a totally different area. With a sense of relief I now knew I could devote my full attention to other projects.

It became apparent that someone or something else was participating in this and helping to direct the flow of information. Although I did not understand it, I was glad to have their assistance. I was unaware at this time that this was only the mere beginning of an adventure that would be full of incredible twists and turns and improbable consequences. Things were to occur that I, as a rational, thinking human being, would have thought were in the realm of impossibility.

Chapter 3

𝕿𝖍𝖊 𝕲𝖗𝖊𝖆𝖙 𝕸𝖆𝖓 𝕮𝖔𝖒𝖊𝖙𝖍

𝕴 HAD INTENDED TO FORMULATE more rational questions about the life of Nostradamus that I would ask Dyonisus the next week, but the tourist season descended on the resort town with a vengeance. Elena worked late each evening and was very tired, so months began to go by without my having contact with the student of Nostradamus. At the time I was involved in many other projects with other subjects and Elena's story was just another possibility to follow up on when we could get together. I am usually working on several possible books at one time so I will have continual projects going on. I mistakenly assumed there would be plenty of time to follow up on this since I thought it would be only an interesting chapter or two in a book of miscellaneous regressions. At the time I never dreamed it would evolve into a book on its own because I could not conceive of obtaining that much information from one of his students.

Summer lengthened into fall and dissolved into winter. I occasionally saw Elena, but we had no more sessions. During winter the resort town shuts down and turns into a ghost town. Most of the residents either migrate to warmer climates or hibernate, awaiting the next influx of tourists in late spring. Elena productively used this time to work on her commissioned portraits. We still could not work because during the winter I also go into hibernation. I live in a rugged rural mountain area and it becomes inconvenient and difficult to go anywhere when the snows come. During this time my sessions cease and I work on the tiresome transcribing of the tapes that I wish to use. This is a necessary but time-consuming and tedious part of my work, so I save it for the dreary winter months when I am snowed in.

Thus it was spring 1986 before Elena and I could finally find time to meet again. She had moved into an apartment in an old building. The residences in that town were very ancient, thus it was not extraordinary that Elena had a trapdoor in her bedroom near the foot of the bed. This caused the floor to creak when anyone walked over that spot. On the day of the session, we were alone although you could occasionally hear people moving around in the other apartments. Before beginning, she put her small dog and cat outside. Since we were expecting a friend, Valerie (or "Val" as she was known to her friends) to come before we were finished, she closed the outside door but did not lock it. These facts are important to what happened during the session. Every session I conducted with Elena had contained something unusual, and this one would be no exception.

Since it had been several months since I had worked on this story, I could not remember the student's name. So I directed her to go back to the time when she was a student of Nostradamus. When I finished counting I found him in his room writing.

E: I'm writing information that I have received from the voices within. I had questions within myself that I felt needed to be answered, so I turned inward. They are questions about myself that would not have any meaning to others.

He was apparently receiving this information through meditation. He said his name was Dyonisus and I wondered about this. Nostradamus lived in France and this name did not sound French. A possibility had been suggested that maybe it was not the student's real name. Perhaps they were given other names in order to protect them. But he insisted that it was the name he was born with.

E: We live with the master. He has a large home. There are five of us students. We have separate quarters. Some by choice share a room, but I do not wish to. However, we all share a common goal.
D: *Where did you live before?*
E: We lived in my native land, in Athens.

This would explain his foreign-sounding name. He wasn't French but Greek.

D: *There are many wise minds in Athens also, aren't there?*
E: There were.
D: *I just wondered why you chose to come here and not study in Athens.*
E: My family was into the merchant's trade. They dealt with different types of spices and cloth goods. And in the course of business decided to move. Some of my family still live in Athens, but my parents moved to Paris. They wished to establish a better communication from one port to the other with the products that were needed.
D: *Did they expect you to go into their business?*
E: Yes, they did. But I had always felt there was something more. That everything was not as ... was written.
D: *Did you have schooling in Athens?*
E: Yes. We came over when I was very young and I studied with the priests at Notre Dame. I was learning to be a ... *(searching for the words)* man of the law. But I felt that the present laws were unjust for the poor class.

D: *Yes, but that's usually the way it is in most countries, isn't it?*

E: That's true. I felt it was necessary to learn something that would be helpful to them. I decided to become a physician. I had heard of Nostradamus and wished to study with him. When I met him I felt this was indeed the person who could teach me many things. I am still what they call an "apprentice." At the university there are people who have been brought from the hospitals so we can watch the surgeons perform. I prefer to work with Nostradamus because he showed a method of making the people not feel the pain when it was necessary to operate.

There has long been speculation about how Nostradamus was able to perform his miraculous cures. He mystified the other doctors of his time. Maybe I would be able to find out his secret. He lived before the discovery of ether when doctors supposedly performed operations without any anesthetic.

D: *Is he the only one who uses this method?*

E: Yes. There were some that I had heard of in my land that did this, but not so much in France. It's a method that lets the person help the surgeon. But it goes beyond that to a quieting of the person's heart and a lessening of the pain in the person's mind.

This sounded very much like a form of hypnosis. I have always thought the hardest part of trying to control pain would be getting the patient to listen to you.

E: There are narcotics that are mostly from the Orient that we can give them; that quiets them. One is a ... opium. It is one of the main types. The other is ladanum. But they are still aware of things. It makes them drowsy but it would not be enough to make them not aware when a leg or arm has to be removed. We have better control. By using the method of working with the mind and the ability to quiet the heart, we can bring them to a point where they have a better chance of recovering and not dying from the shock. We have to use this method in a very secretive manner and make it seem that the other medicines we use are what are causing the patients to respond.

D: *Why do you have to be secretive? I would think the other doctors would want to learn.*

E: This is a time in our land that is very superstitious. Anything that is involved that people do not understand makes them think it is associated with the Devil or witches, and it is very much misunderstood. Society has not learned to understand the unknown yet.

D: *Then he is only teaching his personal students how to do these things?*

E: That is true.

D: *What types of illnesses are the most prominent or most common right now in the land?*

E: Diseases that are caused from the filth that is prevalent in the cities, the unclean conditions. A type of black lung or consumption. There is no way to really treat the poor with this because of the conditions they live in. But we try to tell those who are able to, to drink plenty of liquids, to be in the country and not in the city where there seems to be so much smoke and filth. And there is a type of plague that has caused much concern with us. It is one that even Nostradamus has not a cure for. It causes the throat to swell, much mucus in the lungs and the face turns black eventually. I believe from the lack of oxygen or air.

D: *Is the university the only place where surgery is performed?*

E: No, there are chambers in the hospitals where surgeries are performed. But for learning procedures, some are done in the university.

D: *Is there one type of surgery that is more common than the others?*

E: An amputation of the limbs is not uncommon, because of a gangrene that will set in with wounds and sores that have gone uncared for.

D: *Do they ever do surgery on the abdomen and that area of the body?*

E: Yes, but for so many this is an unsuccessful procedure because of the shock and trauma to the patient.

D: *When women have children, do they have to come to the hospitals?*

E: There is no need.

D: *You told me before that you were taught meditation by staring into the fire. Is this the way Nostradamus does it or have you ever seen him do his own meditation?*

E: This method is the one that has helped me the most. Once we feel comfortable with ourselves, a mental image is sufficient. He has several methods that he uses. I have seem him work with the sand. He uses a very white fine type of sand over a very clear ... *(Had difficulty finding the words.)* I don't remember the material.

D: *Is it like a piece of cloth?*

E: No, it's solid.

I was distracted by Elena's dog barking outside. I assumed Val must be arriving early.

I continued, "... is the material like glass?"

E: What is this?

She seemed confused. He didn't know the word "glass." It is amazing that I have had other subjects who regressed to this same time period and also did not know the word.

D: *Glass would be very smooth and you can see through it.*

E: It's very smooth.

D: *Or is it a type of metal?*

E: No. I don't understand why I can't remember.

D: *(I had an idea.) Do you know what a mirror is?*

E: *(Enthusiastically)* That's it!

D: *A mirror is something you can see yourself in.*

E: That's it, yes.

D: *But what does he do with the sand?*

E: He makes a type of design with it, letting his hand guide him. And through this he is able to see with his inner eye.

D: *All right. I'm trying to visualize it. He has a smooth mirror. And he takes the sand in his hand and then sprinkles it over the mirror?*

E: He covers the mirror with it. And takes a small object like a quill and lets his hand trace designs.

D: *That way it would be a different design each time, wouldn't it?*

E: Right. And then he writes what he hears inside.

D: *Then the making of the designs is just a method of concentration?*

E: Yes. Sometimes he gets visions that he sees in the mirror, but we do not see them. Usually there will be an area cleared by the time he's finished with the free design, and he sees things there.

D: *And he writes down what he sees. Does he do this for very long?*

E: Two or three hours at a time.

D: *We have what are called his quatrains. Is that what he is writing at those times?*

E: Yes. He receives the vision or he hears the voices. And turns to his writing tablet to write down what he receives or sees.

D: While he is doing this, if someone were to talk to him would he hear you?

I was trying to determine whether he was in a trance during these times.

E: We are instructed not to speak to him during this time.

D: *You said sometimes he uses other methods?*

At this point strange things began to happen. Although Elena's dog and cat had been put outside before the session began, they suddenly came into the room and stood together at the foot of the bed staring up at us. I had heard the dog barking outside, so I thought maybe Val, the woman we had been expecting had come into the house and the animals had followed her. I assumed she was probably in the front room which could not be seen from the bedroom. I had heard no one enter or any noise, but this could be explained because we were in the back of the apartment. I had told Val it would be all right if she came back to the bedroom when she arrived. I shrugged it off, presuming she had just decided to remain in the front room rather than disturb us. The animals stood attentively at the foot of the bed for a long period of time which Elena said later was not their normal behavior. I was curious as to how they got into the apartment, but since they were not creating a disturbance, I ignored them and continued with the session.

At this same time Elena's eyes moved under her eyelids. She seemed to be following someone who had apparently entered the room in the past life scene she was involved in. Her eyes followed the person as he entered and sat down on her left next to the bed where a trunk was located in her (real) bedroom. Dyonisus had apparently been alone and meditating in the first part of this session. He had been answering my questions with no hesitation. Now he suddenly became evasive and reluctant to answer. I presumed it was because he was no longer alone.

E: These are things that are secret and I cannot describe now.

Dyonisus seemed uncomfortable, as though whoever had entered the room had caught him in the act of revealing forbidden secrets. I proceeded to reassure him that it was all right to confide in me, but that I would not pressure him to do anything that made him uncomfortable.

I had assumed he would speak no more on this subject if someone else was present, so I was surprised by his answer, "Let me ask him first." Apparently Nostradamus was the one who had entered. This was a very strange feeling, especially since she had her head turned away from me and was concentrating on the empty air above the trunk. There was a long pause as she seemed to converse with someone who was on that side of the room. I almost felt that I, too, was in the presence of another person. She then turned back to me and stated, "I can't share this at this time."

D: *That's all right. I will never ask you to do anything that you do not feel really right about. I'm glad you asked him though. Does he think at some time you will be able to share it?*

E: He says *he* will talk to you at some time.

This was a shock. I felt the hair stand up on the back of my arms and a cold shiver run down my spine. I had the distinct impression he could see me and was looking at me at that moment. During my regressions the subject is seldom aware of me as a separate entity. I like to think that only their subconscious is aware and answering my questions, and I am only a voice buzzing inside their head. It is always amusing and sometimes startling to have the personality suddenly notice me and ask, "Who are you?" But to have a third party suddenly sense my presence was a very strange development.

As calmly as I could, I reasoned that if Nostradamus truly was the greatest psychic that ever lived and had such highly developed mental abilities, why couldn't he be aware that his student was conversing with someone. Would that really be so unusual? It still gave me a very weird feeling to think I might be in the presence of an invisible someone who was aware of me but whom I could not see. Nothing like this had ever happened in my work before.

But even more curious, I couldn't understand what he meant. Just *how* could he talk to me? The odds against my finding the reincarnated Nostradamus and conversing with him through regression were astronomical. I assumed I could continue to question Elena about

Dyonisus' experiences with him. But that was not what he said. He clearly indicated that he would converse with me personally. I was confused and was getting a little dizzy as I tried to comprehend this. "Oh?" I asked. "Does he plan to do this through you? Or does he know how this will occur?"

The next remark was ever more puzzling. "Not only through me but ... through another."

That was even more far-fetched. I didn't know how to take this. How would it be possible to accomplish *that?* Was I going to locate another student of his and gain more information that way? This was the way I worked. If I was lucky enough to find a subject who knew someone famous, *i.e.:* Jesus, Nostradamus, *etc.,* then I would question to find out facts about their life. I could have shrugged this off as being too crazy and off-the-wall to even consider, but there was something about her tone of voice that told me he was serious. I had the feeling that if it were truly to occur, I would have nothing to say about the method or procedure and wouldn't have to worry about it or try to make it happen. (Even if I had the foggiest idea *how* to make something like that happen.) Maybe it would be as spontaneous as this unexpected announcement had been. Oh, well, I figured why question it, maybe anything was possible after all. This was certainly not the time to analyze it anyhow. My head was swimming with confusion. I had to push it aside for now and continue.

D: *I think he should realize that I'm searching for knowledge, for lost knowledge, and I'm always happy for anything I can receive.*
E: He says that he's aware of this.
D: *And I mean no harm at all. I would appreciate anything that you can tell me at any time, or anything that he feels free to tell me. Will you thank him for me?*
E: Yes, I will.

At this point I had to turn the tape over, but I also took this opportunity to quickly go into the front room to see if our friend had arrived. I couldn't understand why I had heard no noises or why she had not at least peeked into the bedroom to see if we were finished. But to my surprise the apartment was empty and the front door was standing wide open. I quickly returned to Elena, more confused than ever. The animals had also retreated and did not return.

I knew I would receive no more information at that scene because Nostradamus had stopped the flow. In order to return the session to familiar grounds, I moved Dyonisus ahead in time to an important day in his life. Elena was answering questions much more spontaneously than in any other session. There was none of the confusion and uncertainty that had crept into the earlier sessions when we touched upon this life. It had been a little bothersome to have the sessions continuously interrupted by Andy or whoever was looking after her benefit. I counted Dyonisus forward to an important day and asked what he was doing.

E: I am receiving information that astounds me.
D: *How are you receiving it?*
E: Through both my eyes and my mind.
D: *Can you share it with me?*
E: *(In awe.)* I dare not.

I was curious enough to attempt to get around her objections. This had worked before under similar circumstances.

D: *Well, it's perfectly all right if you don't want to share it with me. But why is this an important day?*
E: Because it is the first time that I have had the visions. Before I would only hear voices.
D: *Are you going to write down what you are seeing when it's over?*
E: Oh, yes! But this is just for myself.
D: *Are the visions something to do with your own life?*
E: Ohhh, it's far into the future.
D: *I wish you could tell me some of it anyway.*
E: You would not believe me.
D: *Oh, I bet I would. I believe many, many strange things. Is it near where you live now?*
E: I have no idea. I'm looking at what appears to be a city with tall buildings that reach into the sky. There are things flying. They look like birds, giant metal birds. And these objects have people. There are fast things moving within the city. They are also carrying people.
D: *Similar to your carriages?*
E: Oh, no! I've never seen this. Seems to be metal containers with clear ... clear metal.

It is interesting that again he did not know the word for glass. This showed continuity. It was obvious that Dyonisus was looking ahead to our time in his future. He was seeing a scene that Elena would have been familiar with. It was fascinating to hear him describe these things in such foreign terms, as though he was seeing it through new eyes. This phenomenon also happened in my book, *Five Lives Remembered,* where a young girl living in the 1770s saw a vision of the future and described it in very similar terms.

D: *It really does sound wondrous. Do the people look different?*
E: Yes, very—healthier.
D: *They must have very good physicians in that time.*

What would be more natural for a doctor to notice? That the people of the future were healthier than the people in his own time. This added a touch of validity.

E: Healthier. And different garments. So many different types. I could not explain just one. Nostradamus told us there would be things that would be beyond our comprehension.

D: *I wonder if this is the type of thing that he sees all the time?*

E: I believe it is.

D: *Well, you never know; that may be what the world in the future will be like. What do you think of it?*

E: I think it is very different. I'm afraid of it. I've never seen so many people.

D: *I thought Paris was a large city.*

E: It is. But I've never looked at Paris from this view. I'm looking down on it. I see the biggest bridge I've ever seen in my life. It looks like it's made out of metal and ... ropes.

Probably the cables of a bridge like the Golden Gate or something similar which he would naturally not know how to describe in any other way.

E: It's suspended over the water. And these things, these containers, are moving on it.

D: *Is there anything in the water?*

E: Just ... they're boats. Very different, but I know they're boats.

D: *Then you can see all the tall buildings and all the strange-looking vehicles. (She looked confused.) Do you know that word? (She shook her head.) It means something to ride in. It's another word for it. Like a carriage. Even a boat could be called a vehicle. Something that you get into and it moves.*

E: I see. Thank you.

He seemed content with my explanation and happy that I gave it to him.

D: *Do these containers make noise?*

E: I don't hear anything.

D: *Is there anything else you could share that looks different?*

E: *(Long pause)* There's so much. I'm trying to decide which—the lights! The lights are so much brighter than we have here. And there is ... ah ... lights with pictures on them. Very colorful.

D: What kind of pictures?

E: Ah ... so many different. A woman holding an object in her hand. *(A cigarette perhaps, or a bottle of Coke?)* A man in strange clothes on a horse. *(Perhaps a cowboy?)*

I wondered if he was seeing billboards or advertisements made with colored neon lights. I was enjoying this. It was fun to see our world through the eyes of the past.

E: They have lights on the streets.

D: *That would be good; people could see at night. Does Paris have any lights on the streets?*

E: They have burning lights but not fueled the same way these are. And not so *many.*

D: *This is indeed a strange city you're looking at. It sounds like it must be a long way in the future.*

I took her out of that scene and asked him to move ahead to another important day in his life.

E: I am helping sew up. It's a young child. The boy's foot has been run over by a carriage and I had to amputate. I had the boy brought to my own chamber but I was able to make him see that I would help and quiet him. *(Emotionally)* And this is the first time. This has much meaning for me.

D: *What do you mean, the first time?*

E: I was able to put to use the teachings I have learned. I mean, in addition to the practice of the medicine. To put to use what Nostradamus has taught me of how to relieve the pain. It even made the bleeding less than it would have been. Nostradamus guided me with this.

D: *Have you finished all your training?*

E: The physical, but the mental, no.

D: *Where do you practice the medicine?*

E: I have many people that come to me. I also go into the poor section. I want to help them.

D: *What about your family? Do they understand what you are doing?*

E: Yes, they know I want to work with the poor.

He said he had been practicing the medicine for about six years and had been going into the poor section and working with them for about four years. Several of the other students had returned to their own homes in order to help the people there.

D: *Does your country have a ruler?*

E: You mean France?

D: *Yes, that's the country you made your home.*

E: Yes, it does. I can't think ... He came after King Charles. I can't think if it's Louis or not.

D: *I was just curious. Have you ever seen him?*

E: No, I have never met him.

I remembered from what little I had read about Nostradamus that he had predicted the future for his king when the ruler heard about his strange gifts.

D: *What about Nostradamus? Has he ever met the king?*

E: Oh, yes. He is aware of the prophecies. Nostradamus tells him of some of them, yes. Those concerning France. But he does not know *all* of what he does.

D: *Do you know what any of these prophecies are?*

E: I know some of them. But they are not of interest to me.

D: *You don't care about what happens in France?*

E: What I have learned goes beyond the physical.

D: *Have you had any vision of your own that you think is important that you could share with me?*

E: Perhaps another time. I'm feeling weary now.

D: *Is that because of the work you've done with the little boy?*

E: Yes. May I talk with you at another time?

D: *Oh, yes. I'd enjoy that very much.*

Elena might also have been weary because this was the longest we had been allowed to hold a session without being interrupted.

Upon awakening Elena seemed confused. There was only one thing that she remembered while in trance. She asked if anyone had come into the room during the session. I told her about her dog and cat and that I had found the front door standing open. She said sometimes if the animals tried hard enough they could get in, but it was strange for them to come into the bedroom and stand at the foot of the bed and watch her. That was unusual behavior.

She said, "The reason I asked was because I distinctly heard someone come into the room and walk across the floor. Then, they sat down on the trunk."

I drew her attention to the fact that there were many things (pictures and knick-knacks) on the top of the trunk and under normal circumstances no one would have been able to sit there. I told her that her eyes had moved toward that direction as though she saw someone enter and go to that side of the bed. I said she might have heard the people upstairs moving around, because during the session I heard sounds that seemed to be coming from the other apartments.

She shook her head and replied emphatically, "This is strange. I know it doesn't make any sense. But I am certain the sounds came from within the room because there is a trapdoor right there by the foot of my bed. When anyone walks across the room, the floor creaks in that spot. That is what I heard."

The animals were obviously too small to make the noises, especially the sound of footsteps. The tape recorder picked up sounds similar to what she described, but as I have said, they could have been coming from upstairs.

It is interesting to speculate about the possibility of the animals actually seeing and accompanying someone into the room. I had heard the dog barking outside as the phenomenon began. Did they see a presence that was invisible to me? Why else did they force themselves into the house just to stand at the foot of the bed and watch?

When I told Elena that Nostradamus had said he would talk to me himself, she was as puzzled as I was. We couldn't figure out how he was going to accomplish such a feat.

"How could he come through me?" she asked. "It is quite obvious that I couldn't have been Nostradamus if I was one of his students."

We were also curious about the other person he was supposed to come through. The prediction she had made about the extra Jesus material coming through someone else had come true when I received it through Brenda. This had also been an unlikely occurrence. At this point we had no idea where this story was going or what else would happen. I planned to wind it up in a few more sessions when I found out the rest of Dyonisus' life story. I thought there would be nothing else worth obtaining.

In this session her ability to speak more fluidly and give more information had improved dramatically in comparison with the first sessions. Maybe the reason for the forced delay and the interventions by her guide was so she would become more secure and familiar with this procedure.

After this session we sat up several appointments that she was unable to keep due to various personal reasons. She then went to California for a month to be with a daughter who was having marriage problems. Thus, it was again several months before the work on this project could resume.

Chapter 4

Nostradamus Speaks

Since the last session Elena repeatedly cancelled appointments as she was preparing to go to California to be with her daughter. Before she left the thought occurred to me that it might be possible to utilize her abilities as a portrait artist. Wouldn't it be wonderful if she could somehow draw a picture of Nostradamus? I pondered over how I could give her the suggestion that she would be able to see him clearly in her conscious state. I didn't want it to become an obsession and I didn't want her to be haunted by him, seeing his face wherever she looked. Thus, it had to be handled carefully. I decided I could give her the post-hypnotic suggestion that when she wanted to draw him, she would be able to see him clearly and distinctly. The rest of the time he would not even be in her thoughts. His face would only appear when she wanted to see him.

She agreed it was a wonderful idea and it would be a great challenge for her, to see if she could reproduce a picture of him. She did not think a suggestion would even be necessary because when I mentioned him, she could see his face very clearly. She described him with a faraway look in her eyes. He had a high forehead and an aquiline nose, but his eyes were his most prominent feature. She agreed to attempt it when she found time from her busy schedule.

She was gone for a month. When she returned she immediately began a new job in another restaurant and was exhausted from the new adjustments. After a few more cancelled tries we were finally able to get together. It was now May again (1986) and the tourist season was beginning anew.

When I picked her up after work, she collapsed into the seat of the car. She leaned her head back and closed her eyes. She was very tired from a bad day at work. She was having difficulties with the new employer, and the pressures were beginning to show. There were also other family problems that I was unaware of. I reminded her that, although she was tired, the session would relax her more than a good night's sleep and that afterward she would feel wonderful. My subjects always enjoy this work; it's much more refreshing than sleep.

She announced, "I think it's only fair to tell you that we are thinking seriously of moving back to Alaska." Her husband was dissatisfied with his job, and the money situation had not been what they thought it would be. She really liked the peace and slowed-down atmosphere of our mountain country and wanted to stay, maybe even retire here some day. But he thought they should return north, accumulate some more money and be able to buy a permanent home when they came back. She had made many friends and really didn't want to leave, but she could see no alternative. So it was possible they might move as early as July, which was only two months away. "I thought it was only fair to warn you. It wouldn't be right to suddenly announce that I was going to leave next week."

My mind was trying to think ahead. There was no sense of urgency. It might be possible to get the rest of Dyonisus' life story if we had no more delays. I expected his story would make no more than an interesting chapter in a book of miscellaneous regressions, and she could always mail me the picture when it was finished. More than that, I knew I would miss Elena and her loving nature. We had become good friends. But the important thing was for her to do what she felt she had to with her life. If that meant moving back to Alaska, then so be it. I had no idea that my plans would be changed by the end of this session.

Since Elena's apartment would be full of people at this time of day, we decided to go to Val's house where we would have more privacy. Val had never seen regression work done so she was interested in watching. Later I was very glad to have a witness present, as this turned out to be one of the strangest and most unusual sessions I had ever conducted. Without the witness and the tapes to back me up, I know it would be difficult for anyone to believe what happened that day, for I find it difficult to believe myself.

Elena was so tired she eagerly went into trance so she could have a nice rest. I counted her back to the time when she was the student of Nostradamus and found Dyonisus writing. He was doing some translations from the Latin to French for Nostradamus. These were old medical remedies and he was seeing if they could adapt them and use them. He said Latin was a language he was required to know. Actually Elena does not understand either language. Dyonisus said that he had found some interesting theories on brain surgery while doing the translations. I was surprised because I didn't know they performed dangerous operations like that. He assured me that they did. "We can only go so far. Drill holes in the skull to relieve pressure on the brain."

This is called trephining and had been known since ancient times. Mummified Egyptian remains show that it was practiced then and that the patients survived and lived for several years afterward. This was not really what I thought he meant by brain surgery, but I was not aware that any type of surgery was performed on the head in Europe before the days of anesthetics.

D: How do you know when there's pressure on the brain?

E: By the eyes ... and the hands and legs if they're swelling. And pricking their fingers and telling by the amount of blood that's there. There's too much blood in the system.

D: How can you tell if there's too much blood in the system?

E: Like the continuous bleeding from the nose. The nails are extremely rosy. Under the lids of the eyes, the smaller of the veins are congested.

D: Then what do you do?

E: Drill holes in the head. Sometimes there is even a slight swelling. Depending upon where the greatest amount of pressure is. We take measurements of the skull.

D: What kind of an instrument do you use to do that with?

E: It's a metal instrument. Consider it similar to the type of instrument that navigators use on a map. It has a ... *(searching)* I can't find the word for it. It's like a half-moon with a swivel end on it. ... Calibrate? ... I believe caliper. Something similar.

D: But wouldn't this cause pain?

I was thinking of instruments used for the drilling. But he was talking about a measuring device.

E: *(Emphatically)* No! No, there's an adjustment on the top. It turns. That widens it or brings it in. It's open at the bottom. It has two ends in, and a turn on the top. And it's notched so you know where the measurements would be. The closer you get in, you can measure the distance. So you get a circumference of the total measurement.

Her hand motions showed that this was a large instrument, maybe similar to ice tongs.

D: Oh, I see, you're speaking of the measurements; that they wouldn't cause pain.

E: No, the instrument does not cause pain.

D: But I was thinking that the opening of the skull would.

E: Oh! I see what you're saying. Nostradamus has a technique that he uses that causes very little pain with his patients. I believe I've spoken of this before with you.

D: Yes, you have. It is a method similar to the method I use. We call it hypnosis. What do you call it?

E: Trance.

D: I believe you said that the other doctors didn't know he did it.

E: That is correct. It is a secret.

D: Are the other doctors able to perform operations like this?

E: Yes. But they have a greater fatality rate than Nostradamus does. The patient goes into a shock. Sometimes does not live. Nostradamus believes that shock can be a greater cause of post-operative death than perhaps the surgery itself.

D: *It's a shame he can't share his methods with the other doctors.*
E: *(Abruptly)* He has a message for you.
D: *He does?!*
E: Yes. Just a moment.

This was so sudden it was a surprise. Again, I almost dropped the microphone. It was as though Nostradamus had once more picked up that I was speaking to his student. He apparently had seized upon this as an opportunity to speak. Although I thought it was fascinating to learn how physicians practiced their craft in bygone days, he probably considered it trivial and unimportant. Apparently he thought he must interject because his message was more urgent. I looked at Val and shrugged my shoulders. I had no more of an idea than she did about what was happening. During the last session he had said that he would talk to me. Was this what he meant? What could he possibly want to tell me?

What followed was very strange; an unusual three-way conversation. Elena turned her head to the right as though listening intently to someone who was invisible to me. Then she turned back to me to speak. Every time this happened there was a long pause as she appeared to listen before relaying to me what was said. I felt my scalp tingle. It was an eerie feeling to know that somehow Nostradamus knew I was there and was aware of what I was doing.

He proceeded to take over the session.

E: He says that you have to work on translation. The quatrains. That there is something happening now in your time that would be understood more by the translation of certain quatrains.
D: *An interesting idea. But I wouldn't know how to begin.*

I was totally unfamiliar with any of the quatrains. I did not have a book, so I made the only suggestion that made sense to me at the time.

D: *Does he know which quatrain I should talk about?*

I thought he would suggest one. It was not going to be that easy.

E: He says that you are to—I don't understand—use your guide? That they will be able to come to the right ones and translate them.
D: *Can he give me any indication which quatrain it would be? There are many, many of them.*
E: *(A long pause as she turned her head again and listened.)* He says not to question, that to please do it this way.
D: *What? To look through a book?*
E: That's correct. It seems your guide has the facility to be able to read fast.

I naturally thought he was speaking of our invisible guides or guardians, such as Elena's Andy.

*D: All right. I will have to get a book and read through it. And ask him
the meaning when I find a quatrain?*

E: No. Your guide would read it and know that this is the one that has
to be translated. This is to be done as soon as possible.

*D: (This was confusing.) I'm trying to understand how I can do this. If
the guide will do it, how can we get the message?*

E: The guide is the person that you are working with. I'm sorry I did not
make myself clear.

*D: You mean this vehicle (Elena) is to find the quatrain? And we will be
led to know which is the appropriate one for the things that are
happening in my world at this time.*

E: That is correct.

D: Can you tell me why this is so important?

E: There is both an atmospheric condition and planetary changes and ...
(She raised her hand to keep me from saying anything.) There's more,
just ... *(She was listening.)*

I could not believe this was happening. He really knew I was there.
It was so implausible. A man I had long respected and been in awe of was
actually delivering messages to me across time and space. I couldn't have
been more astounded if Jesus himself had begun to speak. My mind was
swirling. I kept thinking that this was impossible.

E: *(A long pause.)* I don't understand, but he is saying that because of the
weaponry that you use in the present time, it has caused a change in
the atmosphere that is going to be felt within a year's time. And if the
knowledge from the quatrains can be translated, it would be beneficial for the people of your time.—There's more. *(A long pause as she
listened.)* He also says that because of the planetary alignment, there
will be earth changes. And with the translation of certain quatrains
it would help people to understand where these changes are going to
be strongest. Then they would be able to make their decisions. He
said that the quatrains will be easily known to your vehicle. He was
hoping it would be done at a faster rate.

This was an interesting possibility and one that would never have
occurred to me without his suggestion.

D: Is he in a trance at this time?

E: I don't understand your words.

*D: Is he meditating at this time? I was just wondering how he knew I
was speaking.*

E: Because he's at a different space right now. I can't explain it. At this
point in time I'm not in a room. When he talked to me there was a
change in the surrounding area.

D: (I didn't understand.) Then he's in a different room?

E: *(Emphatic)* No!—He's with me, but we are not in the room. We are not ... *(Had difficulty explaining.)*

D: Do you mean that when he's talking to you, it's as though you're in a different place?

E: That's correct. It's a place with ... misty clouds. There's no substantial foundation.

D: But it's a nice feeling, isn't it? Because that's important, I don't want you to feel uncomfortable.

E: Oh, yes!

D: That was what I thought. He would be in a different state, a state of meditation or something like that, so he can hear me.

E: That is correct.

D: Does he approve of what I'm doing?

E: *(Emphatic)* Oh, yes!—He does not come through to you direct because of a prophecy he made. That no man shall hear from him again through the ages. In person. He would not speak directly.

D: I didn't know of that prophecy. Is that in the quatrains?

E: Yes, it is. It was not his decision to make this announcement. He was guided to say this in his quatrain so there would be those aware of ... (searching for the word) of imitations?

D: Imposters? Somebody pretending that they are him?

E: That's correct.

D: Yes, I can understand that.—Then I feel greatly honored that he has chosen to come and talk in this way.

E: He says it's not so much an honor as a *need*. He wants you to warn the people.—Just a moment! *(Listening again.)* He says that he is able to see that there is a book, a large volume, containing all the quatrains. He wants you to direct your vehicle (Elena) to study the quatrains. He says that intuitively she will know which ones. You are to give her a suggestion that will give her confidence in the translation and have her work on them. If there is a question on them or a problem in the translation within her, she's to write it down. And the next time you meet with your vehicle, you are to contact us. And he will, through me, look at them, verify them, and tell you.

D: And clarify the points we don't understand. Then she can do this in her own time and she will be led to find the proper ones.

E: That is correct.—He says one thing that is confusing to people is that the quatrains have more than one meaning. It has something to do with ... continuous time, he says. That there is a repeat of patterns within the planets that allows there to be a double meaning. They do not understand this.

D: That will be a new way of looking at them. Then he will explain how they are interconnected and help us to understand?

E: That's correct.

D: We've been taught that we can learn from history. That it does repeat itself, and we can learn lessons from the past in this way.

E: That is what he means. He says also that word meanings have changed somewhat. So that what one would have translated two or three hundred years ago would have a different meaning in your time.

D: *That's true. Even the language I speak, the words are different than they were in your time.*

E: He says that the book he spoke of has the French on one side and the language you speak on the other. And that if the language—English!—if the English is not correct then he will look at the French words and make the correction.

D: *All right. Because we don't know how to speak French or read it. We will have to read the translation. This would be the only way we could do it.*

E: He says that your vehicle will have the gift of knowing.

D: *There is always the problems of whether they have been written down correctly, even in the French, over all these years.*

E: He understands that.

Since I had never really looked at a book of his quatrains, I wondered if they were arranged in some kind of historical order, either by Nostradamus himself or by the translators.

E: Again, he says not to go by the dates that have already passed, as a new meaning could be found in them now.

D: *I have heard that he does list some dates in the quatrains. And some of them contain what is called a "play on words." A name that is twisted around to make a puzzle or a riddle out of it. They say that he did this on purpose.*

E: The translation that will be given to your vehicle will be a clear meaning in your language.

Since he was not going to supply the quatrains, I obviously could go no further with this until I bought a book. I planned to move Dyonisus from the scene. I went over his instructions again.

E: One moment. *(Pause, listening.)* I don't understand everything he is saying. Perhaps you will. He says that one of the first quatrains she is to look for refers to Biblical material that will affirm the work you are doing.

I was startled. Could he be referring to the Jesus material in the book I had just completed?

D: *Do you mean some work that I've already done dealing with the life of Jesus?*

E: This is work from Biblical times that will be discovered in another country that will affirm what you are doing. Evidently these Biblical passages have not been discovered yet in your time.

I was thinking he might be referring to the discovery of the Dead Sea Scrolls in the late 1940s and early 1950s which I refer to many times in my book on Jesus.

D: *I thought you were referring to some discoveries that were made about 40 years ago. This is not true?*

E: No. Because this is work that is going to be discovered in the near future. It's hard to measure time, but within a year or so after your work is published, perhaps sooner. This will coincide with the work that you are doing now in publishing. Do you understand?

I really didn't. Everything about this session was too far-fetched to really understand until I would have time to delve into these strange developments. But at least I knew that he was referring to my book on Jesus.

E: One moment. *(Pause, listening.)* He said that he will also work with ... drawing maps and locations of certain things such as the buried Scriptures that pertain to your work. He can now at this time give an actual location.

This was an interesting development. I reached for my tablet and marker that I always keep handy during regressions.

D: *Could he do it now?*

E: *(Pause, listening.)* He said that it would be more of a clarification and easier done with the quatrain first translated correctly. Then he would work on the map.

D: *Maybe the countries have not changed too much.*

E: It doesn't matter what names the countries are now.

I found this information really exciting. If he were able to do this, draw a map and pinpoint where a valuable archaeological discovery of Scripture similar to the Dead Sea Scrolls would be made, it would be very valuable to the world. It would also prove that we were truly in touch with the actual Nostradamus and that he was a genuine prophet. I could hardly wait to begin work on this.

D: *Wasn't it true that many times he gave countries and nations symbolic names and used symbolism in his quatrains?*

E: That is correct.

D: *This is where some confusion has come in, as to what countries he was referring to with these symbols.*

E: He has been deliberate in his confusion. He says that fewer would have understood in his time, but that you are more into an age of enlightenment. He said that man has grown to a point in time where understanding the quatrains are easier for those who take the time, not only to read but to listen to what is inside of themselves.

D: *And the people in his time weren't like that?*

E: Not as aware as the people of your time.

D: *Maybe that was why he made them puzzles, so they would survive. Do you think that is true?*

E: *(Pause, listening.)* He said that was part of it. He translated in a clearer manner for the King, the rulers of that time. For work that was necessary for them to know about or events pertaining to them.—I am just asking your forgiveness. Being in this space has tired us. It's a newer experience for me. But he said we will be strengthened each time.

He wants you to understand one thing: that this is a time that is present for us *now*. That we are able to project into your time. That we are still surviving in our moment of time. And that you are not talking to people that have passed on, but are as alive as you are now. It is very important that you understand this.

D: *Yes, I've always thought that. People have accused me of speaking to the dead, and I tell them, "No, they are very much alive."*

E: I am glad you understand.

D: *What you are doing is just looking at our time.*

E: That is correct. We are not in the same time frame as when we first spoke with you. But in a different time frame now, to be able to view your world.

D: *Well, there's nothing wrong with that that I can see. But there are skeptics. They're the ones who don't understand.*

E: With the information you will derive from the quatrains, there will be less skeptics. But he says there will always be skeptics. He says that you have important work to do and this is important information for you because of your ability to write. As long as the information is given to you, he will work closely with your vehicle. He said that time is of the essence now. That it's necessary to get the information out to the people.

Since Dyonisus was tiring of being in that strange formless place, I started to move him to another time in his life. She raised her hand again to stop me.

E: He said that when you need to speak with us again, to refer to talking to us at the special meeting place, so we will be at that different space in time, instead of in our own time. It'll be easier for us to talk with you.

D: *All right. But according to the method I use, I will have to first take you to your time. And then I will ask to go to the meeting place?*

E: That is fine. It would be with the understanding of a meditative spot for us to be able to communicate better with you.

It was a good thing that he stopped me to give instructions on *how* to locate them again. When a subject is involved in reliving a lifetime, it is a different process. I was so overwhelmed by this entire procedure that I had not even thought about how we could get together next time. Nostradamus had thought of this detail even though I had not. He had prevented me from leaving until he had given instructions. He was definitely completely in charge of this whole phenomenon. I suppose it would have been more difficult to rely upon Nostradamus sensing my presence each time and interrupting to relay information. This way we had specific instructions on how to reach him the next time. I knew I could not keep them there if they were tiring. Maybe they were both in a meditative trance and it was causing some kind of a drain on their bodies, especially Dyonisus since he was not accustomed to that type of altered state.

Since I still had a little more time left in my session, I removed Dyonisus from that scene and asked him to move forward to an important day later in his life. I knew that once I moved him, the tiredness would leave. At the end of the count I asked what he was doing.

E: I'm watching a surgery I've never seen before. It's part of the hand that has been severed. And Nostradamus is working on putting the hand back together. I'm assisting. I'm listening to his instructions. He is directing me to perform the surgery while he keeps the patient in a trance. He is instructing me to take the tendons and to attach them to the ones that are protruding from the hand itself, and to sew them. The amazing thing is that the patient has been able to slow down the flow of blood, according to Nostradamus' instructions, which is an exciting thing to see. Making it clearer for me to work.

D: *Is it difficult to do?*

E: Oh, yes. It needs all my concentration.

D: *What type of material are you using on the sewing?*

E: A needle and thread. It's thread that's been dipped in tar to make it stronger. The patient will have some use of the hand, but unfortunately I do not have the ability to sew all the nerve endings together.— This is amazing. He has given the patient instructions to visualize his hand healing itself. I have never seen him use this technique.

D: *Is anyone else in the room as you do this?*

E: No, it must be kept secret. The others would never understand.

D: *Let's move forward till the operation is finished and you can see the results, because you are concentrating on what you are doing. I don't want to interfere with that.—All right. We've gone forward some. Was the operation a success?*

E: In most part. The patient has the ability to move the thumb and the finger. The feelings are not in the hand, so he will have to be extremely careful against a cold or a hot, because he would not know if he were hurting himself.—The unfortunate thing is ... *(sigh)* we cannot explain how this work was done. Physicians do not have the ability yet to slow down the flow of blood.

D: *What is he going to tell them?*

E: *(Pause, then a broad smile.)* I am amused because what he tells them will not work for them. He tells them to pack the hand in ice. *(Smiling)* It could only be done in the winter. Where else would he get ice?

D: *(Laugh) That's very true. That's not the secret, but it would numb the hand.*

E: Oh, yes, and it would slow the blood to some extent, but not enough to be able to clearly hold the tendons and the certain muscles in the hand to resew it.

D: *Yes, the blood would block the view and you couldn't see what you were doing.*

E: That's correct.

D: *Do the other doctors think this is the explanation?*

E: They're aware that Nostradamus does not tell them everything. He has many secrets. There are many spies also. *(Emphatic)* Oh, yes! Everyone would want to be able to accomplish the same.

D: *Could this be dangerous, even for a man in his position?*

E: The society accepts so much, but there is a limit to what they will or have the ability to comprehend. Being a religious society, it makes them afraid of things they can't explain. Works of the Devil. He tries to avoid people's questions.

D: *I thought he was such an important person that they wouldn't dare accuse him of anything.*

E: He is still just a man that they would question. He is not the king!

D: *Then he must be careful. You and the other followers protect his secrets. I shall protect his secrets also. They won't learn from me.— I'm afraid I'm tiring you. Is it all right if I come again and speak with you?*

E: Yes. I don't know why but it seems like it's important.

I brought Elena up to full consciousness, and she wanted to tell me what she remembered about the session.

E: It was very strange. I remember as if I was in another room and I could hear voices on the other side of the door. I've had this kind of experience before, like when Andy comes in. And then the door opened but I couldn't see anyone. But I know there were two people on the other side and they were talking to you. One of them was ... Dyonisus *(unsure of the name)* and the other one was Nostradamus. And it was a room ... it wasn't really a room, it was like walking through clouds and mist.

D: *Yes, you said there was no form.—Is that all you remember, just that scene? You could hear the voices but you couldn't see the people w`* were talking?*

E: You know like when you have a dream? You can visualize them ut their form doesn't stay distinct in the dream? Okay, it was like that. But I remember seeing these *eyes,* these wonderful *eyes* looking directly at me. They were turned toward me but they were talking to you.

D: *Whose eyes do you think they were?*

E: Oh, I think they were Nostradamus'. I mean, I *know* they were. I *do* know they were. That was really something, they were so much more magnificent than anything I have ever seen. But it was like his eyes were telling me I have work to do.

I chuckled, "Oh, yes, he gave us an assignment, all right." Val also laughed. It was *quite* an assignment.

"Oh?" Elena laughed. "Well, are you going to tell me?"

This session had been very exciting and unbelievable but it had been Val's first experience of this type. She could hardly contain herself and had been bursting to tell Elena what had happened. I had made her wait until Elena told me any memories she had about the session, because I didn't want them to be colored by anything we might say. I now let Val bubblingly pour out her enthusiastic report of the session to Elena. We told her about the important assignment she had been given, and the instructions that Nostradamus wanted her to follow. When we finished, it was obvious that Elena did not share our enthusiasm.

She sat in deep thought and finally spoke, "Do you mean he wants me to translate quatrains that will predict the future of our world? Gee, that's an awful responsibility. I don't know if I can do that. I don't know if I even *want* to do that."

Val spoke up, "What do you mean, you don't want to? He said it was something that you *had* to do, and you had to do it right away."

I was also surprised by her apparent reluctance. I knew it must be a shock to come out of a trance and be told something of this magnitude. Her face displayed confusion, puzzlement, and disbelief. I knew that she had free will and if she did not want to do this there would be no way to make her participate. I would not even want to try. I would never make anyone do anything they were uncomfortable with.

According to Nostradamus, the bulk of the experiment, the burden of the work, would fall on Elena. She would have to find, meditate, and translate the quatrains on her own. My only part would be helping with the verification by Nostradamus while she was in trance. It *was* a terrific responsibility.

Elena shook her head in disbelief. "The whole idea is impossible. It's almost laughable. There are people who have spent years trying to figure out what Nostradamus meant. And here we come along, who don't even know anything about it, who haven't even read it, and we're going to try to solve the puzzle, to do what they can't. The whole idea is absurd."

"Yes," I said, "absurd, but intriguing." I agreed it was egotistical to think we could solve mysteries that had puzzled mankind for over 400 years. "Maybe it could be to our advantage not knowing anything about it. That way we don't have any preconceived notions about what they should say. Maybe that's what he intended, someone who could look at them with a fresh approach and an open mind."

I had thought it would be a remarkable accomplishment for Elena to draw a portrait of Nostradamus. But now that idea paled before the possibility of translating his puzzles, an enormous and incredibly challenging project.

She said she would think about it. Maybe after the initial shock wore off, she would also see the wonderful possibilities of this experiment. She reluctantly agreed to at least get a book and see if any of the quatrains sparked an interest in her. She thought a friend might have an old book she could borrow.

When I left she still looked confused and lost in thought. I hoped it would not turn her off since Nostradamus had seemed so emphatic that this be done immediately. He said he had hoped it would have been done before this. He had expressed such a sense of urgency and importance that I felt we should try to comply. It would all rest on Elena's reactions to this strange development and her decisions. I felt there was no way it could be accomplished without her. This was an intriguing experiment and one which I would have never thought of on my own. It never would have occurred to me that we would ever have contact with the true Nostradamus. The odds are so inconceivably and impossibly high against this happening. It was also obvious this idea had not originated with Elena, as the prospect frightened and confused her. Although it sounded crazy, it seemed to me the only other explanation was that Nostradamus himself had initiated this whole project. Maybe it occurred to him spontaneously when he found out his student was somehow communicating with a person living in the future.

Why should this seem so far-fetched? Nostradamus was only doing what every psychic down through time immortal has attempted to do: to warn others. Every psychic that has ever had a premonition or vision of the future has felt this same responsibility. To try to stop the event from occurring by warning those involved, in the hope that some way they may be able to take action to avoid the event that was foreseen. What could be more natural than for Nostradamus also to try this? With his truly remarkable precognitive abilities he could see that in our time his predictions were not being translated accurately. He had been forced by the circumstances of his time to be deliberately obscure. Now it had become obvious that he had probably been too obscure and no one could truly understand what he was trying to warn us about. Thus, Nostradamus had seized this opportunity of my contact through his student, to reach forward through time and space and warn us of impending important events.

What did he want to tell us? Would he be successful in making us understand? Would a stubborn mankind listen? It was an intriguing enigma and an exciting experiment. We had no way of knowing where this would lead or what might come forth, but I knew that my insatiable curiosity had once again been sparked and I would follow this wherever it led. This presented itself as a tremendous and seemingly impossible challenge, but it all depended upon Elena. I felt that her cooperation was essential to this project since Dyonisus, her alter ego, was our key to Nostradamus, the master inventor of enigmas. I was as confused as anyone as to what the results of this strange experiment would be.

Chapter 5

The Shift of the World

ALTHOUGH ELENA HAD BEEN THE ONE instructed to find a book of Nostradamus' quatrains and study them, I thought it would not hurt if I also became familiar with them. I wanted a book that was currently in the book stores so that people would be able to find it to compare interpretations. I also had to find one that contained the original French quatrains. I had no idea at the time of the complexity many authors had brought to the translation of this work. I have always thought that translation from one language to another was a simple matter, since a word can only have a certain number of meanings. But I had not counted on Nostradamus' deliberate obscurity. Each book that I found had translated the quatrains into English differently. There were some similarities but often the differences were enough to give the puzzle an entirely different meaning. I did not know at the time, since I am not familiar with French, that Nostradamus often used archaic words and also substituted Latin at times. He freely used anagrams, which are word puzzles where the letters of a word can be moved about and even changed to read as another word altogether.

I chose a book that was the latest published on the quatrains, *The Prophecies of Nostradamus* by Erika Cheetham. Since I did not know which book Elena would have access to, I would use this book as a backup to compare her interpretations. I assumed she would be doing the majority of the work through her meditation and I would only be acting as a guide to discover whether her interpretations were correct. These were the instructions that had been given to us. I could foresee a great deal of work further on down the road because I thought I would have to find as many books written about Nostradamus and the quatrains as possible and compare them. Since it appeared that each author down through the ages had his own ideas, I was aware of the enormity of such a project. But research has always been a major part of my work.

At home I barely had time to thumb through the book. Even at first glance I could see it would be complicated. The quatrains seemed to make no sense at all. I was glad it was Elena and not I who would have to figure them out. The job of interpreting just a few of them seemed to be an enormously ambitious task. I could fully respect Ms. Cheetham's perseverance. There were many quatrains that had no interpretation since they were so obscure. Others were marked with a question mark or an "F" to indicate that they might apply to our future. This was certainly a job no one would want to volunteer for. I put the book in the valise with my tape recorder for future reference and was thankful again that this job would not be my responsibility. How wrong I was! Unexpected developments were already in the works that would change everything dealing with this complicated project. There were to be twists and turns that not even a fiction writer could have envisioned.

Because Elena had had company from out-of-town, we had not been able to have a session since we were informed by Nostradamus that we must immediately begin the translation of his quatrains. If Elena was truly planning to move by July, two months, away, we would have to get started as soon as possible.

Since I had to go to that town anyway for our group meeting, I stopped by her house to set up an appointment and received a great shock.

She answered the door with the announcement, "I'm afraid I have some bad news for you. I have to go to California." I knew she had been there to see her daughter only a few months before. She said she was leaving on Saturday, just five days away. I was disappointed but we had had to delay sessions before, so again I would have to put the project on hold until her return. But her next statement was even more of a shock. I asked when she was coming back and she answered, "I'm not!" I couldn't think of anything to say; I felt dumfounded and overwhelmed.

It seemed that her daughter was getting a divorce and she wanted Elena to come out again and help her with the children. Being the kind of mother she is, of course she said she would come. Elena's family had always been the primary focus of her life. With ten children, someone would always be needing her and Elena would always be there for them. Rather than coming back home, she planned to go on to Seattle in a month or so and travel on up to Alaska by July. Her husband and children were going to take care of selling all their possessions and meet her there. They thought this would be easier and less expensive.

Elena confirmed what I had suspected when she told me the whole idea of this project had frightened her. The urgency disturbed her and she was very hesitant about doing it. She had done a lot of thinking about it and she felt it was an awful responsibility, and a responsibility that she didn't know if she wanted to take on. She didn't know whether she even wanted to know the future. But the more she thought about it, the more she realized that this was an "ostrich with its head in the sand" type of attitude. She had finally decided she would do it if it would help the world to better cope with the future, when circumstances intervened to change her plans. I wondered if she was not secretly relieved to be rid of this responsibility. She could substitute her children's problems, which were difficult, yet more familiar and safer for her to handle.

I really felt that my panic button had been pushed. The subject's free will is always paramount. I had had people back out before, which meant an interesting story would be cut short and put on the shelf, but there was something different about this situation. There had never been the sense of urgency expressed in those other cases. We had been informed that the quatrains must be translated and the knowledge brought forth to the world, and now she was telling me she was leaving. How were we to get the information? She said that maybe she could do some of the translating on her own after she was in Alaska and send me what came to her in meditation. It seemed like a last-ditch effort in order to please me. I felt it was half-hearted because I didn't believe the information could come forth accurately in any other way except deep trance. Even in meditation the conscious mind would be too active for the information to be clear.

The only solution I could find at the moment was to work intensely with her in the few days she had left, if she was willing. I would try to cram as much as I could into whatever sessions I could arrange and be grateful for any information we could obtain under such hurried and unsatisfactory conditions. She agreed more from an effort to placate me than out of interest on her part. It was going to be difficult to find the time. Since she would not be coming back, the next few days would be crammed full of the details of getting ready for a garage sale and arranging the move. There might only be the opportunity for two sessions. We decided to meet later that night after our group meeting was over. I was willing to stay as long as it took because I felt this was very important, and if we could accomplish something before she left, it was worth it. The only other opportunity would be in two days, on Thursday. I would have to accept this and be grateful for anything we could get. Maybe something worthwhile would come through.

Over supper with other members of the group, I was really getting upset. I knew I wanted what was best for Elena and if she wanted to leave I wouldn't protest, but I was also worried about what might possibly happen to her. Her subconscious was trying to impress upon her the importance of doing this project. If she didn't go through with it, she might become ill. The subconscious is very powerful. I thought it was possible that by rejecting what it wanted her to do, it might cause her to get sick. Who knows? The instructions had been so emphatic. I thought the only solution was to have a session and to try to relieve the pressure of the situation, for her sake as well as mine.

Val insisted, "You've got to keep her from going. This is more important. You've got to talk her into staying for a couple of more weeks. Surely she can wait that long."

I understood her sense of urgency and importance, especially since I also shared her feeling of disappointment. But I knew I could never take the responsibility of interfering with Elena's life. If she felt it was more important to be with her daughter, then it would be extremely selfish for me to ask her to change her plans and stay. Elena was exercising her use of free will, and I knew there was absolutely nothing I could do about it.

By a strange unannounced coincidence the group meeting that night was going to be different. Someone was bringing a VCR and planned to show the documentary film about Nostradamus called *The Man Who Saw Tomorrow*. This was amazing in itself since the person bringing the film was not a regular member and didn't know anything about my work with Elena. Elena's main reason for coming to the meeting that night was to say good-bye to her friends. She had never seen this film narrated by Orson Welles, although I had, and she became quite excited about seeing it.

Val whispered to me that maybe this coincidence was to have a purpose. She thought that maybe after Elena saw the film, she would realize the importance of the project and would change her mind, deciding to stay for a few more weeks so we could work on this. I doubted it, I felt she had made up her mind for a variety of different reasons.

One thing I noticed about the film was how little was mentioned about Nostradamus' private life, it mostly concentrated on his predictions for the world. I felt we already knew more about him than they did. Elena was impressed by the film since she had not read anything about him and felt the movie displayed him as a truly remarkable man.

After the meeting, we went over to Val's house again where we would not be disturbed. I knew I wouldn't get home until two in the morning, but I felt it was worth it. We held this session amid the disarray of half-packed boxes because Val was also involved in the process of moving. It was very representative of my feelings about the situation. I felt like everything was coming unglued, that everything was in a state of upheaval.

Elena had borrowed a book from her friend. She had chosen two quatrains from it and had written her interpretations down. They were the only ones she had had a chance to go over. Nostradamus had said she would choose one that would deal with a Biblical discovery. She handed me her book and the notes she had made about the quatrains. I barely had time to glance at them.

I hurriedly leafed through the book I had bought and marked some of the ones the author thought pertained to the future. Maybe we could concentrate on some of those, since I had had no chance to study any of them. It was to be a random, slipshod session without the careful preparation I had hoped for.

When Elena was in trance I repeated the detailed instructions I had been given to contact Dyonisus and Nostradamus in the special meeting place where they could project their minds forward to our time. I was not even sure the procedure would work. I hoped for the best as we began.

D: *1, 2, 3, you have gone to the special meeting place with Nostradamus*

so that we may communicate. Are you there?
E: We are here.

I breathed a sigh of relief and realized for the first time how tense I was. The instructions had succeeded, and we were in contact again.

D: *Last time you spoke of a quatrain that Elena was to find and try to interpret on her own. You said it would refer to Biblical Scriptures that have yet to be discovered. Do you remember speaking of that?*
E: That is correct.
D: *All right. I will read the quatrain she found and her interpretation.*

CENTURY VII-14. This quatrain is worded differently in Erika Cheetham's book.

D: *"They shall show topography faultily. The urns of the monuments shall be opened. Sects shall multiply and holy philosophy shall give black for white and green for gold."*
    This is what Elena wrote: "It concerns the discovery of the Dead Sea Scrolls. This quatrain contains a message for different years. And also the discovery of the Ark (of the covenant) at a later date. Black for white is photographing of the scrolls and the new pages from old."
    What do you think of her interpretation?
E: The first part is incorrect. These are not the Dead Sea Scrolls, but lost work that will coincide with the material that you have been working on and is in the process of being published.

Even though her interpretation was not totally accurate, I think it is very significant that Elena was able to pick one quatrain at random out of a thousand that *did* deal with the Bible. That makes the odds one thousand to one. She had to have been guided subconsciously in this. By Andy? By Dyonisus? By Nostradamus? This was too startling to be coincidence.

D: *All right. You said you would give me some information about where this would be discovered. You said something about drawing a map.*

I had the tablet and marker ready in case we needed it. Although she was an artist, Elena said that she had never even attempted to draw a map before.

E: One moment. *(Pause as she listened.)* He said we will get back to this because of the possibility of the maps being used for monetary gain. Not by you, but by others.
D: *(I was disappointed.) That's always a possibility. There might be treasure hunters, is that what you mean?*
E: That is correct.
D: *But could you tell me in what country it will be discovered?*
E: *(Long pause, then slowly.)* It will be in the mountains where the city

is hidden. The city that has been discovered ... by one who was Caucasian, but passed himself off ... as a person of the desert.

He had answered with a quatrain. This was said very slowly and deliberately as though she was listening and then repeating. He said it was a new quatrain, not one from his book. This was all he had to say on it.

(It has since been suggested that maybe this referred to Lawrence of Arabia, the man who helped the Arabs overthrow the yoke of the Ottoman Empire during World War I. He was the first Westerner to explore these lands, and certainly was a Caucasian who passed himself off as a person of the desert.)

UPDATE: In 1992 as we were preparing the revised updated version of this book, a newspaper article appeared that substantiated this new quatrain. Quote: "The lost city of Ubar, called 'the Atlantis of the Sands' by Lawrence of Arabia, has been found in remote Oman using pictures taken from space shuttle Challenger, explorers said. ... Ruins of that oasis city were discovered mostly buried under sand at a well site named Shisr in southern Oman's barren 'Empty Quarter.' ... Researchers found the city by tracing ancient desert roads detected in pictures taken from several spacecraft, including radar and optical cameras carried by Challenger in October 1984. ... Recent excavations indicate that the city was inhabited from 2800 B.C. until about A.D. 100. If dating of the artifacts are correct, urban development in the region began about 1000 years earlier than once thought. ... The late T.E. Lawrence, the British World War I soldier known as Lawrence of Arabia, called Ubar 'the Atlantis of the sands,' after the legendary sunken continent. According to legend, Ubar—known as Iram the 'city of towers' in Islam's sacred Koran—was destroyed during a disaster about A.D. 100 and was buried by sand. Evidence indicates the city fell into a sinkhole created when an underground limestone cavern collapsed." *End quote.*

E: He has given you all the information on it that you need to know. The rest of the information will come through another source.

D: *(This was a surprise.) Another source? I was wondering about that. I will ask more about that later.*

Maybe this was a glimmer of hope that the project might continue after Elena departed.

D: *There is a quatrain here that Elena, the vehicle, has looked at that she thinks is interpreted incorrectly.* (CENTURY II-48) *"The great army which will pass over the mountains when Saturn is in Sagittarius and Mars moving into Pisces. Poison hidden under the heads of salmon, their chief in war hung with a cord." The interpretation in our book says that this conjunction of the planets occurred in 1751 and the next one is not until 2193.*

E: That is incorrect. It happens in the twelfth month of 1986.

D: *What is it that is to happen? Their interpretation is very unclear. They said it doesn't make any sense. And I know that Nostradamus would not write something that did not make any sense.*

E: *(Pause as though listening.)* There are several things that are being said. Confusing. *(Pause)* There will be a contact from the stars ... A light display will go on. There shall be an occurrence in the sky at that time.

D: *Is that why it refers to these stars?*

E: That is correct.

D: *Instead of saying a conjunction, it means that it will happen in that part of the sky?*

E: No. That is a time element. It gives the date. Astronomers have made *(pause as though searching for the right word)* a mathematical misalignment of the planets. They can very easily make an error when interpreting something from centuries before. As you can see, they have been 20, 30 years off with the exact time.

D: *They are?*

E: When they are using the planets as an interpretation, they can be off ... one or two decades.

D: *This would be important in the interpretation. Do you mean that the planets are different now than they were in the time he was looking at them?*

E: Yes. But mathematically they can interpret it wrong, because of ... *(a big sigh)*

D: *Miscalculations?*

E: That's right.

D: *"Poison hidden under the heads of salmon"?*

E: This has a different association, because of what is happening in the atmosphere today.

D: *It says a great army will pass over the mountains. Is that what you mean by the light display?*

E: That is correct. From the contact being made from the stars, the universe. This contact will bring a great awareness to the people.

D: *And you said this will occur in the 12th month of 1986?*

E: December 22. December 22, 1986.—Please read back the translation I gave you.

This took me offguard. He had no way of knowing that I was using a tape recorder and I had not written it down. I would have to rely on my memory.

D: *It was that ... there would be a great light in the sky. And there would be a light display.*

E: This will actually be a display shown by beings from another planet.

D: *One thing you must understand. I'm not writing these down. I have a little black box that captures the words and will repeat them to me later. So when you ask me to repeat back what you have told me, it's hard for me to remember it. But the black box remembers.*

E: All right, I understand.

(Later when this date had passed we realized that there were some very dramatic and reliable UFO sightings during that time. Could this be what he was referring to?)

I now decided to ask about some quatrains that I had hurriedly marked.

D: *(CENTURY II-46) "After great misery for mankind an even greater approaches when the great cycle of the centuries is renewed. It will rain blood, milk, famine, war and disease. In the sky will be seen a fire dragging a trail of sparks." Can you tell me what that means?*

E: The first part refers to the black nations suffering with a famine. The second part refers to the comet that is happening at this time. The third part refers to the weaponry that has caused illness in the air that will be destructive to the crops and breathing. That will cause people to cough up blood.

D: *The weaponry is causing this to happen in our time, the time of the comet?*

E: That is correct. The weaponry explosion. He says that this has happened recently.

D: *I think I know of the event he means. There was something that happened within this last month of April that has concerned people.*

I was thinking of the nuclear accident that had just occurred at the Chernobyl plant in Russia, April 26, 1986.

E: He says that is what he's referring to.

D: *Of course our scientists and experts keep saying that this will cause no harm. They're trying to make everyone think that it was a minor incident and it will hurt no one.*

E: This is incorrect. He says they are saying this as not to cause a panic.

Another event happened during August 1986 that this quatrain also might refer to. Unexplained gas rising from a volcanic lake in Cameroon, Africa killed about 1500 people. These deaths occurred because the air was poisoned and they were unable to breathe. It was reported that some of the victims coughed up blood. Crops were destroyed that were in the path of the gas. I think this could be a case of a quatrain referring to more than one event, as Nostradamus said they often do, especially when these two occurred so close together in time.

D: *Will anything happen as a result of this accident in our country which is called the New World?*

E: More so toward the north and the northwest. North near Russia. West, on the west side of your country. And toward what is called … Canada. (*Pronounced more like "Kenada." Pronounced slowly as though it was an unfamiliar word.*)

D: *Do you think these problems will be very severe?*

E: Different degrees of severity.

I then read a few quatrains that Dyonisus said did not refer to the immediate future; thus Nostradamus did not consider them to be of importance to us at this time. There were other things to be concerned with now. He seemed to be aware of the shortage of time and didn't want to bother with quatrains about the past.

D: (CENTURY I-16) *"A scythe joined with a pond in Sagittarius at its highest ascent. Plague, famine, death from military hands. The century approaches its renewal."*

He asked me to repeat the quatrain. It was almost as though he couldn't really understand the book's translation. I had discovered that in every book on these quatrains they were translated differently according to the author. No wonder he didn't recognize them. I wondered how much similarity they really bore to his original intentions. After I repeated it, he continued, "This also refers to what has happened in the last few weeks. The scythe being the country Russia."

A sickle is the present-day symbol for Russia. It is also an ancient occult symbol for death.

D: *What does it mean, "joined with a pond"?*
E: He said this refers to how the accident occurred. Through the water pipe. (*She had difficulty finding the proper words.*) Their way of handling the power that they contained. And this being a place run by military. It has gotten out of control. And because the accident will cause this destruction to their country.

This translation made a great deal of sense in light of what had just happened at the Russian nuclear power plant at Chernobyl. At this time, less than a month after the incident, no one had any idea what had caused the accident. The Russians were not releasing any news. It was later suggested it might have had something to do with the plant's cooling system.

The translators had a fondness for translating many of Nostradamus' predictions as meaning war. It was becoming obvious that this was not necessarily so.

D: *People have been wondering what Nostradamus meant by the New City?*
E: People believe that the new city means the one that you refer to as New York. In some of the quatrains this is correct, but not all.
D: *Well, I will read one that they think has to do with the new city.* (CENTURY I-87) *"Earthshaking fire from the center of the earth will cause tremors around the New City. Two great rocks will war for a long time. Then ..."* I can't quite pronounce this right. *"Arethusa will redden a new river."* Does this refer to New York?
E: (*Long pause as though listening.*) I see. He is saying there are three cities involved, a triangle affect. And it will affect the West Coast. That New York *will* be experiencing an earthquake that will be

devastating because of the buildings that are so tall there. But this is not the one referred to in the quatrain.

D: *You said there were three cities involved in the quatrain, and one is on the West Coast?* (I thought he meant that one of these cities was New York.)

E: No, the three are on the West Coast. A triangle. Let's see. I don't understand ... It will affect the city called ... Los Angeles? (*Pronounced with a French accent instead of Spanish.*) San ... Francisco? (*Said slowly as though it was a strange word.*) (*Long pause.*) "Los" something ...

People have since suggested that he might have been trying to say Las Vegas which might form a triangle between San Francisco and Los Angeles. He said the earthquake would affect the three cities during the same time period.

D: *Does that mean there will be a lot of earthquakes during this next year?*

E: It has already started, he says.

That is certainly accurate. Earthquakes seem to be rampant around the world.

D: *Here's another one.* (CENTURY 8-91) *"The Gods will make it appear to mankind that they are the authors of a great war. Before the sky was seen to be free of weapons and rockets, the greatest damage will be inflicted on the left."*

E: This refers to the shift in the planet.

D: *Oh? Is there going to be a shift in the planet?*

I have heard this predicted by several other psychics but I wanted to see if Nostradamus agreed with them.

E: Oh, yes! (*Pause, then she spoke slowly as though listening and repeating.*) The shift will occur toward the closing of the century you know. And will be as abrupt as to be within a six- to ten-hour period. Continents as you know them now will cease to exist or change dramatically. (*A deep sigh.*)

I have heard this dire prediction before, but somehow coming from Nostradamus, it sounded even more ominous.

D: *Is there anything that can be done to avoid this?*

E: The only thing that can be done is to make humanity aware. And to let them prepare themselves spiritually, and intellectually become aware of survival through climatic changes.

This was already beginning to disturb me. It sounded so final.

D: *If it will happen that abruptly, will there be a lot of people killed?*

E: Civilization will cease to exist as you know it now.

Strange how her voice was so calm and serene as she pronounced these words of doom for all mankind.

D: In that short of a time?

E: It will be the beginning of a new age.

D: Is there anything we can do to stop this? Is there any advice at all?

E: Oh, yes! Just stop the explosions that the military feels are so important.

D: These are things that will speed up the shift?

E: (*Uncertainly*) For some reason I'm losing you! I'm floating in a ... it's very gray and ... I can't hear you as clearly.

This is uncommon but it does happen. It may have been caused because Elena was so tired, or it could have had something to do with the special meeting place we were in. The characteristics of that dimension or whatever it was may have been creating a condition that I am unaware of. I did not want to lose contact with Nostradamus because the time for sessions was so short.

I asked, "Is there anything I can do to make the communication better?"

E: (*Her voice sounded very sleepy and groggy.*) Talk to her. Talk to her!

It seemed as though one or the other (Elena or Dyonisus) was trying to fall asleep. If this happened I would lose contact and would have to either move Dyonisus to another time in his earthly life where we would receive only mundane information, or I would have to wake Elena up because she was too tired to continue. I hoped I would not have to do either since I would only have one more opportunity to obtain information from Nostradamus. He was doing an excellent job on the quatrains, so I had to persist. I gave instructions that she would be able to hear me clearly and distinctly and could follow my voice no matter where she happened to be. After a few minutes of this, I could tell she was responding and was once again back with me. Her voice perked up immediately. Whatever had caused the unusual reaction had passed, and I could continue.

This was interesting but time-consuming to try to pinpoint the exact quatrains that dealt with this sort of catastrophe. Since we had just seen the movie about what the translators thought Nostradamus had predicted for the future of our world, I thought I might be able to cut some corners by asking direct questions.

D: I would like to read some more of these, but let me tell you some of the things that the experts have told us his predictions say. Maybe this will make it easier for your to help with the answers. They are saying that there will be earthquakes and worldwide hunger and famine.

E: Yes, that is correct.

D: What will that be caused by?

E: What time period are they referring to?

D: *In the sequence they said, there will be earthquakes and volcanic eruptions and then famine, in that order. It's supposed to be in our future.*

E: The earthquakes and volcanic eruptions are due to the activity caused by the conjunction of the planets, which also affects the shift of this planet. The famine is caused by the weaponry explosions. Accidents that will affect the crops.

D: *Then the experts think we will go into a war in the future after these things happen. That there will be a war involving our weaponry. Does he see anything like that happening?*

E: The events have been changing through the centuries. And because of the new awareness the western civilization has come upon, and because of the accelerated rate of the shifting of the earth's crust, and because of the conjunction of the planets, the war *might* be avoided. Depending on the speed at which the natural events occur. For as in any civilization, when natural disasters occur this is more prominent than the taking over of land.

D: *Yes, especially if everyone is starving too, that makes a big difference.— They say that the quatrains speak of a man from the Middle East who will be the third Anti-Christ who would lead us into war. Do you think this is not correct now?*

The experts all agree that Nostradamus spoke of three Anti-Christs in his quatrains, Napoleon, Hitler and another one in the future. The Bible also mentions a beast that will come at the time of Armageddon. They think it is the same person.

E: This possibility has already taken effect. But whether it will be brought to the point of world war depends on the natural disasters that are taking place. These natural disasters will not only occur in this continent but world-wide, which would affect his country also.

D: *I see. They are interpreting it as war that brings us disaster and world-wide destruction. You think this refers instead to the shift?*

E: That is correct.—Understand! With the earthquakes and volcanoes will be accidental explosion of the weaponry that is buried in the ground. This is going to cause great emotional turmoil within your country and other countries: Brittania and France. And the countries in Europe will want a disarmament. It is important they realize that if this disarmament of the weapons comes about, that it will take place in the Moslem countries also.

D: *Did you say that the shift of the earth will occur by the end of this century or is that when it will begin?*

E: It will occur before the end of the century, this being the year 2000.

D: *Many of the quatrains give dates around that time that the translators have thought meant war.—But you said that when the shift occurs, it will be very rapid and that it will be the end of civilization as we know it.*

E: That is correct.

D: *Will there be survivors to carry on the human race?*

E: Oh, yes!

D: *It all sounds so final. I was hoping you would give me some ray of hope.*

E: There is no death, but a different awareness. Do not feel that people would not know life. There will be those that will be left here to make a new beginning for the earth. But understand, the earth is only a material thing that has a limited life of its own.

D: *Yes, but I suppose because it is our home, we don't like to see it completely destroyed.*

E: Correct.

D: *If there were mass destruction like that, people will be preoccupied with trying to rebuild their lives instead of fighting each other, won't they?*

E: I would hope so.

D: *But you think there will be no cities or anything left?*

E: Not as we know them now.

D: *What about land masses? Will any at all be spared?*

E: All the central part of your continent as you know it will be. Continents all over the earth will be affected. The water mass as we know it now will cover a greater percentage of the earth. Continents that are connected will be split, divided by water that were not divided by water before.

D: *Does that mean that the central part of our country, the water would not . . .*

E: (*Interrupted*) Would be least affected.

D: *What about the other continents? Would there be any areas like that that would be relatively safe?*

E: Which continents are you speaking of?

D: *What about Europe or Asia?*

E: Europe will be affected. (*Pause*) Asia. (*Pause*) There will not be any country that will not be affected.

D: *Will all of Asia be covered with water?*

E: A large portion of it will be.

D: *What about Africa?*

E: Africa shall have a channel cutting through; a new strait.

D: *I keep trying to think of the middle of the United States as being a safe area. But will any place be really safe when this happens?*

E: There will be places that will be affected in a much less traumatic way than others. But understand that what has happened with your weaponry will have a large affect on how much or how soon this devastation would occur.

I had to push aside the horrible images that were flooding into my mind, such terrible scenes of desolation and despair.

D: *Is this what you meant before when you said that you would give us these interpretations and then people could make their decisions?*

E: That is correct.

D: *What do you mean? They will decide whether to stay or go or what?*

E: With a higher awareness, everyone can change their destiny. By making people aware of the damage that can occur to their present weaponry system. By teaching them how to survive. By not having an importance on monetary gain. To be concerned with their spirits. (*Pause*) I will have more for you later.

D: *Then you think that maybe it is possible to change the future if we know these things in advance?*

E: That is correct. The alignment of the planets does not ... it is not known exactly what will happen. What I have told you is one possibility that I see from where I am at this time. The future has been changed many times since our time in space.

D: *Would this make some of your quatrains inaccurate?*

E: This would have changed the meaning of some of them, yes.

D: *Then if this is one possibility, is there another possibility that could happen?*

E: That is correct. As I stated it the last time, because of changes within the event of time there were several meanings in the quatrains. Do not feel that civilization as we know it—or to be more correct—as you know it, has a hopeless future. He says that with the ability to understand what can happen with a planet and to have new awareness within yourselves, that could always change the event of things.

D: *Even a suspected shift in the axis?*

E: Yes. As he sees it now, the shift will occur and there will be great changes. That is from this point in time, your time. But because of people becoming more aware of damage that can be caused by the military destruction, whether voluntary or involuntary, if this can be prevented, the reaction set off beneath the earth's surface would be less damaging.

D: *Is this why he thinks this information should be gotten to the people?*

E: Absolutely!

D: *If only we can make them listen.*

E: There will be those who want to hear.

D: *Otherwise, they would have to rebuild an entire civilization, a whole world.*

E: (*Grimly*) They would have very little civilization left.

D: *This would mean only those who were rugged enough to know how to survive would survive.*

E: That is correct.

D: *Then all the talks of war may not be correct. This shift is the main thing that's important right now.*

E: That is why he wanted to speak with you.

D: *What about these beings from other planets, will they help in any way?*

E: This is dependent on people's awareness. This has been decided to try and bring this planet to a higher awareness.

D: *Would they be able to help stop this thing from happening?*

E: (*Listening*) It depends on how they are received. They can help a civilization. The people must make the decision whether or not they will let them.

D: *I've been told they are not allowed to interfere. Is that what you mean?*

E: (*Listening*) If we cause the planet—we, meaning the people now in your time—to accelerate to an unnatural death, yes, they will become involved. Because it would affect them also. Any time there is a shift in a planet it causes the energy forces to affect the solar system. Thus, the solar system that we are in would be affected. Which would cause a—he says to use the word "domino affect."

D: *Yes, I understand that term. Then you mean this would be felt throughout the universe?*

E: That is correct.

D: *But do these beings, or whatever you want to call them, have the power to stop something like this?*

E: They have the power to raise your level of consciousness and awareness to understand how you could handle this better.—I'm sorry I'm not coming through, expressing myself well.—The natural occurrence when the shift is going to happen, the degree to which it happens will depend on the awareness people have mentally and spiritually. (*Abruptly*) I am going to be leaving but I wanted you to understand what needs to be talked about. There are still quatrains that have to be translated at the next meeting. They will pertain to areas of the earth to be concerned with for this year.

D: *I have one more thing to ask you and then I will let you go. The vehicle that we are working through is going to be moving away from the area and I won't have physical contact with her any more. Is there a possibility that we could communicate through another source?*

E: You have several people that are receptive but the degree is unknown until we try. There is one named Brian who is a student.

D: *I don't think I've worked with him yet. I've worked with Phil.*

E: No, this is Brian.

D: *I'm working with Brenda, who is a student; a music student. I've had good luck with her.*

E: That is the one.

I wondered if he could possibly be referring to Brenda. The similarity of names was just the type of puzzle that Nostradamus was famous for. He may also have been using the closest name he could find in his time period. It was something to keep in mind later when I would attempt to find another way to contact him.

E: But we see no reason why Elena cannot continue the work even though there will be a distance between you.

D: *She thought she would try to do it on her own and write down her interpretations. Then maybe I could ask one of my other vehicles in trance if the translation is correct.*

E: Try to stress the importance of this to Elena, to get this work completed within a minimum of three months. This would allow you to have this ready by Fall. And it would be published before the new year.

That was a pretty fast timetable. I didn't have the material and my subject was leaving. I could understand the importance from the little he had already told me, but he had handed me an impossible assignment. It was also obvious he was not familiar with the workings of the 20th century publishing business. I tried to be realistic.

D: *That'd be pretty fast. I don't know if it can happen ...*

E: (*He empathically interrupted and Elena shook her finger at me.*) This will be accomplished! This *will* be accomplished.

D: *The people in the publishing field say that it takes longer than that, at least a year to a year and a half to get a book published. You must understand there are some things that are out of my control.*

E: (*Emphatically*) This will not be out of ours!

The energy behind this statement was so strong that the surge almost knocked the sound off the tape recording. Her voice dropped so low that I could hardly hear it on transcription.

I shrugged my shoulders. I could see there would be no use trying to argue with Nostradamus, even though I didn't think he was aware of the complexities of the publishing industry in our time. Maybe it was easier in his time.

"All right," I said. "I can tell them of the importance and then see what happens."

E: Understand that we will be relying on other sources also.

D: *I try to do my part, but there are always other people involved that have to be considered.*

E: This will blend together.

D: *I am very concerned that without Elena we will lose contact.*

E: We will try to come through any vehicle you work with.

He then gave me detailed instructions on how to direct someone else to meet with them at the meeting place.

D: *We will have time to work with Elena only one more time before she leaves.*

E: I will give you more instructions at that time.

D: *I sincerely hope that the contact will not be broken. We shall see what happens after Elena leaves. That's really all we can do. Things are out of our control.*

E: (*Emphatically*) It will work!

D: *With your help, maybe it will. I need all the help I can get.*

E: We understand.

With a sense of sadness I brought Elena back to full consciousness. Even with their positive exclamations I felt we would lose contact after

Elena left. I could see no way it could be maintained. How *could* it happen? It appeared to be an impossible situation. Well, at least we would have one more session to try to cram at least a year's work into. It bothered me that we had let so much valuable time slip by. By all rights we could have been working on this fascinating project months ago. But it was really nobody's fault. Circumstances in our private lives had kept interfering and we had no way of knowing these unusual developments would occur. Besides, in the beginning Andy would not allow us to work on this, and probably rightly so. This could be one of the problems now, it was too overwhelming, too much for Elena to want to take on. She didn't have the metaphysical background to allow her to accept such a gigantic responsibility. I could sympathize with that, I think many other novices would have reacted in the same way. Any logical person would run from an assignment such as this. By all rights, I should have too. But I suppose I'm more curious than logical.

She told me what she remembered about the session. "All of a sudden it was like I was in a gray bank and it was really weird. I felt like I heard your voice coming through a tunnel. It seemed like you were fading out and I thought I was losing you." That was the only thing she remembered. I explained to her what had happened and that I had corrected it.

I left Elena at Val's house and did not arrive home until two o'clock. I don't think I revealed to them either by action or by word just how profoundly the session had affected me. Oh, I had heard similar predictions about earth changes from other psychics, but for some reason, hearing it from Nostradamus, it sounded so definite, so final.

I drove home in a heavy fog of depression. I don't remember ever feeling so defeated. The words, "The end of civilization as you know it," kept repeating over and over again inside my head. Did this mean that all our hopes and dreams for that ever-elusive future would be for naught because there would be no future? Then what would be the use of living? What would be the use of trying? Why bother to write my books? What possible difference could it make? What was the use of anything? Nothing had any purpose anyway, we wouldn't be around to enjoy it.

Maybe Elena was right. Maybe we shouldn't try to find out what the future has in store for us. Can we really handle the knowledge of such horrible predictions, especially when they are of such magnitude and we can do nothing about them. Is it better to be an ostrich?

It hit me so hard, this sense of finality. There was no stopping something of this magnitude. If Nostradamus and the other psychics were right, then the world would shift. The terrible earth changes would take place and the remnants of mankind would crawl from the rubble to try to begin building a world all over again. Why? Why try to accomplish anything in life if it could be taken away so easily and suddenly? But then what was the alternative? I didn't have any answers, and two o'clock in the morning is not a proper time to philosophize. I just knew that the idea of my beloved world and way of life being taken away totally depressed me.

Maybe I shouldn't continue the sessions. What Nostradamus had already told me was so horrible. Did I really want to know more?

THE NEXT MORNING WHEN I AWOKE I saw the sun shining in the window and the light streaming across the floor in golden splendor. That was all; I saw that the sun had simply risen just as it always has every morning of my life. The morbid thoughts had been left in the dark closet of night. I thought, yes, the sun will continue to rise. Day will follow day and life will move on, regardless of dire predictions.

With the awakening of this revelation I realized there really was no alternative. You can't stop living, snuff out your dreams and aspirations because of a traumatic something that might happen someday. No, life must be lived. To hide away and give up your dreams is to betray life, to betray everything it stands for.

It has been asked, "If you knew you would die tomorrow, would you live your life any differently today?" I doubt it. We are creatures of habit. I knew I was now more aware of the possible consequences and would try to accomplish something more meaningful with the alloted time left. Besides, no one really knows how much time they have remaining anyway. I could step off a curb tomorrow, be hit by a car and the world as I knew it would cease to exist for me at that time. The world is only real to us while we are in it.

I thought of the people in ancient Italy. On that day when Mount Vesuvius erupted and completely inundated Pompeii with lava, civilization ceased and was completely wiped out for all those people. The people of Hiroshima also had no warning. In a brief moment, in one bright flash, their world was gone and their civilization ceased to exist for them.

Even though the idea of our world coming to such a tragic end was terribly depressing to me, I began to understand. Live life while you can. Love and enjoy the wonder that is all around you. Learn to see with the eyes of a child, and truly strive to understand your fellow man, because our life here on this earth really is a delicate and fragile thing. Nostradamus made me much more aware, but secretly I still hoped in my heart of hearts that he was wrong. The only way of knowing is to wait until we come to that moment in time. What's the alternative? Finding a hole and hiding in it? Either way you die. Far better to spend my days trying to relate to people the wonders I have found through my work and to pass on the secrets I have discovered.

If I could only hold to my beliefs, then the unknown future would lose its power to frighten me.

I knew now I had no alternative. I must continue this project. The curious side of me was stronger than any apprehension I might feel.

Chapter 6

Elena Departs

It was Thursday, the day of our last possible session. It had been only two days since Elena had dropped the bombshell in my lap, and I was forced into trying to cram as much information as possible into a few short days. The session we had had on Tuesday night showed that Nostradamus was willing to work with us and that it was possible to obtain amazing new insight into his quatrains. It was frustrating and disappointing to have such a unique opportunity suddenly cut off. I did not have enough information for a book and to whet the readers' curiosity with just a few translations of the quatrains did not seem fair. Elena had said that since her parents still live in this town she would probably return next summer on vacation. We might be able to work on a session during that time. If this story had to wait until then, if I would have to sit on it for a year or more, then so be it. Of course, this was in direct contradiction to Nostradamus' instructions. He seemed to be emphatic about getting the information to the people of our time as quickly as possible, but at this point I had no other solution. Elena was leaving, and since Alaska is not exactly next door, there was no hope of working with her. She might be able to get some results trying to translate the quatrains on her own, but I thought it was very unpredictable. I didn't think I could rely on the validity of that method. The results in trance while communicating with Dyonisus and Nostradamus had been amazingly clear and concise. I knew these results could not be duplicated by any other method except my working directly with her. I did not know any person called "Brian," but I would keep alert for the possibility of such a person entering my life as a prospective subject. I was working with several people and I had one in mind I thought would be a good guinea pig for the experiment, the music student I had mentioned to Nostradamus. But since I had never heard of anything like this being tried before, I thought I was asking for the impossible. We had such luck with Elena because we had uncovered a past life when she was a student of that great man. Since the odds were enormous against my finding another of his students, I had no idea or plan of how to attempt to contact him through someone else. Impossible was the only word for it; it was utterly within the realm of impossibility.

It did no good at this point to wonder about it. As I arrived in the resort town I knew I must concentrate all my energies on trying to obtain as much information as possible during this last session. I had sat up until one o'clock the night before going over the quatrains. This was the first time I had really studied them. While reading them I at times received an intuitive flash about a possible meaning, but the majority of them seemed incomprehensible and even nonsensical. Nostradamus had certainly done his work well. I could understand why researchers had spent years of their lives trying to untangle them. I could also understand why so many of the quatrains had no explanation. They were just too complex or obscure. I did think that the translators were trying to be too literal. It was obvious to me that Nostradamus was using very involved symbolism in many cases.

I had made notes on several that I wished to try to decipher and remarks on others that seemed curious. I knew there would be no time to do even a portion of them so I would concentrate on just a few. I wrote down questions that I wished to ask about the writing of the quatrains. It would also be important to try to get the rest of Dyonisus' life story and ask some more about the life of Nostradamus. I would have to allot my time carefully if I wanted to do even a portion of what I had planned. This was a case where I would really have to get my priorities straight. But how could I determine which was the most important area to concentrate on? Working under such pressure is far from the ideal condition for hypnosis and I detest competing with a ticking clock.

This was the last possible day to conduct a session because Elena was having a garage sale the next day (Friday) and would fly to California on Saturday morning. There was a myriad of last minute details to occupy her. I arrived early for the session so I could get out of her way, but it made no difference. She had many things that would have to be done before we could settle down to work. I followed as she went to have her hair cut and waited as she delivered a portrait she had been commissioned to do. She would need the money for the trip. Then she had to return home and attend to some things for her daughter. Elena must have felt she was being pulled in several directions as she tried to divide herself between her children's demands. I followed as she performed several more errands, and I waited and watched precious minutes tick away. I knew we must start soon as Elena had plans for the evening.

We finally arrived at Val's house where we would not be disturbed. Val was also moving and things were piled everywhere. As I set up my tape recorder on a suitcase next to the bed, Elena announced that we would have exactly an hour and a half to do the session, then she would have to go to her parents' house for a farewell dinner. Talk about working under pressure. This would really be pushing it to the limit to get anything done in that length of time, but it was better than nothing.

I have gone into much detail about the events of that last day to show that this session was not that important to Elena. It was almost an incidental nuisance. She was more concerned about her impending trip and all the last-minute details that needed to be taken care of. She was merely making time for the session in her busy schedule because she knew it was important to me and she didn't want to hurt my feelings. That was all right with me because I never try to interfere with my subjects' private lives. I felt like an intruder and wanted to get finished and out of her way.

After Elena had settled down on the bed, I gave her the keyword and watched as she went into the familiar deep trance. Then I took her back to the lifetime of Dyonisus and used the detailed instructions I had been given as a method of contacting Nostradamus in the special meeting place. I wasn't even sure if it would work again. At the end of the count Dyonisus announced that they were there and I again felt a great surge of relief that the procedure was successful.

D: *Since the last time we talked I have been going over different books. In our time we have many translations of Nostradamus' quatrains and they all seem to have different wordings. This seems to be creating a problem in our understanding of them.*

E: This has been because of the ignorance of the ages, and why you have reached a more enlightened age. There are still those that have not reached an enlightened mind.

D: *People have wondered why Nostradamus was being so obscure in his quatrains.*

E: This is done deliberately. These things would have been frightening for those of the earlier centuries.

D: *You told me before that some of the quatrains had more than one meaning?*

E: That is correct.

D: *Do all of the quatrains have more than one meaning?*

E: Only some. Not all.

In the limited time I had to study the quatrains the night before, I noticed they were extremely complicated. But an idea had occurred to me. In some of them each line seemed to refer to a different thing. Even the translators commented on this at times. They said that one part would fit with their interpretation while the other would not. I wondered if it was possible that one or two lines might refer to one event and the other lines might refer to another event. This might explain some of the confusion.

E: Each quatrain contains a single prophecy, but it's worded in some so the meaning would be applicable to the time difference in which the event occurred.

D: *Didn't he say that some of these did not occur because of man's ability to change the future?*

E: That is correct.

D: *Some people say that if the future cannot be changed, then there is no such thing as free will.*

E: There *is* free will.

D: *Then he was not incorrect or wrong. He just reported what he saw?*

E: It was what he had seen with the time sequence that was happening. —This is difficult.—May I explain it as, when you see something from a distance you may notice as you approach it closer that details are sharper or not quite as they had seemed from the distance. This means that man's will or beliefs have the ability to change an event as it comes closer to that time. So from the distance that my teacher saw it, it was before man's awareness changed the event or distorted it to a different direction.

D: *So these are the events he saw but man can change them as it comes closer to the time.*

E: That is correct.

D: *It is nice to know that people do have the ability to change things if they know about them. A lot of people think everything is all cut and dried, if you know what I mean, that they can't do anything about it.*

E: This is why he wants you to know about them, so they may be changed.

In Nostradamus' books the quatrains are arranged in what are called "centuries." A quatrain is a four-line poem (or in this case a four-line puzzle) and a century is supposed to be one hundred of them. There are ten centuries, although in Ms. Cheetham's book one of them (VII) contains only 42 quatrains. This means that there are almost 1000 quatrains, 942 to be exact. I wondered if this was the arrangement he intended for them to be put in and if they were in this order for any specific purpose.

E: No, this is one of the misleading puzzles that he put in. He called them centuries but not meaning that there is a hundred years of time. He meant it for a puzzlement, to confuse.

D: *Can you explain what he really meant?*

E: (*Pause, listening*) He meant it so that people, those who were translating for profit, it was to confuse the issue, to confuse the period of time. So they wouldn't, even though they did do it, set each event in a certain century. This is what he meant about a quatrain applying to more than one time period.

D: *The experts today say that a century is a hundred of these predictions and they have put them in that order. One century is a hundred quatrains, the second century is a hundred more.*

E: He does not care what these experts say.

D: *One of these does not contain a hundred. I wondered if he had done this on purpose. I thought maybe there were some quatrains missing that he had not finished or that were not included.*

E: No. All that he wished to be known have come down to you.

I felt I needed to clarify these things. Maybe people have tried to put his prophecies in too much of an order and this takes away from what he was trying to say. He said before that there had been mistakes made because of our misunderstanding of his calculations of different planetary positions. I was thinking that maybe over the intervening 400 years the earth had shifted or changed position enough to make the sky appear differently now, especially as far as numerical calculations were concerned.

E: The calculations he gave *are* correct. The way they have been *interpreted* is incorrect. In referring to an astrological moment in time given from another century, the astrologer of this time would have to mathematically deduct at what point in time this meant. He says that the mathematical part of it was the error that was made. Now in some cases what has happened is that through man's free will it has either accelerated or deleted the prophecy.

D: *I suppose the positions of the stars would have changed over so many hundreds of years.*

E: They have. The sky that he saw was the one in his prophecy. He did not look at the sky of his time.

D: *Do you mean that when he saw the event, he also saw the way the stars were at that time?*

E: Before he saw the event, he would see the heavens. And then it would focus onto the earth. Then, as if looking through a glass that magnifies, the event would be centered in on.

D: *I see. Then the mistake is in the calculations that man is making today.*

E: That is correct.

D: These are things I don't think our experts have taken into consideration.—You spoke last time of our weaponry, or that this power force behind our weaponry was going to cause problems in our time. You said something would be in the air that would cause problems? What kind of changes will this substance cause?

E: (*Pause, listening*) It will change the structure of the clouds, the structure of plant life, the structure of animals. When I say "structure," I mean some physical deformity but ... (*Had difficulty finding the right words to describe.*) ... from within the blood, organs within.

D: *I think I understand what you're talking about.*

Obviously he was referring to the effects of radiation upon the blood and genes. He was using the only words he could find to describe such an alien concept.

(At the time of the Chernobyl accident it was thought that the radiation had not caused much damage and the scientists were not very concerned. They had surmised that it would be washed away by the rains. But several months later it was discovered that it had instead soaked into the ground and contaminated the plant life, especially in Lapland. After the animal life in that area consumed the plants they also became contaminated. Within a few months the scientists announced that the reindeer was now the most radioactive animal on the face of the earth. This was disastrous for the people who make their living from following the rein-deer herds. This might be only the tip of the emerging iceberg. There could prove to be even more startling discoveries in the future to show that these nuclear accidents should not be brushed aside and taken so lightly.)

D: *Our scientists keep saying we have done nothing to hurt the earth. They say this substance is no stronger or no worse than the light that comes from the sun.*

E: (*Her voice was filled with incredulity.*) *How* can they say that? It's a completely different structure, element.

D: *They say that since the sunlight does not hurt us that this substance will not hurt us, except in large doses.*

E: (*Grimly and emphatically.*) They are wrong!

D: *Then does he believe that even small doses of this substance will harm humans?*

E: The smaller the dose, the longer period of time before a difference would be seen. But he has already seen the difference in the fish from the sea. He says, how can they see this physical proof and claim different?

D: *Do you think it's something that takes a long time to appear and maybe that's why they don't understand it?*

E: But what is going to be happening is that the danger to the structure, that will come from the weaponry that affects the air, will be very strong. And immediate changes will be observed within weeks, unless they become aware of this.

D: *But you see, they also think that this is a good power and they can use it for other things besides weaponry. This is why they don't want to give it up.*

E: But they did *not* use it for good when this power was created. They used it for negative, for the destruction of life. Therefore the energy that has come out of it is a negative energy. If it had been used as its inventor had intended it to be, the energy would have no negativity in it at all. And while they have the ability to contain it, when you use it as a weapon, as a destructive thing, you're causing a negative ... (*He had difficulty defining.*) He says you have a word called "karma" or "aura" behind the thing that is what makes something good or bad. So this has been brought into being as a bad thing.

D: *I see. Then because of the way we started out with it, do you think mankind will ever be able to turn this around and use it for good?*

E: In a completely different source. The materials that you use to create this now will not be available in the future. So this will not be able to be used again.

D: *Then they will have to find another source of power or energy?*

E: Evidently there are those who have already done so.

Was Nostradamus referring to solar energy?

D: *I believe the suggestion he gave last time was that we should stop emitting this into the air?*

E: Yes, this is very essential. They are accelerating the changes in the planet and the atmosphere that will totally affect the universe.

D: *Then it doesn't just affect our little planet?*

E: That is correct.

D: *But so many people just don't want to stop. They keep making tests and every time they do this, it releases more into the air. And we've also had these accidents lately like you spoke of last time.*

E: And there will be more.

D: *Does he know where, in what country these accidents will occur?*

E: He says they are in the quatrains.

D: *Will there be any of these accidents in the New World, in the country that I'm speaking from?*

E: Yes. The natural earthquakes will be causing these accidents.

D: *Is there any way we can avoid this?*

E: A removal of the system, of the housing that contains it.

D: *But there's no way to ... (I was trying to find an explanation he could understand.) He knows the power of the King in France. It is the same way in our country. The power is in the hands of a few people and what they decide is the way the world goes. This is where the problem lies.*

E: That's why he wants your people to be aware of the danger involved and why he speaks with us now. He says that the results that would happen from an earthquake near one of your military housing of the weaponry would cause your leaders to definitely realize the dangers. What you can do now is only try and avoid that coming to a reality.

D: *I will try to bring it to their attention, as best I can.—Last time you spoke of some changes that would take place in other countries that would be important for us to know about.*

E: Are you talking about the shift in the earth?

D: *Well, whatever it is that he thinks would be important to know about.*

E: (*Listening*) That parts of the earth will become islands and that the problems of food and survival will be hardest in these countries.

D: *Will this happen at the time of the shift?*

E. Yes. There will be governmental problems prior to this. Again depending on people's awareness. There would be either small uprisings breaking out or there would be a joining of powers to fight uprisings in the Persian countries.

D: *Persian countries? Will these precede or will they happen at the same time the shift occurs?*

E: This is preceding, but the earth change is so much more important because the fighting would stop. I mean, the destruction of the different lands would put fighting a secondary thing.

D: *I see. Does he see us using this type of weapon in the future before the shift occurs?*

E: No, not the most dangerous weaponry. It is the earth changes that will be causing the danger of the weaponry.

D: *Then at least our leaders have that much sense. Do you see our country, the new world, involved in a war before this shift occurs?*

E: *(Pause, listening)* If the leader that's in the Persian country stays strong, this could be a factor.

D: *Here again man's free will is involved, isn't it?*

E: That is correct.

I decided to begin with the reading of the quatrains.

D: (CENTURY II-41) *"The great star will burn for seven days and the cloud will make the sun appear double. The large mastiff will howl all night when the great pontiff changes his abode."*

In this quatrain the translator does not understand what Nostradamus meant by two stars. After a long pause Dyonisus gave the definition.

E: This is one that refers to the coming of the people from the stars. The mastiff would be the symbol of the Devil or evil, and the pope would be changing. Rome would no longer be the home of the Catholic Church.

D: *Then that's what he means by "the great star will burn for seven days"? The coming of these other people?*

E: This is also in reference to the quatrain we spoke of at the last session.

D: *About the light show?*

E: That is correct. The sun appearing double does not mean two suns. It means that the sun would appear both day and night.

D: *The translator has interpreted this as meaning war. I can see why it would be very difficult for them to find the real meaning, especially if they don't believe that there are people other than those on earth.* (I looked for another quatrain that I had marked on my tablet.) (CENTURY VI-5) *"A very great famine (caused) by a pestilent wave will extend its long reign the length of the Arctic Pole. Samarobrin, one hundred leagues from the hemisphere. They will live without law, exempt from politics."*

At times Nostradamus seemed to be confused or frustrated, as though the English translation was causing trouble for him to identify which quatrain it was. Almost as though he was thinking, "Which one could that possibly be."

E: This will occur after the pole shift.

D: *What does he mean by Samarobrin? That is a word they have never been able to understand.*

E: Spell it, please. *(I did so.)* Is it that way in French also?

D: Yes, but it could also be translated wrong in French.

E: Yes. At the time of the shift there will be separation of the great land mass that is at the top of the new country. This will be fragmented into small islands. Because of the distance and the inability to communicate, these will live under their own rule and be aggressive and strong and—"aggressive" is the wrong word—but very protective of their dwellings because of the time to rebuild and to find food. And this is the name that they will call themselves, "Samarobrin," because of the (*searching*) ... fish native to the area. This is in part of the name.

Later when we discussed this, it was suggested that the fish might be salmon which is native in the Canadian and Alaskan area.

I had been watching the clock and I knew that if I were to find out the other things I was interested in, I would have to stop with the translations, even though we were having excellent results.

D: *I said before that the vehicle you're speaking through is going to be moving to a different area, and you said that you would try to come through someone else that I work with?*

E: We will make the attempt. If a vehicle can become receptive, we will gladly make the contact.—May I explain that it has been easiest with your vehicle, Elena, because of the prior connection in lives.—(*After a pause she continued, her voice full of wonder.*) This is so interesting to me. I had never thought of that concept.

D: *What do you mean?*

E: Well, that's what Nostradamus said. That I have a connection with your vehicle.

D: *You had never thought of this, about other lives? Well, it is true. This is why this is happening. That's why I wondered if it might be more difficult coming through someone else that he didn't have a connection with. But he says he will try?*

E: He says that in this meditative place he has brought us to, this should not be as hard.

D: *I am going to instruct the vehicle to meditate upon these quatrains and try to send me, by messenger, her interpretations.*

E: Yes, because unfortunately we have not gone through the quatrains that are essential. Some we have, but not all of them.

I could not imagine what could be more essential and important than those we had already covered, so I was puzzled.

D: *Well, when we make the connection and you come through someone else, maybe we will be able to find those quatrains. We can try it both ways.—But when it comes through someone else, is there any way that I will know that it is really Nostradamus and not someone trying to fool me?*

E: He says that the best way to know is to give this vehicle and the other person the same quatrain. And if they translate it similarly—it does not have to be word for word—you will know.

D: *That would be a very good test. Because I want to make sure I'm not speaking to some other entity or spirit or some other person. I want to be sure that it is him.*

E: He also says that—no, he disregards that. He was going to suggest a certain word that they would say. But if they have psychic abilities they might be able to pick this word up from you.

D: *All right. I think that I work with enough people that I will find another vehicle that he can come through. And Elena will continue to work on her own until we meet again at some time in the future.*

I was preparing to give the commands that would take Dyonisus out of that scene. Val couldn't understand why, since the translating was going so well. She was frantically motioning to her watch and whispering that we still had a half hour left to work on this. She did not know that I had planned to get the rest of the story of Dyonisus' life. As a writer, I have to look at the broader view instead of just what is happening at the moment. If I could really believe Nostradamus when he said it would be possible to get the translations of the quatrains from someone else, then it would happen. But I would never be able to get the story of Dyonisus' life from anyone else but Elena. I knew that this would be essential to any book that I would write about this phenomenon. I also hoped to find out something more about the life of Nostradamus from his student's point of view. Val did not understand that there was not enough time in this last session to do everything. So I would have to concentrate on what I considered to be the most essential. Obviously she considered the quatrains to be more important from the standpoint of curiosity, but I knew we could hardly make a dent in them in the half an hour that we had left to work.

I ignored Val's frustration and instructed Dyonisus to leave that scene and move forward to the last day of his life. I told him he could watch it if he didn't want to participate in it. This is often done to keep the subject from experiencing any unnecessary trauma.

E: *(Her voice became soft and low.)* I see myself laying on the bed. Both my friends are crying.

D: *What is wrong with you?*

E: There's something inside. I have tried to slow its growth but it's taken over me.

D: *Are you very old when this happens?*

E: Fifty-eight. It's a good age, a good age.

D: *Have you been practicing the medicine as a doctor all those years?*

E: No, I decided to study the spirit and knowledge of the mind.

D: *Is Nostradamus still alive at this time? (She shook her head.) Can you tell me what happened to him?*

E: His age. He was ill for a while. He became ill with a ... *(had difficulty)* ... I can't remember the word.

D: *Describe what it was, maybe I can think of the word.*

E: It ... a continuous cough.

Val unthinkingly volunteered the word "consumption" without thinking that Elena might be able to hear her.

E: Consumption, thank you.

Val clamped her hand over her mouth and said she was sorry. I always give instructions that no one in the room speak to the subject while in trance unless I give them permission. I do not want them influenced by anything someone might say. Oftentimes the subject appears to be unable to hear anything else that is going on in the room unless they are directed to do so. Val had blurted out the word spontaneously.

D: *Is that what was mainly wrong with Nostradamus?*
E: He was getting very old. He had several things but it was mostly the body running down. And the mind was tired.
D: *He didn't have any way of curing this himself?*
E: He was ready to go on.
D: *You told me once that he had several houses; that he lived in different places. Did he have a family?*
E: He remarried again late in life. He had a wife and three children.

I remembered from the film that he had been married as a young man and his family had been killed by a plague. I wanted to verify this.

D: *Then this was not his only wife?*
E: *(Sadly)* No.
D: *Did he ever tell you the story of what happened to his first wife?*
E: Yes. This was a hard thing for him. Earlier in his life he had been married and there was a great sickness in the country that took many lives. And though he was able to help many people, while he was away doing ... *(searching for word)* working his medicine, his wife and family came down with the sickness.
D: *And he wasn't there?*
E: No. He was there before they died but he was too late to save them.
D: *Did he think that he could have helped them if he had been there?*
E: Yes. This was the greatest sadness of his life.
D: *Is this why he didn't marry again for a long time?*
E: He was in his forties when he remarried. He was a good doctor. As he grew older his knowledge of the body and the spirit increased a i he was able to help many.
D: *Did he have many students besides you?*
E: Throughout the time that I knew him, he had ... *(thinking)* perhaps 25, 30 of us that trained over the years. In the last ten years of his life, he dedicated it to writing and studying. He had no students during that time.

In the front of Ms. Cheetham's book there is a brief biography of Nostradamus. In it she mentioned a man called Jean Chavigny who was supposed to have been one of his students. It was said that he helped in the compiling and publication of the quatrains. I wondered if Dyonisus might have known this man. I had such difficulty with my sorry pronunciation of the name that he couldn't understand who I meant. After I spelt it for him, he repeated it with a French pronunciation that sounded as though it might be correct.

E: This name is not uncommon. Chavigny , I did not know well. I did not study with Nostradamus till the time that he passed away.

D: *Did you leave about the time he began to write?*

E: No. He had started to write and I stayed with him learning more things spiritual. As his writing continued to develop, he became more of a recluse. And I was eager to learn other things and began traveling.

D: *Did you have other teachers?*

E: Not in the flesh, no. (Does this answer mean that he was taught by spirit guides?) I began teaching a few students that I thought were close and kindred in spirit to me.

D: *I think it would have been hard to find a teacher as fine as him anyway, wouldn't it?*

E: (*Emotionally*) I loved him very much.

D: *Did Nostradamus ever have any problems with the church when he was doing these different things?*

E: Only when he was younger. He became more discreet in what he would say and do in public life. He was a very devout Catholic.

D: *This was a time when the church was not favorable to these things, was it?*

E: Terrible.

D: *Did you ever have any problems in that way from the church?*

E: Yes, I did. It was after I had left Nostradamus. I had started talking to a few people about my beliefs. One was a man I thought I could trust. And he reported me to the clergy in the province. I was very fortunate that the clergy was a kindred spirit and soul. He came to talk with me, and did not allow the incident to go any further.

D: *Wasn't that unusual to find a kindred spirit in the church?*

E: I was fortunate enough that the man had reported me to a priest and not to a bishop or higher. He was more spiritually attuned instead of monetary minded.

D: *Were you more careful after that?*

E: Very much so. The priest was good enough to tell me that he felt I should leave the area so there wouldn't be any repercussions on the matter.

D: *Yes, you were very lucky.—I can tell you're feeling tired.*

E: (*Softly*) Yes.

D: *Has the body ceased to exist yet?*

E: I'm just watching.

D: What do you think you're going to do now that the end is coming?
E: (*Softly*) Oh, I m not afraid.
D: Then let's move ahead a little bit until it's all over with. I just want you to tell me what it's like and what you see.
E: (*In awe*) It's so marvelous!
D: What do you see?
E: (*Her voice filled with wonder.*) Everything! Anything! I can go in any direction.
D: You're free. Are you by yourself?
E: No, there is someone here; but . . . only a sense, of person, of loving. A guide.
D: Do you know what you're going to do?
E: I'm going to follow. Follow the love.—Oh, it's so beautiful!
D: What do you think of the life you just left?
E: I think it was a good one. Things that I was uncertain about were made clear to me.
D: Yes, it was a life of great knowledge. I think you learned a lot and grew spiritually in that life. But now you're happy where you're at?
E: Yes. But I'll be back.
D: Do you know this?
E: Yes, they tell me this. They say that there's more work needed on the earth plane.—Oh, I feel so honored that they're telling me this.
D: Are they telling you what you're going to do?
E: That I will help mankind.
D: What do you think about that?
E: I think it would be wonderful.
D: I thought maybe you didn't like living on earth, that you wouldn't want to come back again.
E: No! I didn't dislike living on the earthly plane.
D: Do you think it will be long before you have to return to earth?
E: I don't know.—I feel honored that they feel the way they do about me.
D: Oh, I do, too. I think it is very wonderful. And I have learned much from your knowledge also.
E: Thank you. We may speak again.
D: We may, yes, we may. You never know when I may come again and ask questions. And I wish you peace and love and joy wherever you go on your travels.

I had come to feel very close to this kind man but I somehow knew that I would never speak with him again. I felt that when Elena left, this chapter would be closed and would not need to be reopened. I knew Elena's life was going in another direction. At least having these two sessions may have relieved the pressure that her subconscious was exerting upon her. I felt now that she could safely say she had tried to do her part in this strange scenario and that circumstances had intervened. I had been afraid that without any sessions at all, she would leave with the subconscious burden of unfinished business and this might cause her to become ill. I knew I had now done all I could with this story from Elena's point of view. The only regret I had was all the wasted months we could have been working on this. But there was no way of knowing the story was even there. Life is like that. Circumstances have a way of taking over and before we realize it too much previous time has slipped away. So we could just say that life got in the way and go on without regrets and the "ifs," "ands," or "buts."

After I brought Elena back to full consciousness, Val was upset because I had not continued with more of the quatrains when Nostradamus was translating them so well. She was afraid there would never be another chance like this. Naturally she was unaware that I was trying to get the rest of Dyonisus' life, which would be impossible to obtain from anyone else but Elena. I had to make the most of the limited time we had for today's last and final session. It had to be my decision as to what was the most important information to pursue.

Val was still trying to encourage Elena to stay for a few more weeks so that we could work on this. I did not talk to her about that at all. I knew that she had made a decision, and I would never want it on my conscience that I had tried to influence her to change her plans just to suit me. I had no idea where this story was going, and even if it just went into a drawer to await her return, I knew she had made the best plans for her life because they were *her* plans and not influenced by me.

I did encourage her to find time to draw the picture of Nostradamus when she was finally settled. This she eagerly agreed to do. When she gave me a big farewell hug, I knew that my work with her was finished.

She said fondly, "Oh, we'll keep in touch. One thing you must promise me, that you'll tell me if it ever does come through anybody else. That would be the most fantastic thing. If that ever happens, then I'll believe anything."

As I walked out of the house and headed my car down the road toward home, I had no answers, just some tapes containing the beginning of an interesting experiment. It was just enough to whet my insatiable curiosity and then have the door slammed shut on it. Nostradamus had insisted that it was possible to continue, but at this point I couldn't see how. What he was proposing was impossible, it had never been accomplished before. As I drove, the trees became a continuous blur and my mind echoed Elena's last words.

I silently answered her, "Yes, if that ever happens, then I too, will believe anything."

Chapter 7

Through the Magic Mirror

AFTER ELENA'S DEPARTURE I continued to work with various other subjects as I was involved in several other projects. I am always working on many different things in various stages of development. I was disappointed that the Nostradamus material had begun so fruitfully and now seemed in all reality to be lost to me forever. The odds were tremendously against me finding another student of his at random. The only other way would be to try to contact him through another subject. This was something I had never tried to do and I had never even thought about doing. It had worked before because I had been involved with one of his students. By following his instructions I could direct the student to ask him to meet with us in the special meeting place that Nostradamus had designated. In order for it to work with someone else, I would have to find a way for them to contact Nostradamus during his lifetime in the 1500s in France and also ask him to meet us in this special place. Would this place exist and be accessible to anyone else? How could I direct someone else to try to contact him? If they were not someone who could physically speak to him as Dyonisus had, how could the contact be made?

It was definitely a challenge and one I would dearly enjoy experimenting with. It would be vastly more complicated than trying to contact your dead Aunt Lucy and speaking with her in spirit form through a medium, if such a thing is possible. I don't know: I've never participated in a stereotypical seance. I believe what I do is totally different.

In order for this to succeed, I would have to contact Nostradamus during the same time period through a different channel or vehicle who had no knowledge of what had gone on before. Nostradamus would have to remember me, that we had begun an experiment, and be willing to continue. The whole thing was strange and virtually impossible. But if it could succeed, wouldn't this prove that I had truly been in touch with the real Nostradamus during his lifetime? Wouldn't this at last prove that it was possible to travel through time with this unique method? In the past I've been able to find two or three people who were involved in the same lifetime and could give me their individual versions of the story, thus proving that they actually lived that life together in the past. But this was something totally different. It would prove that it was possible to reach an individual by using someone unknown to them and who had no association with them during their lifetime.

A fascinating challenge. As I worked with my different subjects, I studied them to isolate the one I thought might be the most successful to use as a guinea pig in this experiment. I told none of them of my plans. I finally decided to try it with Brenda, a young music student at the local college. I have known her for years since she attended school with my children. She kept very busy working part-time at the college and attending classes in order to obtain her bachelor's degree in music. What spare time she could find she devoted to composing, her first love. She had expressed curiosity about my work and wanted to try regression. During the very first session she proved to be an excellent somnambulist subject and wonderful material began to come forth immediately. This was most unusual to have such quality material released during the first session. Perhaps the reason this happened so quickly was because the trust level had already been established, as I was not a stranger to her. This was the reason I wanted to try the experiment with her first because she was such a clear and concise channel. We had been working together for over a year on various other projects and she had already proven her flexibility to work on experimentation.

One remarkable example of her adaptability and ease of obtaining answers occurred at the time of the Chernobyl nuclear accident in April, 1986. On the day the explosion was announced the news reports were sketchy; no one seemed to know what was going on. More thorough news did not come forth until several days later. I thought it would be interesting to ask Brenda questions about it while she was in trance and try to find out what was happening.

When I arrived at her house on that day, I asked if she had heard the news reports. She said that maybe she is just a crazy composer but she would rather play the piano and write her music than watch TV or listen to the radio, so she seldom has them on. It may be hard to believe but there are still a few people who aren't trapped into the boob-tube habit. The circumstances were right for an experiment.

Toward the end of our regular session I asked if she could see what was happening in Russia at that time. She immediately picked up on the nuclear accident and reported it as an observer, saying that it was caused by several minor equipment failures that had escalated into major ones. She said that several people had been killed and that more would die later as a result of the radiation and from cancer and such. There would not be a great deal of danger from the radiation since the majority of it went into the earth and therefore the water in the area would be poisoned. She provided a great deal of detail that no one in our country knew at the time.

None of this information was public news, but her remarks were verified in the days that followed. Another example of her abilities concerned her prediction of a massive earthquake throughout the middle part of the United States that would be triggered by the New Madrid fault. Thankfully, this has not occurred yet, but she gave a great deal of detail about it.

It was because of remarkable examples such as these that I had chosen Brenda for my first choice as guinea pig.

A MONTH WAS TO GO BY before I could attempt the experiment. I had been working with her on another project. We were exploring the interesting past life of a young girl who lived during the time of the Inquisition in Europe. This life contained a great deal of information about the persecution by the church during that time period and I wanted to finish that before I started on a new project. Once a week we worked on it and the other entity became like Scheherazade, the princess in the Arabian Nights. The woman who told stories to the Prince for a thousand and one nights in order to save her life. Every week I prepared to kill her off, so to speak, to come to the end of her life so I could go on to the new experiment. And every week she kept supplying me with more and more interesting information. Thus, I let her live for another week. Finally after a month we were able to wind up her story, put her to rest and allow her to retreat back into the pages of time. Her story will be told in my book, *The Horns of the Goddess*. This girl could always be resurrected later if more information was needed. This makes it sound like I have some kind of life and death power over these other personalities, but it actually shows the ease with which they can be contacted again and again. I will leave the logic of it to be debated by others. I only know that my techniques work.

On the night I was to try the experiment I was no more prepared as to the method I would use to contact Nostradamus than I had been when Elena had left so unexpectedly. It is important to emphasize that Elena and Brenda live in two different towns about 30 miles apart and they had never met each other. I seldom tell any of my subjects about the stories I am working on with someone else. When I am with them I try to concentrate on the work I will be doing at the time. So on this night I merely told Brenda that I wanted to try an experiment. If it didn't work, we could always try to contact another life that she had lived in the past.

She knew my reasons for not telling her about it. If it were successful then there was no way anyone could say that I had influenced her because she was totally in the dark about what I was looking for. We had done this before so it did not bother her. She was agreeable and said, "That's okay. But will you tell me about it when I wake up?" I laughed and said that I surely would.

After I used her keyword and watched as she slipped into a deep somnambulistic trance, I asked her to go back to a time when she was in-between lives, in the so-called "dead" state. I have found that much more information can be obtained when people are in that state because they are not directly involved with a life. When someone is living a life, their perception is narrowed and the physical environment is usually all they are aware of. They cannot supply any information that does not pertain to the life they are living. After they die, the veil, so to speak, seems to be ripped away and they have access to greater knowledge, often remarkably so. There will be more information about this amazing state in my book *Conversation with a Spirit*. Brenda had already proven to have a great capacity for finding this knowledge for me when I have directed her to go to this state. I didn't know how to proceed but I thought this would be a good place to start, once she had removed the shackles of the limiting physical body.

When I finished counting, I found her in an unearthly place of ethereal beauty.

B: I am on one of the higher earths. An earth at a higher vibration. It is very beautiful here. I am sitting beside a crystal clear stream that is tumbling over rocks and crystals and gems. The colors are a lot brighter and more vivid than on the earth we spend our lives on. The grass is extremely emerald green. I'm under an oak tree and nearby there is a waterfall. And one of the unusual things about this waterfall, it is also a natural formation of crystal wind chimes. Some of them chime together like wind chimes do, and some of them act like a wind harp or wind whistles. There's all sorts of music from them and the waterfall. It's an extremely lovely plane. It's one of my favorite places to come.

It did indeed sound like a very beautiful and peaceful place. I wondered if she would mind helping me or if she was busy.

B: *(Laugh)* I'm busy listening to the wind chimes. But I'm by myself.
D: *I mean, you're not involved with anything that I would take you away from if I ask you some questions?*
B: No, I don't think so. In case I have to change location to find an answer to a question, I can always come back here afterward. It's a special place to me.
D: *All right. What I would like to do is present you with a problem and see if you can help me with it in some way.*
B: As long as it's not math.
D: *(Laugh) No, not math, I don't like math either. It's a problem that I have been presented with, a situation-type problem. Maybe you can help me.*
B: I'll see what I can see.
D: *You are aware that I work with this method with many different people to get information?*
B: What method do you mean?

D: *Well, it's a method I use that allows me to speak to you in these different states. I obtain information from many different people in this way.*

B: Yes, you have found a gateway.

D: *Well, this is the problem. I was working with a young woman who, in a past life, was a student of the great master Nostradamus.*

B: Michel de Notredame.

D: *We call him Nostradamus in our time, but do you know who I mean?*

B: Yes, you use the Latin version of his name. He's a very developed soul. In that life he had a very difficult path to walk. He was the most talented and gifted of psychic abilities on that level, *ever.* He had so much psychic ability that he was ... just dripping with it. In other ages he would have been deified as a god.

D: *In his time he was also misunderstood in a lot of ways. Well, I was working with this young woman who was giving me information of her life as one of his students. And while we were doing this, Nostradamus spoke to the student. He did not speak to me directly, but he said that it was very important to translate his quatrains, his prophecies. He said they have much meaning to the time period that I'm living in now. He was very emphatic that I do this work.*

B: I understand the situation.

D: *He was giving me a great deal of information about the quatrains, and then the person I was working with moved away. Before she left, Nostradamus said he would contact me through someone else so we could continue our work. And I wondered if I gave you the instructions he gave me, would it be possible for you to contact him?*

B: From what I can see, it appears there might be a way. In addition to having psychic abilities, he also called upon his guides on this side of things. And during the time that he's calling upon his guides, I think I might be able to go and present myself and see what happens. As a friend, not as a guide. Just as a friend to help communicate with him. I could present myself as a gateway through a dimension in time.

I began to get excited. She sounded so confident. Would this possibly be the way to re-establish contact with him? I hardly dared hope it would be so easy.

D: *He wanted a vehicle that he could use to continue the work we were doing on the translations. He said it was easier with the other woman; she had a connection with him because of being a student of his at one time.*

B: Yes, that would make it easier. Did he specify the vehicle he wanted or did he leave it up to your discretion?

He had mentioned the music student that I was working with. Even though he said "Brian," I believed he really meant Brenda. I was going to assume that anyway, for the sake of this experiment.

D: *Well, he did specify this vehicle. He said he would try to come through her in the same way that he came through the other person.*

B: That is good that he specified this one. Then he must feel that there is a sympathetic vibration that will assist with the communication.

D: *I could tell you the directions he gave me to contact him. I don't know if we need the other person, the student, or not.*

B: It does not appear so. From what I can see, it appears that he is prepared to speak to me like he does to his other spirit guides. And for me to either relay it or to speak as though he were speaking directly as if I were not in-between, which generally works out best.

I impressed on her the importance he had stressed in revealing this information to our time. The sense of urgency he conveyed about getting this work done. She said she understood.

D: *We met him in a place that he called the "special" meeting place. I don't know if you know where that is.*

B: I think he's referring to a certain dimension that he can reach.

D: *I believe so because when he described it, it was not on earth. And he was able to stay there for only a limited period of time to converse with me.*

B: This is true. He does this; he'll go to this meeting place when he's conversing with his guides.

D: *Then should I give you the instructions? Or will I need to count you there? Which will be easier? Afterward you can always return to your beautiful place.*

B: Yes, I can return to this place at another time. This is a fascinating situation. Zero me in on a year so I'll know when.

D: *When he lived?*

B: Yes. Where I am, time doesn't mean anything and I can view his whole life, and afterward and before, like a moving panorama.

D: *I'm not sure of the exact years, but I believe he lived in the 1500s.*

B: All right. Give me a moment to focus in on him, so that I can get the message across to him.

D: *I know this would be difficult to do with the ordinary human being, but he was* not *ordinary.*

B: No, he is not ordinary at all, so it can be done. But this being the first time, it might take a little bit longer. It might help if I describe what I see as I zero in.

D: *All right. Maybe we can go back to the same time or situation when he was speaking to me before.*

B: Or close enough to it to where he would remember the connection.

I was really getting excited. Would she be able to locate him and contact him? The odds were so tremendously high against it that any rational person would have to say that it couldn't be done. But succeed or fail, it was well worth the attempt and I was almost holding my breath in anticipation.

B: I'm zeroing on earth, and I'm over Europe now. And there's France. I'm getting closer. Do you know where in France he was?

D: *I'm not really sure of the name of the city.*

B: His name is Michel de Notredame. ... Okay, I see him at his place. There is a house where he does his work. The house is made out of stone. According to the standards of the time it's comfortably large. But according to your standards, it would be a little bit small. Everything is relative. There is a special room where he liked to do his work. In this room he has various instruments set up. And I see ... he has come in ... and he has lit a flame. He's burning alcohol so that the flame is blue. And he's setting up his various instruments to help him concentrate on the higher spheres.

D: *Is this what helps him to see his visions?*

B: Yes. Somehow it helps him with these various instruments of measurement. It helps him to get in tune with the higher vibrations of the universe which are very precise mathematically. He's able to tune in on these, much like tuning in a radio. And from there he can see many things, or he can astrally travel to other dimensions for a period of time. He is a very unusual man.

D: *What type of instruments do you see?*

B: He has some writing instruments and he has ... *(Hard to describe)* I can see them but I don't know what they're called. Pointers that are connected at an angle like for measuring distances on maps. And he has some calipers. And he has some crystals of various sorts on hand as well. I think the crystals are for focusing the light in particular ways to come up with certain vibrations of light.

D: *Do you think he uses them to stare at or what?*

B: He doesn't stare at the crystals. He focuses the crystals to get a particular vibration, or rather a particular color of light and he meditates on this to encourage a certain frame of mind.

D: *And you don't know what the calipers or the other measuring instruments are for?*

B: No, I'm not sure unless it's for trying to diagram what he sees and he wants to do it accurately.

D: *Do you see anything else?*

B: Well, the whole room is pretty well cluttered up with things. There's parchments and manuscripts all over and writing instruments. And there's a table with things on it. He's at a writing desk, or rather there's a writing desk nearby. And there's a few books sitting around.

This description of the room and house sounded very similar to the other one given by Dyonisus. I asked for a description of Nostradamus.

B: He's a very distinguished-looking man. He's of average height for the
time. He has a higher forehead. He has a very fine-featured face.
Piercing gray eyes—or blue—they're light colored. He's in his early
fifties at this point. His hair is gray and he has a full beard and
mustache, and it flows into the hair. And he keeps it clean which is
unusual for this time. He keeps himself well for this time. I think
that's partially due to the things he has seen in the future for I think
he has seen the advantage of good hygiene. He's wearing robes but
that is usual.

D: *Does he have any prominent features?*

B: Very fine featured. His face is proportioned real well. He has straight
brows, and his nose is straight and it's shaped well. His brows kind
of shadow his eyes some and his cheekbones are prominent enough to
make them look very deep-set. And with them being a silvery-gray
color, they look very piercing. They just kind of reach out and grab you.

I took a quick intake of breath as a tingle of excitement ran through
my body. Elena had also mentioned that there was a special quality about
the man's eyes. From the description it appeared that Brenda was seeing
the same man in the same setting.

D: *But he doesn't look threatening, does he?*

B: No, because he's a kind man. Just very piercing and intelligent.

D: *What is his occupation when he's not doing these predictions?*

B: He's a doctor. He doesn't have any of his medical instruments in this
room. I think they're in another part of the house. He does a little bit
of everything but that seems to be the usual pattern for this time, for
educated men to be able to do and be conversant with all the major
branches of arts and sciences.

D: *Did he teach medicine?*

B: Do you mean, did he have any apprentices?

D: *Yes, any that he taught medicine to?*

B: I don't think so. It doesn't appear to be that way. He has some
students who study metaphysics with him. They have to say that
they're studying medicine because of the Inquisition and such.

From these statements it appeared that the students lived in the house
with Nostradamus just as Dyonisus had said.

D: *There was one student in particular that I was interested in. I don't
know if you can see his students there or not.*

B: There are no students there at this time. He's working alone.

D: *Nostradamus had cures and methods of helping people medically that
the doctors of the time could not understand. Do you know anything
about that?*

B: This is directly related to his psychic abilities. When he would enter
another dimension he was able to see anything and everything that he

desired to see. Any field, any subject. He would be able to see things that he could do with what he had. Things others had not thought of but which would be more effective for treating his patients.

D: *I have always wondered why he didn't tell the other doctors some of his methods.*

These were "test" questions to see if she could come up with the same answers that Elena had.

B: The doctors would scoff, because these things would go against age-old ways of doing things. If the doctors were open-minded enough to try something then they would demand to know, "Well, how did you find that out? Where did you learn it?"

D: *"How did you come by this knowledge?"*

B: Yes. And they would be very suspicious about it. They would say that he was in league with the Devil. Everything has an inner suspicion between the church stirring things up, the political unrest, and the various plagues that sweep through from time to time.

D: *That was a shame, wasn't it? Because he had much he could have taught them.*

B: Yes, indeed. Basically his talents were wasted at this time. He did the best he could with the time period he was at.

I have focused in on another instrument he seems to have. It's not exactly a mirror. It's sort of between ... it's sort of a mirror and it's sort of a cloudy glass. I can't really see what it is.

I almost gasped. Could this be the same mirror Elena had mentioned that Nostradamus used to see his visions?

B: This mirror is an archaic instrument and he knows the art of using it. It's controlled by your mind. I think this is what is referred to as a "magic mirror" in folklore. This mirror was made in ancient times before the civilization fell.

What civilization was she referring to? Atlantis?

D: *I wonder how he came by it?*

B: I'm not sure. There are various relics like this scattered throughout Europe that are prized and treasured. And each one has a story as to how it got passed down and survived through the centuries.—He's fixing to use it. And I think this is how I'm going to be able to contact him, through this mirror. Because apparently he'll concentrate on the mirror with the help of the light that he has focused. He concentrates on the mirror and the cloudiness clears. And in the cleared space he'll either see a person that he'll be speaking to or he'll see a path to enter another dimension. Rather like your story, *Through the Looking Glass,* where the little girl went through the looking glass. He will mentally walk through this looking glass down whatever path he sees.—I think when he concentrates and it clears, I will present myself, then speak to him and invite him to walk down the path to you.

D: *Maybe this is what he means by the special meeting place.*

B: Perhaps. This mirror could be the path.

D: *The last time he and his student both met me there. This would be good if we can do it without the student. There won't be so many people involved.*

B: Yes. We go to speak directly. Let me wait on him until he gets in the proper state of concentration. (*Long pause.*) It's difficult for me to focus in, but I think it's because it's the first time.

D: *Yes, I think after we do it once, it will be much easier. When he sees there's a new contact.*

B: He'll be happy for that, I know. It's very vital. It's like ... there's a description given of the amount of energy behind the work that *you* are doing. Multiply that by ten or a hundred times and that's the amount of energy behind the work *he* is doing. It must come through! And it must be as accurate as possible.

D: *I think it is normal for psychics to try to warn people when they see things that are going to happen.*

B: Yes, because he's so ... I seem to be picking up on some of his thoughts. Perhaps this will assist in our communication. The main thing he's concerned about is that, in spite of his warnings, the people make the wrong choices anyway and walk the very path that he has foreseen. He is trying to get the news to people in enough time so that they can perhaps change their minds about some things and avert the worst of it.

D: *There were many things he saw that I don't think he understood. He tried to get them through to me, and it's difficult because his quatrains are puzzles.*

B: They had to be obscure. They *had* to be.—I get the feeling that's what he wants to do. To give a prose explanation to go along with the quatrains.—Ah! He's at the proper point now, I believe. Let me try to contact him. I will try to report on what happens. (*Pause*) He sees me now! (*She addressed him respectfully.*) Michel de Notredame. I am the one sent to contact you. I have been asked to be the communicator with the one that has contacted you on the other side of time. (*Pause*) Yes, I am the one. I was asked to repeat to you to meet us at the special meeting place. So that we may insure the interpretation of your quatrains into plain language. So that all of us may be warned in time. (*Pause*) Well, we can either try to get started or at least set up our line of communication so that it will work out well. Are you prepared to go to the special place, Michel de Notre Dame? (*Pause*) All right. We will wait for you there.

My excitement could hardly contain itself. Could it really be possible? It actually appeared that we had made contact with him.

D: Did he understand you?

B: Yes. Apparently this communication is in the mind and it's of concepts rather than with spoken language. So it doesn't matter what language you think in; it's the basic concepts that go across and are interpreted into whatever language his conscious mind thinks in and vice versa.

D: Did he remember what you spoke of?

B: Yes, although his facial expression did not change, his eyes became very fiery. I could tell he is excited. And he remembered. He said he had been waiting to be contacted, and he was wondering when and how we were going to contact him.

I felt giddy. I could hardly keep from laughing out loud from pure joy. I thought we had lost contact with him and it worried me that we would not be able to re-establish it. I really thought it would be more difficult, if not outright impossible.

B: I think that this time the main thing we're going to do is try to make sure we can communicate clearly and make sure things can go across well, because the next time it will be easier. I'll know to focus in on the mirror. It took me a while to find it.

I agreed, the most important thing was to get the line of communication going again. I was too excited to think about translation tonight anyway.

D: Do you want to ask him how he wants to do this, or can he hear me?

B: I'm having to repeat right now. What I have to do is, repeat to him what you say because he doesn't hear you. He knows you're there but he cannot directly observe you. He's using me for that purpose. I get the feeling the way he wants to do this, instead of my always saying, "He said thus and such," and then me turn around and saying, "She said this and such," for me to ... it would be like the magic mirror but with words, and just speak as though it was him speaking.

D: That would be a lot easier because before there was a lot of conversation back and forth. A three-way conversation.

B: There may still be some of that. I'm not sure. But he's very anxious to communicate. I'm still doing things in the third person because he's *here*, but he hasn't said anything yet. He's just working out how he wants to set this up.—I know he has said that he would never speak through another human being, so that people could beware of imitators claiming to be him. But, although the vehicle I am using is a human being, the part of me that he is speaking to here is a spirit. And so, from his point of view he's speaking to a spirit and not a human being. The final link that contacts you happens to be a human being, but my spirit is in between.

It is amazing that she also mentioned this prediction which warned about imitators.

D: *Can you see what the special meeting place looks like?*
B: There's really nothing here. It's a void, a part of a particular dimension. It seems to be kind of a little pocket where people can come and interact between two or three different dimensions and communicate. There's no physical features about it to describe. It's just a particular vibration in the universe.

That seemed to fit the same description that Elena had given of this place. She said it was like a gray bank with misty clouds but had no form or substantial foundation. I was delighted because it sounded like we had found the exact same place where we had met before.

B: It appears to me that it is the same place. Mostly I feel his presence, but I picture his face there so as to make it easy for me to identify. And I hear you although I do not see you.

I wanted to make sure she was comfortable in this strange place and not start to lose contact with me as Elena had done when we entered that dimension. I gave her instructions to prevent any disruption.

B: It's comfortable, but I feel like I'm in two places at once. It's an odd feeling but it's ... not bad. If I can describe it for you, it's like when you're between being awake and asleep. And you think you're awake but you're really asleep. And you feel real strange because you think you're awake. So you feel like you're kind of in two places at once. It's two states of mind simultaneously.

This description also sounded remarkably similar to Elena's. It was the only thing she remembered upon awakening. She also was aware of Nostradamus' face.

D: *The student that spoke through the other vehicle also said it felt strange. It was a little hard for him to maintain it because he wasn't used to it.*
B: I can see where it would be. He had a different conditioning than this vehicle has. He was trained by Nostradamus but he had a lot of cultural things to overcome.
D: *Does Nostradamus know that I am the same person that spoke with him before?*
B: Yes. He sends his greetings.
D: *I send mine.*
B: And he says, "I am very happy that we've been able to set up this line of communication. Although I have predicted that I will never speak through another person, I'm speaking to the spirit here. And the spirit says that she can relay my words as I speak them. To where it will *sound* like I'm speaking through a person, but it's simply because this

relayer is cutting out the third person aspect. The 'he saids and she saids.' I'm allowing her to do this to make it quicker, so we can communicate more in the amount of time we have here. Because I can only stay here for a small portion of time before *my* body gets tired and I must go back."

This was again verification that we were speaking to him while he was alive during his physical lifetime because a spirit would not get tired.

D: *I appreciate any amount of time that you can spend with me.*

B: You don't know how *I* appreciate your being able to get in touch with me, so that I can make sure my quatrains are properly explained.

D: *I was worried when the other vehicle left.*

B: Well, I get the feeling from my studies that if something must come to pass, there is always a way figured out to where it will come to pass.

D: *Yes, for I want to pass this knowledge on in my time period.*

B: There are several who will be eager for the knowledge and it is needed. It's needed to be passed and spread so that people can take heed and try to protect themselves from the things I can warn them of.

D: *You did say before that you would give me the corrections on the quatrains because you were aware that some of them had been translated incorrectly.*

B: Right. And on most of them, even the ones that have been translated nearly correct, on all of them, I want to give additional explanation of what I saw when I was writing these. I had to leave out a lot because of the form I was having to write them in. I would like to clarify a lot of things to help them become clearer. Because in several of them I would have to combine two and three events and write about it as if it were one event, so that I could fit it into the quatrain.

D: *Do you mean they were events in different times, or events all happening at the same time or what?*

B: Both. A lot of times events in different times that were following similar patterns could be written about in one quatrain.

D: *This is something people don't understand. The majority of people who study your quatrains think you're speaking of only one event.*

B: It's very easy for them to make that mistake because of the way I had to write them. So I am not offended at this.

D: *It's really human nature to try to understand in the simplest way.*

B: Yes. It is difficult to find the more complex way if you don't know where to look.

D: *If the events were happening in different time periods, why would you include them in one quatrain? Do they bear a similarity to each other or what?*

B: Michel de Notredame has tried to draw a demonstration. In this dimension we are in there is a way of physically demonstrating time. It's hard to describe. Apparently one of the aspects of time is that it moves in a spiral. And at similar positions on each of the loops of the spiral, events have the possibility of being similar, or at least following similar general patterns. Whenever he would see some of these general patterns, particularly if it is affecting the same culture, he'd write about it in one quatrain. I think one reason why he did that was to confuse those who would persecute him. And another reason, I think he felt that if he was able to write about it in one quatrain instead of three or four, the time spent writing the three or four could be spent writing about other events. He was trying to get as many events down on paper as he could, because he saw so many things. There's a lot that he did not get down on paper. So he was trying to get as vast a scope as he could because he felt it was extremely urgent that as much information be passed down as possible.

D: *We have the saying that history repeats itself, it follows patterns. Is this what he means?*

B: Basically. There are other aspects to it that I can see in this dimension that are not readily visible in the physical dimension. But, basically, yes. For example, an obscure person rises to power and becomes a tyrant and is eventually toppled. This is a pattern that is repeated several times. And so he found that if there are two or three that are going to have a particular affect on world history, he can write a single quatrain about more than one of them, say, about two or three of them. And have obscure references within the quatrain to where one can see that, yes, it refers to this person and to that person, because this happened to this person and this other thing happened to this other person. But they both follow similar patterns.

D: *I think the problem is that our experts think he is referring to one event or one person, and it's very difficult to figure out what he means.*

B: One problem is that your experts look at it from the physical plane. He says that he understands this. Particularly if they are writing within the influence of the overwhelming historical event. They tend to interpret all the quatrains in relation to that historical event. This is only natural and understandable. That's why he was so anxious to set up this line of communication, to be able to take the biases out and to balance the viewpoints on the quatrains.

D: *Many of them are not even understood until after they happen.*

B: Yes, indeed. That's another reason why he is wanting to give additional explanations with his translations.

I decided to ask a few questions that would be test questions. I was so much in awe of this man and so overwhelmed by this breakthrough that I really did not need any proof. A great deal of verification had already been provided between what Elena said and what Brenda was now saying. But he had told me it would be all right to do this in order to verify that I was speaking with the same person. I was a little afraid that I might insult Nostradamus by questioning his validity.

B: Let me explain this situation to him. *(Pause)* Yes, he urges you to go on. He tells me that he's not doubting my honesty, that he just wants to make sure that the communication is clear.

D: *He used a lot of time factors dealing with astrological signs in his quatrains. Do you know anything about that?*

B: Do *I* know anything about it? Or does *he?*

D: *Well, does he? Can he tell me anything about how he set the times that these events were to happen, when he used these astrological symbols in his quatrains.*

B: Let me put this to him. *(Long pause as though listening.)* The answer that I'm getting is in pictures of concepts rather than in words. And I'm not sure if I'm going to be able to explain clearly what I am seeing. First of all, I get the idea that he's going to show me a general picture and then lead me down to the specific. He says that—or rather the pictures show me that everything is interrelated. The positions of the planets in regards to time and such. And when I say "everything," I'm seeing a picture of our galaxy at this point, and its position is tied in with time. The galaxy can be divided up into wedges, so to speak, each wedge representing a certain amount of time. This also applies to the grand sweep of time in the solar system. And each of these wedges of time is principally influenced by the vibrations of a certain celestial body. And these wedges come in an orderly fashion, one precedes after the other. Whenever he mentions a particular celestial body he's referring to that wedge of time that the body's vibrations permeate. And since it comes along in a certain order, that would be thus and such many years after the time he is speaking, because there would be other wedges of time in between. The language is not sufficient for wording this well. I'm calling them wedges of time because everything, all energy, emanates from a central source, and time is a sort of energy. These different celestial bodies in their different positions all emanate their own particular vibrations. And their positions with each other as regarded from outside the solar system, as well as regarded from within the solar system, gives clues as to how they interact with each other. And hence would affect the wedges of time that they permeate.

I received a much more complicated answer than I had expected when I asked that question. Although it was obscure to me, when I later showed it to an astrologer, he said it made sense to him. He said the description used archaic phrasing but Nostradamus was definitely describing astrology. I especially thought that the phrase, "these wedges come in an orderly fashion, one precedes after the other," had to be a mistake. Because how can anything precede *after* something? To precede means to go before. The astrologer agreed that this is correct in normal language, but in astrology the planets do appear to precede after each other. This was proof that the mind of an astrologer, in this case Nostradamus, was conveying this concept since neither Brenda nor I know anything but the bare rudiments of astrology.

D: *Why are the experts today having difficulty dating the events in his quatrains?*

B: I think it is because from the concepts that he uses they consider it to be nonsense, and so they don't even consider them. In doing that they have thrown away some vital data that would help them in dating his quatrains.

D: *Another question I wanted to ask, is there ever a possibility that his quatrains are wrong? That some of them didn't come to pass?*

B: He says that if some of his quatrains appear to be inaccurate, it's not because he didn't see accurately but because of the inadequacy of the language to communicate what he has seen. He says that is the major stumbling block. The only way for some of his quatrains to be wrong is if mankind in general were to realize the path they are walking and make a crucial decision at a junction in this path to take a different path. That will change history totally. Which would then make it different than what he viewed the path as being, from the direction mankind was already walking in his time.

D: *I see. Then does he believe it's possible that man can change the future?*

B: (*Sigh*) He's hoping it is. He says that's the main reason why he wrote down his quatrains. So that some of the horrible things he saw would not come to pass.

D: *Could man have changed the future at different times in the past between our times?*

B: Apparently there's been a few minor changes but nothing to alter the overall pattern.

D: *I thought this might make the quatrains uninterpretable if an event that he saw didn't come to pass because man had taken another path.*

B: This is true. This is a possibility. But apparently at this point the major pattern still holds.

I was still asking test questions.

D: *May I ask if you know a person known as Dyonisus?* (*I had to repeat it twice trying to get the pronunciation right.*)

B: Your pronunciation is close enough. He's a student of mine. He studies well. Sometimes he has difficulty understanding, but he's doing well for opening up his mind. And he tries. And so, I think he has promise. He's doing good with his medical studies but he mainly has a strong interest in ... metaphysical, I believe. Yes, the communicator calls it "metaphysical." In metaphysical studies. He doesn't have the natural ability for it that I have. But I have discovered there are things people can do to open up parts of their minds that they're not aware of. And so we have been successful with this.

D: *Do you know where Dyonisus came from?*
B: (*Pause*) I'm not real sure. His parents are emigrants. And he's from somewhere out of the country. He came here to study with me.
D: *By emigrants, what do you mean? That they came from another country or what?*
B: Yes. I am allowing this vehicle to use words from beyond my time if they fit. If the concept calls for what you would consider a modern word, I'm perfectly willing for the vehicle to use the word if it conveys what I mean. Better that than to try to talk around your elbows saying something when there's a word at hand already.

Again I experienced a cold shiver. His description of Dyonisus was far too perfect to be coincidence.

D: *Can you tell me what city you are living in? I know sometimes this is difficult.*
B: Yes, it's being difficult. I'm wanting to say Paris but I don't think it's Paris. It's another major cultural center that's not too far away from Paris.—Perhaps the name will come. Sometimes I've noticed that will happen with some of my patients. They're trying to think of something that's difficult to remember. And when they start speaking of something else, it will sneak up on them and they will suddenly remember it.

Later, after Brenda was awake and we were discussing this eventful session, the name "Lyons" suddenly popped into her head. (Pronounced: Lions.) She blurted it out for no specific reason. Looking very puzzled, she asked what it meant. I told her I thought it was the name of a city in France. Could this be the name he was trying to remember and it truly did emerge in the head of the vehicle later when she was thinking about something else? An interesting possibility. Also an example that we were not dealing with the part of the brain that contains mundane dates and names.

D: *Have you ever been to the university?*
B. Yes, I have, many times. The city that I'm in has a university. The major university is at Paris. And there's a university here as well where one can study sciences and theology and such. The main reason I go there is to use their library.
D: *Did you ever teach medicine at either one of these universities?*
B: I've taught courses there. Not necessarily always medicine. Sometimes they ask me to teach in philosophy.
D: *When we meet again, would he want to translate the quatrains or would he want to just tell me the things that are going to happen?*
B: He's going to use a combination of both, just whatever comes. To be able to spark the communication and get it started, he'll probably have you read a quatrain and he interpret. And at some point he'll probably … (*laugh*) he says, knowing him, he'll start lecturing on it and he'll just

kind of keep blabbing. *(Laugh)* That's *his* word, "blabbing." I did not put that in.

D: *(Laugh)* *Well, I want him to blab all he wants to. I'm here to listen and to pass it on.—We have many, many books of translations of his quatrains and I've noticed that none of them seem to agree. This is what makes it difficult.*

B: Yes. He says to find an interpretation that you're comfortable with, then it will be easier to communicate the concepts. And if the concepts are not the same as what he was trying to put forth, then he will tell you what he was trying to say, that was perhaps lost in the interpretation. He says if you're more comfortable reading them aloud in English then that is fine, for I'll be communicating across the concepts of what you say in English. And he will see how they compare with the concepts he was thinking of, even though he was writing in French.

D: *Okay, because I don't understand French. I have noticed in comparing various books that the English is different in each one, according to whoever did the translating.*

B: Yes. That's why he's wanting to deal with the concepts and he's not worried about what language we're dealing with.

I was afraid some of them may have been changed so much that he would not even be able to recognize them.

B: He says he's intimately familiar with all of his quatrains. He's aware of how some of the concepts may have gotten twisted around. So when you read a quatrain and I send across the concepts, if this seems similar to a quatrain he wrote, he will speak of that quatrain. But if they do not seem familiar, he may ask for you to read it in French to help him zero in on the particular quatrain.

That idea certainly did not appeal to me since I don't know French. I asked if it would be possible for him to zero in on the book in some way.

B: I'm not sure as that can be done.

I protested, "But I can't pronounce the French words." He was not about to let me get off of the book that easily.

B: Well, he points out to me that French has changed. When they're reading, the French in your time, they leave a lot of the sounds out. But in his time most of the sounds were pronounced. The French in your time leaves out a lot of the consonants and slurs the vowels together. He says just go ahead and pronounce them. Make your vowels pure and pronounce it the way it's spelled. And even though it may sound atrocious to him, he'll know what you're saying.

D: *(Laugh)* *That's what I'm thinking. I'm afraid it* would *sound atrocious.*

B: He doesn't care. If his physical body were here he'd be jumping up and down at this point. He says he doesn't care. He wants to get across the concepts.

D: *His quatrains were not totally in French, were they?*

B: No, there are some Latin influences.—He says, I will warn you. I might get emotional at some point about some of the things they have done to my quatrains. But I will try to keep it under control because this is my vehicle for undoing what they have done, and so I am going to take full advantage of this and try to communicate. It's very important that the message get across.

D: *Just promise that you will not get angry at my butchered French.* (Laugh)

B: No, I will not get angry at your French. I will just simply get angry at the publishers and the editors and the translators.

D: *It would be good if I could find someone who knows French, then they could read it to you.*

B: I don't think that would do much good because language changes through the centuries. And their French would sound butchered to me as well.

It looked as though I was not going to get out of it.

D: *All right. Then the next time we meet, I will read it in English. And if you can't grasp it at all, I will try the French as a last resort.*

B: Yes. I think it should work out in English. This vehicle that we are using is familiar with the language of English. And at my end of things we are dealing with mental concepts. So you read it in English, the vehicle is able to grasp the concepts of what's being communicated and show them to me. And if the concepts are not quite what I wanted to get across, I will give the vehicle the concepts I meant. Then the vehicle will give it to you in English since we are dealing with concepts here and the vehicle normally translates concepts into English or German whenever the vehicle is communicating. And if I decide that I want to add some additional concepts, I will start lecturing, so to speak.

D: *I would feel much more comfortable with that.—Also, you have used words that we call anagrams. Why did you do that?*

B: I usually used anagrams whenever I was writing about something that was politically sensitive.

D: *From your time or for other times?*

B: Both. I used some of the anagrams because they would be politically sensitive in my time and it would be somewhat untactful to use the straight words. And in my time, you understand, the noblemen carry a lot of power. I would not want to get them angry with me because they would have me arrested and then I couldn't write any more quatrains. So I'm willing to go to certain lengths to disguise what I write, so long as it does get written. Now in some of the other quatrains I use anagrams because the subject matter is very sensitive for the time that it's referred to. It would not be good for the general public to know what I'm writing about, because I might cause a panic or something like that. So I use anagrams so that those who are knowledgeable on such things can figure it out. Because those who are knowledgeable are usually in a position to do something about it.

D: *I am thinking he may be getting tired. The main thing I wanted to do tonight was re-establish this contact.*

B: Yes, he agrees that this time of communication is to an end. His control and concentration is wavering, and he notes that the vehicle being used is also getting tired.

D: *This is about as long as we will do it at any one time. (About an hour.)*

B: He says that will be fine. Time is meaningless in this place. He'll be able to space out the encounters at a pace that he can handle. The amount of time that elapses at his end won't necessarily be the same amount of time that elapses at your end. And he considers that from his point of view he will be initiating the communication. Basically he will do what he did tonight to enter this special meeting place. And he knows that when he comes here that you will be here. Although it may have been two or three weeks at his end, it may only be a day or two at your end. But it does not matter. He knows that he'll be able to meet you here to communicate. Tell the vehicle to go to the special meeting place and to think of the mirror because that helps to open up the path. To picture the mirror and the room he'll be in and mentally picture him coming through. That helps set up the energy to draw him through. The way this dimension is set up, when the vehicle thinks of him being at the mirror to contact you, somehow it works out to where it will automatically be at a time when he is ready to contact you anyway.

I wondered what would happen if he were waiting to contact us at a time when we weren't working. I certainly didn't like to mentally picture him waiting there in vain and growing impatient. This procedure sounded strange but apparently the contact would all be taken care of automatically. Everything about this whole situation was strange so there was no sense in questioning the plausibility or logic of it.

D: *Then the next time we meet I will start reading some of the quatrains. Shall I just pick them at random or what?*

B: He's not sure. It's getting more difficult for him to communicate because he needs to go back. He says that we will clarify that next time. He's going back now and he has returned to his body. He is in his laboratory now. He feels deeply exhausted but very pleased. He sends you warm feelings.

I didn't want to tire him either. I told him I had been afraid that the contact would be broken when Elena left and I had thought there was no possible way to contact him again.

B: He still has the mirror open even though he has returned to his body. He communicates the concept that when it comes to metaphysics ... well, he's given me the go ahead to use a colloquial phrase here. (*Laugh*) There's more than one way to skin a cat. He says that if this way had not worked, he would have figured out another way and it would have been much more difficult for him. But he was hoping that this way would work because it was the easiest way for him and possibly for you, too.

D: *Yes, because this is a very good vehicle, a very clear channel.*

B: Yes. He realized that. He says he wanted to find a vehicle that was educated enough to have a good vocabulary, that could be used to communicate the concepts in the most succinct manner.

D: *I believe it was a little frightening to the other vehicle. It was a little overwhelming. She thought it was a big responsibility to take on.*

B: That is true. He feels that the mind set of this vehicle will be able to handle it because it's a very eager and open mind. Eager to learn new things and grasping for knowledge. He says that the more this method of communication is used, the easier it will become. It's like a well-loved pipe, the more it's smoked the better it works.

D: *In the time allotted to us we will try to get all the information about the quatrains he wants to give us. And then we can each go about our own business, and he will feel he has accomplished a mission.*

B: Yes. He says it may take quite some time. He's not really sure how long it will take. But he's prepared to devote however long it takes to do it, as long as there's a vehicle of communication to use. He says he realizes that you probably have other projects going on with this vehicle and other vehicles. And to feel free to continue with these because he will be continuing his other projects. He does want to stay in close communication with you in order to keep working on this project because it is vitally important. But he realizes that he mustn't ... "hog the vehicle," I believe is the concept. He's doing his closing ... I'm going to say "ritual," before returning to a normal state of consciousness.

D: *I too, am prepared to devote as much time to this as it takes and I really think we can do it. I feel very confident now. I appreciate you (the vehicle) doing this, too.*

B: It is my pleasure. I have admired this man for quite some time. Such subjects interest me anyway. And the life that this vehicle is presently in, she has also been very involved with such things. So this will be interesting for her, too. I feel honored that I have been chosen for such an important task.

I told her she could again return to her beautiful place, but she had beat me to it and was already there, once again enjoying the crystal stream and musical waterfall.

B: I believe next time if you just ask to go to the special meeting place it will work out because that place is not linked to the wheel of life. That would automatically catch me, meaning this entity, in between life cycles.

After Brenda awakened, before I told her anything about the session I wanted to know what she consciously remembered. She kept seeing a strange glass or mirror. I asked her to describe it.

B: I'll try to give the measurements, too. I see an oval, I'd say about fourteen inches long and about ... four and a half, five inches wide. (*She was making measurements with her hands.*) An oval of ... I want to call it "glass," but I'm not sure. It's kind of like a surface between two dimensions. One side of the glass is on our dimension and that side looks kind of milky white. And when you flip it over and see the other side, which is connected with the other dimension, you see nothing, a void, black. Maybe occasionally a little bit of shimmer if the light hits it just right. But there's just nothing there because the other side of this glass is not in this dimension. Like a window or a doorway or something. And I see a man's face kind of floating, suspended, with no particular background.

D: *Is it a pleasant face?*

B: He's good-looking. He really is, he's handsome. His forehead is kind of straight, and his hair goes back from his forehead. He has a beard and a mustache that is flowing and real pretty. And he has piercing eyes. I seem to associate him with some sort of laboratory, things cluttered up, instruments, junk like that. But the main thing that fascinates me personally is the concept of this glass oval of whatever it is with two dimensions. I don't know what kind of technology or knowledge would produce such a thing, but it's interesting to try to conceive of the civilization that would have instruments like that. (*Laugh*) I wouldn't mind having one of those gizmos myself.

I then revealed what had happened. I told her, "We have just done the impossible!" I explained to Brenda about my experience with Elena and all the complications that led up to my wanting to try this experiment with her. She was very excited and wanted to continue working on this. The only thing she could remember reading about Nostradamus was an old book about his prophecies that was printed after the Second World War in which they tried to associate all his quatrains with the war. She remembered thinking at the time how silly that was, because many of them didn't really seem to apply to the war but had been stretched by the translator to fit.

MY EMOTIONS AFTER THIS SESSION ranged a whole gamut from incredulity because I had thought the project impossible to achieve, to wonder, to ecstasy, and exhilaration over the actual accomplishment and breakthrough. I felt if this could happen then truly nothing was impossible. Nothing could hold us back now for we had been able to transcend the barriers and boundaries of time and space. I knew we would be permitted to return again and again, as many times as we wished, to seek and find hidden knowledge. I could not even conceive of or imagine what wonderful adventures and insights might lie in store for us beyond the portal of the magic mirror.

Chapter 8

ffəan of ffəystery

𝕁 HAD NOT HEARD FROM ELENA since her departure. After this tremendous breakthrough, I wrote her to tell her about the fantastic developments. I also wanted to let her know that she was now "off the hook." She did not have to feel any further responsibility in this project. I had come to the conclusion that her part in all of this had been to act as a bridge, a catalyst to get the whole thing started.

Her answering letter contained the following revelation, "I knew within a few weeks after leaving you that I was finished with that part of it. But I did have an inner knowledge that things would be continued even though the intellectual side of me didn't understand. I *know* I have to do the portrait, I've been seeing his face more and more in my mind's eye."

The picture arrived a few weeks later. For some reason she saw him wearing a wool cap that was pulled down over his ears. She said it was a difficult portrait to draw and she was not totally satisfied with it. Her main disappointment was that she felt she did not reproduce the intensity of his eyes. When Brenda saw it she said it was very close to the way she pictured him in her mind. Whether it's totally accurate or not, it's still a remarkable accomplishment that Elena was able to reproduce the portrait of a man who has been dead for 400 years.

Rather I should say "so-called" dead because when I began to converse with him on a regular basis, the word "dead" would never have described him. To me he became very much alive and displayed all the various mixed emotions that mold us into individual human beings. At different times he would be irritated, impatient, worried or intense. He would often become angered at how the interpreters had translated his quatrains. At other times he would convey a genuine sense of humor. At these times he would joke with us and even become feisty. He was quite a personality. He was also very human. I knew at all times that I was communicating with a living, physical human being and not a spirit. He was also very emphatic about insisting that he was very much alive, that I was not speaking to the dead. This point was very important to him. He deeply wanted me to understand this. That he just had this unusual talent that enabled him to see the future and thus communicate with me. Does this mean that the theory of simultaneous or parallel time is a fact? I will leave it to others to try to explain the how and the why and the logic of it. I will just try to carry out the project that he assigned me.

J WANTED TO KNOW MORE about Nostradamus so I often asked questions about his life. I will put these all together here out of context.

D: *Would he mind if I ask him some questions about his life?*

B: He says that he'll answer the questions he can. Since he's not at the end of his life yet, he doesn't know the full story.

D: *(Laugh) But I'm interested in the early part. He should know about that.—One of the things people have always wondered about is how you were able to perform your medical cures. How you were able to control pain and bleeding and things like that. Can you share that with me?*

B: It depends on which way I use. Sometimes I use physical means and sometimes mental means. I seem to think that this ... whatever you want to call it, to where I'm able to see the things that will happen. Sometimes that carries side effects, invisible energies that can do other things like damp out pain or suppress bleeding. As far as physical means are concerned, a lot of times I use this talent for that too. If I put my mind in a certain frame I can see the life energies that flow through a body. If there's a point where they're not flowing the way they should, if you press that place or rub it or use other types of manipulation to where they flow freely again, many times that helps to eliminate pain. I usually use a combination of physical and mental ways of controlling pain in operations. One thing that I do is *very* effective. I get the patient to help me with it. I get them in the right frame of mind as well, to where they don't feel the pain. With them not feeling the pain from their end, and me helping them with my mind and pressing the places I can see that will help control the pain, that keeps the pain down to a minimum to where I can operate without the nerves of the body experiencing shock.

D: *These are things that the other doctors don't know about, aren't they?*

B: No, they don't have this talent that I have. And besides, everyone is very ignorant about what the mind is capable of. I have been conducting experiments to find out what the mind *can* do. That's one of the things I've been doing with my students. These studies that we do with the mind are both medical and metaphysical at the same time. These studies are very popular with my students.

D: *I can see where they would be. But don't the other doctors wonder how you're able to do these things?*

B: They wonder, but whenever I try to explain to them, their superstitions get in the way and they immediately start crying "witchcraft." So I don't bother. I just smile and shrug my shoulders and quirk one of my eyebrows and let them wonder. And my reputation grows.

D: *I thought they would try to imitate you, to copy you in some way if they knew.*

B: They don't know what to do *to* copy me.

D: *Couldn't they pick it up by watching you?*

B: No. Often at the beginning of an operation I'll stare into a patient's eyes to get them in the proper frame of mind. I don't really know why I'm able to do this, but I am. And they (the doctors) apparently can't concentrate their eyes well enough to do this.

D: *I thought if they heard you talking to the patient they would know you were doing something.*

B: I do murmur to the patient but they, the doctors, are usually not close enough to hear what I'm saying.

D: *What do you say to the patient?*

B: Oh, it depends on what the situation is. Generally I tell them good things. Like, they're feeling good, that it's very pleasant, that they have no reason to be afraid, and that everything's going to be okay and they'll be just fine afterward, and things like that.

I remembered that Dyonisus said these were dangerous times and they had to be very careful because of the Inquisition.

D: *I always thought that a man as powerful as you are would not be in danger. I consider you to be powerful anyway, with all your knowledge.*

B: I'm respected because I'm educated and because my medicine—my doctoring—works. I'm respected because I'm considered to be knowledgeable. I'm a well-rounded, educated man. But that does not give me the political clout that I need in order to insure that I'm not in any danger at all. I was born to plain and simple parents. I have no titles. In my point in time noble people carry very real power and people honestly believe the King to be God, or next to God, because the King has absolute power. And so it works like that. Also, in my time the church is *extremely* powerful. And I have to be careful for that, too. Because the church can wield enough political power to cause kings and noblemen to do what they want in certain situations. So my task is very important. I'm not flaunting myself as I say this. It should be obvious to anybody that my task is vital. Else why would I have this ability that I have? I've had it all my life. I did not ask for it. It was there and so it must be there for a purpose. God works in mysterious ways, and this is one of his more mysterious ways, I suppose. And so, I'm going to do the most I can, the best I can, so as to help mankind in general.

Nostradamus seldom spoke in direct first person after this. The information was relayed through Brenda in third person.

D: *Can Nostradamus give us any information about healing that can be applied in our present time?*

B: Yes, he can. That is, he can try to explain some of the things that he would do. If you find them applicable you are welcome to apply them. He says that he got many of the physical techniques that he uses from things he saw from future times. And he would say, "Ah! I can do that now myself. It may not be accepted by my colleagues but I can go ahead and do it, and it will help the people. And I'm going to help the people as much as I can." Most of these are not necessarily complex procedures but just things to help better his chances of saving some of his patients. However, being as strong psychically as he is, he says he is able to mentally see what is wrong so that he would know what to treat. He would use a lot of positive energy with the person, and have the person help him by imagining themselves with the problem no longer being there. He would build them up and help them develop confidence in themselves as well as trust in what he is doing. To help the psychic fields to be conducive toward both the physical and the mental and the emotional aspects of healing.

Even if Nostradamus didn't call it that, he was obviously practicing an advanced form of hypnosis combined with acupressure and the ability to see the weak spots in the aura. It appears that he was such an advanced natural metaphysician that he also had other talents which he used without realizing exactly how or why he was doing it.

D: *Does he ever use color as a factor in healing?*
B: Yes, very much so. He says one of the things he would do to help create the right atmosphere is that, by using a prism, he would demonstrate the colors of light to a patient. He would demonstrate how what appears to be white light has other colors in it. He would point out one of the colors to them and ask them to imagine that they were standing in a light of this color shining down upon them. Whichever color was necessary for the desired result to help set their psychic fields in balance.
D: *Is he aware of the method that I'm using to contact him?*
B: He says he doesn't know specifically but he has the strong feeling that it's similar to some of the methods he uses for healing.
D: *Yes, the method is called "hypnosis" in my time.*
B: He says he has used that method to help lessen pain in people.
D: *It is used for that in our time, too. But it also has many other uses.*
B: He says it's most wondrous. It's a handy tool and he's glad that it has not been lost through the ages.
D: *He may know how to use it better than we do and he may have uses for it that I don't know about. But I have discovered this method of using it to contact people through time. It's working with the mind and the mind is a very marvelous creation.*
B: He says there are really no limits to what can be done with the mind.

D: *It's a shame that the others in his time can't learn these things. It would make it so much better.*

B: They *could* learn it, they just *won't.*—At this point I get the feeling of a great grief from Michel de Notredame. He knows there are so many things his people could do that would make their lot better. But they don't or can't because they don't know of it or can't handle the knowledge or they're just kept in ignorance. This saddens him very much.

D: *Yes, it's the time he lives in and we have no control over that.—I was wondering where he learned how to do these things. Did he receive training from anybody?*

B: He says that he'd always been a little bit odd and that visions of the future were always with him. He'd look at people and see superimposed upon them visions of how it was going to be for them. And he realized that he could use this gift to help people. So he started trying to seek out knowledge and training. He says there wasn't much to find. Most of what he does he discovered on his own. He had discovered that he was able to focus well if he stared into a candle flame. And so he reasoned that it would be even better if he used a spirit lamp to burn alcohol in or something similar, to make a purer flame.

D: *People have thought that maybe he traveled and learned of these things from great teachers in other countries.*

B: He says he has studied with a few teachers but not as many as what is thought. Most of the teaching he has had has been from great teachers of the other plane. He says sometimes when he would meditate he would receive knowledge.—But he seems to be rather confused as to where he got the mirror. He says he's not really sure how that happened. He seems to think that a being of some sort from another plane or another dimension bestowed it upon him, in order to be able to make contact between different planes.

D: *I wondered how he found it.*

B: He says he didn't find it. He was meditating one day and he saw this being standing before him, talking to him and teaching him. The being told him he would be able to recontact him and other planes whenever he wanted to. And Nostradamus asked, "How? I am not that disciplined yet." And the being said, "You will know when you return to normal consciousness." When he returned to normal consciousness, the mirror was lying before him.

D: *So he really didn't know where it came from.*

At the beginning of one session she announced:

B: He had a little bit of trouble coming through to the meeting place this time, but he feels his problems should not interfere with what he's wanting to do with you.

D: *Why did he have trouble?*

B: I'm not sure that he knows. He suspects it may have something to do with the fact that some of the skeptics have been questioning him. They've been putting out negative forces and influences which would interfere with what he's trying to do. He says that skeptics are as eternal as weeds, and about as viable. He kind of snorted at this point and shook his head.

D: *Are they questioning him about his medical work or about his work with these prophecies?*

B: Both.

D: *I can understand because sometimes I get negative feedback, too. I probably can't really appreciate his position but I try.*

B: He appreciates your understanding but he says you must realize that he has to deal with a lot more ignorance than you have ever had to try to conceive. He says that some types of ignorance are the same across the centuries and others have changed, but that is life.

D: *Has he ever been in any danger from the church because of the things he does?*

B: He says there have been some threats made. Different ones of the church trying to manipulate him and get him to do their bidding. But he says that he has managed to outwit them and be his own person.

D: *Did they try to have him predict things for the church?*

B: They've tried to get him to not publish certain predictions. They've tried to trap him with some of his predictions, trying to make it sound like he has committed heresy. They've tried to bribe and blackmail him with money. And they've tried to get him to alter certain predictions to suit their needs. He says that the church is not a religious institution. It's one of the largest political institutions on the earth. And so they really—he's borrowed a phrase from me at this point. He says they don't care, they don't give a fig. When he saw this phrase in my head, he asked me what a fig was. (*Laugh*) The church does not give a fig about the religious aspects. He says they use that to help do the political manipulation. And they do so to make things to be to their convenience.

D: *Does he mean they might try to change the quatrains?*

B: Yes, that too. Since they're wanting to change them anyhow and they're not going to be caught trying, he knows that if he words them the way he does they don't really make much sense to the priests and such who would be reading it. So they wouldn't know where to change it in the way that they want it.

D: *Very clever. But some of these may have been changed. That's wl* ɩ *we're trying to find out.*

B: He says so far as he can tell, the priests really were not ever very effective at changing his quatrains. Some of the changes that have taken place have been due to poor typesetting rather than deliberate errors. He's assuming that we knew there had been some poor translation as well.

He says that whenever he is viewing the future, those places where nothing very important is happening appear to be smooth like silk. But those places where something of major importance is happening, look like a pucker in the cloth—a snarl in the cloth with all the threads tangled up. It draws his attention to it, and he looks closer to see what it is. He gets glimpses of what is happening through the various loops and knots of the threads that are snarled there in the cloth. And the events that are larger make a larger mess of things and so it's easier to spot them. That's one other reason why so many of his quatrains have to do with things that are heart-breaking, such as war. Because they're very obvious to be spotted and sometimes it's hard to go around these places in time without going through some of it to see what will be happening. He says it's difficult to explain but he will try from time to time, like just now, to explain what happens when he looks into time.

D: *The translator in the book I'm using says she has the idea that he wrote the quatrains in Latin in the original form before he put them into the French. Is that true?*

B: He says the way the situation was, his consciousness would be like a blank slate to be written upon and the words would appear to help him decipher the concepts that he would be seeing. He would not be conscious at the time of the language they were in until he had already written them down. They often were in Latin but not always. Then he would translate them into French because he was writing this for the ordinary people and not for the clergy.

D: *Then he would not be truly conscious of anything he had written until he came out of trance?*

B: This is true. He says that while he was in trance he had control over his hands for writing, but he would not know why he was writing. The forces from beyond the mirror would be guiding his hand. When he would come back, he would know what he had seen but he would not know what he had written.

D: *Then the puzzle he put them into, was that done while he was in trance or while he was conscious?*

B: While he was in trance.

D: *Then he didn't consciously make up these puzzles.*

B: No. He says he was capable of doing it, and he often did his private correspondence in this manner, but it would not be nearly so complex as these done while he was in trance. When he would come forward from the mirror, he says that he would be amazed at the complexity of the puzzle. He would know all the meanings and the graduations of meanings and the subtleties involved from what he had seen. But he says there is some other element, other than his conscious mind, that is better at manipulating the words into these puzzles. He says when he's in trance he'd see several things, one scene right after another. And when he'd come forth, sometimes only one quatrain will have been written. And he would see that even though he'd seen several different events that they were all related to that quatrain.

D: *They are so complicated, it would seem to be beyond the average person's ability. One would have to be a master puzzlemaker. I can now appreciate a little more the difficulties the average human has trying to decipher these.*

B: This is true. He says this is the reason for the importance of this project. To help some human being to reestablish contact with that aspect of existence that could help interpret these quatrains.

This sounded like a remarkable case of automatic writing. Many people are able to do this while both awake and in trance, and often things come through to the individual in this manner that are completely foreign to them. It has been argued that it is simply the person's subconscious at work and not a separate entity manipulating their hand. It can be debated as to what is occurring in the case of Nostradamus.

D: *Down through history sometimes different rulers have tried to change some of the meanings to say that he was predicting things about them.*

B: Yes. He chuckles and he says that is a common game to be found amongst the rulers of men.

D: *His puzzles, the anagrams and the different meanings of the words also create problems.*

B: He says that is one reason why he is glad to be able to initiate this project.

This was true. He really did initiate it. The idea would have never occurred to me. I was very surprised when he first began to speak to me through Elena.

B: He says he knew you would be, but he knew that you would be open to the communication, which was to his advantage.

D: *Yes, because of my curiosity I wouldn't pass up a chance like this. (Laugh) He picked a curious one.*

B: He says to give him a curious person any day of the week over one who is self-assured. Because one who is self-assured has themselves walled off and they're smug because they know everything already. But the curious one says, "I may know quite a bit but there's always more to learn, and I want to know what makes something happen."

D: *Then he understands me.*

   Why is it so important to him that he get these quatrains translated correctly in our time period?

B: He says, what good is a prophecy if the words are wrong? A prophecy must be accurate for it to do any good. When you foresee the future and you prophesy to help the people involved, how can it be of help if they don't really know what you're trying to say. If they don't hear the forewarning as it's truly worded, how can there be anything done about it?

D: *That's true. Because his quatrains are so obscure, most of his prophecies are not understood until they happen, then it's too late.*

B: He just quirked his eyebrow and kind of smiled and said, "Well, we know who's to blame for that." I think he's referring to the Inquisition or the church.—He said one problem was that the things he was trying to describe were so beyond the ken ... beyond the knowledge of mankind, and he only had a limited vocabulary to describe them with. They're so beyond the knowledge of people, they didn't recognize what he was trying to describe until after they have seen it— because he described so many things never known to mankind before. So they will have no way of recognizing them until they are already known to mankind.

D: *Yes, and then they say, "That's what he meant." But this is also true of the Bible. It had to be written in symbols because sometimes the things they saw were too difficult for them to understand.*

B: Yes. He points out a minor prophet in the Old Testament, and he chuckles at this. He says this minor prophet also predicted some of the things that he predicted, so far as the technological achievements are concerned. For some reason he finds that amusing.

D: *Who is the minor prophet?*

B: I get the name Zephaniah. Is there a Zephaniah?

D: *I think so. Of course, some of his writings may have been removed from the Bible.*

B: This is true.

I thought he might have meant Zachariah. I didn't think I had ever read any book called Zephaniah. Later when I looked it up, I found it consisted of only a few pages. It was a long tale of mass destruction apparently brought about by the wrath of God.

D: *Let me know if he is getting tired.*

B: He says he's holding out so far. He doesn't know how long he'll be able to last today since the communicating connection does not seem to be as clear as it was last time. And he's having to work harder to get the image across. But this is an important project to him, so he says he doesn't mind pushing himself a little bit, if need be.

D: *I don't want him to hurt himself. I'm very concerned about that.*

B: He says he has this system set up to where it would be impossible for him to do permanent damage to himself. If he starts to go too far, he'll be snatched back to ... I want to call it his "laboratory." And he says that he may have a headache for a few days and dizziness, but it will pass. He says that's one reason why he connected to this method of communication. He knew that there were several different ways of adjusting communication and contacting our time period. But he wanted to make sure he got in touch with those who could work with this knowledge without damage to themselves or without perverting what they find out.

D: *Yes. There could be a lot of wrong things done with this, in many ways. And there are other people too, who wouldn't care about the vehicle. I'm very careful in this way.*

B: He says that is important. Good vehicles are difficult to find and you must take care of the ones you do find.

D: *And I will also be very careful in the ways I write these things down, to be as true to what he is saying as possible.*

B: He says he appreciates the care that you will take. It will cause trouble for yourself, but he says that apparently you agreed to take this on before you entered this lifetime. Since you agreed to take it on, the forces of the universe are behind you in such a way that that's all the protection you need.

D: *All right, because I'm just too curious to let it drop now.*

This question was asked by an observer at one of the sessions. I did not know who Catherine de' Medici was. Later when I began to do research I found that she was the mother of three kings of France, and wielded a great deal of power behind the throne. She often asked Nostradamus to tell her what he foresaw for the future of her sons and their country.

John: *Knowing a little bit about your life, what was it like to be a service to Catherine de' Medici, the mother of the kings at the time?*

B: He's shaking his head and chuckling. He says it was like walking a tightrope over a firepit at times. That she had a sharp mind and was interesting to be around. But you never knew what direction she was going to strike from next. He says she was very shrewd and she had the interest of her family and how they could gain more power foremost in her mind at all times. He says she was very manipulative. But that she had to be in order to exercise the power and control that she craved. He says that she really should have been born a man. But she was born a woman and in his culture at that time she had to resort to various means to exercise the influence that she felt she must exercise. He says that with the combination of the type of horoscope she had and the type of karma she had for that lifetime, it was a really interesting result. When he is with her he always must exercise his best diplomacy and speak with soft words but still with the ring of truth because if she thought he was trying to prevaricate or fib about something, she would get most upset.

J: *She sounds like a hard person to deal with.*

B: She was. He says that she would have been a lot more interesting friend, someone that one could really have exciting mental exchange with, if it weren't for the fact of her position.

D: *I was interested in his personal life. I didn't know if I'd be prying if I asked some questions about that.*

B: He doesn't seem very comfortable with the idea. He's perplexed. He's saying, why do you want to know about things like this? It is not important to our project. It has nothing to do with what we have to get done.

D: *Well, there have been biographies printed about his life and I was curious if they were correct. I wanted to get some facts to back those things up.*

B: He says that it really doesn't matter to him whether they're correct or not. He doesn't care if they tell the most heinous lies about his life, as long as they translate his quatrains correctly. He also says that it is time for him to leave. I, the vessel, suspect that he is wanting to get out of further questions of this nature.

D: *Okay. I didn't want to upset him. But we do have curious minds about him as a person too, as well as a prophet. I never know if I'm asking an offending question.*

B: I don't think he was offended. It's very easy to tell when he's offended about something. It seems to echo within the communicator's body.

Nostradamus not only made each quatrain an individual puzzle, but compiled the entire book as one gigantic puzzle. There seems to be no discernible order to their arrangement. By the time I asked this question we had translated over 100 of them and I was trying to decide how to arrange them.

D: *I'm trying to put these quatrains we have covered into some kind of order. Chronologically, if possible. And this is a big job.*

B: He's in a good mood this time and when you said you were wanting to put them in order, he asked facetiously, "A logical order or an *il*logical order?"

I enjoyed it whenever he was in a mood to joke with me. It was so much better than being chided for making extraneous comments.

D: *(Laugh) Is there a difference?*

B: He says it depends on your point of view.

D: *(Laugh) Well, it's a big enough job trying to put them in some kind of chronological order.*

B: He says a chronological order would be a logical way of doing it. One way that you could do it that would be an illogical order is to put them in alphabetical order according to the first word of the quatrain.

D: *(Laugh) Or the way that he did it. Which I think was illogical.*

B: He says it was quite logical. It was based on fine and precise mathematical principles as defined by the throwing of die.

D: *Was that how he figured out what order to put them in?*

B: I'm not sure. He's full of vinegar tonight. He's in a very good mood.

D: *(Laugh) I just thought he threw them all together and shuffled them like a deck of cards. And said, this is the way they're going to go. That is how much sense they make to me.*

B: He says actually what he did was put them in six stacks, each according to one side of a die. And he would throw the dice, and when he got a double number he would take one at random from that stack that that number delineated, and put it next to his book. But if he got two different numbers he would add the numbers together and divide them by some decimal to come up with a number to pick one at random from another stack.

D: *I suppose that's as good a system as any. I didn't know they had dice in his time.*

B: He says that dice have been around for centuries. Their shape and dimensions may change occasionally but the principal is the same. He was calling them dice because that is what we have that is related to what he used.

D: *I thought maybe when I finally finished this project I would see some kind of pattern he had used, maybe using mathematics, if there is any pattern there.*

B: He says there is undoubtedly a pattern there, but it would be rather difficult to find it. And he says, do not be alarmed if you do not find it. For he was trying to make it deliberately obscure so as to make it difficult for certain parties—and those are his words—certain parties to figure out what he was saying.

D: *Okay, then I will not expect to find any pattern. It is just like shuffling them and throwing them out.*

B: He says there is a pattern there. It's just that it's too complex mathematically for ordinary people to see.

D: *Well, that was the main thing I was wondering about, how he decided on their order.*

B: He says that he hopes that his lecturing has assisted you in this.

D: *But you can see the job you've given me now, to try to rearrange them in the order they're supposed to be in.*

B: He says chronological order is sufficient.

D: *Sometimes it's difficult to figure out. It's complicated because they often refer to more than one event and the events are in different time periods.*

B: He says, so you put them down twice. One for each time period.

D: *That's what I've been trying to do, refer back and forth to the different ones. It's difficult. It's a big job to do this.*

Apparently that was the wrong thing to say. At this point Nostradamus interrupted me. Brenda began to speak very fast, as though he was aggravated.

B: He says he does not want to hear of your difficulties for writing. He says, he is learning at this point that you 20th-century people have it so easy. You don't appreciate how easy you have it. I don't want to hear any of it. *She* doesn't have the Inquisition breathing down her neck all the time. *She* doesn't have to put everything in riddles just to keep her body and soul connected. She—He's just generally ranting—She doesn't have to do this, she doesn't have to do that.—I don't want to hear it. I want to get this project done.—He is saying that the complaints you have about things getting in the way of your writing is very minuscule and unimportant compared to the problems he has when he's writing.

I had to laugh; the outburst had taken me completely offguard. He could often display unexpected shifts of emotion. I certainly hadn't meant to upset him.

D: *And my writing equipment is much easier to use.*
B: Right.
D: *All right. I apologize. This is the part that I have to work out.*
B: Yes, he says that's your problem. He says, I can't just give you everything for your books, you know. You have to put a little bit of yourself into it.

I felt like a schoolgirl again, being chewed out by a teacher. Sufficiently reprimanded, I could still feel a sense of affection and understanding beneath his gruffness. He was right, he had done his part on this project 400 years ago. This part of it had to be my responsibility.

He often did this when I would ask him about the order of certain quatrains and their relationship with each other timewise. He would say that he was only interpreting the quatrain we were working with at the moment. Putting them together was my problem. So he certainly didn't just hand me all of the answers.

Note: More information was given on the numbering system of the quatrains in 1994 when the question was asked again for a television show. This is presented in the Addendum at the back of this book which was added at the 1996 reprinting.

Section Two

The Translation

Chapter 9

The Translation Begins

D: *Should I count or will you be able to just go there and see if you can find him through the mirror?*

B: Sit quietly and meditate on something for a moment and I'll be able to go there and do it. I'll let you know when everything is ready. I'm focusing in on his dwelling place now. He is in his—I'm going to call it a laboratory. It's a combination of laboratory and study. He's in there focusing on the mirror. "Michel de Notredame, I have returned. It is time for us to meet again, if it is your wish." *(Pause)* He says that he'll meet us at the meeting place. *(Pause)* All right. I am there, and he is here now, too.

He says to read the quatrain and pause slightly between each line to give the communicator time to absorb the phrases well so that he can communicate the concepts.

D: *I know you will try to translate into our terms. But tell me first the way he words it, so I can better understand the way he is thinking.*

B: In this special place we're not using words, per se. I say "he says thus and such" and I really mean he communicates thus and such. He's been communicating mostly with mental pictures with a feeling of words underneath, if that makes sense. I'll do the best I can. He says every little bit helps. He doesn't mind if the bits have to be small because it's a drain on him to come to this place. So he says as long as we keep at it steadily, the job will get done.

D: *I wish there was a faster way to do these.*

B: He says if it is meant to be done, it will be done. That we may just as well move at a comfortable pace and all of us involved with this will do the best we can.

D: *Does he want me to begin at the beginning of the book or just pick some quatrains at random or what?*

B: Let me ask him. *(Pause)* To begin with, choose the one that feels like it's the one to begin with. He says to still the body and still the mind and look into the inner core of yourself, that's where all wisdom resides. And by following the guidance of this you'll be able to pick the correct one. He's talking in circles. I don't really understand but that's what he says.

D: *I would like to tell him that the book I am using has the French and the English translations in it, and it is divided into centuries. It has ten centuries and each century contains 100 quatrains. Was that the way he intended it to be?*

B: He said, "Of course, that's the way I arranged it. That's the way I put it on the manuscript."

D: *I thought maybe this might have been an arrangement someone put them in later.*

B: He says, "I repeat that is the way I put it on the manuscript."

D: *But one century doesn't have a hundred in it.*

B: No. He says he knows that. He arranged it in centuries out of convenience. But not all the centuries were complete because he wasn't able to clarify the time channels to get all of them.

D: *I just wanted to be sure that someone else hasn't tampered with it.— So that would give us almost a thousand. That's why it would be very difficult to begin at the beginning and go through. That would take an awfully long time.*

Later this was exactly what we ended up doing. After picking out a hundred quatrains at random, we decided to become more organized. At that time I started at the beginning of the book and took them in order. Even using that procedure there appears to be no logical order as far as time sequence is concerned.

D: *Would he be able to elaborate later without the use of the quatrains? Or does he need them to focus in, so to speak?*

B: He says that he thinks he will probably need them to help focus in, since he's having to communicate in an indirect manner. Sometimes he might be able to extemporize but he says he's not going to count upon it.

D: *Then we do need the quatrains to help him remember what he has seen.*

B: Well, not necessarily to help him remember what he has seen but to help him focus in such a way that I can communicate what he's trying to say. He says if he occasionally sounds rude, it's not because he has anything against you or I, the communicator, personally. It's just that he's trying to get the job done. He said that sometimes you put in too much extraneous comment between quatrains or while he's trying to think. If occasionally he tells you to stop it, it's not because he's being mean, because he is extremely grateful for this contact of communication. It's just that there is so much information to be put through that he sometimes gets impatient. Especially when he's trying to put through an idea and to speak, and you're speaking too. (*I apologized.*) He says don't worry about it. Whenever new experiments are tried things have to be worked out. If there is something he does not under-

stand, he'll ask about it. And he says you needn't apologize so much.
D: *Okay. But I am very much in awe of him and I don't want him to become angry with me.*
B: He says that he is glad to have some accomplices.
D: *It's not good to do this alone, is it?*
B: He says it can be done; it's just more difficult.
D: *I mean ... it's lonely.*
B: He says when he's troubled and concerned with higher things, he doesn't worry about loneliness.

There was a lot of trial and error in the beginning when I first began to present the quatrains to him for translation. After much fumbling around, I learned the procedure he wanted to use. During this time I began to know when he was mentally communicating with Brenda and I was told to please stop yakking and interrupting. I was instructed to read the quatrain slowly, pausing between each line. If there were words he did not understand, and there were many, I would spell them for him in both the English and the French. These were usually proper names or words that he was using for anagrams. Then I would often be asked to repeat the quatrain again. I would then wait a few seconds for the translation to begin to come through. I had to hold my questions many times because he did not like to have his train of thought broken. I wondered at first if I was offending him with my fumbling efforts, but he said that was not a problem. He was so intense because he was trying to get a lot done in a limited amount of time.

It was amazing how quickly I was able to accept this unusual project. How easy it is for the strange to become commonplace. It soon seemed as normal to converse with Nostradamus across 400 years of time and space as it does to talk to a neighbor by telephone.

After the first sessions the translations became much more detailed. In the beginning I was only able to do four quatrains at a session. Later, as we settled into a pattern, we were able to handle about six to eight and sometimes as many as ten.

The first quatrains that I used for this experiment were picked out at random. I chose the ones that impressed me for some reason. I was intrigued by the most difficult ones, the quatrains the experts had never been able to find any explanation for. I thought that would make this project even more of a challenge. I also picked the ones the translators thought pertained to our future. After completing a hundred of these, I became more systematic and started at the beginning of the book and proceeded in a more organized manner. By that time we had become so adept at this we were covering as many as 30 quatrains in an hour session.

I have never been in doubt that I am truly in contact with the physical Nostradamus while he is alive in his lifetime in France during the 1500s because he has physical limitations imposed upon him. He can only stay in contact with me for about an hour before he must return to his physical body. He quite obviously tires toward the end of the session and says he must leave. Sometimes he leaves abruptly with no warning. At these times I suspect he has become so involved he accidentally overstays his time limit. Or something might have happened at his end of the connection that pulled him back into his body.

He said that if he stayed too long he would have physical symptoms, headaches and dizziness the rest of the day. But he is quite willing to suffer these if it will get the job done. Since I would not wish to cause him any discomfort, I respect his demands. I couldn't hold him there anyway because when he gets ready to go, he just leaves. I know this doesn't happen because my subject, Brenda, is tiring because often after Nostradamus has returned to his physical body in his laboratory, we continue to work on something else.

Once the initial contact was made and the instructions were carefully followed, it turned out to be a surprisingly simple task to meet Nostradamus in our special meeting place. From there we began a very ambitious project, a project I would never have volunteered for: the translation of his quatrains into modern-day language.

Elena had been hampered in relaying his meanings because she was also looking at the prophecies from the 16th-century viewpoint of his student, Dyonisus. The things Nostradamus showed him were mystifying and frightening, and he could find no words in his limited experience to faithfully describe them. He had to result to crude symbolism to try to convey the meanings. Brenda was not so hampered. She was not involved and tied into a life as Dyonisus was. She was speaking from the in-between-lives state where the viewpoint is greatly broadened and expanded. She thus would have a greater recognition and understanding of any visions or symbolism she was shown. She would be able to supply modern words for things that had no names in Nostradamus' time. In this way maybe we could at last make sense out of his puzzles and comprehend the true depth and wonderful powers of this unusual and remarkable man.

I will begin with our first fumbling efforts. The results were truly amazing even though we were experimenting and trying to find a working pattern and procedure.

The first two in the book are fairly easy for anyone to decipher, but I will put them here in the beginning for the same reason that Nostradamus began his book with them.

CENTURY I-1

Estant assis de nuict secret estude
Seul reposé sur la selle d'œrain;
Flambe exigue sortant de solitude
Fait prosperer qui n'est à croire vain.

Sitting alone at night in secret study; it is placed on the brass tripod. A slight flame comes out of the emptiness and makes successful that which should not be believed in vain.

B: He says it is simply a description of what he does in his laboratory. He put that one at the beginning as a word of explanation as to where he got the things that he was writing.

CENTURY I-2

Le verge en main mise au milieu des BRANCHES
De l' onde il moulle & le limbe & le pied:
Un peur & voix fremissant par les manches:
Splendeur divine. Le divin pres s' assied.

The wand in the hand is placed in the middle of the tripod's legs. With water he sprinkles both the hem of his garment and his foot. A voice, fear; he trembles in his robes. Divine splendor; the god sits nearby.

B: He says, ditto. The first quatrain explains his instruments and the second quatrain explains how he starts the process of opening himself up to the other realms.
D: The translators said that Nostradamus is afraid of the power that he invokes when it comes to him. "A voice, fear, he trembles in his robes." They thought this meant he was afraid of these things he saw.
B: Uh-oh! He's indeed angry with that interpretation. He says that fear does not mean afraid, fear means respect. He says that he's in wondrous awe of what he sees because he doesn't understand all that goes on. But he says that he isn't afraid, he's just very respectful. And he knows he has to work cautiously to make sure he doesn't make a mistake.

CENTURY III-92

Le monde proche du dernier periode,
Saturne encor tard sera de retour:
Translat empire devers nation Brodde,
L'œil arraché à Narbon par Autour.

The world is near its final period, Saturn will again be late on his return. The empire will shift towards the Brodde nation; An eye at Narbonne plucked out by a goshawk.

B: He's organizing the thoughts and concepts to be given to me so that I may be able to speak them clearly. He says working through a third person, meaning myself, he must try to minimize any foul-ups in communication. (*Pause*) He says that in this quatrain he's referring to a period of time in which there is a war. And the event happens near the end of this war, at the final stages, when Saturn is again late. He says that statement has a double meaning. On the one hand it refers to an astrological event of Saturn being in retrograde, to help narrow down the time involved. It also refers to some of the technology in this war. In this war, as in all wars, there are great advances done in research of science, both weapons research and things like that. In this war the scientists are researching how to warp and alter time to help change some events, to swing the war over to their advantage. And they have failed yet again. As a result of this second failure, the entire complex is destroyed in a large catastrophe. That is the eye being plucked out by a goshawk. Because they are dealing with powers they don't know how to control and it rips them apart. The people who are not there assume that they were hit by a missile of some sort because of the great destruction. But what happened was that the vortexes of energy they are trying to deal with were not fine tuned enough to work with and they got out of control. Those words Narbonne (pronounced: Nar-bone) and Brodde (pronounced: Broadda) are referring to the nation and the place. But he said what he tuned in on was that the government involved is most devious and it has false names for things. I think he's meaning "code names" here, and what he received was the code names when he saw this. I'm trying to find out from him if he had any idea of the location of these places. He said that he's focusing in on it to see if he can tell me. (*Long pause*.) He says it's difficult to do because the picture that he always got on this one was the research complex where they were doing it. He says that it seems to him that it involves England and Northern Europe. Narbonne is a place name, the town close to where it happens. I believe that both of the names are anagrams from the way he is talking. He's finding it difficult to get the concept across to me of specific places because he's thinking in anagrams and the anagrams don't come across as clear concepts.

D: *Does he have any idea when this will happen.*

B: He says it's still in our future but the groundwork has been laid already. Scientists working on secret projects are already working in this direction, but it will be a while before anything comes of it. He said something may come of it within our lifetimes but we won't know of it because the government will keep it under wraps.

D: *In the translation they think that Brodde is an old French word meaning black or dark brown. Because he used that word, they think the quatrain deals with the African nations or the black people.*

B: He says this is not true. He's chuckling at this point. He says he used that word on purpose because it does indeed resemble the word for a dark color, but it's actually an anagram for a place name. He didn't want to get too specific because he didn't want to make it too easy for the Inquisition and other nosy people to find out where he was talking about.

D: *Well, this shows the difficulty they've had trying to understand his quatrains. We've made a beginning anyway.*

B: Yes. He says beginnings are always difficult. But as we work together as a team, we'll get more accustomed to our ways of thinking and we'll be able to work better. This time you and I both are struggling to communicate because I don't have any visual reception of him today like I did before. However, with me concentrating and him concentrating, he gets the picture across of what he's trying to say. He sent me a picture of a part of a research complex where this is going to take place.

D: *Will it affect the rest of the world or just that area?*

B: So far as the catastrophe is concerned it will be very localized and will have some strange side-effects in the dimension of time in the general area there. He can't really describe it and he can't really tell us how to prepare for it because it's very bizarre. But he said that it will eventually have far-reaching effects because the government was counting on that line of research to give it an edge in this war. And some of that edge is taken away and it will end up affecting the outcome of that war.

D: *Does he know what war this will be?*

B: War Three, he says. The Third War.

D: *I didn't know we were going to have another war. We're hoping we won't.*

B: He says that he has seen several wars for us to have, and he's hoping to help us avert some of them.

D: *Can he see what countries will be involved?*

B: He says that it will involve the northern hemisphere and a piece of the southern. I'm trying to find out what piece of the southern. I'm thinking he means Australia because he keeps saying the piece of the southern hemisphere that is involved is an island.

This was the first mention of this war. Over the next few months I was to find out much more than I comfortably wanted to know about it. This information is reported in the chapters on the terrible Anti-Christ.

CENTURY II-62

Mabus puis tost alors mourra,
viendra,
De gens & bestes une horrible
defaite:
Puis tout à coup la vengeance
on verra,
Cent, main, soif, faim, quand
courra la comete.

Mabus will then soon die and there
will come a dreadful destruction of
people and animals. Suddenly
vengeance will be revealed, a
hundred hands, thirst and hunger,
when the comet will pass.

He asked for the spelling of Mabus and then corrected my pronunciation. He pronounced it: May-bus.

B: He says that the death of a world leader, perhaps a religious leader, will coincide with the coming of a major comet. I think perhaps he's meaning Halley's Comet. He says the comet will be clearly visible in the country where this world leader died. The country involved is in the Middle East. The dying of the world leader in this middle eastern country and the passing of the comet will provoke a revolt. Part of the reason why the revolt is provoked so easily is that there will also be major crop failures that year. Many people will be hungry.

D: *Will this all happen in the year that the comet will be visible?*

B: It will *start* in the year the comet is visible, but it will continue for 500 days, a hundred hands. He's using that symbolism to indicate how long it will last, as well as indicating that there are a hundred people who will contribute toward the revolt in such a way that it will break forth and become open enough and wide-spread enough to capture the world's attention.

An interesting idea that a hundred hands could mean 500 days. The five fingers on a hand multiplied by one hundred. Also, even today we use the word "hand" to refer to a person, such as a "hired hand." Thus, a double meaning. It was becoming obvious that Nostradamus thought in very clever ways.

I considered that this quatrain might possibly refer to the downfall of President Marcos of the Philippines because of the similarity of his name to Mabus, and the timing would be correct. But Marcos did not die, he was deposed from power.

Since Halley's Comet passed in 1986 and did not create the expected dramatic display, and since nothing happened in that year that would fit this quatrain, it would appear that it was inaccurate. But Brenda was the one who assumed it was Halley's. This quatrain could refer to an undiscovered comet. There are many possibilities besides Halley's.

Update: When the Persian Gulf War began to materialize in August 1990. I received letters and calls from readers of this book. They had noticed that the anagram Mabus became Sudam when read backwards in mirror image. This was quite remarkable and fit in perfectly with Nostra-

damus' thinking. If Sudam Hussein was the Middle Eastern leader referred to in this quatrain, then it meant that he would die. Throughout the war President Bush suggested that his own people should arise and assassinate him. This did not happen, but the quatrain also contained the number of 500 days. How does that relate? It was also suggested that the comet passing could have referred to the missiles that were used during the war. They certainly resembled comets as they soared through the night sky.

CENTURY II-65

Le parc enclin grande calamité.	In the feeble lists, great calamity
Par l'Hesperie & Insubre fera:	through America and Lombardy.
Le feu en nef peste et captivité,	The fire in the ship, plague and
Mercure en l'Arc Saturne fenera.	captivity; Mercury in Sagittarius,
	Saturn warning.

B: He says that the first line refers to the fact that the leaders involved are not competent. They're there because of family prestige. He says that on a joint venture between America and France ... he's having difficulty describing. I'm thinking he's trying to describe a space shuttle.

D: *Oh? What does the picture look like?*

B: He's not picturing it. He's just trying to describe the concept of what it does. He says that it's a ship but it's not an ocean-going ship. And I asked him, "An airplane then, a ship that goes in the air?" He says, not *in* the air, on and above it. He says, so the airship flies above the ocean and regular ships, so this ship flies above the airship. He says there will be a calamity. This ship will have some scientists on it doing some biological experiments to see how these take place beyond the pull of gravity. An accident will happen, a malfunction which will cause this ship to tumble back into the atmosphere and break up as it does so, and it would burn in the atmosphere. But some of the vials and containers being used in the biological experiments contain organisms hardy enough to survive the fall. Since these have been exposed to the cosmos they will be different than they were before. And these organisms have the potential of causing plagues. He says the astrological notations there at the end are like a horoscope of the date. He says that Mercury in Sagittarius, that is easy enough to observe. Just look at the sky at night with—he calls it "a far-seeing eye"—I think he means a telescope. And Saturn warning, he says for a drawer of horoscopes to draw up a horoscope when Mercury is in Sagittarius and Saturn is in a bad house for both America and France. It will be then. I think he's trying to say that Saturn will be at ... in relation to Mercury, the angle will have a bad meaning.

D: *It will be a joint venture between America and France. The translator said that by interpreting his astrological signs as a conjunction that this quatrain would happen in the year 2044. Do you know what a conjunction is?*

B: Yes, he says he just got through describing it to you. And he says that the disaster will sadden both these nations and sympathetic nations, and they will work together to find out what happened.

This was the first indication that I would need an astrologer or "drawer of horoscopes" to help on the translations. But where would I find one who was skilled enough to do it and who was also open-minded and familiar with metaphysical concepts?

Again unusual circumstances were to come into play. The very next week one of our members brought a young man to our metaphysical group meeting who had never been there before. He turned out to be a professional astrologer and was also interested in Nostradamus' quatrains. When he heard what I was doing he was most anxious to work with me on this. Coincidence? Later he said, "I knew there was some reason for me to go to that meeting that night." Because of other circumstances he has never returned to the meetings. It appears it was intended for him to be there on that night so we could make the connection.

At first I took the interpretations to him to look over. But later, he wanted to sit in on sessions to ask Nostradamus questions personally. At those times, I tried to focus only on those quatrains that contained astrological references. This proved to be deceiving because many times what appeared to be an astrological quatrain actually referred to something else.

John Feeley studied under the famed astrologer Isabelle Hickey, and has been drawing up horoscopes since 1969. He has been invaluable in understanding these astrological concepts that are foreign to both myself and Brenda. When it is applicable I will include his findings in the translation of the quatrains. He has offered much insight into the dating and time factors involved.

CENTURY II-91

Soleil levant un grand feu l' on verra,
Bruit & clarté vers Aquilon tendants:
Dedans le rond mort & cris l' on orra,
Par glaive, feu, faim, mort las attendants.

At sunrise a great fire will be seen, noise and light extending towards the North. Within the globe death and cries are heard, death awaiting them through weapons, fire and famine.

B: He says that this one has a double meaning, a double date. One of them has already come to pass and the other one has yet to come to pass. He says that the first event this one refers to is the Tunguska disaster in the early part of our century.

I was surprised. He was referring to the terrible explosion of unknown origin that occurred in Siberia in the early 1900s. It leveled the forest over a 30-mile radius, killing mostly wildlife since this area was sparsely populated at that time, and rendering the land radioactive and useless. There have been many theories brought forth to explain this. The most common one is that a meteorite hit the earth at that point. But would that explain the radioactivity? Russian scientists have now offered the possibility that a spacecraft may have crashed there. Would Nostradamus be able to pinpoint the real cause? His next statement startled me even more.

B: He says the other event this quatrain refers to is a similar occurrence. He says that because a group he calls the "Others"—and I sense he has that capitalized—were trying to contact us. And when they enter the Earth's atmosphere, they try to do it on a circumpolar orbit. But the Soviets have done some secret weapons research and they have some energy fields guarding their northern approach corridors. When this ship enters these corridors, it causes the ship to malfunction in such a way that many of the crew are killed. And when they crash there will be soldiers there on hand to either capture or kill them and cause them to perish. But the ship will be harboring some microscopic organisms that will react in bizarre ways in earth's climate and cause some not-understandable plagues. Plagues that cannot be understood because the scientists cannot recognize the causative organism.

His mention of the "Others" really struck a note in me. I was surprised when he used that term. I have been told many times during my sessions about the Others and the Watchers. It usually refers to beings from outer space. I immediately assumed that Nostradamus was also using the word in that context.

D: *I would think that they would not want to kill them; that they would be curious enough to want to study them.*
B: He says the country where they crash will either be at war or fixing to go to war. They will have the wartime set of mind, so that anything from the outside is an enemy and will cause potential harm. Instead of being curious, they are—he says our word "paranoid" would fit. They suspect a new type of weapon from their so-called "enemy," and so the beings involved are killed. Apparently, a soldier will have an itchy trigger finger and with a weapon of some sort—I think he's putting across the concept of some sort of machine gun—will start shooting at everything with it.
D: *I would think they would want to try to study them. I think our country would, at least I hope they would.*
B: He says you can never count on anything because you never know what's going to happen in war.

Apparently he indicated without directly saying so that *both* incidents (Tunguska and this one) involved the crash of a spaceship.

One thing that bothered me was his mention in two separate quatrains of microbes or germs. I knew that in Nostradamus' time period the doctors did not know of the existence of bacteria or germs. They were very ignorant on this subject and really did not know the cause of diseases that were rampant during that time. The common belief was that all lower forms of life were created by spontaneous generation, and doctors went to great lengths to prove it. This was a strange belief, that all smaller life-forms, from mice and rats down through frogs and toads to worms and bugs, had no parents. They were created spontaneously by sunlight out of the mud, slime, stagnant water or decaying matter they seemed to emerge from. So I wondered how Nostradamus seemingly knew of such things that he could not have possibly seen. I asked if he had used those terms "microbes and germs" or if that was Brenda's interpretation of what she was being shown.

B: He says that it is generally accepted in his time that such things do not exist. But he says he first received an inkling that they may exist from reading some of the writings of some of the Greek philosophers. They theorized that such things would exist. That even as forms of life can get bigger and bigger: men, animals, plants, the planet ... in space, the ether and such. That why can't it go in the other direction and things get smaller and smaller. So he says the Greeks believed there are very small particles called "atoms." And why couldn't these small animals and such called "atoms" act the way some plants act? Some plants act as poison. Well, he theorized, why couldn't some animals act this way too? And with his theorizing this, it helped him to understand what he was seeing whenever he saw these things from the future. He has found that I understood these concepts and that there were labels for these concepts in my language. And so he told me to go ahead and label them microbes and germs. In his own understanding he has different words. Sometimes he calls them "atoms" the way the Greeks would. And sometimes he calls them "the little ones" and "the little animals" that do this. He says he really doesn't have a specific word for these because he's never seen them. He really doesn't know what they are. So when he's not in a trance it's just a theoretical or mental exercise, a mental diversion to think about such things. And so whenever he sees in the future generations that such things are acknowledged to exist, he has the feeling like you have when you successfully work a puzzle.

D: *I'm very surprised the Greeks knew of these things. I don't think we are aware in our time period that they were so knowledgeable.*

B: He says some people in your time period are aware that they knew of such things. It's not generally acknowledged that the Greeks knew a lot of things they did because there were several schools of thought in ancient Greece. And some of them were not popular. The ones that were popular, particularly with the Romans, were the schools of thought that got passed down through the centuries and these often did not include the concept of atoms and such, even though there is written evidence of such schools of thought.

D: *It's commonly believed that because they couldn't see these things they could not have known about them.*

B: IIe's laughing at this somewhat scornfully. He says the scientists in your time are very narrow-minded and stupid to be thinking that. He says the Greeks, above all else, were thinkers. They were always thinking about things and figuring things out. They didn't have to see something to be able to logically conclude that something existed.

Another thing I was curious about was his mention of the Others. I told him I was familiar with the term but I wanted to know what he knew about them.

B: He says he doesn't know much about them. Only what he has seen in his visions and what he has been able to logically surmise. He says they hold several heretical beliefs. That if he would give voice to half of them he would be burned at the stake. He's getting excited at this point. He says, for one thing, the earth is not flat; it is round.

D: *And he is correct.*

B: Well, he rather arrogantly says, "I know that!" (*Laugh*) And for another thing, he says that anyone with any knowledge, anyone with eyes to see can tell that the earth is not at the center of the universe. And he very much doubts the sun is at the center of the universe either. The sun just happens to be the center of this portion of the universe. He says that with God being an infinite God and being infinitely powerful, who's to say that we are the only creations there are of God. It seems to him that with God being an infinite God that there must be infinite creations of God. He has seen things in his visions that the only way he can explain them is to say they are some more creations of God: other men, animals and beings from other parts of the universe. He says the priests would consider these things heretical, but he personally considers the priests to be heretical since they are trying to limit God. And the Bible says very plainly that there are no limits to God.

D: *Well, tell him that I agree with him. And he is asking the same questions we are still asking today, only now we're a little more open-minded to search for the answers.*

B: He said he has assumed there will be a few that are not as open-minded. There always seems to be a segment of society that make a practice of staying as narrow-minded as they can.

Upon awakening, I asked Brenda if she knew the term, the "Others." She said it could mean many things, but she did not particularly associate it with anything that stood out in her mind. When I told her what it meant to me, she said she would not have thought of it in that context.

B: The man has a good sense of humor when he's not being intense.—
    Uh-oh! He just reprimanded me for being impertinent.

D: *(Laugh) Well, there's nothing wrong with having a good sense of
    humor. It relieves the tension.*

B: Oh, that wasn't what he was complaining about. He was calling me
    impertinent because of what I said about him, when he wasn't busy
    being intense.
        He says there will be future sessions. He has seen this. He says
    that things will be settling down into their patterns. And we will con-
    tinue to go along these patterns for a while with little changes coming
    and going. But gradually shape our lives in the various directions that
    our lives will take.

D: *What I'm thinking about doing is eventually trying to translate all of
    the quatrains.*

B: He says that if our paths work out in that direction that will be good
    because he would like to do that. He says he knows for sure we will
    get the important ones translated anyway. He says to be sure to con-
    centrate on the quatrains and the information they contain, and not on
    the miscellaneous surrounding information. He realizes that the way
    the communication was established may seem amazing to you, but as
    far as he's concerned that's not important. The important thing is to
    get the information in these quatrains available to people.
        He's very intent on the work and purpose. He just concentrates
    so on getting it down that he forgets that you feel insecure about it. He
    is like an artist in the middle of a painting. He is concentrating on the
    end of the effort, to the entire effort and bringing it through to a finish.
    And he doesn't bother with what he considers the trifles along the way.
    He's concentrating on the one goal.
        Michel de Notredame realizes that it is sometimes frustrating for
    you because of the obstacles that are in the way. But the thought was
    in his mind as he was leaving that the more you have to struggle to
    accomplish something, the longer the accomplishment lasts.

Imagine a puzzle composed of several hundred pieces. This is the
dilemma I was faced with as I attempted to arrange the quatrains in some
kind of logical order. It was possible but difficult. Especially when there
is an occasional piece which refuses to fit anywhere. I decided to rely on
any dates given and the subject matter. After much shuffling and
rearranging, I settled on the following order. It is amazing and almost
unbelievable that when the chapters are combined they make sense and
form a continuing story. There do not appear to be contradictions, as
though Nostradamus had them in some kind of order before he shuffled
them and forever mixed them up. When we remember that they were
interpreted in such a helter-skelter fashion, the odds on this continuity
emerging must be astronomical.

Chapter 10

Quatrains Dealing with the Past

B: He's in the process of arriving. You don't see what I see, so you don't know how it is. It's like seeing someone coming up out of the fog. When you first start seeing them, in a sense they are there. But they're clarifying the connection by appearing out of the fog. So he's already here; it's just that he's still coming.

D: *Then when he becomes clear or closer you know he's there?*

B: Clearer. There's no such thing as distance here because there's a different set of dimensions at work on this plane. I thought that description would interest you. Sometimes I forget you can't see them, because they appear so plainly to me. And so he is here.—He says that when you were in the process of choosing the quatrains that you felt drawn toward, he knew there would be some from the past included. This was necessary to help add perspective to the ones that have not yet come to pass. So that those who are reading of this will start to understand the way of his thinking, and thereby be convinced of the events that are yet to come.

D: *I have no way of knowing if they relate to the past.*

B: He says that is no problem. Because your hitting upon one that has already happened will help you to check the accuracy of translations and interpretations of the various ones. It also serves to illustrate how he means that quatrains can refer to more than one thing. Because if it is a quatrain that has already come to pass, people can have a more complete picture of what happened in both of the events and can see how one quatrain can serve for both.

A S WE BEGAN TO TRANSLATE more and more quatrains I found I would have to start making decisions about which ones to include in this book. I was convinced there would have to be sequels if we wished to print them all, as one book would never be able to hold them. Nostradamus advised me on this and suggested we omit those that dealt with the far past and concentrate on the ones describing events during the last 100 years or so. He especially wanted me to zero in on those that would pertain to events coming up during the next 20 years. These he felt were vital and the most important element of this project. I found the ones dealing with the past to be interesting and thought the readers would also, but I agreed that he was probably right. He suggested they be included later in a book for the historically curious.

I do not want the reader to get the mistaken idea that all the quatrains translated by Nostradamus during this experiment dealt only with modern times. This would be a gross mistake. The ones I have chosen to omit dealt with the French Revolution, Napoleon, the fates of various lines of royalty in Europe, the Spanish Civil War, World War I, *etc.* Nostradamus also has a fondness for predicting trends in religions and philosophy. He felt that this also had a profound effect on the future of the world. I decided to omit many of these since they dealt with cultures in the past.

I will only include a few quatrains pertaining to the past in this chapter to show his line of thinking. The rest will someday go into another book where there would be more room to study these and observe his remarkable accuracy. I think the ones I have decided to include in this book will more than demonstrate his profound use of complex symbolism.

CENTURY I-25

Perdu trouvé, caché de si long siecle,	The lost thing is discovered, hidden for many centuries. Pasteur will be
Sera Pasteur demi Dieu honoré:	celebrated almost as a god-like
Ains que la lune acheve son grand siecle,	figure. This is when the moon completes her great cycle, but by
Par autres vents sera deshonoré.	other rumors he shall be dishonored.

D: *That's interesting that he uses that name, Pasteur.*

B: He says that the name refers to whom you think it refers to. The pharmacological secrets that Pasteur discovered are simply rediscoveries of things that were known before but lost during the great dark age. He says that some of the things that Pasteur does ... did ... he says he's getting confused with his tenses.

D: *(Laugh) Because it's in his future and our past.*

B: Yes. He says that some of the things that Pasteur does will later be superseded by better practices. And the things that he did will be known to have not been the best way to do it. That's what he means by being reviled, because better ways will be found of doing what Pasteur discovered.

D: *Is that what it means, "when the moon completes her great cycle"?*

B: No. He says the moon has many cycles that the scientists as a whole do not seem to be aware of. If the scientists were fully aware of the cycles of the moon they would not be confused with the purpose and the construction of such structures as Stonehenge. For one, the great cycle of the moon encompassed the time from the fall of the Atlantis civilization to the gradual rise back to civilization again and the rediscovery of knowledge that was lost centuries before.

D: *So that's what it means. Pasteur was just rediscovering things that were known at the time of Atlantis. And "by other rumors he shall be dishonored" means they will find other ways of doing these things. The translators could connect this quatrain with Pasteur because he uses the name. He doesn't have very many where he actually names someone.*

B: Sometimes a particular person will stand out. He says modern medicine as you know it would not exist had it not been for the work of Pasteur.

*D*URING THE MONTHS THAT WE WORKED, we translated several quatrains dealing with World War II. Nostradamus commented on the major figures that were involved in that conflict. Strangely, when he referred to President Franklin Roosevelt he painted quite a different picture than we who were alive at that time saw. I had always considered him a great man who brought us through the war. Nostradamus referred to him as a man who was able to manipulate his presidential powers to be almost a king. (CENTURY VIII-74) He did serve more terms in office that any other president, and there was talk at the time that he might become similar to a king. It was at that time Congress limited the number of terms a president could serve. He also referred to Roosevelt manipulating to get us involved in the war. In CENTURY I-23 the leopard represents England and the boar is the Nazis because they were a piggish bunch. America is referred to as the eagle playing around the sun, indicating that we were *supposedly* neutral. This quatrain mentions a time, "the third month at sunrise." This was not astrological but referred to the time that England began to feel threatened by Germany and was trying to get the United States involved in the war. He indicated that Roosevelt had to find a way to enter the war with the people's support. Research proves this to be accurate. In *March, 1941*, Roosevelt offered all aid "short of war" to England. His most powerful opponents accused him of preparing the nation for a declaration of war. The reason for getting us involved was to help the economy. In CENTURY I-84 Roosevelt was described as the great one hidden in the shadows holding a blade in the bloody wound. This meant that he did things to provoke Japan. England is referred to as his brother in this quatrain. There were several other instances where Nostradamus refers to England as our brother. Roosevelt is again referred to in CENTURY II-9 as the thin man who has a peaceful rule for nine years before developing a bloody thirst. He was elected in 1932 and we entered the war in December 1941. Although these nine years encompassed the Depression era, they were relatively peaceful. There were several other quatrains, but these are enough to show the way Nostradamus saw Roosevelt and the entry of our country into the Second World War.

CENTURY III-75

Pau, Verone, Vicence,
Sarragousse,
De glaives loings terroirs de sang
humides.
Peste si grance viendra à la
grand gousse,
Proche secours, & bien loing
les remedes.

Pau, Verona, Vicenza, Saragossa,
swords dripping with blood from
distant lands. A very great plague
will come with the great shell, relief
near, but the remedies far away.

B: He says this quatrain refers to World War I and II. The place names
named at the beginning refer to places that played key roles in World
War I. The way the politics had become tangled up in Europe was
what caused World War I and II. He says if World War I had not
taken place, World War II would not have. The plague released by the
great shell was the atomic bombs dropped on Japan. They had a little
bit of medical relief there for the victims, but the remedy had to be
brought in by the United States which was far away.

D: *They have interpreted this as something that would happen in the*
future. They thought he was talking about chemical warfare, gas or
something like that.

B: He says that he can see where they'd get that aspect of the interpretation because of the gas warfare used in World War I. He was also
hinting at that. He was speaking of both events, World War I and World
War II, with World War II being the most calamitous of the two.

I could see now that this quatrain was a perfect example of his prophecies having double meanings. Of history repeating itself by referring both
to the chemical warfare as a plague and also the plague of radioactivity.

In this quatrain the place names had significance, but often when
Nostradamus used city names they indicated a country. The quatrains
have been consistently misinterpreted because the translators often
thought he was referring to an event that would happen in a certain city
when actually he was using those names as symbolism for a country.

The next one also referred to the atomic bomb.

CENTURY V-8

Sera laissé le feu vif, mort caché,
Dedans les globes horrible
espouvantable,
De nuict à classe cité en
poudre lasché,
La cite à feu, l'ennemi favorable.

There will be let loose living fire and
hidden death, fearful inside dreadful
globes. By night the city will be
reduced to rubble by the fleet, the
city on fire, helpful to the enemy.

B: Living fire inside dreadful globes refers to radiation from atomic
bombs dropped on Japan. That it burned like fire but the people

would not die right away like they would from regular fire, and they would have to live through the agony of it before dying. The fleet refers to the German planes flying over and bombing London and reducing it to rubble. The fearful globes were incendiary bombs. They wanted to provide some light to be able to find their targets. And so they would drop globes of explosive liquids that would ignite on contact, to help provide light to aim their other destructive bombs by.

D: *That makes sense because they had blackouts during the Second World War.*

There were many quatrains referring to Hitler. Many of these could be accurately translated, especially when Nostradamus used the anagram "Hister" to refer to Hitler. I will include one that was not so obvious.

CENTURY III-36

Enseveli non mort apopletique,	Burned, apoplectic but not dead, he
Sera trouvé avoir les mains	will be found to have his hands
mangees:	gnawed; when the city will condemn
Quand la cité damnera	the heretic who, it seemed to them,
l'heretique,	had changed their laws.
Qu' avoit leurs loix se leur	
sembloit changees.	

B: This refers to Hitler's suicide and death and consequent remains being discovered there in the bunker. His hands appearing to have been gnawed is symbolic of his once great power crumbling about him where he does not have the far reach that he had earlier. And the allies were, so to speak, chewing away at his borders.

D: *Apoplectic usually means somebody in a coma or something similar, doesn't it?*

B: It is someone who is popeyed with rage, someone who is struck down with a cerebral accident due to high blood pressure, possibly caused by the losing of temper. He says that this man (Hitler) could not control his emotions or passions, and that he would be carried away. He would start talking about a subject that would upset him and let his emotions carry him away to the brink of nervous breakdown.

D: *So this is the way Nostradamus saw him. I think people have said that Hitler was very emotionally unstable.—What does the second part mean: "When the city will condemn the heretic who, it seemed to them, had changed their laws." Is that also referring to Hitler?*

B: Certainly. He thought that would appear very clear to you so he didn't bother to give you the explanation. The city had always been saying, "Heil Hitler," and emulating him and saying how he was perfect and everything. But it was very quick to condemn him after his death, for he had changed the way of doing things from a democracy to a dictatorship.

D: *There was always a lot of speculation that Hitler didn't really die in that bunker. There was the idea that maybe he got away somehow and someone else died in his place.*

B: He did die there. The bigwigs of the Nazi party who survived and escaped to South America and other locations kept that idea circulating to help them keep control of what was left of the Nazi party. And also to give hope to the followers that were left that they would once again rise to power and glory.

CENTURY IV-95.

La regne à deux laissé bien peu tiendront, *Trois and sept mois passés feront la guerre.* *Les deux vestales contre eux rebelleront,* *Victor puis nay en Armorique terre.*	**The rule left to two, they will hold it a very short time. Three years and seven months having passed they will go to war. The two vestals will rebel against them; the victor then born on American soil.**

D: *The translators couldn't understand the word "vestals." They think it is a corruption of another word.*

B: He says that this quatrain has multiple meanings but they all refer to the same series of events dealing with World War II. The rule left to two refers to the two main dictators who were trying to conquer the world, the leader of the German Empire and the leader of the Japanese Empire. Between these two they were trying to take over the world. Hitler was trying to take over Russia and Europe, and eventually he was going to try and take over the United States. The Japanese were taking over Mongolia, Siberia, China, India, Australia and that part of the world. They planned to help take over the Americas from the other coast, so that the people of the Western Hemisphere would have a two-front battle to fight. However, he says that meanwhile in America, the victor, the element that was to determine which side of this conflict would win, was already being developed. That was the atomic bomb. There were two main scientists whose brains figured out the theoretical information needed to develop the bomb. In this quatrain he dated this conflict. The time element involved was from the time that the Americans became involved in World War II. He is saying that three years and seven months later would be when the Americans, bearing the victor, would end the war by dropping the bomb.

D: *The translators say that "three years and seven months having passed, they will go to war," means that is when someone will start a war.*

B: He says they are misinterpreting that. He knows what he is talking about. Three years and seven months later is when the victor goes to war. That is when the *bomb* enters the war and changes the concept of violence forever. Three years and seven months later is when the bomb is first dropped. The bomb being represented metaphorically as a champion knight going into battle for the allies. This champion, the bomb, first goes into war three years and seven months later. And this particular knight, so to speak, would henceforth be around to affect war politics and the face of battle forever after. Because after World War II was ended, the effects of the bomb were still felt throughout by the cold war and the way that things were still tense. Then the world was not at peace the way it had been at peace before. Because the threat of war was still there from this knight representing the bomb.

D: *The "two vestals that will rebel against them" are the two scientists?*

B: Yes. These two scientists not only rebelled against the dictators who were trying to take over the world, but they also rebelled against conventional ideas at the time. Saying that the way the scientists pictured the world was not the way existence truly was. They were able to break through conventional thinking and bring forth the various theories and mechanizations of nuclear power.

This explains his use of the word "vestals" to represent the scientists. I discovered that according to Roman mythology Vesta was the goddess of the hearth and the hearth fire. In ancient Rome there were six vestal virgins who tended the sacred fire in her temple. This is another remarkable example of the clever way Nostradamus used words and mythology to create the image within the puzzle he wanted to achieve. The scientists could be compared to vestals since they were tending a sacred fire when they invented the bomb. The bomb could also be considered a vestal virgin at the time since its success had never been proven.

D: *The translators say that the two powers will be America and Russia and they will go to war at some time in the future.*

B: America and Russia *will* be at war in the future, but this particular quatrain does not refer to that.

CENTURY II-89

Un jour seront demis les deux grand maistres,	One day the two great leaders will be friends; their great power will be seen to grow. The new land will be at the height of its power, to the man of blood the number is reported.
Leur grand pouvoir se verra augmenté:	
Le terre neufue sera en ses hauts estres,	
Au sanguinaire le nombre recompté.	

B: This refers to the event of your President Nixon establishing diplomatic contact with Communist China. He says that they are the two men of power. And at that time the new land—that is, the United States—was at the peak of its military power. Economically, monetarily, the United States dollar was still very powerful on the international market. He says the number being reported to the man of blood, are the casualties from the Vietnam War being reported to President Nixon. Particularly the final numbers reported to him after he ended the American involvement in that conflict.

D: *Then he is called the man of blood because they thought he was the most responsible?*

B: He is not the one most responsible for it. That lies on the shoulders of the president preceding him, President Johnson. But they call him the man of blood because he was Commander-in-Chief during the bloodiest years of that war, even though he was successful in ending *openly admitted* American involvement in that conflict.

D: Openly *admitted. You mean it hasn't really ended.*

B: Not only that, but secret organizations of American control are still involved. They never became *un*involved in that conflict.

D: *It's still going on like a quiet war, so to speak. Would that be right?*

B: Yes. That is why there are sporadic discoveries of American prisoners still being held over there. For even though the United States has supposedly stopped its involvement and the American public is not aware of the secret organizations that are involved, the people over there *are* aware of these organizations. And they *are* aware that they are American organizations. So they still consider Americans as being involved and thus they consider it right and proper for them to hold American prisoners.

D: *Why are these secret organizations still involved?*

B: The reason has to do with the imaginary spheres of power between that which is labeled "democracy" and that which is labeled "communism." The leaders of these organizations feel that if they withdraw altogether it will cause a threat to the balance of power in that area of the world. And they do not wish for this to take place.

D: *They have translated this quatrain as referring to America and Russia. That some time in the future they might become friends. And they think the man of blood might be the Anti-Christ.*

B: He says that it is true that someday America and Russia will become friends. But that will be due to the efforts of the man who comes *after* the Anti-Christ.

CENTURY V-78

Les deux unis ne tiendront longuement,
Et dans treize ans au Barbare Satrappe:
Au deux costez seront tel perdement,
Qu'un benira le Barque & sa cappe.

The two will not remain allied for long; within the thirteen years they give in to barbarian power. There will be such a loss on both sides, that one will bless the bark (of Peter) and its leader.

B: He says that this has already taken place. This refers to America and Russia after World War II. Although they were allied together during World War II and immediately afterward during the occupation of Germany, by five years after the war had ended these two powers had split ways and were on opposite sides of the fence. The 13 years referred to ... he says to start dating it from 1950 or thereabouts, from the time that these two powers split the blanket, so to speak. The 13 years refers to the most intense time of the cold war. From the time they split the blanket to the time of the Cuban missile crisis where it came close to erupting into open warfare. This was a time of great unrest in both countries. The one country, Russia, was trying to rebuild the damages from the war and modernize simultaneously, and this was causing a lot of social stress. Stalin was having his purges at the time, and people kept getting killed for no reason from the secret police killing imagined enemies of the state. Also at this time the United States was having great social unrest due to the paranoia about communism, as stirred up by McCarthy and others thinking along the same lines. Both countries had building paranoia. At the time people realized they had come within a very close distance of breaking out into open conflict, but nobody on this level can realize just how close they came to getting involved in open warfare. He says that was a major turning point along the branches of time. A major dividing branch where they would go one way and start working out their problems and come to peace, or at least to being on speaking terms, as they are today. Or they could have broken out in warfare and in the process destroyed most of Europe from throwing weapons and bombs at each other. He says that since this was a major branching point along the pathways of time, it stood out very clearly and it was fairly easy for him to spot. It also clearly demonstrates that man can change the consequences of his future, especially if he knows what these consequences are.

UPDATE: These observations were given to us in 1986 while interpreting the quatrains. But in January 1992 it finally came to light that Nostradamus was correct. The 1962 crisis was touched off by the Soviet installation of nuclear missiles with a range of 800 to 1000 miles. Kennedy saw this as a definite threat to the United States. These missiles were eventually withdrawn after days of tension, during which time Kennedy was under heavy pressure to invade Cuba. Soviet General A.I. Gribk   *announced that during the Cuban missile crisis the Soviet Union also s   it short-range nuclear weapons to Cuba (with a range of about 40 miles)   d authorized their use against any U.S. invading forces. He said the two super powers were drawn closer to nuclear war at that time than was previously thought. Robert McNamara, President John F. Kennedy's defense secretary, said he was unaware of the presence of the short-range missiles in Cuba at the time. But he was absolutely certain that Kennedy would have ordered nuclear retaliation on Cuba—and perhaps the Soviet Union as well—if nuclear weapons had been used against U.S. forces. A spokesman said, "We came closer to nuclear war than anyone had ever imagined. There is absolutely no question that we were right at the brink."*

D: In the French the word *Barque* is capitalized. It says, "they will bless the bark."

B: He says that a man whom one çountry will bring to the United States would approve of the efforts of the pope of the Catholic Church trying to make peace between the two nations, as well as trying to intervene in other armed conflicts as well. Russia, claiming to be an atheistic country, would be suspicious of anything that the Catholic Church would do, thinking it to be a capitalistic trick. Whereas the capitalist, so-called Christian country, the United States would approve of the efforts thinking that this is a third party who could be somewhat objective and help them to work out their problems. I get the feeling that the pope he is referring to is the present pope who seems to be quite involved with politics and trying to bring about world peace. Yes, he says that my feeling is correct. Another reason why he says he represented him as being a Barque is because that is a type of boat, something that travels. And this pope will not stay cloistered up in the Vatican.

D: Yes, that makes sense. This one travels everywhere.

UPDATE: It was revealed in 1992 that the present pope has been involved in political negotiations with the United States and Communist countries in the past. Such a discovery gives this quatrain more plausibility. It was revealed that President Reagan approved a secret program of aid to Poland's outlawed Solidarity movement a decade ago after consultation with Pope John Paul II and a heated argument among administration officials.

D: They have interpreted this as an alliance between the U.S. and Russia instead of the time they were at their most divisive.

B: He says to go onto the next quatrain, these interpretations are ridiculous.

CENTURY IV-28

Lors que Venus du Sol sera couvert,	When Venus will be covered by the Sun, under the splendor will be a
Soubs l'esplendeur sera forme occulte:	hidden form. Mercury will have exposed them to the fire, by a
Mercure au feu les aura descouvert,	rumor of war will be affronted.
Par bruit bellique sera mis à l'insulte.	

B: He says that in this particular quatrain not all of the references that sound astrological are necessarily so. He's having difficulty getting the concepts through but he will try. He says that this quatrain has a multiple meaning. One of the interpretations refers to an event that has already taken place. It is an event that actually did happen, but at the time it did, it was considered to be a rumor rather than an actual event. One aspect of this quatrain has to do with the Russian space program. He says that back in the early seventies when Russia and America were trying to outdo each other in regards to accomplishments in space flights, particularly *manned* space flights, Russia embarked upon an ambitious project. They decided that since they had not been successful in having a manned flight to the moon, in the process of trying to salve their hurt pride they reasoned that they would do something better and not worry about the moon. They attempted to send a manned flight to Venus. He says that when they did this, contact was broken for a period of time and the ship was presumed to be lost or destroyed. At the last minute communication was reestablished just before the ship burned up in the atmosphere of Venus. He says that at the time the United States suspected it had happened, but they were thinking it might be just a trick of propaganda for the Russians. This was at a time when diplomatic relations between the two countries were very touchy.

Nostradamus saw that the Challenger accident was not an isolated incident of space tragedy. It was merely the most publicized. He saw that astronauts had been lost since the beginning of space exploration, by not only the United States, but Russia and other countries. He said that unknown to the outside world, other countries besides the two super powers were conducting space experiments in the early days of space travel. Many of them stopped experimentation after disastrous results. Nostradamus reported that many of the so-called "unmanned" flights actually contained astronauts who died or were lost in space during unsuccessful missions. These accidents were never made public for obvious reasons. When I thought about this, I remembered rumors in the early 1970s that the Soviet first soft landings on Venus actually contained astronauts who died. There was much speculation at the time because of mysterious radio broadcasts. But no proof was ever brought forth and these speculations have remained only rumors. Did Nostradamus see what actually happened on some of these space missions?

Chapter 11

The Present Time

B: He says to tell you he has his tools and instruments and his ink pot and his scrolls with him.

D: *He does? Why did he bring them this time?*

B: Figuratively speaking. A figure of speech. He says he always brings them. Plus he brings his ... he calls it his book of questions. And he's showing me an image of a book that has nothing but question marks in it.

(It was obvious he was joking with me.)

D: *(Laugh) Okay. Tell him I have my scrolls and my writing instruments and my little black box.*

B: He says you're a fibber. You have nothing but your black box.

D: *(Laugh) I beg your pardon. I have his book.*

B: He says that doesn't count, because that's *his* book, and he has it, too. Ah-ha! But you have no ink pot and no book of questions. He just added, however, the infernal woman *asks* enough questions. She doesn't *need* a book of questions. *(Laugh)* I think he is teasing you.

D: *I get the impression he is.* (Laugh) *Yes, I'm full of questions. I've got a terrible curiosity.*

B: He says, terrible is the word for it.

D: *(Laugh) Well, I'm glad he puts up with me. He is the one who started this whole thing.*

B: He says the wheel of karma is endless. It does not begin and it does not end. Therefore you cannot accuse him of starting the whole thing, for things are endless. He says, he could just as easily say you started it by getting involved with regressive hypnosis to start with, so you see it is endless. If everybody were to realize that, it would make courts and law obsolete.

D: *Well, if he has finished joking with us, is he prepared to continue the work of translating his quatrains?*

B: He says, with a grand gesture of the hand, he is always ready to continue the work. He says, let us do it. *(Smiling broadly)* He appears to be in a very good mood.

Over the months we worked together, Nostradamus gave me the translation of many quatrains that apply to our present time. I will include the most unique here.

CENTURY III-13

*Par fouldre en l'arche or &
argent fondu,
De deux captifs l'un l'autre
mangera:
De la cité le plus grand estendu,
Quend submergee la classe
nagera.*

Through lightning in the box gold and silver are melted, the two captives will devour each other. The greatest one of the city stretched when the fleet travels under water.

B: He says that this quatrain refers to some inventions that you would call "modern" inventions. These, of course, will be found to have military applications. He says, for example, the box with the flickering light refers to the taming and controlling of electricity. Gold and silver in the box being melted refers to some of the applications of electrical technology, such as electroplating things with gold and such. And how this in turn led to technology such as communications technology using microchips and such as this which in turn is what is used to communicate with what you call "submarine"—the fleet of submarines that each country has. So he says that he was just simply trying to produce a picture of all the many wondrous inventions he saw for the future.

D: *And that goes along with the part that says, "the two captives will devour each other."*

B: He says that has to do with, yes, the energies involved because they have to be balanced. They are opposite energies but they have to be balanced for it to work. And so they, in a sense, devour each other in that they are balanced.

D: *The translators thought that he was talking about alchemy.*

B: He says that the practice of alchemy gave rise to chemistry and astronomy, as well as astrology also contributing to this. And he says that physics, as well, was affected. He says that some of the early alchemists were looking for metaphysical knowledge and some were just simply looking for physical knowledge. This led eventually to what you would call modern-day sciences which invented all these things.

D: *So in a round-about way it is referring to alchemy. Although the translators think he is talking about some kind of a process that he used in his day.*

B: He says that he can see where they would get that interpretation since they insist on putting blinders on him.

Often he would not give me all the answers. He would still leave us with some of the puzzle to figure out on our own.

B: He says that is for you to figure out. He's not going to tell you everything. Now that he has given the clues one should be able to find it. He says that one must exercise the mind for it to grow or one would turn into a dullard. (*Laughter from the group.*)

D: *So he wants me to use my own brain.*

B: He says you would not want to have copious amounts of Swiss cheese in that region of your body.

D: *(Laugh) True. I don't want to have a holey brain. You can't have all the answers just handed to you, can you?*

B: He says he has had too much practice with being mysterious. It's hard to open up all the way.

There were several quatrains referring to the deposal of the Shah of Iran and the rise to power of the Ayatollah Khomeni because these were forerunning events to the horrible "time of troubles." (CENTURY II-10 and I-70.)

CENTURY VI-34

Du feu volant la machination,	The machine of flying fire will come
Viendra troubler au grand	to trouble the great, besieged chief.
chef assiegez:	Within there will be such sedition
Dedans sera telle sedition,	that those abandoned will be in
Qu'en desespoir seront	despair.
les profligez.	

B: He says that this was a prediction of the accident that happened earlier this year at NASA with the Challenger crew. (This occurred at the end of January, 1986.) He says that the aftereffects of that tragic accident caused a great division of opinion in power, both within NASA and the Strategic Air Command, in regards to the aims and goals of the American space program. He says that there has been a faction fermenting for quite some time in favor of unmanned probes with sophisticated instruments on them. This accident gave them the fuel they needed to start a fire of dissent. And those idealists who hold to the dream of man exploring space directly have become very discouraged about the development of the matter. For they were wanting to construct space stations and develop solar power to help relieve the energy needs of the earth.

D: *"It will come to trouble the great besieged chief," by that does he mean the leaders of NASA?*

B: He says the great besieged chief is both the leaders of NASA and the President of the United States.

D: *Is he able to see what caused the accident?*

B: I will ask him. (*Pause*) He says it's hard to see clearly but one of the major contributing causes to the accident seems to have been computer error.

D: *Of course he wouldn't know what computers are, would he? Did he see something with machines or what?*

B: Well, he looked at the situation and he picked the concept from this vehicle's mind. He was thinking of mathematicians and thinkers, and he was thinking of machines. He was thinking of machines that did the thinking of mathematicians and thinkers. And what would happen if a system depending on such a machine were to break down and make a mistake the way humans do. And he, instead of asking for a colloquialism, asked for a term that would fit that concept. He is satisfied with the term "computer error."

D: *That was very cleverly done.*

B: He says that even though the majority of the evidence was destroyed in the conflagration, what pieces are found and what story is pieced together will not be made public. It will be kept within the highest circles of NASA as they try to figure out what caused such a horrible accident.

D: *They have released some things, but we never know if it's the truth or not.*

B: He says what they have released is propaganda.

D: *Will this be a setback to our space program?*

B: Yes, it will ... somewhat. He says it will set it back temporarily. But the time element involved will be longer than what is originally anticipated. Because right now it has caused a great division in the ranks. It's like a two-headed serpent fighting itself. Each division is trying to get the upper hand so as to direct the space program in their desired direction. By the time this is resolved the implementation of the decision will be delayed by war. It won't be until after the war is over and things have settled down and the country has recovered from the war, that the space program will be implemented in the direction of the development of solar power and space stations. The idealists will eventually win out, but it will be a very close decision. The advent of war will help strengthen their position.

CENTURY IV-30

Plus onze fois Luna Sol ne voudra,	More than eleven times the Moon will not want the Sun, both raised
Tous augmenté & baissez de degré:	and lessened in degree. Put so low that one will sew little gold: after
Et si bas mis que peu or on cendra,	famine and plague the secret will be discovered.
Qu'apres faim, peste, descouvert le secret.	

B: He says that this quatrain refers to an event, the roots of which have already been laid but the outcome will not come to light for a while yet. He says the phrase "more than eleven times the moon will not want the sun," refers to the United States' space program and the manned flights to the moon. The moon at that time was very prominent in men's thoughts, thereby raised in glory and more important. Therefore she was not needing or wanting the influence of the sun to add to her glory. But then the space program will fall into disfavor so that the glory of the moon is lessened through policy changes in the government, and the emphasis is shifted in a different direction. And the change of emphasis is due to some—he insists on using the word "nefarious"—nefarious policy-making behind the scenes the voting public is not aware of, but would not approve of if they knew of it. These policy changes of redirecting the money toward military things rather than scientific things will contribute to the horrors of the changes that are to come. But the machinations behind the scenes will not be exposed until a later date.

UPDATE: One of my readers spotted something in this quatrain that I did not. Quoting from his letter: "The moonshots went up to number eleven before Neil Armstrong landed on the surface. The missions were, of course, named after Apollo, the Roman sun god."

D: *What is the meaning of "one will sew little gold"?*
B: When the change of policy takes place it affects the money available for contributing to the moon's glory; that is, the money available for space programs. It is diverted for other uses and since no money is contributed into the space program, they cannot return in kind. Because when money is contributed to research that the space program is involved in, they return it ten-fold by the discoveries that are done to help improve the lot of mankind.
D: *"After famine and plague the secret will be discovered."*
B: After the time of troubles.
D: *I'm thinking of another quatrain we covered about the Challenger tragedy and that they were trying to put space stations in space. He said it would all be delayed because of a war. Do you think these two are connected?*
B: Yes. He says this situation concerning space exploration is very complicated and tangled.

D: *This next one has some astrological signs in it. I do want to tell him I have found a young man who is an expert astrologer. He wants to work with me on these to determine the signs that Nostradamus mentions.*
B: He says that will be good if the young man will keep his mind open to novel interpretations of what he sees and not be too hard and fast to the established rules of astrology. The planets form their patterns and given enough time they will come around to those patterns again. Therefore more than one path will be indicated, just as more than one interpretation can be given to the quatrains.
D: *The young man suggested that at times I ask for more astrological information.*

B: He says that he will do what he can to help. Sometimes it's difficult to translate the concepts precisely enough to be of any real help. But he will do what he can.

John was present and wanted to ask a question about a quatrain that I had received from Elena. I asked him to look up the astrological signs and he wanted to get more information about it. He was concerned about it because it was supposed to be happening very soon, December 22, 1986, about two months away. Elena had interpreted through Dyonisus that the quatrain concerned spaceships. John did not agree with this.

CENTURY II-48

La grand copie qui passera
les monts,
Saturne en l'Arq tournant
du poisson Mars:
Venins caches soubs testes
de saulmons,
Leur chef pendu à fil de polemars.

The great army which will pass over the mountains when Saturn is in Sagittarius and Mars moving into Pisces. Poison hidden under the heads of salmon, their chief in war hung with a cord.

B: He says once again this quatrain has more than one meaning. Through a mistake made by a leader, an international incident will occur. He says the main trouble with the situation will be caused by a breakdown in communication between the two powers involved.
John: We know that during that time period Mars and Saturn will be in square aspect. "Poison hidden under the heads of salmon. Their chief in war hung with a cord." Does this mean that the chief will hang himself? That he'll commit suicide because of the mistake?
B: "The chief in war hung with a cord." He says that the situation is a lot more complicated than what will first appear on the surface, symbolized by the assumed knot in the cord. To hang oneself with a cord, one must tie a knot in it somewhere. He says that the chief, the leader involved, will feel great regret about what happened and will want to continue his career and help correct the situation, to help make up for the adverse affects of it. However, he will be symbolically hung by others wishing to take his position in the organization. He will be hung so far as politics and his career are concerned. It will be almost like his committing suicide because the end result will be that he will be a broken man and not be able to do anything about the situation. It appears, he says, that all in all the entire event will end up being a fiasco as viewed from both sides. But it will have cataclysmic and very harmful consequences. There's another word he's wanting to use here and I can't find it. It will have very ... profound consequences to both countries involved.
D: Would "far-reaching" be a good word?

B: No. Profound, deep-reaching, stabbing deep to the quick, because it will affect world policy in general for many nations.

D: *We wanted to clarify this first part again. "The great army." In one French translation it was, "The great horde which will pass over the mountains."*

B: He says the word "horde" is closer to the description than "army." The way the situation develops, an enemy or one who does not wish the United States well will take advantage of the situation by extending their power in an unethical way. And they will do it by sending a horde of agents working for them into this area. He says this is not clear to him, but that aspect of the situation will not come to light until a little bit later. And much of the world will be offended by this action.—Michel de Notredame asks if you have anything you would like to add.

D: *Well, is that date, December 22, 1986, correct?*

B: He says, yes, or so close as to not make any difference.

D: *We were interested because this is going to be very soon in our future. (We were asking these questions in October 1986.)*

B: Yes. He says from his perspective it looks so very immediate that the time from which we are speaking today and the time that it is going to happen appear almost simultaneous.

Ms. Cheetham translated the astrological signs mentioned in the quatrain as a conjunction, but this is not true. John had found that these signs would occur from the last week of November, 1986 through December into the first week of January, 1987. It's interesting that Elena came up with this date for this quatrain when she didn't know anything about astrology.

I believe this quatrain refers to the problem President Reagan had with the discovery of the arms deal with Iran. This fiasco began to unfold around the end of November and continued through December into January. The rest of the nation watched the story develop on TV and probably felt the emotions of disbelief, anger or frustration. Some may have felt the entire scenario was being blown out of proportion. That part of the drama did not touch me. With a sense of detachment I listened as a senator suggested that President Reagan resign and appoint a successor. The phrase, "their chief in war hung with a cord," kept running through my mind. It's true, the President is certainly the head of the armed forces. My sympathy for the President being symbolically hung was replaced by the amazement and wonder of watching Nostradamus' 400-year-old prophecy come to life before my eyes. Then a cold chill rippled through my body. If he was correct about this prediction, would his horrible visions of the Anti-Christ also come to fulfillment?

Ms. Cheetham says in her book that "saumon" means a donkey head in Provencal. She could not see any way of translating that to make any sense in this quatrain, so she used the word "salmon." But I wonder; could this be referring to the donkey, the symbol of the Democratic party? By "poison hidden under the donkey head," could it mean that the Democrats were somehow responsible for the negativity in the news concerning this event? John said also that a donkey head was a favorite type of mask worn at festivals in France—here again suggesting that something hidden was going on. These are my observations and not Nostradamus' but he did tell me to try to use my own deductive powers at trying to solve these puzzles.

J: *You said this quatrain might have more than one meaning. Saturn in Sagittarius to me represents almost like a fire arrow. And Mars into Pisces is water like the oceans. Does this have something to do with trouble at sea or with battles with naval ships?*

D: *Or do you want to explain it in your own words?*

B: He says that he doesn't mind his asking questions like this because that is what discussion is all about. Give and take. He's been looking forward to discussing with this young man rather than merely communicating to him. He says there is a difference between discussion and communication. One thing that seems particularly pleasing to him is that the line along which you appear to be thinking seems to parallel his own train of thought. This makes discussion a lot easier and direct. He says that you are right to follow your feelings about the matter when interpreting horological symbols. Your feelings are your psychic guides helping you as they observe from their higher planes. They thereby contribute towards your insightfulness in the matter. He says this particular event will involve the ocean. He's giving me a picture of what I interpret as a submarine. It's going to be involved as well as armed ships on the surface of the ocean.

D: *What country is this that's involved?*

B: He doesn't say for sure. The feeling he's putting across is that he feels there will be an American involved and that it will take place in the Atlantic Ocean. The image that Michel de Notredame projects to my mind is like looking down upon a map, the center of which is the Atlantic Ocean. And I see what appears to be cylindrical missiles splashing into the water and what appears to be a partially submerged ship and a submarine nearby. It's like seeing a photograph of this superimposed on the map of the Atlantic Ocean, so that the objects in this photograph are out of proportion in their size in regards to the ocean. But the location of it is in the Northern Hemisphere of the Atlantic Ocean, in the southwest quadrant. I get the feeling that this is where the incident will take place.

It is interesting that missiles were mentioned because they were also involved in the Iran arms scandal. Could he be again referring to both incidents?

D: *The reason we are asking about this quatrain is because the other vehicle thought it dealt with spaceships. It was Dyonisus who was telling us of this and I personally think he may have misinterpreted what he was seeing.*

B: He says this is perfectly reasonable because of the great preponderance of cylindrical objects in the picture, the submarine and the missiles. He could have mistaken these for space going vehicles since they tend to be cylindrical as well.

J: *What does "the poison hidden under the heads of salmon" mean?*

B: He says that represents a two-fold thing. Poison hidden in the heads of salmon refers to a nuclear submarine, as well as referring to the war-like tendencies of the commanders of these submarines. They'll be somewhat antsy to push the button, so to speak. Both of the incidents referred to in this quatrain result in a fiasco.

J: *I think the southwest quadrant would be near Cuba or in that area. Could this mean that a Soviet sub pulling maneuvers off the coast could threaten or even bomb the United States?*

B: Yes. He says that particularly there will be an American surface ship in danger. The Soviet commander of this sub will have secret orders the rest of the crew are not aware of, basically saying to antagonize and instigate as much as they can get away with, without necessarily going over the line. What happens is that he gets carried away and goes too far, but he's not afraid of punishment because of the general nature of his orders. The American commander, on the other hand, is in a situation where he had been ordered to defend the coast of the United States but not to do anything to start a war. The commander, in the process of defending his ship from the submarine, manages to strike the submarine and he feels he may have sunk it. He feels like his hands are tied, that perhaps this may be interpreted as an action to start war rather than an action of defending the United States.

J: *Will this lead to war?*

B: It will be one of the events leading to a conflict, preparatory to the time of troubles. It won't be an out-and-out war at this time, just one of the pre-events leading up to it. He says, for example, there are several things that happened previous to World War II that at the time were considered isolated incidents, but were later realized as being a set of events leading up to World War II. He says it is this type of situation. It's difficult for him to say from his perspective, but when the time of troubles is through and we are looking upon it and are documenting that period of time, the connection will become apparent.

Could this prediction have some connection with the Soviet submarine that sank in the ocean October 3 to 6, 1986? It was said that there was a fire and nuclear explosion on board the sub and it sank east of Bermuda while being towed back to Russia. Our help was refused and U.S. planes and ships were ordered to stay away. Could there have been more involved than was made public?

Also, as this book was going to the publishers, there was an incident involving the American submarine *Bonefish* in April 1988. The ship was disabled due to an explosion of undetermined origin in exactly the area of the ocean that Nostradamus indicated. There were some other parallels with the quatrain. "Poison hidden under the heads of salmon" in this case could refer to the toxic fumes that were released inside the submarine that threatened the lives of all on board. Also the word "salmon" could refer to the submarine (a fish) and its unusual name *Bonefish*. Surface ships were also involved in the routine exercises that were taking place in that area of the Atlantic. The *Bonefish* was an out-dated diesel-electric submarine that was due to be decommissioned soon. There are only four of this type left on active duty. The Navy uses this type to simulate Soviet submarines in these exercises because the Russians have many of this type still operating. Could this be why Nostradamus indicated to Brenda that it was a Soviet submarine? Could he actually have been showing her an accident that occurred during war "games" and not an actual confrontation? It would have been difficult for him to distinguish the difference and for Brenda to draw any other conclusions from the pictures she was being shown. Again I wonder whether or not he was seeing more than we will ever be told about.

B: He says it was very difficult to communicate through Dyonisus. For one, he didn't think in French as well as Michel de Notredame does. He says a lot of times he would misunderstand the concepts he was trying to get across. He says also it was a very indirect way of communicating. But he had to establish the communication somehow, and this was the most primary way he could think of to do it. Because he knew it would develop into *this* sort of communication. He felt it was very important to open up a way because at your point in time it's very crucial. You're at a point where these things will be taking place within your lifetimes. They'll be having a very profound effect on your lives and on everyone's lives. He wants to get the information out to try to, at least, help some of the people.—He hopes that the young astrologer whose acquaintance he has made today is not unduly disappointed because of the lack of definite astrological references so far. But he says he will be happy to continue working with this young man through this medium. To work together on this to help bring to light the puzzles involved.—He knows that in his own day there are various dialects of French in his country, and even though your country is relatively young, he finds it amusing that various dialects of your language seem to exist in your day and in your country as well. He says he has noticed the young astrologer speaks differently than what he has been accustomed to hearing in this language from your plane.

We laughed. John is from Boston. I didn't think his accent was that noticeable, but apparently Nostradamus thought so.

CENTURY VII-41

Les oz des piedz & des main enserrés,	The bones of the feet and the hands locked up, because of the noise the
Par bruit maison long temps inhabitee:	house is uninhabited for a long time. Digging in dreams they will be
Seront par songes concavent deterrés,	unearthed, the house healthy and inhabited without noise.
Maison salubre & sans bruit habitee.	

B: He is saying that this refers to various events in American history, and some events to come. This is one of those quatrains with several interpretations. He says the house refers to the White House. One of the associations with this quatrain, one of the things he was seeing that he did not bring out very strongly, was the events of Watergate. The reason why he didn't bring it out very strongly is that the quatrain is associated with other events that seem to be more major and more important. He thought the people needed to be warned against these, rather than just the events of Watergate. He wanted to give them a hint about Watergate because that would be a bad thing to have happen, but not necessarily avoidable. In secret the presidents of the supposedly free country have been steadily abusing the power to a greater and greater extent. And something needed to happen to shake them up and to shake up the people so they wouldn't be so complacent. But he says it also refers to events in the future. There will be a time in another period of great social unrest, even more major than the social unrest that occurred during the Vietnam era, to where due to a—the concept he's trying to put across is a combination of two concepts that cannot be explained in one or two words. He first shows the concept of a hung jury, so that a sentence cannot be decided upon in court, but he's applying that concept to an election. A hung election with the nation being the hung jury, and with the vote being very finely divided between two different men for president. The electoral college will not be able to make the decision either because the vote will be so even, so finely divided throughout the entire nation, that it will temporarily freeze the processes of democracy. The hands and feet, the very core of the operation, that is the election, will be locked up, frozen. He says the people will be clamoring for whichever candidate they voted for and it will cause a great noise across the entire nation. It will be a touchy subject due to the world situation in general at the time. Thus, if one or the other candidate is put in office it would be at the risk of causing another civil war or at least a revolution. He says it will be a time of great social pressure, social unrest, and even more explosive than during the Vietnam era. It will be a while before they work out a compromise and hold another election to come up with a candidate acceptable to all, one who can be installed in the White House without the threat of all the noise and confusion and such caused by a revolution or a civil war or what-have-you.

D: *What does "digging in dreams" mean?*

B: He says that in the process of trying to find a solution to the problem there will be a lot of oratory. Bringing up a lot of concepts about patriotism and love of country and such, and bringing up the dreams of the founding fathers of the nation.

I thought this could possibly happen in the 1988 presidential election. In 1987 there was no clear-cut favorite candidate and who could successfully carry an election. When Bush and Dukakis were announced, it was met with lukewarm enthusiasm. But the hung jury concept did not materialize as George Bush was elected to the office of President. So it appears that this strange prophecy describes an event that is still in our future. How far we can only speculate.

D: *But you said it could also refer to Watergate because of the confusion?*

B: Yes. He says if you would like he will give a few of the associations of Watergate but he doesn't feel that it is essential. He says that in the case of Watergate, the bones of the hands and feet being locked up together refers to the president abusing the powers of the CIA for the interests of his political party against the other political party. It was like cutting off your hand or cutting off your nose to spite your face, for both parties want to work for the good of the country. And they let petty things, party differences, get in the way and become too big. The president abused his powers at the time of election against the other party so that it created a great noise. Watergate, in other words. (*A play on words. The opening of a water gate would make a loud noise.*) It was not settled until the president stepped down from his position so that things could be quietened and another put in his place.

I could understand the comparison now. In both cases someone would have to be appointed to fill the office until a president could be duly elected. This is what he meant by the house being uninhabited. There was a period of time, in Watergate and in this future case, when the country was being run by someone who had not been elected by the people.

B: He says that the man who took the office (Gerald Ford) was in a very delicate position for he had been appointed vice president after the other one had been impeached. Then the president resigned so he became president without ever having received a vote from anybody, except for his constituency in Michigan. He says that particular man (Ford) was in a very uncomfortable position. He did not ask for that to happen to him. He had not aimed for the presidency. The man did well in the circumstances and the way he handled the entire situation on his part caused a lot of good causes for his karma.

D: *I understand. The house was inhabited but it was not inhabited by an elected president. This other meaning about the election is more important because the Watergate episode has already passed.—He'll probably get mad again if I tell him the translation of this quatrain. It says, "Nostradamus seems to have believed in ghosts, because this is a description of a haunted house which is exorcised when the bones of the victim are removed. Perhaps an occupant of the house dreamt of the grave which led to the discovery of a skeleton?"*

B: He's not mad at this point. The image he's projecting is him rolling all over the floor laughing. He says that if she wants ghosts, he'll show her ghosts. He'll come and haunt her in her dreams.

D: *She did interpret it quite literally, didn't she?*

B: Yes. He says that's why this project was instituted. He knew that this would happen.

In all fairness to Ms. Cheetham, many other translators have also thought that this quatrain referred to a haunted house. I think this is a wonderful example of Nostradamus' marvelous use of symbolism.

This next quatrain is most amazing because it appears to have come true while this book was being written. This translation was received in December 1986 and it seems to be an obvious reference to the Bakkers and their trouble with the PTL Club which began in March 1987. It also appears to relate to Jimmy Swaggart's problems in the beginning of 1988. Apparently Nostradamus thought it was important to comment on it because he believed it would have a negative influence on the church in general. I believe that he saw more far-reaching consequences than we are now aware of.

CENTURY II-27

Le devin verbe sera du ciel frappé,	The divine voice will be struck by heaven and he will not be able to
Qui ne pourra proceder plus avant:	proceed further. The secret is hidden with the revelation so that
Du reserant, le secret estoupé	people will walk over and ahead.
Qu'on marchera par dessus & devant.	

He said this had a double meaning. The first meaning is not applicable to this chapter so I will only include the second one here.

B: He says this also refers to an event in which, due to the pressures of the times, the great powers that fundamentalism will have attracted to itself will be taken away because of information revealed about the leaders. Unsavory information will take the wind out of their sails, so to speak, and they will lose support to their movement. People will go on and life will go on as if they never existed. He asks that you please do not gloss over this interpretation of the quatrain. You must keep it in mind and be interested in it because it's much more immediate and closer in the future. To make sure your mind didn't shut it out. For you to be mulling on it afterwards.

CENTURY I-40

La trombe fausse dissimulant folie,
Fera Bisance un changement de loix:
Istra d'Egypte qui veut que l'on deslie,
Edict changeant monnaies & alois.

The false trumpet concealing madness will cause Byzantium to change its laws. From Egypt there will go forth a man who wants the edict withdrawn, changing money and standards.

B: He says that this is a multiple meaning quatrain. One of the meanings does refer to past events, but it also applies to events to come in the future that will be of help to you. He says that the false trumpet refers to powerful leaders who are both religious and political. Men who have made their living being involved with religion, who in the prime of their lives get involved with politics. He says he could name names, but that the skeptics of your book will not care for this too much. For your own personal information he's willing to tell you some names if you don't print them. He says he can't help but think that traces of the Inquisition still exist in your time.

D: *Maybe not as bad, but still ...*

B: He says that it's going to be getting worse with the times. First, he says that in sentences where he doesn't call them by name, you're welcome to go ahead and use those sentences because it's information that is needed. This is partially for your own protection also, because these men are powerful enough to cause you grief through libel suits and what-have-you. Others like you, such as this vessel and different ones, will know who you're talking about without having to have names named because these men are easy to find with your communication devices. (*I agreed to his restrictions.*) He says that the false trumpet refers to fundamentalist-type religious men who distort the word of God and use it for their own ends. He says that several of these men are striving for political power and they are banding together to help as many of them as possible to attain *key* posts in the government. A lot of these posts are not necessarily splashy or public. Maybe a quiet post tucked away in the bureaucracy somewhere that's in a key spot so far as the information and power flow is concerned, where they can use it for their own ends and subtly affect world events to their favor. He says these men attaining political power will have repercussions all over the world. It will cause many countries in the middle—he's calling it the Middle Earth, and he's showing me a picture of eastern Europe and western Asia and the Middle East, the whole area there. Leaders of this part of the world will become very alarmed by the development of things. They will start changing their laws in reaction to this, making it more difficult for Americans to travel in that part of the world. Some laws in particular that will be changed will be those having to do with the conversion of American money into other currencies and with trading with the United States. It will have negative repercussions. He says that as a result of this it will end up affecting the young Anti-Christ, referred to as Byzantium. The young Anti-Christ in his own country, in the process of building up a power base, will be influenced by the perverted actions of these fundamentalists. Influenced in such a way that it will make it more difficult on Christendom in general later on. The fundamentalists will be an element in their own undoing in this way. He says that these men who appear to be very religious are very shrewd and calculating. When they go to seminary schools to learn how to be a Reverend and such, a lot of the things they learn can be used for crowd control and brainwashing and manipulating people. This is basically what they are doing, but they are for private, secular things rather than just religious things.

D: *Then what they're really after is power.*

B: Exactly, he says.

The rest of this quatrain will be interpreted in Chapter 17, "The Monster Appears," pp. 222.

CENTURY VI-62

Trop tard tous deux les fleurs
seront perdues,
Contre la loi serpent ne
voudra faire:
Des ligueurs forces par gallots
confondues,
Savone, Albinque par monech
grand martyre.

Too late both of the flowers will be lost, the snake will not want to act against the law; the forces of the leaguers confounded by the French, Savona, Albenga through Monaco great martyrdom.

B: He says this quatrain concerns Ireland. The two flowers can either be thought of as referring to Ireland and Northern Ireland, or to the Protestant Irish and Catholic Irish. He says that poor Ireland, that poor island is so divided against itself that it's best represented by *two* flowers rather than by one. Both groups in Ireland feel they are fighting for the good of their beloved country. And when it's too late they will realize they have been tearing her down, so that she will be lost totally. He says at the last minute they will try to compromise in an attempt to save the situation. The snake refers to the leader of the rebellious forces and the law refers to the forces that are cooperating with Great Britain. But they will have been foiled in their efforts by various schemes implemented by members of the underworld in the various locations named in the quatrain. These will be tearing down the situation, both with supplying faulty arms to both sides and also smuggling in hard drugs and such to mess up the minds of the people who are fighting. Monaco is the point where it's being channeled through to Ireland. He says that members of the underworld are in the various locations described in the quatrain, but they coordinate their efforts and channel what must be done through Monaco. He says it seems like an illogical way of doing it, but through the tenuous connections of the underworld it is the most direct and logical way of doing it.

D: *The translator called this an "erroneous quatrain."*

B: He says there is no such thing. I cannot repeat his reply to this exactly but it was a non-verbal rude noise. He says, "Try an error on that woman's part."

D: *The translator thinks he was talking about some kind of a league between countries. She says, "Nostradamus seemed to intend a league against the French in this verse, in which the French triumph. But Monaco was bound to the Spanish by treaty and Savona and Albenga belong to Genoa. Nostradamus probably had one of the 16th-century Italian leagues in mind, but in this case, wrongly."*

B: He's shaking his head in mild exasperation. He is saying that the impertinent girl should go back to school and learn her three R's all over again. He says occasionally he would have a quatrain that was fairly clearly referring to something in his own time, simply to keep his credentials up. But the political situation as it was during his lifetime was so petty and impermanent compared to the events to come that he didn't really concern himself with it much. The events to come are so much more tragic and world shaking.—He says that if she insists on associating it with a league, the quatrain could somewhat be associated with the League of Nations. Its faulty conception by World War I and its breakup by World War II. Perhaps she could logically associate that. He says she insists on thinking 400 years too late, but that's her problem.

D: *They have tried to limit him by saying he was more interested in his own time period, and that is what many of his quatrains pertain to.*

B: He says that he sees far, far in time and in distance. He has seen to the end of the earth totally and to the end of this solar system. He says why should he concern himself with just the petty goings-on in southern Europe during his time?—I'm going to interject something. I suggest we change the subject. He's getting somewhat angry. I am communicating with him on the spiritual plane and he can project images that would not literally be true. He's projecting an image of him stomping his feet and smoke coming out his ears.

D: *(Laugh) Then I think you are right, we had better go on to another quatrain.*

CENTURY V-75.

Montera haut sur le bien plus à dextre,	He will rise high over his wealth, more to the right, he will remain
Demourra assis sur la pierre quarree:	seated on the square stone; towards the south placed at the
Vers le midi posé à la fenestre,	window, a crooked staff in his hand,
Baston tortu en main, bouche serree.	his mouth sealed.

B: He says that this refers to a man in the United States. A man who is very wealthy. Wealthy to the point that anything he wants done can get done instantaneously, for he has the money to get it accomplished. He says this man will be well known and famous because of his wealth, but his true mission in life will be secret, for this man will be a fanatic of sorts. He will be involved with such organizations as the American Nazi Party and the Ku Klux Klan. That's why he put in the phrase, "the crooked staff," to represent the burning crosses of the Ku Klux Klan and the swastika of the Nazi party. This man's sole ambition in life is towards the overthrow of the American government as it is presently constituted in the 20th century. He says this man naturally enough will also be involved in politics. But even though his main ambition is to change the form of the American government, he has to stay low-key in politics so that he may continue spinning his webs of power and continue making new contacts and expanding his range of influence. The groundwork that he has laid will come to fruition at the time of the troubles caused by the Anti-Christ.

D: *At this present time does anybody know who he is?*

B: Those who follow him know who he is.

D: *But the other people don't know the danger he poses?*

B: No, for he has been very sly, very careful.

D: *Would that explain the phrase, "he will remain seated on the square stone"?*

B: Yes. He will be in the center of the entire organization, but he won't be the figure of power that people see. He will have a puppet, someone who will appear to be the one in power, but he will be pulling the strings. He will have a figurehead, but he will remain seated behind, on the square stone that is, in the center of this organization.

D: *"His mouth sealed" would mean that he is secret.*

B: Yes, he is secret. The phrase, "toward the south at the window," means that due to his political beliefs, what open activities he does indulge in and the mayhem he likes to cause is more often to appear in the southern part of the country where such mayhem has been somewhat traditional.

D: *Then no one's going to know who he is until he comes to light at the time of the Anti-Christ.*

B: This is true.—He says that he's hoping these messages he's trying to convey will get across in time. He is hoping the people will be open enough to accept this and perhaps help with spreading this core of knowledge to help avert the disasters that he has seen, for they are avertable. This is why he is always willing to communicate.

D: *We had a question about something that I don't know if you would know anything about. It concerned the stock market. Is he familiar with our stock market?*

B: He says that he has heard tales that in Florence the traders buy and sell things according to what they will get on future trading trips and not what they have immediately on hand. He asks if it is like this?

J: *That's what the stock market is. What I wanted to know is: On October 31, 1988, the planets will be at the same alignment as they were on October 29, 1929. That was the stock market crash in 1929. Will something similar happen in 1988 because of the similarity of the signs?*

B: The vibrations will echo through it. He says he's not really sure what you're asking about the stock market, but he can tell you that the effects you're asking about that took place in 1929 will happen again, concerning society in general. It will have great social, economic effects. He doesn't know anything about the stock market, *per se,* but he says that which fouled it up that time will foul it up again.

D: *It did have a great effect on the economics of the world the last time it happened.*

Afterwards we wondered if this could mean the possibility of bank failures because the stock market is supposedly protected against a similar occurrence. During this time the savings and loans corporations were experiencing trouble. The similarity of signs could refer to a monetary or financial problem, apparently of large proportions.

Note: At the end of October 1987 the stock market took a record-breaking plunge. We waited to see if it would be repeated in October 1988. At that time there began the huge corporate takeovers, buyouts and auctions of enormous proportions involving huge sums of borrowed money. The market faltered when this started, but it was nothing compared to the dive the year before. This was the date that John had found in his astrological calculations. It was not Nostradamus' prediction. Nostradamus merely confirmed that the similarity of signs could mean a similar event.

Chapter 12

The Near Future

SOME OF THE QUATRAINS were difficult to date yet they seemed to pertain to events that would be happening soon, or within the not too distant future. I have included these in this chapter.

CENTURY II-53

La grande peste de cité maritime,
Ne cessera que mort ne soit
vengée,
Du juste sang par pris damné
sans crime,
De la grand dame par feincte
n'outragée.

The great plague in the maritime city will not stop until death is avenged by the blood of a just man taken and condemned for no crime; the great lady is outraged by the pretense.

B: He says that this refers to two different events. He saw—from his viewpoint, in the future from his time—that London was going to have another bout of Black Plague. But he says that is already far in the past for us, so he will not touch upon that at this time. The other event also refers to a great plague. He says that whenever he uses the phrase "the maritime city," sometimes he's referring to London and sometimes he's referring to New York. Because they're both, in your time anyway, two of the major cities on earth and they're ports. He calls them maritime cities because they are ports as well as big cities. He says what we must watch out for is that before and during the time of troubles there will be many diseases going around and many epidemics and plagues. Particularly the one you have labeled "AIDS." He says it will spread out from the cities and grow like wildfire over the whole country, and it will affect a goodly portion of the population.

D: *It says, "the plague will not stop until death is avenged with the blood of a just man taken and condemned for no crime." Can he clarify that part?*

B: He says that if he were to try to explain that part it really wouldn't make any sense, but it will become clear in time. He apologizes about being so vague about that part of it.

D: *Will it have something to do with a cure or something like that?*

B: He says there will not be a cure for it in time for this plague. Death will just have to run its course.

D: *The translators have identified this as the Great Plague of London.*

NOTE: *This quatrain is further clarified in Volume Two.*

CENTURY II-35

*Dans deux logis de nuict le
feu prendra,
Plusieurs dedans estouffes
& rostis:
Pres de deux fleuves pour seul
il adviendra:
Sol, l'Arq & Caper tous seront
amortis.*

Fire will take hold in two houses at night, several people inside suffocated or burnt. It will happen near two rivers for sure when the sun, Sagittarius and Capricorn are all diminished.

B: He says this quatrain contains a date in that last line. The fire taking hold in two houses indicates a breakdown in communication between two major powers, particularly in this case referring to the United States and Russia. The fire taking hold in two houses will be the uprush of hard feelings due to a misunderstanding in the two Capitol buildings, the Kremlin and the White House. The people getting suffocated or burned indicates that there will be people in both places wanting to keep feelings from rising high, to try to keep things on an even balance, to talk things out. And some will simply be put in a position where no one will listen to what they have to say so they have been suffocated, so to speak. Others will speak out anyway and their careers will be ruined. They will risk their careers by trying to keep the situation from getting worse and so they will have been burned, so to speak.

D: It says *"it will happen near two rivers, for sure."*

B: He says that the Potomac is one of the rivers, and the other river is the one in Russia, symbolic in a similar way in Russian history.

D: *"The sun, Sagittarius and Capricorn are all diminished."* Can you give me a little information on that?

B: He says this is at a time when these three zodiacal forces are not in their houses and thus they are not exerting influence on the affairs of man. Each of the zodiacal signs exerts influence to a greater or lesser degree, depending on their relation to the other zodiacal signs. At this time other signs will be exerting more power, more influence, and these three signs will be exerting less. Hence, the influences they would have on the situation will be diminished. He says picture casting a horoscope for the world in general, and at a time in this horoscope where the influence of these three signs are at a low ebb, that should give you an idea of approximately when this would take place. Particularly in regards to the horoscopes for the two countries involved.

D: *Russia and the United States? I was thinking it would be pretty hard to do a horoscope for the whole world.*
B: He says it can be done but it's very complicated. You would have to have his mirror to be able to do it.
D: *(Laugh) John, the astrologer, couldn't do that, but he could draw one up for Russia and the United States.*
B: He says for him to do a comparative horoscope between the two countries, using the date of inception of the present political systems. That is July 2, 1776, for the United States, and the appropriate date for Russia, close to the beginning of this century. He says it will be a fun thing for him to do, for he will enjoy doing it.

According to Nostradamus' instructions, John did a comparative analysis of the horoscope of the United States and Russia. The following is his own description of what he found:

The most widely used horoscope for the United States has Gemini on the Ascendant, the Moon in the sign of Aquarius, and the Sun in the sign of Cancer. Gemini rising shows that we are a people who enjoy novelty, fads, knowledge and communications. Mars in Gemini means we can show the world our dualism in many matters in an aggressive way. Venus in Cancer in the same quadrant indicates our love for motherhood, children, glamour and nostalgia. It also reveals our nourishing and protective nature toward the rest of the world. Jupiter, the Sun, and Mercury all take place in the sign of Cancer in the 2nd house of money and values. Our emphasis is on material wealth and the accumulation of possessions. With Jupiter in this house it makes it very easy for us to do this. Mercury, our intellect, is geared to scientific advances as long as it has a material reward as the outcome. Since we have the North Node in the sign of Leo in the 3rd house we should concentrate on our problems rather than embroiling ourselves in the affairs of other countries. This has led to our downfall (Vietnam) and could be our final disaster. Neptune and Saturn take place in the 5th house. Neptune in Virgo points to the tremendous advances we have made in medical care, food preservation, and electronic industries. Saturn in Libra influences our judicial system which is very lenient compared to other countries. These planets also show our obsession with all forms of sports and entertainment. Pluto in Capricorn in the 9th house forewarns us not to get entangled with other countries. It could lead to our destruction. The Moon in Aquarius in the 10th house influences our fickle popularizing of celebrities. We are an easily swayed nation and our media exploits this fact. Uranus in Gemini in the 12th house is our hidden talent, our genius for producing wonderful new inventions that have revolutionized the world. In comparison with Russia's horoscope, we are more adaptable and not as fixed in ideology.

The horoscope for the Soviet Union (November 7, 1917) has the Sun in the sign of Scorpio with the Moon in Leo, as well as a Leo Ascendant, all very fixed signs determined to make their own way. Saturn on the

Ascendant in Leo indicates that the birth of the Soviet state was difficult and full of tension. Saturn here shows a troublesome beginning followed by a maturity that eases up on tension. The Moon in Leo with Mars in Virgo in the 2nd house reveals that the people in power will hold onto the purse strings of the nation. As money pours in, it is spent, with Mars here maybe to keep up with the latest innovations. The Sun and Mercury are in Scorpio in the 4th house which points to the abundant wealth that this, the largest country, has hidden under its vast tundra. This great wealth could be the hope of the future for this nation. Venus and the North Node are in the 5th sector indicating that the entertainment of the people is very serious and conservative. The hope for this land is in its people's creativity and resourcefulness. With Uranus in Aquarius in the 7th house this foretells unusual and sometimes hostile relations with other countries. Jupiter in Gemini and Pluto in Cancer in the 11th house forewarn that relationships with other friendly countries could turn around to become a "stab in the back." Neptune in Leo in the 12th house shows that the leaders should not deny the strong spiritual nature of the people. Mysticism and spiritualism as well as inefficiency are shown by Neptune in its ruling position.

There are positive and negative aspects between the two charts of these world powers, but with cooperation and better understanding maybe we can build jointly a better tomorrow.

CENTURY I-21

Profonde argille blanche nourrit rochier,
Qui d'un abisme istra lactineuse:
En vain troublez ne l'oseront toucher,
Ignorans estre au fond terre argilleuse.

The rock holds in its depths white clay which will come out milk-white from a cleft. Needlessly troubled people will not dare touch it, unaware that the foundation of the earth is of clay.

B: He says that this refers to an event. Somewhere in western North America there will be some miners digging for ore. And this ore they find will be a different ore than that which they are looking for. They will be afraid that it is some sort of radioactive material brought in or introduced by a meteorite centuries ago. But he says there is no need for alarm because this material, although it will end up being a new element to put on the periodic table, will not be harmful for mankind and can be put to good use.

D: *Was it brought in by a meteorite?*

B: That is what he said.

D: *The translators wondered if this quatrain might be alchemistic.*

B: He says you could look at it that way. But since the general reading public would not understand his theories of alchemy, he says he will not give them to you at this time.

CENTURY X-49

Jardin du monde au pres du cité neufve,	Garden of the world near the New City, in the road of the hollow
Dans le chemin des montaignes cavees,	mountains. It will be seized and plunged in the tank, forced to drink
Sera saisi & plongé dans la Cuve,	water poisoned with sulphur.
Beuvant par force eaux soulfre envenimees.	

B: He says that by "garden of the world" he refers to the New World since so much food grows there and we have so much surplus that we could feed the whole world. He's showing me a picture of the United States. In the Rocky Mountains there has recently been or will be a city being built as part of a government project. It will be a complete city with all the services that are needed for the people who live there. This will be adjacent to extensive underground chambers blasted into the mountains for the storage of secret records and such. What will happen is that ... okay, the pictures he's showing me are of a nuclear reactor. Apparently there's going to be some sort of meltdown. He says that the water being pumped into the reactor to cool it will not be totally purified. There'll be a mistake made and an element in the water will react with the radioactive elements of the reactor and will cause an accident to take place. The poison part that he refers to in the quatrain is referring to radioactive poison rather than conventional poison.

D: *Does he call it a nuclear reactor?*

B: He doesn't call it anything. He doesn't have a word for it. But he's giving me a picture of what he sees. He shows it in layers. First he shows a picture of a stylized atom. Then he shows a picture of a clump of ore that glows at night. And then he shows a lot of apparatus around this clump of ore and the whole thing bathed in a blue light. It shows all of this submerged in a huge tank of water.

D: *Then this nuclear reactor is within this hollowed-out mountain, or did you say that was a city?*

B: He says the reactor is within the hollowed-out mountain but since the city is right there adjacent to it, it could be a danger to the inhabitants of the city. The city is there because of the reactor, with the technicians and such.

D: *So this is what he means by the New City. They have interpreted the New City as New York and the hollowed mountains would be the tall buildings in New York.*

B: He's chuckling at this point. Just because a place is called "new" like

New York doesn't make it new. He says that from what he has seen through his mirror, he is given to understand that by your time New York is quite an old city. He says that he has seen some visions concerning New York, and that there are going to be calamities befalling this city. But this particular quatrain does not refer to them.

I had never heard of any city of this type, which would not be unusual if it is indeed a secret government project. It has since been suggested that he might be referring to the NORAD facilities in the Rocky Mountains of Colorado. Then I discovered that in the book, *Bigger Secrets,* by William Poundstone, he mentions the secret city that will be used to house the top officials of the government in case of nuclear attack. It is located within the hollowed-out Mount Weather, 45 miles west of Washington, D.C. It is a true underground city consisting of office buildings, cafeterias, and hospitals. It is completely self-contained with its own waterworks, food storage, and power plant. It is presently staffed with hundreds of government and maintenance workers. There is even an underground spring-fed artificial lake. This all sounds too much like Nostradamus' description to be coincidence. I wonder if this could be the city that he envisioned? True, Brenda did mention the Rocky Mountains but there might be more than one of these secret underground government cities that we know nothing about.

CENTURY III-21

Au Crustamin par mer
  Hadriatique,
Apparoistra un horrible poisson
De face humaine & la fin
  aquatique,
Qui se prendra dehors
  de l'amacon.

Near the (river) Conca by the Adriatic sea will appear a horrible fish with human features and an aquatic purpose, it will be caught without the hook.

B: He says this refers to a scandal that will take place in regards to military secrets. On an experimental basis, the Soviets have built an underwater dome and an underwater submarine base in the Adriatic sea. He says they are using this underground place to send out their submarines for subversive purposes. When this is discovered, due to pressure from statesmen, diplomats and politicians, this will all be brought to the surface. And the submarines will be taken away from there without the use of the hook, so to speak. Because instead of taking the submarines away by destroying them with weapons, they'll take the submarines away through political maneuverings.

D: *"The horrible fish with human features," means the people involved?*

B: Yes. He says that refers to both the base and the fact that there are submarines involved. They have to have people to run both.

D: *Their translation really bothers me. They think he may be referring to a real creature, something similar to a mermaid or something of this sort.*

B: He has put his index fingers into his ears. And he's huffing and puffing and making his beard wave back and forth. He's saying, "I'm not going to listen to this! I didn't come here to listen to this!" (*Laugh*) He says if they think he is talking about a mermaid, then he will show them a genuine model of the *flat* earth. He says any man of education knows that the earth is round. So if they think he's definitely talking about a mermaid, then he's sure they'll be glad to receive from him a model of the flat earth, too, because they probably believe in that as well.

D: *Yes, that translation seems ridiculous to me too. They think it could have been a creature that looks like a mermaid. They said there are some aquatic creatures that resemble a mermaid to some degree. Something like a seal. (Actually they are referring to a manatee or a dugong. I didn't think he would know those words.) They think he means something along that line.*

B: He says he wouldn't have described them as being horrible then because natural creatures are a beauty to behold.

D: *(Laugh) He makes more sense than they do.*

B: He says, "Of course!"

D: *It's funny how the only explanations they can come up with are usually something literal like that.*

B: He says they just refuse to believe that he's actually seeing some of the things he sees, and they don't trust in the powers he's working with.

D: *They think he's tied into his own time.*

CENTURY I-22

Ce que vivra & n'ayant ancien sens,	A thing existing without any senses will cause its own end to happen
Viendra leser à mort son artifice:	through artifice. At Autun, Chalan,
Austun, Chalan, Langres & les deux Sens,	Langres and the two Sens there will be great damage from hail and ice.
La gresle & glace fera grand malefice.	

D: *The translators think that because he is a doctor he is speaking of something medical here.*

B: No. He says this is an event in the future. That mankind will have developed some devices to moderate the weather and be able to have some say as to how the weather will be. The machines that are in charge of these computations and calculations will become too clever for their own good, for they will not have common sense. Common sense is what is gained through the experience of living. Consequently, through the fault in their programming, which will not be spotted until too late, they will accidentally cause the weather to misfunction so as to cause a great deal of damage through unseasonal ice and hail. The men running this will not realize that if one tries to force the weather to do one thing for too long that the natural pattern will finally overcome the interference and perhaps cause some unseasonal weather in the process of trying to get things back in balance again. As a result, these computers, while trying to overcome the natural forces that are trying to get things back in balance, will blow a fuse, so to speak, and become damaged beyond use.

D: *What do these names mean?*

B: He was naming places that will suffer the worst damage from the unseasonal weather.

D: *This is one that the translators couldn't understand at all.*

B: He says he wrote it down fairly clearly because he knew the concepts involved were already obscure enough that no one in his time would be able to understand them.

D: *They were not thinking of machines at all. They thought because he's a doctor that this was referring to something medical, like a petrified embryo removed from a woman's womb. That would be a thing existing without any sense.*

B: He says this is true. That would be a thing without senses. However, he says that man's devices such as computers and such have no senses either. He just shrugged his shoulders and said, "Well, if people insist on being narrow that is their choice to make."

CENTURY II-2

La teste bleu fera la tete blanche	The blue leader will inflict upon the
Autant de mal que France a faict	white leader as much damage as
leur bien,	France has done them good. Death
Mort à l'anthene grand pendu	from the great antenna hanging
sus la branche,	from the branch, when the king will
Quand prins des siens le Roy	ask how many of his men have been
dira combien.	captured.

B: He says that this refers to events that will take place during the time of upheavals. There will be an accident, a great tragedy. It will start out as plans for a war game, plans for an "in case of" incident. Like "in case thus and such happens, this is the defensive measures we'll take." In this particular war game, the teams are labeled the white team and the blue team with a white leader and a blue leader, as in the manner of military strategy and planning. The various sides are labeled with colors so there'll be a generic situation. He keeps saying that Great Britain will be involved with this, and that the leaders will be running this war game in the computers. There will be a malfunctioning circuit in the computer that will misfire in such a way that it will cause the computer to think that it is a real life situation instead of a war game. Hence the computer will set off the defenses and the weapons involved, and will start dropping real bombs on the areas involved and cause a tragic international incident. He says that this particular incident will throw Europe into chaos, trying to figure out what happened and why.

D: *Will this involve U.S. troops as well as European troops?*

B: No. He says it will basically be European troops. The only U.S. troops that will be involved will be those stationed in that part of the world at the time. Extra U.S. troops will not be called in at that time. Because the action of what takes place is so senseless and so bizarre, it will be obvious that either a madman got loose with the weapons or that it was a freak accident. And there is no reason to call in extra troops for fighting purposes. He says that after the dust starts to settle, so to speak, some peace-keeping troops may be called in to help reestablish civil order.

D: *"Death from the great antenna hanging from the branch." I wanted to clarify that part.*

B: He says that has a multiple meaning. On the one hand it refers to a new type of weapon that will be developed. A type of radio wave that at certain frequencies and intensities can be lethal. It can cause intense pain in the nerve endings and destroy certain portions of the brain. He says at the same time it also refers to their orders being broadcast by radio from the computer. The "branch" refers to that part of the computer which misfunctions and it branches off in a different direction than it should have. He says the two countries mainly involved will be Great Britain and France. Great Britain will be aggressive toward France for no apparent reason, and France will be hurt very badly by this, physically as well as economically and politically. The relations between France and Great Britain will be very strained until it is figured out what went wrong.

CENTURY II-14

A Tours, Gien, gardé seront
yeux penetrans,
Descouvriront de loing la
grand seraine:
Elle & sa suitte au port
seront entrans.
Combat, poussez, puissance
souveraine.

At Tours and Gien watchful eyes will be guarded, they will spy far off the serene Highness. She and her suite will enter the harbor, combat joined, sovereign power.

B: He says this refers to an event that should take place in the near future, no later than 1991. It refers to an incident between the British Navy and a North African, Middle Eastern power. I believe he may be referring to Libya. He's showing me a map and he's concentrating on the portion that is labeled on your maps as Libya. Even though this map he shows me has no countries outlined, the portion of Africa that his gaze is centered upon is labeled "Libya" on 20th-century maps. He says the people in those ports in France, with their radar, will see a picture of the situation and see it develop and unfold. A flagship of the navy, one of the major ships of the line, is referred to as "she" since ships are referred to in the feminine. As she's the flagship of that particular fleet, she is the queen of that fleet of ships. He says this flagship will encounter some ships of a foreign power and that a confrontation will take place. This will be happening in the Northwestern part of the Mediterranean. It will be a minor confrontation so far as fighting is concerned because no one will be killed. It will be mainly shells and torpedoes lobbing back and forth, but it will be blown into an international incident by the press and the diplomatic world. In this particular incident Britain will come out as the leader of the situation, the winner, so to speak.

This seems very possible since trouble with naval ships in the Persian Gulf began in 1988.

UPDATE: It has been suggested that this quatrain referred to the British involvement in the Persian Gulf War in 1990 and 1991. Brenda thought he was referring to Libya, but she was guessing because Nostradamus showed her a map with no countries outlined. It could also refer to a future incident involving Libya caused by increasing tension in the Middle East.

Chapter 13

The Time of Upheavals

ΝOSTRADAMUS FORESAW a time of dramatic and violent earth changes which he called "the time of upheavals." Some of these were difficult to date because he also foresaw an even more terrible time in the far future when the changes in the earth would be very drastic. At times I could not differentiate which time period he was speaking of. I have tried to categorize them to the best of my ability.

CENTURY VIII-29

Au quart pillier l'on sacre à
Saturne.
Par tremblant terre & deluge
fendu
Soubz l'edifice Saturnin trouvee
urne,
D'or Capion ravi & puis rendu.

At the fourth pillar which they dedicate to Saturn split by earthquake and by flood; under Saturn's building an urn is found gold carried off by Cæpio and then restored.

B: He says this quatrain refers to two different events. He has not made it clear if these two events are related or not. The four pillars represent four major nations. Each nation in its own right is a pillar of the culture that these nations share in general. One of these nations, the one that comes under the auspices of Saturn, will have some great natural disasters, as mentioned in the quatrain, earthquakes and flooding. It will rend the nation from end to end, and there will be great crying out. Also there will be the breakdown of general services that will cause much conflict and pain. The great urn filled with gold taken away and then restored, he says that line has a double meaning. The one meaning is the nation that is rent apart by the earthquake and flooding. It's a rich nation but these natural disasters will empty its coffers in the process of its trying to deal with these natural disasters. After it has exhausted its own resources it will turn to other nations for help. And the other three pillars will send aid to restore the coffers so that the people may survive.

UPDATE: This has certainly started to come to pass. The end of the 1980s and the beginning of 1990s have seen a rash of terrible devastating earthquakes all over the world, as well as the awakening of long-sleeping volcanoes. These have certainly "emptied the coffers of these nations." Nostradamus said it would not take a war to deplete the economy; it could be done very easily by these natural disasters.

B: Another meaning for this last line refers to the gold plundered from Central America by certain European countries during the colonization age. Some of it was taken to Europe and some of it went to the bottom of the sea. He is saying that in the future as technology advances there will be greater successes in finding these treasures that have gone to the bottom of the sea. These treasures and artifacts will be restored to the countries they were stolen from.

D: *Are you talking about the time of Cortez and the Conquistadores?*

B: Yes. He was specifically speaking of Spain and its rape and stripping of Central America and South America of their gold and silver treasures.

There is an amazing parallel between this definition and the symbolism used in the quatrain. "Gold carried off by Cæpio and then restored." According to Ms. Cheetham, Cæpio was a Roman consul who plundered Toulouse in 106 B.C.E. However, the treasure never reached Rome and Cæpio was impeached and expelled from the Senate. It becomes obvious that Nostradamus has once again used symbology based on an event in Roman history. He has explained that he often did this to confuse the Inquisition.

D: *Then it does have a double meaning. Would he be able to tell me which four countries are represented by the four pillars?*

B: He is saying that it is difficult to say because between the present and the time that the happening will occur, some of the countries will have changed their names, even though the nationality will stay the same. But he will say that the four pillars have to do with western culture.

CENTURY IX-31

Le tremblement de terre à Montara,	The trembling of the earth at Mortara the tin island of St. George
Cassich saint George à demi perfondrez,	half sunk; drowsy with peace, war will arise, at Easter in the temple
Paix assoupie, la guerre esveillera,	abysses opened.
Dans temple à Pasques abismes enfondrez.	

B: He says that the earth, after a period of peace, as indicated in the line "drowsy with peace," will suffer a great natural disaster. The earth will have some particularly severe earthquakes. So severe that the crust will rip open all the way through the mantle and the hot lava will spew forth. That particular earthquake will be so disastrous that it will set off earthquakes all over wherever earthquakes happen. These earthquakes will be so large and dangerous they will be destroying things right and left. He says half of the English Isle will be ripped away and buried into the sea. As a result of all this disaster, famine will set in almost right away and people will start fighting. The war will be fought over the few resources of earth that will be left after this disaster. There won't be enough food to go around, and people, from countries who are starving, will be marching upon the people of countries who have surplus food. He says that the country you live in will be fortunate in that it is protected by oceans. But even at that, the country will just barely survive because it will be one of the hardest hit by the earthquakes. Since it has a surplus of food it will not be hit by the famine. It will just be a problem of distribution. Other countries, such as India and China, will also be ripped up with earthquakes but they have too many people and not enough food. And they will turn and march on Russia and eastern Europe where the corn and wheat fields lie.

D: *Are those words (Mortara and Cassich) names or anagrams of countries?*

B: He says they are anagrams for something that he found most puzzling at the time. But from associating with a 20th-century person, he is beginning to understand. He says that there seemed to be places on the earth that had names attached to them but he could not discern it as being a country or what-have-you. And now he finds that, through the workings of scientists after his time, there are places on the earth that have names to identify them, not because they're countries, but because they're a geological feature. The San Andreas (*pronounced strangely*) Fault, for example, has a name of its own but it's not a country. He said these names are anagrams referring to the major fault lines that will be crucial in this event.

D: *They have identified St. George as referring to England.*

B: Yes, that is a clear reference since it was a natural disaster not a man-made disaster. He just wanted to disguise it enough to get past the Inquisition, but not to make it too puzzling to future generations.

D: *"At Easter in the temple the abysses opened." Does that tell when it's going to happen?*

B: He says that it is an allegory. Due to this great disaster where communications and such break down and people are marching on other countries to fight and such as that, the abysses that open at Easter at the temples refers to the fact that, since the priests are not able to come up with a comforting explanation for these things for the people; they will lose credit with the people and the abysses will open up in the foundation of religion. He says Christianity will falter on the shards of its own foundation.

CENTURY IV-67

L'an que Saturne & Mars esgaux combuste, *L'air fort seiché longue trajection:* *Par feux secrets, d'ardeur grand lieu adust* *Peu pluie, vent chault, guerres, incursions.*	In the year that Saturn and Mars are equally fiery, the air is very dry, a long meteor. From hidden fires a great place burns with heat, little rain, a hot wind, wars and raids.

B: He says that he personally refers to this as the *dry* quatrain. (*She laughed.*) I think he's trying to be humorous. He says that in this year he's speaking of ... he will give you the circumstances of it and perhaps John can find the year involved. He says it's in the not-too-distant future. When Saturn is in a fire sign and at the time the sun moves into a fire sign, there will be a comet. This will be a very bright, easily-seen comet. But it will be perhaps previously unknown. This coincides with the time of great geological troubles. There will be earthquakes and volcanoes erupting, and this will mess up the weather systems so there will be great famine and drought. He says this will cause social upheaval in unexpected places. Nations that are considered prosperous and powerful, particularly western nations, will be revealed as being not as prosperous as everyone had thought. And they will be torn with civil strife and rioting as people try to move out of the areas of drought toward areas that still have some water and where they can grow food. He says this has been alluded to before, and this will be a very traumatic time. This will cause upheaval in various parts of the world because this will be a widespread condition. The social upheaval caused by this will assist the Anti-Christ in gaining power in certain areas of the world. It will be one of the contributing factors of things being weakened and ready for the takeover by the Anti-Christ.

J: (He had been looking up these signs.) *Mars and Saturn will be conjunctioning in Sagittarius very shortly, sometime in ... February of 1988.*

D: *Why, that's just a few years away from now!*

B: He says that from what he can see, that appears to be very close to the time that he is seeing. It will be a very fiery time, very dry and very hot and fiery astrologically. And he says that the common every-day people will feel mentally and spiritually battered because of all of these cosmological disasters coming one right after the other from all directions, beating them down.

This sounded very similar to the "Rainbow Quatrain" (CENTURY I-17) which is covered in Chapter 25, "The Far Future," pp. 307. Nostradamus indicated that one of the signs that the Anti-Christ was coming would be a whole year without a rainbow. This sounded symbolic rather than actual. Nostradamus said there would be droughts with little rain until this dramatic year without a rainbow, indicating extreme dryness. That year would be the sign that the Anti-Christ had come and the predictions concerning him would start to come to pass. These two quatrains are connected in this symbolic way.

J: *Mars and Saturn conjuncting in Sagittarius would also show us some type of religious-type of strife or some type of religious fervor or fanaticism that could be very harmful to others. Does this quatrain refer to that as well?*

B: Yes, he says that it's one of the social upheavals that will contribute to laying the way open for the Anti-Christ to take over. Certain countries, their social and political structure will be turned totally upside down. And religious fanatics—he says he's not referring to spiritual people but to religious fanatics. He's making the distinction: poles apart, this is very definite and clear. He says religious fanatics will come into power and believe that they are doing what should be done. There have been other groups come into power believing they were doing what should be done, even if it takes drastic means, and they've always come to a bad end. He says this religious fervor also affects the Anti-Christ's side of things, too. It helps him to come into power for he has a very guileful tongue. And the people whom he influences will venerate him as a religious figure, as well.

D: *It's interesting that he calls this his dry quatrain.*

B: He says that the world will be very thirsty. They'll be thirsty for water and they'll be thirsty for comfort—spiritual comfort. Because the religious fanatics will offer no spiritual comfort, only power plays.

The date, February 1988, came while this book was at the publishers, and we were able to see yet another of Nostradamus' quatrains come to pass. I do not believe he meant that all of the portions of his explanation would come to pass in that month, or even in that year. I think he gave the astrological signs in order to date the beginning of his vision. The winter of 1987 and 1988 was declared to be one of the strangest in 100 years. The summer of 1988 was said to be the driest in 50 years. We were in the midst of a terrible drought that equalled, if not surpassed, the drought of the Depression era. For the first time in shipping history barges could not navigate the Mississippi, but became stranded as the river receded to the lowest levels in record. In the Arkansas River 100-year-old shipwrecks were exposed to the light of day and archaeologists were able to examine them. Was all this coincidence? Or is it the beginning of the times leading to the year without a rainbow?

Also no one can dispute that the year 1988 was filled with religious turmoil and upheaval, brought on by the Bakker and Swaggart scandals. A general feeling of mistrust was spreading through the church community.

CENTURY III-3

Mars and Mercure & l'argent joint ensemble, *Vers le midi extreme siccité:* *Au fond d'Asie on dira terre tremble,* *Corinthe, Ephese lors en perplexité.*	**Mars, Mercury and the Moon in conjunction towards the south there will be a great drought. An earthquake will be reported from the depths of Asia, both Corinth and Ephesus then in a troubled state.**

B: He says that those events refer to what you would consider the present state of the world. If you want a date on that, look up that particular joining of planets.

John wanted to know what sign the conjunction would be in.

B: One moment please. (*Pause*) He's giving me two signs. He's saying Cancer and Leo. (*John was busy looking through his Ephemeris.*) He's complaining about my subconscious. He is shaking his head in perplexity. (*Laugh*) It could be two different dates involved, but he says these events will be taking place within the very near future.

D: *The quatrain says, "toward the south there will be a great drought" during that time.*

B: He says that this refers to the drought in Africa.

D: *"An earthquake will be reported from the depths of Asia."*

B: Yes. He says the major earthquake's from China, killing many people.

D: *"Corinth and Ephesus then in a troubled state."*

B: (*He corrected my pronunciation.*) He says this refers to the fact that there are always troubles going on in the eastern Mediterranean, in that part of the world. It will be very vulnerable for the Anti-Christ to flex his muscles in that direction.

These cities do refer to the eastern end of the Mediterranean. Corinth is in Greece and Ephesus is part of modern-day Turkey; its ruins are located near Izmir. In the following chapters the Anti-Christ is repeatedly associated with these two countries.

J: (*Excitedly.*) *I've got the date now, July 13, 1991 in Leo.*

B: He says that is only five years away from your time. And from his point of view that appears to be almost simultaneous.

D: *It sounds like the Anti-Christ will be coming into power when all these earth changes are also happening.*

B: He says, yes, it will be a very traumatic time all around.

UPDATE: As the 1990s began there were many reports of increased violent earthquake activity throughout Asia. Terms such as "the strongest, the worst," were common descriptions. In the summer of 1991 there were terrible floods which triggered massive mudslides in China that killed thousands and caused millions of people to be homeless. I would certainly classify mudslides in the same category as earthquakes because the earth did literally move.

Later when the astrologer had time to thoroughly study these planetary placements, he said this combination would occur on other dates through the 90s. The only other one in Leo would be August 21, 1998. It might be helpful to list the other possibilities because Brenda had such trouble with astrological information, and Nostradamus seemed to be giving her more than one date. For the astrologically curious: January 3, 1992, October 16, 1993, January 11, 1994, April 8, 1994, December 22, 1995, May 16, 1996, June 12, 1996, December 3, 1997, February 27, 1998, and March 28, 1998 are also possibilities according to the signs given in this quatrain. The astrologer personally thought December 22, 1995 would be the best choice because it had the closest degrees of conjunction. That date would also fit more closely with the fruition of the "time of troubles."

CENTURY III-12

Par la tumeur de Heb, Po, Tag, *Timbre & Rome* *Et par l'estang leman & Arentin* *Les deux grands chefs & citez* *de Garonne,* *Prins mors noyez. Partir* *humain butin.*	Because of the overflow of the Ebro, Po, Tagus, Tiber and Rhône and by the lakes of Geneva and Arezzo the two great and chief cities of the Garonne taken, dead, drowned. Human booty divided.

B: He says that this refers to the earth changes that will be taking place, that the Anti-Christ will be taking advantage of in the process of his world conquest. In central Europe, southern Europe and in the Near East, particularly around the eastern end of the Mediterranean, there'll be several severe floods. As a result of the disruption of local governments and such due to the natural disasters, the Anti-Christ will move his troops in under the disguise of helping the people restore civil order in the wake of these disasters. He will use that as a device to take over the countries, and use population like slaves and such as this. That's why they are referred to as human booty. He says this will also be a time of economic problems, and this will be one of the things contributing to the time of troubles. With things being in great unrest, with things not working right and failing all over, this will contribute to the ease with which the Anti-Christ comes to power. He says it will be a time when dynamic young men with golden tongues can sway the populace to their way of thinking because the populace is wanting something to hope for.

D: *It sounds like everything is going to be coming unglued at that time.*

B: He says it will be a very traumatic time. The souls that are on the earth at this time were aware of these consequences before coming into this life. This is why there are more old souls in proportion to young

souls living today than any other time in history. People will need
steadiness of purpose to make it through these times.

D: *I have some questions I would like to ask him. I want to clarify some
of the quatrains we've already gone over.*

B: He says that is the purpose of this, to clarify.

D: *Most of these deal with the predictions about earthquakes. I'd just like
to know if these are going to happen before the Anti-Christ or during
the time of the Anti-Christ.*

B: He says the earth changes refer to the earthquakes and the volcanoes,
the changes in the level of the oceans and the differing amounts of
glaciers and such. This will be taking place in the late 1980s, early
1990s. He says these events are separate. They are acts of God, they
are not related to the Anti-Christ. But the Anti-Christ will turn them
to his advantage because several countries will be disorganized due to
the severity of the natural disasters. It will make it easier for the Anti-
Christ to get spies in and people to work from within, to help him to
overthrow that country later on. At the time these events are happening, the Anti-Christ will already have begun the building of his
base of power in his area of the world. But these natural disasters will
be taking place all over the world, and in several cases they will help
the Anti-Christ lay the groundwork for taking over certain countries
later on in his career, like in the mid- and late-1990s.

As this was being published a disastrous earthquake struck Armenia
in December 1988. The amount of people killed and the damage created
was incomprehensible. Entire cities were wiped out. The estimate of the
death toll was 55,000 people killed, and survivors were dying from the
terrible cold. Countries all over the world were sending supplies, and for
the first time the Soviets were accepting the help offered. Is this the
beginning of the fulfillment of Nostradamus' terrible prophecies concerning natural disasters?

D: *In the beginning of our work we had quatrains that pertained to the
earthquakes that were going to hit the United States. He told us this
through Dyonisus. There was something about a triangle. There
would be three cities on the West Coast that formed a triangle and they
would be hit by earthquakes. Can you give us any information on that?*

B: He says, as you could very easily ascertain, two of the points of the
triangle are in the place called "California." The third one—he says
that he's very unfamiliar with trying to put place names for that part
of the world since it is the New World—but you will be able to do it
yourself. He says find a place not too far to the east that has also been
prone to earthquakes in the past.

D: *Okay. That's what he said before, that they formed a triangle. He also
mentioned there would be earthquakes in New York City too.*

B: He says that will be part of the more drastic earth changes that will be taking place later.

D: *Will the ones in California happen first?*

B: Yes. They will be closer to the more natural order of things because that place is prone to earthquakes as it is. So the places that are prone to earthquakes or are in areas that have earthquakes sporadically but very violently, will have them first. And then the places that should not have earthquakes will have them also.

D: *There has been a lot of theory that the axis is going to tilt around the same time. Does he see anything about that?*

B: He says it's hard to say. A lot of things are very clouded at this time, but he would not be surprised if it were to happen. This shift of the axis is not a gradual thing like some would say. He says it happens suddenly. And when it happens it could be very catastrophic.

D: *But he thinks these events with the Anti-Christ are so predominant on the time lines that they will happen anyway, regardless of the earth changes or a shift?*

B: This is true. He says that in the part of the earth the Anti-Christ is in, there will be less damage sustained than in other parts of the earth. These changes will affect his land but they won't devastate it like some lands will be. So he'll be able to turn this to his advantage. At a little later time when other countries are still trying to recover, he offers assistance. And once they accept assistance, it is too late for them, for he will eventually end up stabbing them in the back.

D: *That's what I thought. If the countries were all being ravaged by earthquakes and such, his would also be. And he wouldn't be able to think about conquering.*

B: His will have its problems too, but it will be in a state of strong martial law so they will already be organized and can pull together, whereas other countries will be under civilian law at the time of the earthquakes. After the disaster strikes, martial law is declared to bring order to the streets and stop the looting.

I believe these statements do not really contradict anything that Dyonisus told me through Elena. I think it merely shows he did not fully understand what he was seeing, and he may have gotten the time sequences mixed up between these first events and the more radical earth changes that Nostradamus saw in the far future (which are reported in Chapter 25).

I think that hearing so many terrible predictions of one horrible event after another would have really upset me if I had not already come to terms with this that night after I left Elena's house. When Nostradamus first began to tell me of these awesome visions that seemingly fill our future, the human side of me was naturally repulsed. But now that I have accepted my role in something that I have no power to change, I can act as an objective reporter, distasteful though the task may be.

Chapter 14

The Coming of the Anti-Christ

THROUGHOUT THE SESSIONS there were little bits and pieces revealed about this personality known as the Anti-Christ. He seemed to be a secretive figure shadowy even to Nostradamus himself. I have tried to include in this chapter what details we could find out about him, in order to try to understand this person who is destined to loom very large on the future of mankind.

D: *When the translators refer to the Anti-Christ that we've been talking so much about, they say that Nostradamus called him the* third *Anti-Christ. Is that correct?*

B: He says that it depends upon your point of view whether he would be the second or the third Anti-Christ. From a European point-of-view he would be considered the *third* Anti-Christ. From the other viewpoint there would only be two Anti-Christs rather than three.

D: *Whose viewpoint would that be?*

B: He says anybody non-European. Asiatics, Third World countries, the Americas.

D: *I thought maybe he said something in his quatrains that made them assume that there would be three.*

B: He says there are quatrains that are referring to the third Anti Christ. He says he doesn't specifically enumerate them, but there have been quatrains that have come to pass and people have realized that the quatrain applied to a particular event, and they were able to interpret that he was speaking of three different men when he is speaking of the Anti-Christ.

D: *By his definitions, who were the other Anti-Christs?*

B: He says Napoleon was one, but that's strictly from a European viewpoint. Because Napoleon mainly affected Europe and that was it, although it was devastating enough. And so only the Europeans would consider Napoleon an Anti-Christ. But the other Anti-Christ, regardless of your viewpoint, is very clear. He says that would be Adolf Hitler. What Hitler did and what the coming Anti-Christ will do will affect the whole world and not just Europe.

D: *And he considers the Anti-Christ that's coming, to be the third.*

B: Yes, and he says he's even worse than Adolf Hitler was.

D: *Is there any information we would be allowed to have about the Anti-Christ?*

B: How do you mean? What sort of information?

D: *Identifying perhaps where he would be located at this present time in our world, and perhaps his age.*

B: He says that it's hard for him to spot the location because of the turmoil of the time lines at this point in time. Since we are nearing close to the events to happen it causes an effect somewhat like a thunderstorm in the time lines. He knows that the Anti-Christ is in the Middle East somewhere. He can't spot him exactly because of all the violence and the negative events in that part of the world which cloud his vision somewhat. He says this Anti-Christ at the present time is a young man at a very crucial time in his life. Any strong impressions he gets at this time will have an effect on his future lifepath. And where he is at this time in the Middle East, there is a lot of political maneuvering, violence, and corruption. Due to the atmosphere during this crucial time of his life it's having an effect on him, and he is coming to realize what his life's destiny is to be.

D: *But you said he was such a major figure it would be pretty hard to prevent him from coming to power.*

B: This is true. The events leading up to his coming to power were set into motion centuries ago, as far back as the first conception and inception of the Ottoman Empire.

CENTURY I-76

D'un nom farouche tel proferé sera,	This man will be called by a barbaric name that three sisters will receive
Que les trois soeurs auront fato le nom:	from destiny. He will speak then to a great people in words and deeds,
Puis grand peuple par langue & faict dira	more than any other man will have fame and renown.
Plus que nul autre bruit & renom.	

B: He says this refers to the Anti-Christ. The three sisters refer to the three Fates: the one who spins out the line of life, the other who measures the length of the life, and the third who cuts it off at the proper length. He says this man is destined to become a world leader even though he will be misusing this power. His name, in the manner of some countries, will be somewhat lengthy. And some of the names he bears, if you look up their root meanings, will give some clue as to what he is destined to be. He says various names mean various things: for example, names like Leonard and Leo refer to lion-like qualities, regal qualities, and such as this. This man's name, even though it will sound somewhat barbaric to European ears, will also have root meanings to the names that will give some hints as to what he will be capable of accomplishing. Whether he chose to turn good or bad, he'd be able to accomplish a lot either way. It's just simply whether he chose to go in a positive or a negative direction.

D: *Then at the time when we begin to hear of these people, we should look up their entire names and see if we can find some clues there?*

B: Definitely.—He says this man will be influenced by certain old customs that have been somewhat forgotten. They're still known of in literature but they're not followed anymore. But he can't get any more specific than that.

D: *The translators say this quatrain refers to Napoleon. They said that his name was derived from a Greek word which means "destroyer" or "terminator."*

B: He says that illustrates what he's meaning about the Anti-Christ.

CENTURY I-50

De l'aquatique triplicité naistra.	From the three water signs will be
D'un qui fera le jeudi pour su	born a man who will celebrate
feste:	Thursday as his holiday. His
Son bruit, loz, regne, sa puissance	renown, praise, rule and power will
croistra,	grow on land and sea, bringing
Par terre & mer aux Oriens	trouble to the East.
tempeste.	

D: *"From the three water signs," does that mean those will be the signs in his horoscope?*

B: He says that has a multiple meaning. Those signs will be predominant in his horoscope but he also was using that to indicate what location of the world the Anti-Christ would come from. For there'll be three major bodies of water somewhat nearby—mainly the Mediterranean Sea, the Red Sea, and the Arabian Sea.

D: *I can see now that he tries to put as much as he can into these quatrains. He condenses a great deal into just a few lines. It must be very difficult for him to do that.*

B: He says you get a knack for it after a while. The Inquisition does wondrous things for causing you to develop knacks for things.—This quatrain refers to this man and how he will be successful in gaining immense amounts of world-wide power. He says that, as he has indicated in his quatrains, Thursday will be an important day to him and his followers. He will be a threat to all, but particularly to the East because he will be successful in conquering both China and Russia, and will have the entire Asian continent under his control. He says this will be the first and only time that the entire continent has ever been under one leader.

I took this quatrain to John, the astrologer, and asked if he could get any information from it. He thought the three water signs might refer to a grand trine. He said this would have considerable influence if they were located in a horoscope. Upon searching through his ephemeris he was able to find out that a grand trine of water signs will occur on July 1, 1994. John feels this may be the date of the Anti-Christ's coming to full power.

D: *We've been speaking a lot about the coming Anti-Christ, and trying to piece together his story. It has been asked, does the Anti-Christ have any connection with the city of Damascus?*

B: One moment please. He says he must gaze into the mists of time to tell you. (*Pause*) He says he has been to Damascus, but he's not from there originally. He is from another place. He will keep his origins obscure for security reasons. He will use it as a part of his mystique. But he will have connections with Libya and with Syria. He will use many channels to come to power. Whatever channels are available for him to use, he will take advantage of. And if there are any channels to be used in Damascus, you can be sure that he will be using them.

D: *But that eliminates one possibility of where he's located now at this time in his life.*

B: He has spent his entire life in the cultural area known as the Middle East. He has had some exposure to various political systems, and one political system which has particularly influenced him is that of Libya. It fits in with his studies about Adolf Hitler. He is very dictatorian in his outlook. (*Pause*) At the present time he is in Egypt.

This was an unexpected surprise because earlier he said he couldn't see where he was.

D: *Living in Egypt right now?*

B: Yes. This period of his life is spent in Egypt learning because Egypt is in a good location so far as the Arab world is concerned. He has equal access to both the Middle East and North Africa from Egypt, as well as the culture that is available in Egypt. Egypt is also strong enough to protect itself from the other countries, so it is not apt to be run over by armies.

D: *Then he's not a native of Egypt, he's just studying there. I suppose when the time comes for him to begin coming to power, that he will return to his own country. I'm just guessing.*

B: No. When it comes time for him to come to power he will go to the place where he sees chinks in the armor. He will go to a place where he can take advantage of the political system in such a way as to start gathering power unto himself. He will not worry whether or not he is a native of the country. He will find ways to take over countries and take advantage of the loopholes in their system, and twist their power to his own means.

D: *I figured it would be hard for an ordinary person to do this. He would have to already be in a position of some kind of power—through his family or something.*

B: He will be able to contrive positions.

D: *Will the Anti-Christ be taking over for a family member who dies and then puts him in power?*

B: He says the Anti-Christ will have several paths to choose from for coming into power. That path would be the easiest way for him to come into power, and the possibilities are strongest that he uses this method. Where he is, the key is that it will be socially acceptable to come into power in this manner, to take the place of a dead family member.

D: *A line of succession?*

B: Not necessarily a line of succession. He says quit jumping to conclusions. This is a military dictatorship. It could be a case of power with the nephew being within the military organization and the uncle dying. And the nephew through a very aggressive and audacious move taking over the uncle's holdings and powers and cowing everybody under him.

D: *Then it doesn't necessarily have to be a son.*

B: Whatever path opens up to him first. If it's through his father, so be it. If it's through his uncle, so be it. Or if it's by some other means. He says the young man is obsessed with power and the attainment of it.

D: *Well, we've gained a few more little pieces. We're trying to understand his personality.*

B: It's difficult to do. He is a complex person.

CENTURY II-3

Pour la chaleur solaire sus la mer
De Negrepont les poissons demi
cuits:
Les habitans les viendront
entamer,
Quand Rhod, & Gannes leur
faudra le biscuit.

Because of heat like that of the sun upon the sea, the fish around Negrepont will become half cooked. The local people will eat them when in Rhodes and Genoa there is a lack of food.

B: He says that in future times there will be most terrible and wondrous weapons. And one type of these weapons is like bringing a piece of the sun down to the earth, in its intensity and power. Whenever one of these weapons are set off, the destruction spreads for miles around. He says that this quatrain refers to the fact of the continuing unrest in the Middle East. As a result of this unrest it will escalate into yet another one of the wars that take place there. One of the leaders will be able to get hold of … the modern term for it is an atomic weapon. First he shows a long gray cylinder and then he shows me a picture of a mushroom cloud.

D: *Then there's little doubt of what he's referring to.*

B: Right. That's why I did not hesitate to call it an atomic weapon. He says there is a leader in that part of the earth that will be crazed, and will go to great lengths for the smallest thing. And this leader will not hesitate to use such terrible weapons because he will use terrible methods in war. So the people he is warring against retaliate with an atomic weapon. The country is right there; it has a coast on the Mediterranean. And when this country is bombed, one of the bombs will land in the Mediterranean instead of on the land. When it goes off, it will poison almost all the fish in the Mediterranean, and kill a lot of them from the heat. Due to this war the regular passages of trade will be disrupted, so that the people on the other coast of the Mediterranean will be desperate enough for food they'll eat the fish anyway, even though they know they should not.

D: *What does he mean by "Negrepont"?*

B: He says that it refers to a characteristic place there on the Mediterranean. He has the strong idea that this place, Negrepont, is at the eastern end of the Mediterranean. There is a place there on the coast where there are some cliffs that are of a dark color. So the local people have a particular name for the cliffs: The Dark Point—"Negrepont."

D: *That's interesting because I thought Negre usually means black or dark in Latin.*

B: He says it's the word for dark or black in many languages, most of them related to Latin somehow.—I'm going to take the liberty of asking him a question. Just something out of curiosity on my own part. And depending on his answer ... if he answers "no," I'll feel foolish and I won't want you to know the question.

D: *Oh, no; don't feel foolish. No knowledge is ever foolish. You can tell me what you asked him.*

Later when Brenda awakened, I told her about this incident and she thought it was interesting that her subconscious was also curious.

B: When he was saying the leader would go to great lengths to do anything, it reminded this one of a leader in your time who is known to do the same thing, who is in that part of the world. I was asking him if it was the same person. And he was saying that, no, it wasn't but it was someone very much like this person.

D: *What person were you thinking of?*

B: The leader of Libya. Kadaffi. He said he doesn't think it is him; the time element is off a little bit. But he says it is someone very much like him, perhaps someone related to him.

D: *That was a good question because many people think this leader, Kadaffi, is crazy.*

B: Michel de Notredame says that he is indeed crazy. (*Laugh*) He is saying he has syphilis of the brain.

D: *The world leaders are finding out that he is very difficult to communicate with and to work anything out with.*

B: He says that Kadaffi might be part of the original cause of the conflict, but when this point is reached, it will be many years later. He says Kadaffi will be part of the root cause. His present actions, the things he is doing, are leading toward this conflict. But as the years progress he will become increasingly more crazy to where when the major conflict is reached he will no longer be capable of handling anything or functioning. He will still think he's in power but his "yes-men" around him will actually be shielding him from the rest of the world. The way they will be treating him will be a diplomatic way of having him in a padded cell, so to speak.

D: *They won't let him make decisions by that time?*

B: Oh, he'll think he is making decisions; they just simply won't carry them out. And so the conflict will pass from their hands into other hands.

D: *Many people have thought that Kadaffi is the third Anti-Christ that Nostradamus spoke of.*

B: He says that Kadaffi is a posturing fool. Had he played his cards right he could have been the third Anti-Christ in order to reach the power he wanted, but he's always sabotaging himself. There will be someone else from the same culture, from the same part of the world who will learn the lessons that Kadaffi did not.

D: *There is another leader from that part of the world who is also feared at this time, the Ayatollah Khomeni.*

B: He says once again the Ayatollah Khomeni will be contributing to the beginning of this problem, the way that Kadaffi will. The Ayatollah has the capability of carrying it through, but his problem is his great years. He says the conflict will be carried on to the finish by younger hands.

D: *That makes sense. I thought I would ask because those are two leaders in that part of the world that are creating a great deal of trouble at this time. But this will occur after their time.*

B: Yes, one will be dead and the other will have passed from power.

(The Ayatollah Khomeni died in 1989.)

D: *The quatrain which follows this one has been interpreted as referring to the same thing. They think they go together.*

CENTURY II-4

Depuis Monach jusque aupres de Sicile	From Monaco as far as Sicily all the coast will remain deserted. There
Toute la plage demourra desolée:	will be no suburbs, cities nor towns
Il n'y aura fauxbourg, cité ne ville,	which have not been pillaged and robbed by barbarians.
Que par Barbares pillé soit & volée.	

B: He says it's the same part of the world, or rather he's saying it also has to do with the Mediterranean. It's not the same event exactly. He says that the first event, the atomic weapon being dropped by one of the Middle Eastern countries, will spark off yet another war on top of that war and they will be fighting back and forth. Other countries, particularly European and Western nations, will feel they need to interfere to try to stop the war because of the supplies of fuel. So when the European countries try to interfere, the same crazed leader that dropped an atomic weapon before, will use up the rest of his arsenal on Europe. Most of it will be striking southern Europe since that is the closest part of Europe. As a result, the European Mediterranean coast, particularly that of France and Italy, will be almost uninhabitable, and Italy will get the brunt of it. He says the barbarians are the people under this crazed leader. This leader is not the Anti-Christ. What purpose this leader serves, since this leader is crazed and he uses his weapons injudiciously and gets the world involved with the war, is that he weakens the major nations to where the third Anti-Christ will be able to rise to power with little or no opposition. He sets the stage for the third Anti-Christ. He will rise to power in that part of the world, but no one will really know where he is from. He will be a mysterious figure and no one will know much about him. All they will know is that he wields great power and that no one can argue against him.

D: *It seems like there are lots of quatrains about the Middle East.*

B: He says the Middle East is a place of strife. It seems to be their karma or something.

CENTURY III-60

Par toute Asie grande proscription, *Mesme en Mysie, Lysie &* *Pamphylie:* *Sang versera par absolution,* *D'un jeune noir rempli de* *felonnie.*	Throughout Asia there will be great proscription, also in Mysia, Lycia and Pamphilia. Blood will flow because of the absolution of a young dark man, filled with evil doing.

D: *Pardon my pronunciation; I do the best I can.*

B: He realizes that the educational standards in your time are not as high as they should be; hence people are not familiar with the classics. He says those names that you have had trouble pronouncing were from the classics. Had you studied the classics, you would know how to pronounce them. Therefore he knows that you have not been blessed with high educational standards.

D: *It's not my fault. It's just that they don't teach them in our time. They don't emphasize them—let's put it that way.* (Laugh) *That's why it takes so much to try to understand these prophecies. He must be very knowledgeable.*

B: He says it's not a matter of being knowledgeable. It's just a matter of what you know. The body of knowledge he has encompasses different knowledge from the body of knowledge that you have.

That was certainly correct, because these were only strange sounding names to me.

D: At least he knows what I'm talking about.

B: Fairly. (*Laugh*) He says those names are the equivalent of what those areas of the country were called during the time of the Greek civilization. He was using the classical references so that the Inquisition thought he was merely making a comment on history. He says a leader will arise in that area of the world which you refer to as the Third World countries. This leader's main goal in life will be to unite the Third World countries of the *whole* world, but particularly those of the *old* world, into a force to be reckoned with, in order to battle with the so-called "super"powers. The area of conflict will be the gray area between that which is considered eastern Europe and that which is considered to be the Middle East, particularly around the Adriatic and Caspian Seas and the eastern Mediterranean. He says it will be a fruitless conflict. There will not be any definite outcome from it. There will not be a winner or a loser, just a bunch of strife all around. He says this series of events that take place there will have some relation to some of the prophecies in the Bible.

D: Which Biblical prophecies is he referring to?

B: He says some of the ones in Revelation will apply but not all, as well as some from the minor prophets of the Old Testament and some of Isaiah. What people don't realize is that when St. John was writing Revelation he was of the same breed as Michel de Notredame, in that he did not write of one continuous series of events or one large happening. He wrote of several different things that will be happening in the future, independent from each other. From his perspective, it may have been difficult or he may have been unwilling to differentiate between them. All he knew was that they would all be happening in the far future. So he may not have felt the need to differentiate the fact that this event will happen here, but it is not necessarily related to this other event which will be happening over here.

D: We have always been told that Revelation was one great vision with each of these events following in sequence.

B: This is true. He did get it in one vision but it's not a sequence of events. It's merely a view of many things that will be happening in the future. He says some of the descriptions that John gives in Revelation, particularly that of Armageddon, will apply to this quatrain, this event in the eastern Europe, Middle East area. Such as there being so much blood flowing that it comes up to the horses' bridles and such as that, for there will be much bloodshed.

D: *I believe the scholars think that all of the Old Testament prophecies always pertain to Israel. They never think of them pertaining to anything else.*

B: Israel will be involved with this. The Bible prophecies may have been Israel-oriented or Israel-centered simply because they were from Hebrew prophets. But he says that does not mean they prophesied about Israel only. The Old Testament prophecies were having to do with many things. He points out that some of the wondrous devices present in the 20th century and further into the future were predicted by such people as Ezekiel and Isaiah and various prophets such as that.

D: *They have just not been recognized as that.*

B: Not by everybody.

D: *In this quatrain, this young dark man filled with evil doing, is that the Anti-Christ or another leader?*

B: He says it is a leader that will arise. In a sense he can be called anti-Christ, in that his main ambition would be to tear down Christianity, for he will not be a Christian. But he will not be Anti-Christ in the sense of the other leader that he has mentioned, whom he calls Anti-Christ because he is against humanity in general and humanity *is* Christ.

D: *Will this dark young man come before that time?*

B: He's thinking on it. Just a minute. (*Pause*) This dark young man will come shortly before the Anti-Christ. And he encourages me to use a colloquialism here. The ruckus that this young man raises will help set the stage for the Anti-Christ to take over.

D: *I'm thinking of Kadaffi. He's not so young but he is dark.*

B: He says Kadaffi or one like him is a good candidate for this, but he will not name names.

My research disclosed that Mysia, Lycia and Pamphylia were located in ancient Greek times on the western and southern coasts of Turkey where it meets the Ægean Sea and the Mediterranean Sea. Thus, I think he is referring to modern Turkey by his mention of these names. This is a remarkable example of Nostradamus relaying correct information that was not available from either my mind or Brenda's since we have very little knowledge of ancient Greek history.

UPDATE: Nostradamus said this dark young man would be a leader who would arise shortly before the Anti-Christ. Could this be Sudam Hussein? The conflict area referred to as being around the Caspian Sea and the eastern Mediterranean was definitely involved with the Persian Gulf War. The gray areas between eastern Europe and the Middle East around the Adriatic Sea definitely pinpoints Yugoslavia and the satellite countries. These areas were experiencing conflict during 1991.

CENTURY II-98

Celui de sang reperse le visage,	He whose face is spattered with the
De la victime proche sacrifiée,	blood of a newly sacrificed victim.
Tonant en Leo augure par	Jupiter in Leo forewarns through
presage,	prediction. He will be put to death
Mis estra à mort lors pour la	for the promise.
fiancée.	

B: He says this refers to the time of the Anti-Christ. The promise referred to is, on the one hand, the promise he made to himself to take over the world. And the promise, on the other hand, from the great karmic wheel that his power for bad will be counterbalanced by a power for good. If you will compare the effect of Jupiter in Leo against his horoscope, that is the forewarning through prediction that you can have.

J: *(After studying his ephemeris.) Jupiter is in Leo from August of 1990 to September of 1991. Is this the period when the Anti-Christ will be taking power?*

B: He says this is when he is beginning the realization of his ambition. This is when he is able to start his political career, so to speak. He will start on a so-called "local" level; that is, within his own country. From there he will just keep growing and becoming more greedy.

D: *We're beginning to put all these dates together. We'll be able to have a time schedule, so to speak, step-by-step of what he's going to do.*

B: He says that is the purpose of the project. If the people can find out ahead of time what is to happen, perhaps some things can be altered to avert the worst effects. Because if you're totally unprepared, the bad things that will happen will just knock you flat on your back. But if you're prepared ahead of time you'll have—the way he puts it—he says you'll have a stack of hay behind you to fall on. *(Laughter from the group.)*

UPDATE: *There can be no dispute that the dates given (August 1990 to September 1991) remarkably coincide with the Persian Gulf War. Whose "face is spattered with the blood of a newly sacrificed victim"? Sudam Hussein's or George Bush's? That is open to speculation.*

We were given several quatrains that detailed the Anti-Christ's invasion plans. These contained several symbolic references to Greek names. One such reference was in CENTURY V-27. He said the Adriatic Sea would be covered with Arab blood because there would be fighting all over the eastern end of the Mediterranean, including the Adriatic, Black and Caspian Sea areas. He said the leader from Persia was the one that eventually makes trouble for the rest of the world, but in the beginning he is not taken seriously because he appears to be "just another one wobbling in the mud pile." He told me to look up the modern names for Trebizond, Pharos, and Mytilene to have clearer locations.

My research shows that Trebizond is an ancient name for the city of Trabzon located on the northern (Black Sea) coast of Turkey. Pharos is an island off Alexandria, Egypt. And Mytilene is a city on the Greek island of Lesbos off the coast of Turkey. So I would interpret these references to mean that the Anti-Christ would come from Persia to occupy Turkey while Egypt and Greece trembled. (Also see CENTURY II-86.)

He explained that he often disguised his quatrains in this way, so that the Inquisition would think he was only making references to ancient history.

CENTURY X-75

Tant attendu ne reviendra jamais	Long awaited he will never return in
Dedans l'Europe, en Asie	Europe, he will appear in Asia; One
apparoistra	of the league issued from great
Un de la ligue islu du grand	Hermes, he will grow above all
Hermes,	other powers in the Orient.
Et sur tous rois des orientz	
croistra.	

B: He says this quatrain is linking up the future changes of the political balance caused by the Anti-Christ with the development of communism. The one who never reappears in Europe refers to the philosophy and thought system of Marx and Engels, who developed the theoretical basis of communism. They were hoping that system would take hold in the industrial world, but its main stronghold is the Asian continent. He says that philosophy developed most strongly in Russia and China. The Anti-Christ, though from the Middle East, will take advantage of the aspects of this philosophy that allows complete control of a population. He will take advantage of that and develop a thought system of his own based on communism. But he will be able to work it in such a way that he will rise in power and take over to unite the entire Asian continent before setting out to try to take over the rest of the world.

D: *What does the name Hermes mean? "One of the league issued from great Hermes."*

B: He is saying there are many people who will follow the philosophy system as thought out by Marx and Engels, and they will all believe they have true interpretations of what these men were envisioning in their political system. They will consider these two men to be their own, their prophet, and they will believe in their system. Their writings will communicate to them—therefore making them great Hermes. Great Hermes refers to one of the Greek gods who was in charge of communication. He says that the name is used metaphorically to refer to the founders of the philosophy these people will be following. "He will grow above all other powers in the Orient." One man amongst all these many (the Anti-Christ) will rise up above them and come into power due to his own particular manipulations of different institutions in political power.

CENTURY III-95

La loy Moricque on verra deffaillir,
Apres un autre beaucoup plus seductive:
Boristhenes premier viendra faillir,
Par dons & langue une plus attractive.

The Moorish law will be seen to fail, followed by another that is more pleasing. The Dnieper will be the first to give way through gifts and tongues to another more appealing.

B: This has to do once again with the beginning of the career of the Anti-Christ. "The Moorish law will be seen to fail," indicates that the Anti-Christ, in addition to shaking up the Christian religion and helping to destroy it, will also be shaking up the Islamic religion. The way of living and of conquesting that this Anti-Christ has will be a replacement for religion, and this will assist him in his conquest. The Dnieper represents Russia because it is a river in Russia. Russia will be his first major Asian conquest and he will not do it through force but through guile, through the limberness of his tongue. He will trick the Russians so they will come under his power and there will be nothing they can do about it. Since he comes from the Middle East, that area will already be fairly under his power before he tackles Russia. Then he'll turn to China and bring China and the rest of the Asian continent under his control. At that time he knows he will be in a position to take over the rest of the world.

D: *You said before that he would take over Russia and China, and that it would be the first time that Asia would be under one ruler. I was wondering how he would do that since Russia is so powerful.*

B: He'll do it through trickery and guile. He will trick the Russians to where they'll think they're doing what they want to do until it's too late for them to break free. But he knows that will not work with the Chinese since the Chinese are masters of guile themselves. He will have to use a different method with the Chinese.

D: *Does he know what method that will be?*

B: That's in another quatrain. He says he'll get the information to you in good time.

UPDATE: During 1991 Russia and her satellites began to undergo sweeping changes. Is this a natural evolution or is there a power behind the scenes manipulating the events through "trickery and guile," making them think "they're doing what they want to do, until it's too late for them to break free"?

CENTURY IV-50

Libra verra regner les Hesperies,	Libra will be seen to reign in the
De ciel & terre tenir la	West, holding the rule over the
monarchie:	skies and earth. No one will see
D'Asie forces nul ne verra paries,	the strength of Asia destroyed
Que sept ne tiennent par rang	until seven hold the hierarchy in
le hierarchie.	succession.

B: He says "the strength of Asia being destroyed" refers to the Anti-Christ taking over Asia through his methods of guile. He will appoint subcommanders to rule these vast tracts of land for him. And the world in general will not realize they are mere puppets and they won't realize what is going on until they observe a succession of them being so-called "fired and hired."

There are definitely seven or more leaders in that area who could be considered puppets: Kadaffi, the Ayatollah, Arafat and many others. But how far back do we go to begin counting? Maybe as far as the Shah of Iran?

B: "Libra being seen to rule in the West" is the sense of fairness and justice as epitomized by the United States Constitution. At first they will not interfere because they will feel this type of government was freely chosen by the people and that this is what they want in Asia. Then they will see that this is being forced upon them, and that a succession of leaders are being appointed as mouthpieces for this Anti-Christ.

CENTURY III-34 also refers to how the Anti-Christ spends many years working silently behind the scenes consolidating his power. Then once the structure is built, he will make his appearance in the international arena. He will have planned so well that the countries he goes against will be totally unprepared for the man with the golden tongue.

CENTURY VIII-77

L'antechrist trois bien tost	The antichrist very soon annihilates
anniehilez,	the three, 27 years his war will
Vingt & sept ans sang durera	last. The unbelievers are dead,
sa guerre.	captive, exiled; with blood, human
Les heretiques mortz, captifs,	bodies, water and red hail covering
exilez.	the earth.
Sang corps humain eau rougi	
gresler terre.	

B: This refers to the Anti-Christ, the one, the power behind the powers at this time. He is not in power at this time. He says he's behind the powers pulling strings. He has not made his move to reveal himself yet. He says he is like a spider waiting for his time. He will take advantage of the world situation to make his move for power. And he will succeed. But there will be a lot of terrible bloodshed and war in the process. The Anti-Christ, surprisingly enough, will refuse to use nuclear weapons and do this through conventional warfare. He saves the nuclear weapons for other unspeakable deeds. That's why he mentioned all the blood and gore in the quatrain too. There will be so many people being killed that the burial details won't be able to haul them off fast enough. He says that everybody in the world will become accustomed to the sight of corpses, and the sight of death will not make people squeamish as it does now. They will become numbed to it because it will be around so much.

D: *That sounds so horrible.*

B: He shrugged and said, "That's war."

D: *Will this war be confined to their part of the world?*

B: He says the entire world will be involved with it at one point in time or another. Sooner or later, it will involve the entire globe.

Chapter 15

The Last Three Popes

STRANGELY, although the Anti-Christ was supposed to emerge from a Moslem country, the Catholic church was to play an important part in his devious plans. He would use the church for his own ends in the same manner that he would use other countries to gain the power he desired. He appeared to have a very warped and diabolical mind. Without Nostradamus' warnings through these predictions, I believe it would have been impossible to imagine that any human could be capable of such twisted thinking. I have tried to arrange them in a chronological sequence. This is a difficult task because they often refer to several events separated in time.

CENTURY VIII-46

Pol mensolee mourra trois lieus
du Rosne
Fuis les deux prochains tarasc
destrois:
Car Mars fera le plus horrible
trosne,
De coq & d'aigle de France,
freres trois.

Paul the celibate will die three leagues from Rome, the two nearest flee the oppressed monster. When Mars will take up his horrible throne, the Cock and the Eagle, France and the three brothers.

B: He says that the present pope will be on one of his many journeys when he dies. He will be away from the Vatican on one of his trips when his life is no more. This will be at the time the Anti-Christ has begun to stir and to flex his power. The two cardinals nearest the pope will realize the danger to their church, and they will close themselves up in the Vatican to try to protect themselves from what is to come.

D: *Then the oppressed monster is the Anti-Christ. Does this mean that all this will take place during the present pope's lifetime?*

B: He says these events will start towards the end of his lifetime. He will die when this has begun to come to pass. He says that is why there are only two popes left to go up to the destruction of the church.

D: *(This was a surprise.) Then the majority of these prophecies about the Anti-Christ will take place after the present pope dies. And here are only two more popes after that?*

B: He says that neither pope will last very long, due to the troublesome times. One moment please. *(Pause)* He says the present pope will be assassinated. He is a good man and he honestly is striving for world peace. However, he is not in touch with his spiritual center the way he should be for this position. But he is desirous enough of world peace, so that—unbeknownst to the world in general—he is working against some established power parties within the Roman church. So a point will come at which those in the Roman church who want to hold on to their wealth and power will advise the Pope—they will *mis*advise the Pope—so that he will be placed in a situation that is dangerous to him, but he will not be aware of the danger. Due to this assassination of the present pope there will be a lot of unrest and rioting and such in Rome. And he says the next pope will not last very long.

(The rest of this quatrain will be interpreted in Chapter 22, pg. 273.)

CENTURY II-97

Romain Pontife garde de t'approcher,	Roman pontiff beware of approaching a city watered by two
De la cité que deux fleuves arrouse,	rivers. You will spit blood in that place, both you and yours, when
Ton sang viendras aupres de là cracher,	the roses bloom.
Toi & les tiens quand fleurira la rose.	

B: *(Sadly)* He says that this quatrain should be engraved in metal and sent to the present pope. For at a city watered by two rivers, in the time of late spring when the roses bloom, that is when and where he will be assassinated. He and several of his entourage will be killed.

D: *You said before he would be assassinated when he was away on one of his trips.*

B: Yes. He says find a major European city that is at the junction of two major rivers, and tell the pope to beware of that place. He says it will be easy to spot on any decent map of Europe.

D: *But there are many cities that sit on rivers.*

B: He says a *major* city at the junction of two rivers. That narrows it down more than you can know. It will be a major city that will just stand out at you.

D: *That's all we can do, I suppose, is just try to warn him. The quatrain was pretty clear. It was just a matter of relating to the correct pope.*

CENTURY I-4

Par l'univers sera faict un monarque,
Qu'en paix & vie ne sera longuement,
Lors se perdra la piscature barque,
Sera regie en plus grand detriment.

In the world there will be made a king who will have little peace and a short life. At this time the ship of the Papacy will be lost, governed to its greatest detriment.

B: He says that although this quatrain has multiple meanings, the main one that you need to be aware of is that it refers to the pope that will come between the present pope and the last pope. This one will have a short reign. He says that some of the political blunders and mistakes made by this pope is what makes it easier for the last pope to be a tool of the Anti-Christ. He says apply what you have learned from the other quatrains to this one and you'll get enough from it. He was just wanting to point out that the reign will be very short and that it will not be good for the church because it will bring about the final downfall.

CENTURY X-70

L'œil par object ferra telle excroissance,
Tant & ardente que tumbera la neige,
Champ arrousé viendra en descroissance,
Que le primat succumbera à Rege.

Because of an object the eye will swell so much, burning so greatly that the snow will fall. The watered fields will start to shrink when the Primate dies at Reggio.

He asked for the spelling of Reggio and I told him it was Rege in the French.

B: Yes, he says that is correct.—He says that as usual this has a multiple meaning. One thing he was referring to was the object that causes the eye to swell and burn so greatly. It is a type of atomic device, not exactly a bomb, that when set off it will do something to the planetary climate. It will displace an air mass that will upset the balance of hot and cold so that a greenhouse effect will get out of balance and run to the extreme and do drastic things to the climate, which in turn will affect agriculture.

This sounds like the modern concept called "Nuclear Winter." This is the theory that if we were to have a massive nuclear war, the clouds of dust and radioactivity would circle the earth and interfere with the climate to such a degree as to create a perpetual winter.

B: He says that would take place at the time when the pope dies at Reggio or Rege.

D: *Is that what he means by, "when the Primate dies"? I thought he was using symbolism because I think of a primate as a monkey.*

B: He says that refers to the Pope of the Catholic Church because another word for the pope is the Primate. He says if you will look it up in the dictionary you will find in addition to meaning an ape, that another definition will be a pope of the Catholic Church.

D: *Is Reggio a city or what?*

B: Yes, it is a place in Italy.

I am assuming this refers to the death of the second pope because he indicated that the present pope would be on one of his journeys when he is assassinated.

B: He says that the alternate meaning for this verse is a metaphysical type of meaning. It is also foretelling some ruin to befall the Catholic Church. They will become ambitious again and seek to grasp more power than they should. Their eye will swell with pride and vanity, thinking they can handle whatever they desire to try after, and that will be their downfall. The light shining so brightly will be the ambitions they are grasping after. The snow falling is the cooling of those ambitions when they fail, and that will cause great upheaval in the structure of the Catholic Church with a pope being dethroned. He says that as a result the members, the people who follow the Catholic Church, will fall away in great numbers, to where the influence of the Catholic Church will shrink. And their watered fields, so to speak, their sphere of influence, will become much less.

D: *Yes. I can see that this quatrain does have two meanings. Does he think they will both happen at the same time?*

B: He really doesn't think so.

D: *But he put them in the same quatrain because they are similar in meaning. I think I'm beginning to understand his thought processes.*

When these quatrains first began to come through, I just could not imagine how it would be possible for the church to get into such trouble. It is a strong and powerful institution. But then the events concerning Jim Bakker and the PTL Club began to surface, and the problems with Jimmy Swaggart followed close behind. This was predicted in Nostradamus' quatrains about the false trumpet. (CENTURY 2-27 and CENTURY 1-40 in Chapter 11.) The uproar that these events have created within the church makes it seem well within the realm of possibility that Nostradamus could be correct with these drastic predictions concerning the church.

CENTURY X-71

La terre & l'air gelleront si
grand eau,
Lors qu'on viendra pour
jeudi venerer,
Ce qui sera jamais ne feut
si beau,
Des quatre pars le viendront
honnorer.

The earth and air will freeze so much water when they come to venerate on Thursdays. He who will come will never be as fair as the few partners who come to honor him.

B: He says the first part of this quatrain is related to one of the meanings of the other quatrain. The second part of this quatrain is related to some other quatrains he has already translated for you. He says you will know which ones when he gets through speaking. The earth and air freezing is another effect of the atomic device that will throw everything out of kilter, mentioned in the previous quatrain he just translated for you. He says that all manner of solutions will be tried to counteract what happened but they will not be successful, in spite of the fair words of the governments to their peoples to try to keep them from panicking. He says the other part of the quatrain—the person referred to who will come who will not be as fair as those who give honor—refers to the leader he spoke of who will arise out of the Middle East. In spite of his propaganda forces putting out all the fair words and falsehoods about what grand and wondrous things he will be doing for the world, it will not completely disguise the fact that the man is an Anti-Christ and doing all sorts of heinous things. The man will not be able to live up to the image his followers try to put forth of him.

D: *Will this man come forth at the same time these weather changes occur?*

B: No. He says that if events are going to happen at the same time, he'll let you know. If he doesn't say anything then you can assume two different times are involved.

CENTURY II-15

Un peu devant monarque trucidé
Castor, Pollux en nef, estre
crinite
L'erain public par terre &
mer vuidé,
Pise, Ast, Ferrare, Turin,
terre interdicte.

A short while before a king is murdered, Castor and Pollux in the ship, a bearded star. Public treasure emptied on land and sea, Pisa, Asti, Terrara and Turin are forbidden lands.

B: He says this refers to events that will happen due to the intervention of the Anti-Christ. Castor and Pollux, which are the Gemini twins, here represent the Prime Minister of Great Britain and the President of the United States.

D: *It's not an astrological quatrain then?*
B: Not in this case. But the bearded star refers to a comet.
D: *I thought so. They figured that part out, too.*
B: He says it is a major comet that will be clearly visible in the sky of the Northern Hemisphere. He says actually these are signs leading up to the assassination of the pope.
D: *Oh? The present pope?*
B: No, the one following.
D: *Do you mean the one following will be assassinated also?*
B: Apparently. That is what he is showing me. He says the present pope will be assassinated but this will be before the comet comes. This present pope will be assassinated simply because he is concerned about the human condition and he travels so much that he gets into dangerous situations. The next pope will be assassinated because he will be in the way of the Anti-Christ and he won't buckle under to his demands. So the Anti-Christ has him assassinated to get his tool in office.
D: *You said he would have a short reign.*
B: This is the reason why. At the time the second pope is assassinated, the Anti-Christ will start his European campaign. As a result of these events the Prime Minister and the President will be in consultation about the matter. They will meet at sea the way Churchill and Roosevelt did, for better security and secrecy for their meetings.
D: *That last part, "public treasure emptied and ..."*
B: (*Interrupted*) He says that refers to warfare. The public treasure being emptied on land and sea refers to all the weapons that are turned out and destroyed in the course of warfare.
D: *And that part where the countries are said to be forbidden lands. It sounds like those are cities in Italy.*
B: Yes, they are. He's already interpreted this. He says that refers to his beginning his European campaign.

CENTURY II-36

Du grand Prophete les lettres seront prinses,	The letters of the great prophet will be interpreted and fall into
Entre les mains du tyran deviendront:	the hands of the tyrant. His efforts will be to deceive his
Frauder son Roy seront ses entreprinses,	King, but soon his thefts will trouble him.
Mais ses rapines bien tost le troubleront.	

B: He says this refers to some incidents that take place during the time of troubles. Before the Anti-Christ comes to full power, when he's still rising in power and still scheming, to the rest of the world it will appear there are still some other men above him when it comes to the power structure. In reality the Anti-Christ will just be using them as step-ping-stones on his way to the top of the heap, so to speak. And while he's doing this, one of the things he will do is have some traitorous cardinals in his pocket. And one of these will be spying on the pope.

D: *This won't be the last pope?*

B: No, this will be the next to the last pope. The cardinal who is spying on the pope will be stealing information from him, plus he will be altering the pope's correspondence. Whenever the pope receives a letter, he alters the wording of it a little bit so the pope thinks it has said something else other than what it has said. He does it to make the situation worse, so the pope will react inappropriately to the various situations. So the people will think he is a bad pope, and he's more apt to get assassinated or something sooner. This cardinal will be troubled about what he is doing, because it seems to be bringing dissension into his beloved church, but he is doing it because he's on the side of the Anti-Christ.

D: *Then "the letters of the great prophet" refers to the pope. The transla-tors thought this quatrain referred to Nostradamus or one of his inter-preters. It says, "It may just as well be Nostradamus talking of some personal vendetta of his own."*

B: He says he's not going to waste his time and effort writing quatrains on things as petty as that when there's the whole world situation to worry about.

D: *They thought he was the great prophet referred to.*

B: He says it is flattering that they realize he is a great prophet, but when he's looking into the future he's not going to be projecting himself into the future. He's just writing what he sees.

CENTURY III-65

Quand le sepulcre du grand Romain trouvé,	When the tomb of the great Roman is found, a pope will be
Le jour apres sera esleu Pontife:	elected the next day; he will not
Du Senat gueres il ne sera prouvé,	be approved of by the Senate, his blood poisonous in the
Empoisonné son sang au sacré scyphe.	sacred chalice.

B: He put that line concerning the tomb of the great Roman in to help ordinary mortals pinpoint which pope he is talking about. The tomb is in Rome amongst the layers and layers of archæological ruins under-neath the present-day buildings.

D: *Does he know who the great Roman is that is in the tomb?*

B: He says he can't narrow it down to the name because several names keep popping into mind. But this Roman was a famous philosopher and he theorized about all things. He is mainly known for his philosophy and his discourses on the nature of things. He had a profound effect on Western thought and his writings are still in existence today. So consequently the archæologists will know who he is and what he did. That is why he called him the great Roman. He says when that happens and a pope is elected immediately after, it will be a clear sign. It won't necessarily be the very next day. That is symbolic of a very short time after the discovery of that tomb. In less than a year a pope will be elected. And whenever this takes place you will know that this is the last pope that will bring about the destruction of the Catholic Church. When he is elected it will be seen that he is a tool of the Anti-Christ. This will be the reason why the ruling bodies will not approve of this choice of pope. The fact that he will help bring the downfall of the Catholic Church is what is meant by his blood being poisonous in the chalice. The chalice representing the church and the poisonous blood representing the harm he will do to this organization.

CENTURY IV-86

L'an que Saturne en eau sera conjoinct,
Avecques Sol, le Roi fort & puissant:
A Reims & Aix sera reçeu & oingt,
Apres conquestes meurtrira innocens.

In the year Saturn is in conjunction with Aquarius, and with the Sun, the very powerful king will be received and anointed at Reims and Aix. After conquests he will murder innocent people.

B: He says this refers to the last pope of the Catholic Church. This event will take place sometime during the next decade from your point of view, the 1990s. He says to use your chart of stars to plot those positions in order to obtain the date of this, to give you an idea of what will be happening in that realm of power.

John wasted no time and had already referred to his ephemeris.

J: *Saturn and the Sun are in conjunction in Aquarius on January 30, 1992.*
B: He says that the present pope will be assassinated, and the next pope will not last very long. Then the following pope should either be pope already or will be sworn in on or about the date you have found.

UPDATE: As this date was rapidly approaching (in 1991 when this book was being reprinted), and the present pope John II was still very much alive, it seemed impossible that so much could happen in so short a time. I asked the astrologer to go over the ephemeris again. He said that was the only date during the 1990s when these planets would conjunct in Aquarius. Then I remembered a similar problem we had while writing Volume Two of this work. We had discovered that Ms. Cheetham had made a mistake in translation from the French to the English, and this affected the dating in a dramatic way. This took an entire chapter to unravel and explain. (See Volume Two, Chapter 29, "Finding the Date of the Shift.") It suddenly occurred to me that this could be a similar case. When I checked the French portion with a dictionary, I was amazed to find she had indeed made the same error. In both cases she had translated "eau" or "water" as referring to Aquarius. Aquarius is not a water sign. It is called the "Water Bearer," but it is an air sign. The astrologer said this, of course, would make a dramatic difference in the dating of this important quatrain. Upon checking the ephemeris he discovered that this conjunction would occur in only one water sign, Pisces, during the rest of this century. There would only be two times that the Sun and Saturn would conjunct in Pisces: March 5, 1995 and March 17, 1996. I personally favor the 1995 date because that coincides with other predictions that state the Anti-Christ could be recognized by 1995 by those who are aware. This definitely gives more time for these important papal events to occur. It is regrettable that we humans are not as accurate in our reporting as the master himself. It shows that we are very capable of making an error; in this case an error from the original French.

D: *Before you said this last pope would be the tool of the Anti-Christ.*

B: This is correct. He says the Roman church is already a tool of the Anti-Christ. They may not necessarily be aware of this yet but they're helping to make the Anti-Christ's way easier, for a time. They are already predisposed towards working into the Anti-Christ's hand of cards. And he says he's referring to Tarot cards, not poker cards.

D: *(This was a surprise.) Oh, is he familiar with Tarot cards?*

B: Yes, he says he is. He says that when he sees pictures, when he has visions of the Anti-Christ, he sometimes sees him holding a hand of cards.

D: *Can you see what the cards are?*

B: He says he will try to show me what they are. One card is the Hanged Man, it is inverted. There is the Valet of Batons, it is upright. There is the inverted Emperor and the inverted Hierophant. And there is the inverted Ten of Swords and inverted Justice. And the Wheel of Fortune, it is upright.

D: *The majority of those cards are inverted.*

B: This is true.

D: *I think we can get a reading from that.*

B: He says sometimes the cards change, but at this point in time when he's communicating with us, he sees him holding this hand of cards. The thing that concerns him is that most of the time the hand of cards he holds are usually Major Arcana. Occasionally there may be some Minor Arcana. He says this is very unusual. Usually a hand of cards is Minor Arcana with the influence of one or two Major Arcana to indicate their overall pattern. But the Anti-Christ, being such a crucial figure in this confluence of history and time, his hand of cards tends to be mostly Major Arcana with some, maybe a few Minor Arcana to help provide some details.

The Tarot deck is essentially two decks of cards in one. It has 78 cards and is divided into the Major and Minor Arcana. Our modern playing card deck with its four suits has evolved from the Minor Arcana. The Major has 22 picture cards and their presence in a layout adds more importance and significance to the reading.

Since Nostradamus was apparently familiar with the Tarot, I wondered if when he saw an important figure in his visions whether he did a Tarot reading on that person to gain more information into their personality and the deeds they would perform. It was a possibility since the Tarot is very old, dating back into antiquity. It is known to have been used since Egyptian times. From the cards he mentioned, it appeared the deck he was familiar with was very similar to ours in modern times.

B: He says the deck of Tarot is a very valuable tool. It is very good for developing your psychic self and your spiritual self. And it is good for communicating. In his day many symbols from the Tarot were used for communicating secret messages in correspondence. He says the Tarot is very versatile, and it will be very important during the time of troubles. Those who have any familiarity at all with the Tarot will be very helpful, particularly working in underground movements, to help keep communication clear, because they will be relying on psychic communication as well as physical communication. The Tarot will play an important part in both.

D: *We still have the cards in our day and time.*

B: He's aware of this and he's aware that the cards have been diversified into several systems using various symbols so that each person may be more apt to find those symbols which they can relate to clearly on the psychic level. And thereby get a clearer picture of what is needed to be known.

D: *It would be very good in the future if he can tell me when he sees any symbols like this, because we will be able to understand those symbols.*

B: Yes, he says he is not aware of everything, but the more this communication continues, the more familiar he becomes with the vessel. He says that while he was in the process of exploring this vessel's subconscious, he became aware that this vessel was familiar with the symbols of Tarot. And he realized that he could use this symbolism as well to transport from his place to your place.

D: *Yes, John and I are also familiar with Tarot symbols.*

B: He says this is good. This helps make the communication even clearer. Even though he's known as an astrologer and a doctor, that's not all he knows. He's aware of other systems of knowledge as well. He feels himself free to draw upon these other systems of knowledge if they can intermesh with that knowledge we understand.

D: *I suppose this was dangerous knowledge in his time.*

B: He says it's dangerous knowledge in your time too, but you are not aware of this yet. He says the time of suppression is very soon and any knowledge that broadens the mind and causes people to think will be considered dangerous. The way he puts it, events in recent past history in your century that seemed very horrible will seem child's play by comparison to what is coming.

I laughed nervously. I certainly didn't like to imagine what he was describing.

B: He says that you chose to be here at this time. There is now a higher proportion of old souls in the world than there has ever been before because the old souls will be needed to help the world to survive. You will find them everywhere, permeated in the oddest places. The old souls will be in communication with each other and they are the ones that will help things hold together and survive.

D: *I just hope these books can come out before all of this really begins to happen.*

B: He says it's a very close thing. That's why he's so anxious to try to get information through, even though he stops like this to digress from time to time, he feels that it too, has a place and an importance in addition to the interpretation of the quatrains.

J: *Will this last pope be French?*

B: He says he has a strong feeling that he will be. The man will be of swarthy complexion and his character can be likened unto the Tarot card "inverted Hierophant." He says this man is a man of mystery, of dark waters. This man will have a physical deformity of some sort. He's not sure if he'll have a shoulder that is slightly crooked or hunched, or a clubfoot, but it will be a deformity of that nature, either of the shoulder or of the foot. It will be a congenital defect in the bone. It won't be caused by injury but he was born that way. Consequently, his mind has been scarred by this through the cruelty and callousness of people toward people who are different. He says this man of swarthy complexion and blue eyes entered the church at a young age out of bitterness and desperation because he knew he would never get a girl to love him and marry him. He entered the church so he would not have to deal with this. His parents were involved with the Nazi movement in France. Consequently, he is scarred by this as well. He says he had to bear the taunts of his schoolmates and such in the years after World War II, of their calling him "Nazi-lover" and such as this. He says had it not been for the cruelty and callousness of the people he was exposed to in his environment, he could have turned out to be a good man, perhaps even kindly. But as it was, he has been warped into cruelty from pain, and he wants to get back at the world because of the pain he bore when he was young.

D: Is this why it is easier for him to become a tool of the Anti-Christ?

B: Yes. This makes him very susceptible to this.

D: What does this last part mean, "After conquests he will murder innocent people"? I believe that doesn't refer to the pope but to the Anti-Christ. Is that correct?

B: He says that is referring to the pope figuratively in that the pope, due to these hurts in his early childhood, will want to show them, saying, "Look at me, I'm powerful. I can do it. I'm better than you." And "after conquests" means that after he attains the power he is desiring, he will be responsible for the murder of innocent people, just by being the tool of the Anti-Christ. He will not actually murder people himself, but he will cause avenues to be opened through which people will be murdered. Particularly, he will see a chance to hurt those who hurt him when he was young. He says this pope has the appearance of being a kindly man at the present time, for that is advantageous for him. But the hidden is very prominent in his makeup.

CENTURY II-57

Avant conflict le grand tombera,	Before the battle the great man
Le grand à mort, mort, trop	will fall, the great one to death,
subite & plainte,	death too sudden and lamented.
Nay imparfaict: la plus part	Born imperfect, he will go the
nagera,	greater part of the way; near
Aupres du fleuve de sang la	the river of blood the ground
terre tainte.	is stained.

B: He says this refers to the last three popes of the Catholic Church. He says the third from last will fall from an assassin's bullet. He says the second from last will be swallowed up by the schemings of the Anti-Christ. And the last one is the one he has mentioned before who was born misshapen. The pope who will be in charge of the church for what time is left for it. He'll go the greater part of the way. But he, too, will fall in the end because he has been a tool. The Anti-Christ will use him as long as he needs him, until he gets in the way and then he'll get rid of him. And when he gets rid of him, that will essentially get rid of the church too.

D: I thought when I read this, "born imperfect," that it might refer to the last pope because he said he would have a defect of some sort. That wraps up all three of them in one quatrain.

CENTURY II-76

Foudre en Bourgongne fera
  cas portenteux,
Que par engin oncques ne
  pourrait faire,
De leur senat sacriste fait boiteux
Fera scavoir aux ennemis
  l'affaire.
	Lightning in Burgundy will reveal
	portentous events. A thing that
	could never have been done by
	trickery. The lame priest will
	reveal matters of the Senate to
	the enemy.

I felt excited because I sensed this was referring to the last pope.

B: He says, needless to say, the lame priest refers to the French pope who is of service to the Anti-Christ referred to as the enemy. The deeds done by this man are done because he voluntarily contributes the inner resources of the information that he, as pope, has access to. Information that the Anti-Christ could not have gotten in a million years just through his spies, had the pope remained true to the other side. He feels that with the other information he has given, this quatrain should be fairly straightforward.

D: *Yes, it does relate. "The lightning in Burgundy" is the war beginning. Is that correct?*

B: No. The lightning in Burgundy refers to the fact that treachery has come from Burgundy before and this particular pope has his ecclesiastical roots in Burgundy. If he had his preferences, he would prefer to have the Papacy based in France rather than in the Vatican.

CENTURY IX-36

Un grand Roi prins entre
  les mains d'un Joine,
Non loing de Pasque
  confusion coup coultre:
Perpet. captifs temps que
  fouldre en la husne,
Lorsque trois freres se
  blesseront & meutre.
	A great king captured by the
	hands of a young man, not far from
	Easter, confusion, a state of the
	knife. Ever-lasting captives, times
	when the lightning is on the top,
	when three brothers will be
	wounded and murdered.

B: He says this quatrain for the most part refers to events yet to come. Yet is also refers to some events that have already happened that started the ball rolling, so to speak. That started the chain of events to lead up to these events. The high king represents the pope and the young man is the Anti-Christ. This refers to how the last pope will be a tool of the Anti-Christ. He is captured into his influence, so to speak. It will be a time of great unrest and of war and desolation. There will be many horrible things going on. He says the entire latter half of this century—meaning this period of time you are in—has been a series of catastrophic events, each topping the ones before, leading up to the time of troubles. During the time of troubles assassination of world leaders will become so very common that people won't even bother to learn the names of the present leader. Because he will soon be assassinated and a new leader in his place. He says that's why he referred to the three brothers being wounded and then murdered. At one time it was considered very horrible, for example in your case, very horrible for a president to be assassinated. Such as your President Kennedy and others at that time that were assassinated. But he says that toward the end of this century people will look back and think, "Well, gee, that's nothing. That happens all the time now." And he says that "the lightning towards the top" refers to the warfare going on and the great danger to anybody with ambitions to lead, with the exception of the Anti-Christ, since he will be the moving force behind most of these assassinations.

D: *The translator connects this quatrain with the Kennedys. That's the only connection they have made.*

B: He says that is correct so far as it goes, because that one line does refer to the Kennedys. He was using that as an example of how horrified the nation was when those assassinations took place.

It might be interesting to conjecture that Martin Luther King might be one of the brothers Nostradamus refers to as being assassinated at the same time as John and Robert Kennedy. He may have been using it metaphorically. These were three leaders and brothers in the sense of what they believed in.

D: *Something occurred to me about the phrase "the lightning at the top." It reminds me of the Tarot symbol of the Tower.*

The Tower is a dramatic-looking card. It shows the top of a tall tower being struck by lightning, and it symbolizes change and destruction.

B: He says that is very astute of you to notice that. That symbol does relate in that way because the entire time of troubles could be represented by the overriding power of the Tower. There will be other cards with the powers they represent influencing events as well, but it will be a time of dramatic and traumatic change.

D: *What does the reference to Easter mean?*

B: He says that the phrase "not far from Easter" refers to the pope's religious standing rather than a particular time. He says this man will appear to be very close to the precepts of the Catholic Church. But inside he still will hold pretty close to the pagan ideas that were believed by the Christians early on. He says that Easter started out as a pagan celebration that the priests Christianized so as to help convert the barbarians to the church. And this man will be basically a barbarian with Christian trappings.

B: He says that trying to use astrological symbols is very difficult with this vessel. It is not because of fear on the vessel's part, it's due to ignorance. But using this sort of symbolic communication, that this vessel is familiar with, such as the Tarot, makes it very easy to communicate the concepts he needs to get across in a very efficient way. Because he, too, is comfortable with the Tarot, and he may refer to this heavier in the future, rather than astrological symbols, so as to be able to communicate the easiest. He says he will leave some pictures of hands of Tarot cards with the vessel so that she may pick them out from a deck for all involved so that readings may be done. After she awakens, she will be able to pick out hands of Tarot cards for the Anti-Christ and for the pope and other major figures that you ask her about. He says this will work very well. He's acting very excited. He's jumping up and down and his beard is waving back and forth as he jumps. He's saying that he should have thought about this a long time ago.. It's a matter of feeling your way and finding the easiest way to communicate. Remember how long it took just to make contact when we first started communication. He's been feeling his way and exploring into the subconscious of this vessel and he says now he's found some wide open avenues, six lanes wide, for communicating through. This way he will be able to communicate longer because it won't be as much effort on his part. He's so excited he can hardly contain himself. He says he's ready for you to come back and communicate again right now.

I laughed because he had never been able to remain with us this long. Maybe he had found an easier way.

Upon awakening, Brenda had vivid pictures in her mind. She described the scene.

B: I have this picture; it's like I'm floating in limbo someplace where time and space and place don't really exist. And in this place I see this round table top. I'm calling it a table top because that's what it looks like to me, although there are no legs to hold it up. The table itself is white but it's like it's made out of pearl or mother-of-pearl. And engraved on this table is a central circle with spokes radiating out.

D: *Like a horoscope wheel?*

B: You could say that but the symbols I see are like the symbols that the alchemists use. Those type of symbols are engraved on this table in various places. And around this table I see four hooded figures sitting. Each of these figures holds a hand of Tarot cards, but each hand is individual and applying to them. It's as if each figure had a complete deck to deal with and this is the hand they have chosen to come to this table with. On this table they are seated around, there seems to be a layout of Tarot in progress but involving several decks. I would never be able to duplicate that if my life depended on it. It's very complex and the cards are positioned according to where they should be on this whcel. I get the feeling they are playing out some world event. The only cards I am able to pick out are the ones the figures hold in their hands.

She immediately proceeded to pull the cards out of the deck for the first hand she could remember and laid them on the table for John to interpret. The layout was strange and like none I had ever seen, but it turned out to be very symbolic. It was obvious to us that these first cards were the same cards Nostradamus had mentioned as representative of the Anti-Christ. Brenda said she had lain the cards down the way the figure had been holding them in its hand.

J: Can I make a comment? This layout is also strange to me. But I've seen French readings, the traditional gypsy-type, the fortune tellers of old. This is similar to how they would lay the cards out.

D: *Could it be this was the pattern that Nostradamus was familiar with?*

J: Possibly, yes, because they wouldn't use the complex patterns of Tarot that we've progressed into. They only use past, present and future.

Strange as it seemed, the only explanation would appear to be that these layouts of cards had come directly from the mind of Nostradamus. I asked Brenda to read off the cards for the tape recorder.

B: I have laid down an inverted Hanged Man, an upright Valet of Batons, inverted Hierophant, inverted Emperor that is in a superior position (on top of) to the others. Inverted Ten of Swords that is over-shadowed (underneath) by the Emperor. An inverted Justice and an upright Wheel of Fortune that kind of culminates the entire hand.

These were laid down like a typical playing hand of cards, except that some (the ones mentioned) were in front of or behind the others. John proceeded with this interpretation.

J: I would interpret this as how the Anti Christ is coming about. (*He pointed to the different cards.*) This is what is present right now and this is what is to take place as his life goes on. And it really does fit in. First of all, we see the Hanged Man reversed. When I see the Hanged Man in its upright position it represents circumspection, wisdom from above. It represents learning to trust in the inner spirit that guides all of us. In its reversed position, it represents trusting the inner spirit that would be a downward struggle rather than for something positive. Then we have the Valet of Batons which would represent a young man. It would represent to me a traveler in life, someone beginning on the journey of life. The baton would represent a cutting from a tree. You put it (or the person) in whatever type of medium and it will grow. But he's growing in the sense of spiritual downwardness because of the reversed Hanged Man. I look at the Hanged Man as a very spiritual card because it represents that we're taking our body and sacrificing it to become more spiritual. When it's reversed, we're sacrificing it, but maybe for all the wrong reasons. That's how I would see he is taking his life at the present. Then going on to the next two cards, this probably represents his ascendancy. You see the Hierophant and the Emperor and they're both reversed. To me the Hierophant in its upright position represents conforming to what the world wants. But in its reverse position it represents wanting to *rule* the world. The Hierophant was like a symbol for a Pope or a very high priest. So the Hierophant reversed represents a priest using negative forces. Sort of like being a priest of some higher energies that are not part of the source of life. And then the Emperor card reversed represents great power but misuses of great power.

This was amazing. Out of all the cards in the deck Brenda had picked out the ones that really fit what Nostradamus had been telling us of the personality of the Anti-Christ.

J: Then we come to the Ten of Swords reversed. When this card is upright it represents, "Hey, it's bad times, it's bad news for you." But in its reverse position it represents, "Around you is death, around you is despair and desolation."

D: *Well, he would be causing it; it wouldn't touch him.*

J: It wouldn't touch him because we have the Wheel of Fortune upright which means, "This is the day; this is part of fate. The Wheel of destiny has made this take place." And the reversed Justice means perversion of justice. Creating and living by his own laws. He will feel no obligation to justice; it cannot touch him. So it really does fit in with what the Anti-Christ supposedly gets into.

D: *I wonder if Nostradamus might have done a reading on his own to find out about the Anti-Christ, and this was the reading he came up with.*

J: It's a possibility.

She continued by laying out the hand of cards that were representing of the last pope.

B: One thing about this one that is really kind of neat and interesting is that you see what's visible here but there's a card back here (behind the others) and it's totally hidden by these other two cards. There is the inverted Judgment and the upright Magician and the upright Ten of Cups. The upright Queen of Coins is almost but not quite totally hidden by upright Justice. The next visible card is the inverted Eight of Batons. And behind upright Justice and inverted Eight of Batons we have inverted High Priestess, totally hidden, but influencing those cards. And the hand ends with the inverted World.

J: This is another interesting layout. When Judgment shows up in traditional Tarot it represents awakening change of consciousness, a new way of starting things. It represents a consciousness ready to blend with the universal. Well, in its reverse position, it would be the reverse of that. It represents a consciousness that *doesn't* want to blend with the universal but wants to blend with its own power. And that power would be the Magician card. In other words, "What *I* manifest, what *I* make, what *I* take from above and make below." And having the good fortune of the Ten of Cups coming with it. I think the Ten of Cups represents the satisfaction of one's material desires. To me, it represents great satisfaction, great happiness coming to the person. When I see it in a reading, it represents having your heart's desire. He's going to be pleased with what he's accomplished. And there's going to be an influence of a woman of money and power in his life. She'll probably be dark in coloring. She's going to be like an earthmother-type. She's going to have nourished his career or she's going to be some type of support. I don't think she's a holy woman, but she's a woman of power and position and money. She's going to definitely have some type of influence in his life. I feel psychically that she probably is one of his soulmates or a spiritual companion from another lifetime. They meet again and they can't be lovers but they can be confederates. So she is more of a mentor to him. Justice upright usually represents balanced forces because it represents the scales, keeping things in balance and in check. In traditional Tarot the sword is double-edged, it can be either used to kill, to maim, to hurt, or to harm in the cry of Justice. (On the card a blindfolded woman is holding scales in one hand and a huge sword in the other.) He might unknowingly make some really poor judgments during his career. This woman could have something to do with this; his making his bad decisions. She is like someone behind things. Even though the Vatican is such a preserve of maleness, she's going to be very closely involved in his life in some way. I don't think she's his mother. I feel there's some spiritual karmic link.—It's interesting that the High Priestess is completely covered up and she's reversed. To me, in an upright position she represents secret knowledge that is hidden, that is only revealed to the initiates. And here we're going to see secret knowledge revealed to all.

The full implication of this interpretation will be revealed in the next chapter, "The Ravage of the Church," and the manner in which the Anti-Christ uses this pope for his cause.

J: The Eight of Batons represents things that are a great burden. I don't like the Eight of Batons. It represents taking on more trouble than you should get involved in. But it's inverted, so maybe he might pass on the responsibility of the burden to others. Then the World reversed represents a world in chaos instead of enlightenment. A world gone amok. The Anti-Christ's power is going to come through people like that. I think this pope is going to cause a lot of mischief and misfortune.—It's real strange that the Queen of Coins showed up there. I see that and I feel real strongly that it's going to be a secret type of thing that no one knows about because she's partly hidden, and the High Priestess being hidden all together. He doesn't want anybody to know what he is going to do until the time comes. But I'm getting the feeling that maybe Nostradamus did do readings to help him with his visions.

The third hand of cards belonged to the present pope. I will not repeat the reading here because I don't believe it contained anything essential to the coming horrors of the Anti-Christ. But it was again interesting that the cards were very appropriate. They mostly dealt with his personality and travels. It accurately portrayed him as a good and just man with the right motives.

The fourth hand of cards will be interpreted in Chapter 22, "The Turning of the Tide," for it represents the man who will lead the fight against the Anti-Christ.

I have included all cards here so that others who are familiar with the symbols of the Tarot can see what insight they can gain into the personalities of these two major characters in the scenario of our future.

UPDATE 1999

The implication that a Pope of the Catholic Church could be used and manipulated by such an extreme personality as the Anti-Christ was made more believable when a book was written in 1999 indicating that it has happened before. *Hitler's Pope: The Secret History of Pius XII,* by the British Catholic scholar John Cornwell chronicles the events during World War II when the Pope knowingly aided Hitler in his persecution of the Jews. Their association began in 1933 when Hitler controlled Germany, and Pacelli (Pius) was the Vatican's secretary of state. The accusations were shocking to the present-day Catholic Church, but were backed by the location of pertinent documents and letters. The Church's explanation: "Pacelli was a man of his time, brought up in the pre-Vatican II teachings that all other faiths were erroneous." Will this also explain why the next Pope will be drawn into the web of the third Anti-Christ? He will be "a man of his time" thinking he is doing the correct thing. If it occurred once, will it happen again? Is this another example of Nostradamus referring to two similar events in the same quatrains? Two popes unwittingly assisting two Anti-Christs during troubling times.

Chapter 16

The Ravage of the Church

THE TERRIBLE THINGS that Nostradamus saw the Anti-Christ doing to the Vatican and to the cultural centers of Europe were almost unbelievable. I would hope that man had become too civilized for such horrible deeds. But maybe it is this unbelievability that gives them the ring of possibility, because they are truly the work of a demented power-hungry madman. It must have upset Nostradamus as much as it did me to see cultural heritage, knowledge and religion, the cornerstones of civilization, destroyed wantonly in the name of control. The Anti-Christ had learned his lessons well. He knew how to completely undermine the morale of the people; he would strike at the heart of their belief system.

I will list the events separately here, although in time sequence they should be dispersed among the events in the following chapters.

The following quatrain was partially interpreted in Chapter 14, pp. 189.

CENTURY V-25

Le prince Arabe Mars, Sol, Venus, Lyon, Regne d'Eglise par mer succombera: Devers la Perse bien pres d'un million, Bisance, Egypte, ver. serp invadera.	The Arab Prince, Mars, the Sun, Venus and Leo, the rule of the Church will succumb to the sea. Towards Persia very nearly a million men will invade Egypt and Byzantium, the true serpent.

B: He says the church succumbing to the sea refers to an accident that will take place in Rome. I'm not able to receive the images clearly of how this will happen. But somehow in the process of this accident the base of the Catholic Church will be totally destroyed, as if the city sank into the sea and existed no more, or never had existed. From what he is showing I get the feeling that this will be a separate event from the events happening in the Middle East.

D: *Do you think they will happen at the same time?*

B: Not at the exact same time. He says they'll happen pretty close together so that some people will connect the two events in their minds, thinking, well, the Arabs have always been against Christianity anyway. But actually the causes will be separate from each other. The Arabs will be quick to take advantage of the situation but they did not originally cause the situation. He says the restrictions of the Vatican will cause the church structure to crumble. Although they may rally, it will be a blow that the church will never fully recover from. It will eventually be seen in future ages as the beginning of the end for the church. It will be seen as the reasons why the church collapsed after successfully surviving so many centuries.

D: *Can any of that be made any clearer? Does he think this will be a natural accident or a man-made accident?*

B: (*Pause*) He seems to think it will be a combination of both. A man-made type accident that triggers a natural accident or *vice versa.* The images are not coming through clearly today.

D: *But it does have to do with the sea.*

B: Yes. And not only with the sea but also with some sort of terrific force coming down out of the sky. I'm talking about an energy force, not a force of army but some sort of energy force coming down out of the sky ... and dissolving things. It will be termed a natural disaster because it's beyond the technical capability of anyone on earth to produce that force. So it would have to be termed a natural accident because they will not be able to find any cause for it.

D: *In the French part of the quatrain, he abbreviated: "ver. serp.," and they have translated this as "the true serpent." What did he mean by this?*

B: He is saying that although the people will mostly be concerned with what happened to the church and will be trying to figure out the cause of that, what they truly should keep their eye on is the events in the Middle East. Particularly that leader who would be invading Byzantium. Because he says future events will show that leader to be a very dangerous man.

When he mentions Byzantium he refers to Turkey. Istanbul (Constantinople) was built on the site of this ancient city. It became increasingly apparent that when he mentioned a place name in his quatrains, he was often not referring to that city, *per se,* but to the country it was located in.

CENTURY II-81

Par feu du ciel la cité presque
aduste,
L'urne menace encor Ceucalion,
Vexée Sardaigne par la Punique
fuste,
Apres que Libra lairra son
Phœton.

The city is almost burned down
by fire from the sky, water again
threatens Deucalion. Sardinia is
vexed by the African fleet after
Libra has left Leo.

D: *In this quatrain they think there was a misspelling in the original French.*

B: He says that it is entirely possible since sometimes the printers are careless.

D: *The word they think is misspelled is "Deucalion." The French had it as a "C," "Ceu" instead of "Deu."*

B: He says, yes, since C and D are almost mirror images of each other, if the printer's eyes were tired at the time it would be easy to substitute one for the other and not spot the mistake. He says it is true that it should be a "D."

D: *These names are not the same words that are in the French.*

B: What names are they in the French?

D: *Sardinia is Sardaigne. Is that the same as Sardinia?*

B: (*He corrected my pronunciation with a definite French accent.*) He says that is the pronunciation as near as he can get this vehicle to pronounce it since the vehicle also does not know French. Sardinia is the way it is called in your time, in your language.

D: *They have translated Tunique to mean African.*

B: (*He again corrected me.*) He says this is correct.

D: *They have translated Phœton to mean Leo.* (*He corrected me and I tried it several times until I got it right.*)

B: Phæton (Fee-ton), with an "F." He says that is the Greek version, the Greek conception, of that particular entity. Phæton was in charge of the sun and fire, and the higher symbol for Leo is the sun. The translations are correct. He says that initially the Anti-Christ will obtain power within his sphere, that is Asia, the Middle East. When he starts to rise in power *out* of his sphere, that is in Europe, the first place of unrest will be the area of the Mediterranean. For it will be best for him to approach Europe from the south, from his geographical orientation. And due to his Middle Eastern heritage he will have already united North Africa, being culturally sympathetic, with his Asian and Middle Eastern conglomerate. Hence he is in a strong, secure position to take on Europe from the south since his own forces are at his back. Due to the weapons he uses and the ravages of war, the Anti-Christ knows that one way of bringing a potential enemy under control is to threaten cultural destruction rather than just strict physical destruction. For cultural objects have great meaning to a culture, and people will go to great lengths to try to preserve certain places and things. His main tool will be the use of terrorist tactics but on a larger scale. What he will do to put Europe into its initial shock, to make it easier to take over, is that he will start destroying the city of Rome. He will start systematically smashing it to rubble using various sorts of bombs dropped from airplanes. He will destroy it to such an extent that the seven hills of Rome will be leveled. That will be his desire, not only destroying the cultural objects that Rome contains, but to level the hills Rome is built upon to try to totally destroy the city. He will do such a good job that Rome will be threatened by the encroachment of the sea, destroying what is left. In addition to trying to destroy Rome, he will also threaten the great cultural centers of Greece, represented by Deucalion in the quatrain. (Deucalion was the equivalent of Noah in Greek mythology.) He says he will also be destroying places such as Athens and the great Greek cultural centers of learning and history. The world will be so shocked by these actions that it will momentarily be paralyzed. Thus, he will be able to make great strides in taking over and obtaining power before the other governments figure out just how they want to react and how drastically they want to react. He says this man will use such tactics throughout the entire conflict. That he will always be doing daring and shocking things to obtain what he wants.

D: *And where does Leo enter in? It says, "after Libra has left Leo."*

B: He says that once again that is a multi-meaning phrase. It is difficult to explain that line because the situations involved have not yet happened to make it clear. He says that the signs of Libra and Leo will be representing geographical locations as well as political forces involved in this conflict. A certain aspect of this man's forces will be represented by Libra. And when the political forces represented by Libra have done what they have decided to do with the political forces as represented by Leo, he will start with his campaign on Europe. He says that at the time when these events start shaping up the astrological implications will also become clear. But when he sees that point in time it's like a storm cloud that's building upon itself and flashing out lightning in all directions. It's difficult to really describe what's happening at this point because it's too tumultuous. The concepts involved are not clear enough to apply vocabulary to it for verbal description. The only thing that is clear is that there will be great destruction in Rome and other major cities of that peninsula that contain cultural treasures. For the Anti-Christ has in mind to wipe out the established culture and to supplant it with his own, rather like what the Moors tried to do when they invaded Spain. This man will try to do this to the entire continent.

CENTURY II-93 and III-17 also refer to this destruction.

CENTURY V-86

Par les deux testes, & trois bras separés,	Divided by the two heads and three arms, the great city will be troubled
Le cité grande par eaux sera vexee:	by water. Some of the great men among them, wandering in exile;
Des grands d'entre eux par exile esgarés,	Byzantium is hard pressed by the leader of Persia.
Par teste perse Bisance fort pressee.	

B: He says this refers to the same situation but from a different point of view. He says the help that could have saved the situation did not arrive in time. This is due to political and diplomatic ranklings amongst the western powers that could have nipped the situation in the bud, so to speak. He says there will be two countries—he seems to be referring to England and the United States—working together who are equally powerful so far as military might is concerned. But he says that when it comes to a military operation there must be *a* leader at the head to make the decisions. And if there are two leaders rankling over them, they may not be made in time. In this case, this particular military alliance between the United States and England will be a newly established one for use in time of emergency. They will not yet have worked out just who is in charge and who will back down. So they are rankling over what they should do in this situation. The three arms refer to the three basic branches of military service: sea, air, and land. They will not be able to get their strategists to decide what will be the best way to deal with the situation. Meanwhile, the Anti-Christ will be making progress, from his point of view, by leaps and bounds.

D: *"The great city troubled by water."* He has had other quatrains about the water encroaching upon Rome whenever he bombs it. Does it refer to that?

B: Yes. He says that amongst the confusion some of the thinkers that could provide answers for the leaders, to help them figure out the situation, will not be able to get to them in time due to breakdown in communication and in transportation and such. He says he wishes to add a note here. He has become aware from working with us that a lot of times when he uses terms like "the great city," the interpreters of his quatrains think he is referring to New York in the United States. He says this is not necessarily so because he had not heard of it in his lifetime. A lot of times when he refers to the great city, he refers to a city that is great in terms of time and achievement, not just in size. In this quatrain he's referring to Rome.

CENTURY V-43

La grande ruine des sacrez
ne s'esloigne,
Provence, Naples, Sicille,
Seez & Ponce:
En Germanie, au Rhin
& la Cologne,
Vexez à mort par ceux
de Magonce.

The great ruin of the clergy is not
far off, Provence, Naples, Sicily,
Sees and Pons. In Germany at the
Rhine and Cologne, vexed to death
by those of Maine.

B: He has mentioned to you before how this man will destroy the cultural
centers of western Europe to help cow the people, and that he will try
to level the seven hills of Rome. Another thing he will do in the process
of all this destruction is to ransack the Vatican totally to the ground
and destroy the library. He will do this mainly to undermine the
authority and break up into little pieces the Catholic Church. For that
will be a major obstacle in his plans. One way he will do this is by
revealing all the controversial things he finds that are hidden away in
the Vatican Library. Things the church has declared people should
not read for it would be threatening to their faith. He will be sure that
these things are distributed about. It will cause much dissension with
the church. Theologians and priests and students will turn one against
the other, each with their own theories and interpretations concerning
this new information. And all will be confusion. That way the
Catholic Church will no longer pose the obstacle that it did before for
this man and his plans.

When Nostradamus said the Anti-Christ would ransack the Vatican
Library and steal important documents relating to the church, I wondered
how this would be possible. Then it occurred to me that if this last pope
were a tool of the Anti-Christ, he might allow him entry into the most
sacred and secret archives. This would explain the treachery the pope
might do to cause the downfall of the church. The Vatican would not be
aware that the traitor was within their midst in the highest office until
after the terrible event had taken place.

D: *In these names, I thought it strange that he mentioned Maine.*
B: He says don't rely too heavily on what the translators do. It is not the
state in your country that you are thinking of. It's another place name
along with the others which are various major centers of learning in
Europe.

I think Maine is a typographical error as Nostradamus indicated. Ms.
Cheetham's book says that Magonce translates into Mainz or Mayenze.
This is a city in West Germany, the home of Johann Gutenberg, the first
printer of moveable type and the Bible. Through his activities, Mainz
became the center of printing during the late 1400s. In this context it

makes perfect sense in this quatrain as a symbolism of education and learning. If Brenda's mind had been involved in this, she would have picked up on the state and not an obscure foreign city because that was the way I read it to her.

D: *Speaking of the translators, the interpreter calls this one "a totally unsuccessful quatrain."*

B: Uh-oh! His eyes are flashing and my analogy is, you've seen these posters of Uncle Sam with his fingers pointing to you? (*I laughed.*) He is pointing to the book in that manner and he is saying, "*Who are they to say this?*" He keeps saying, "Give me time. I must have more time." He is saying the translators who said that do not have as many centuries standing in the way of their understanding as he does.—Does that make sense?—I've tried to remind him we've been able to come to the source and they couldn't.

CENTURY II-5 referred to submarines, symbolized by a fish. In a double meaning, they referred to the Germans' use of them in World War II but also by the Anti-Christ in his war. He would use the submarines to take the Vatican papers past the Italian fleets.

The people who are truly religious leaders are referred to as "a victim, its horn gilded with gold" in CENTURY III-26. They are the opposites of the "hollow priests." "The entrails will be interpreted" refers again to the secret records of the Catholic Church being exposed to daylight. He said he used this symbolism because priests used to cut open animals and expose their entrails to daylight to try to tap into metaphysical mysteries.

In CENTURY III-6 the destruction of Rome and the ransacking of the Vatican Library are again mentioned, referred to as "lightning striking inside the closed temple."

CENTURY I-62

Le grand parte las que feront les lettres, *Avant le cycle de Latona parfaict:* *Feu grand deluge plus par ignares sceptres,* *Que de long siecle ne se verra refaict.*	Alas! What a great loss there will be to learning before the cycle of the Moon is completed. Fire, great floods, by more ignorant rulers; how long the centuries until it is seen to be restored.

B: He says that that has a multiple meaning. One meaning is that during the time of troubles, during the earth changes, in all the countries, the fundamentalist sects of the various religions will become very powerful, claiming to offer people the comfort they need to get through the hard times. He says he does not care what religion these sects are affiliated with, be it Muslim or Christian or Shinto or what-have-you. These fundamentalist sects always suppress learning and education so there will be great censorship of books and such. He says that is one meaning of the quatrain. Another meaning of this quatrain refers to the sacking of the Vatican Library by the Anti-Christ. It will bring to light information and facts and knowledge that have been suppressed for several centuries. He says that, ironically, in a way the Anti-Christ will be doing a good thing by ransacking the Vatican Library because later on that knowledge, which has been suppressed for centuries, will be open to the whole world and available for everyone to use. He says even though the Anti-Christ goes about it the wrong way and uses violence to accomplish his ends, the fact that he does release this knowledge to the world will help him by starting the beginning of the cycle of his working off this karma, and working towards a higher level of karma.

D: *I suppose that is something in his favor anyhow.*

CENTURY II-12

Yeux clos, ouverts d'antique fantasie,
L'habit des seuls seront mis à neant:
Le grand monarque chastiera leur frenaisie,
Ravir des temples le tresor par devant.

Their eyes closed, open to the old fantasy, the habit of priests will be abolished. The great monarch will punish their frenzy, stealing the treasure in front of the temples.

B: He says this refers to the Anti-Christ and the destruction of the Catholic Church. The people involved with the Catholic Church, particularly the priests and such, will not be aware of the winds of change and will be hanging onto the old order even though it is no longer viable and dead, so far as being able to work within the framework of reality. He says "great monarch" has a double meaning. It is referring to the Anti-Christ plus it is referring to the pope who is the Anti-Christ's tool, because the pope is the great monarch of the church. They will be robbing the church blind, so to speak. Because the Anti-Christ, in addition to taking over the material possessions of the church to help fund his armies, will also be desecrating and raiding the Vatican Library.

D: *I didn't want him to get angry but I want to ask him something.*
B: He said, ask.
D: *I know he is under the persecution of the church and the Inquisition because of the time period he lives in. It has been suggested that when he speaks of the complete dissolving, the complete destruction of the Catholic Church in our future, that it could be mostly wishful thinking because of the persecution he is under.*

B: He says he has done a lot of wishful thinking in that direction, it is true. However, he asks that you observe the basic nature of the universe. When the pendulum swings one way, in one extreme direction, then it must swing back in the other direction to balance it. And he says when it swings back in the other direction it will cause this Catholic Church to become no more. The pendulum controlling the rise and fall of the Catholic Church is extended across a longer period of time, but the outcome will ultimately come about. Because the Catholic Church will become totally superfluous which will contribute to its disolvement.

D: *I thought he might get angry if I suggested that he was making up quatrains as wishful thinking and not as something he had actually seen.*

B: No, he is taking this very calmly. He says he can see where one would come up with that since he does have such a great amount of trouble from the Catholic Church.

Chapter 17

𝕮𝖍𝖊 𝕸𝖔𝖓𝖘𝖙𝖊𝖗 𝕬𝖕𝖕𝖊𝖆𝖗𝖘

CENTURY II-23

Palais, oiseaux, par oiseau
deschassé,
Bien tost apres le prince parvenu:
Combien que hors flueve ennemi
repoulsé,
Dehors sousi trait d'oiseau
soustenu.

Birds at the palace, chased out by a bird very soon after the upstart prince. How many of the enemy are repulsed beyond the river, the upheld bird seized from without by a trick.

B: He says this refers to when the Anti-Christ takes over Iran. In order to be able to take over the country, he has to use a decoy to trick the Ayatollah in charge. The birds represent the hangers-on at court, the chattering magpies, the sycophants, the ones that tell the leader what he wants to hear. The bird that is upheld is the decoy that the Anti-Christ uses. When he starts to take over Iran he will drive away internal supporters of the Ayatollah by starting a civil war. Then he will put forth a man as a leader. A man for Iranians loyal to the Ayatollah to concentrate their hate on. This man will end up being assassinated in the process of Iran being taken over, and they will think they have succeeded in foiling the attempt by assassinating him. Only to find out that he was a decoy all along, and that they have played right into the hands of the Anti-Christ.

CENTURY I-40, which was interpreted in Chapter 11, pp. 155, had a portion that applies here.

D: *"From Egypt there will go forth a man who wants the edict withdrawn."* Can you give any comment on that sentence?
B: He says later on in the course of events the Anti-Christ will start uniting the currencies of the various countries of that world to make it easier to submerge them into one political entity. Since his ambition is to take over the world, one of the ways he will accomplish this is to try to get one currency circulating throughout this area and have the

other currencies become defunct or what-have-you. There will be those who will protest against this. Particularly a charismatic popular leader from Egypt will be resisting this. He will want that particular edict or law withdrawn so that all the countries in this league of Arab nations can keep their own currencies and their own trade and such, rather than be submissive to this one political entity.

UPDATE: Referring to CENTURY I-40, *there was much discussion, both pro and con, during the 1990s about replacing the currencies of Europe with one currency. World leaders think it will be inevitable.*

CENTURY I-61

La republique miserable infelice	The wretched, unfortunate republic
Sera vastee de nouveau	will again be ruined by a new
magistrat:	authority. The great amount of
Leur grand amus de	ill will accumulated in exile will
l'exile malefice,	make the Swiss break their
Fera Sueve ravir leur	important agreement.
grand contracts,	

B: He says this will be taking place when the Anti-Christ is in the process of taking over Europe. The second wretched republic refers to Germany. He says it's called a wretched republic because it is split across her heart. He's showing me a picture of east and west Germany, the land of Germany being split. He says that those in exile gathering up hard feelings refers to the fact that for his own purposes the Anti-Christ will put the Nazi party back in power in Germany. The movement in Germany in your present day, the popularity of Nazism amongst Germany's youth, is laying the groundwork for this. As a result of this, this will cause Switzerland to break her centuries-old neutrality. And her breaking her long-standing agreement will be her taking the side against the Anti-Christ and actively fighting.

UPDATE: During 1991 there was a renewed interest in reviving the Nazi Party in Germany, especially among the young people of that country.

CENTURY II-96

Flambeau ardent au ciel soir	A burning torch will be seen in
sera veu,	the sky at night near the end and
Pres de la fin & principe	source of the Rhône. Famine
du Rosne:	and weapon; help provided too
Famine, glaive: tard le secours	late, Persia will turn and
pourveu,	invade Macedonia.
La Perse tourne envahir	
Macedoine.	

B: He says the interpretation of this quatrain is somewhat complicated because it refers to a complicated situation during troubled times, which would tend to make even ordinary situations complicated. This refers to some of the diplomatic foul-ups that lead to the Anti-Christ attaining more power. It is at the beginning when he does not have a broad base of power yet but he is building on it. The torch seen in the sky at night refers to his demonic hatred and his magnetism. This combination will help to make him powerful. He says this torch seen burning at night indicates that people will see he has power and they will be aware that he wields it for the dark side rather than for the forces of light. Those in power who can do something about it will realize that something needs to be done, but they will not come to a decision until too late. Meanwhile, he will have already started his campaign by invading neighboring countries and taking them over, and building a broader base of power with which to tackle yet other countries. And eventually take over the Asian continent.

D: *Why is Persia mentioned specifically?*

B: Because this is the part of the world from which he will start his campaign of power.

D: *In several quatrains he has mentioned the word "Perse." John though "Perse" might be a name or an anagram relating to the Anti-Christ.*

B: Sometimes it is used as a name and sometimes it is used as an allegory. In this case it's mainly an indication of that part of the world in which there is enough political turmoil where someone can rise to be in control quickly, through a military coup or what-have-you. And from there take advantage of unrest in neighboring countries to become more powerful.

John had not been present when the quatrains referring to the destruction of the cultural centers were translated. He spotted the mention of Macedonia and asked whether the Anti-Christ would invade Greece. In ancient times Macedonia was composed of parts of modern-day Greece, Bulgaria, and Yugoslavia. Nostradamus explained to John about the Anti-Christ's plan to demoralize Europe and western culture by destroying respected sites. He would also invade there first because he felt he could handle the military forces on hand in that part of Europe.

UPDATE: Is this quatrain an indication that the Anti-Christ is somehow involved in the internal conflict in Yugoslavia? This erupted into war in 1991.

B: Michel de Notredame says that he does not mind expounding to clarify things. He is so delighted to communicate with a sympathetic spirit in another plane of time that he does not mind a bit going back over things he has given before, by way of explanation.

D: *One time he said he didn't like to repeat himself.*

B: Well, he's saying that when he's talking directly to the black box, unnecessary repetition is somewhat tedious. But when he is talking to a person who is not filled in with the full story, he does not mind throwing in a little bit of explanation to help him get a better grasp of the picture, so that they may communicate better.

J: *Does the flaming torch have an astrological symbolism?*

B: He says, yes, it does. Now the main problem is to try and get it communicated. He may have to put it into allegory so that it will sound like ordinary language to my stubborn subconscious. And John can use his wits towards applying it to astrological symbolism. He says whenever he himself personally pictures a flaming torch in the sky at night, he's also speaking of a comet that is visible. In this case particularly visible to the Northern Hemisphere since these events will be predominantly taking place in the Northern Hemisphere. He says that with good reason comets have traditionally been used as harbingers of doom, and in this case it will be particularly applicable. He keeps giving me the date 1997. I don't know if this applies to this quatrain or not, but I keep seeing this number in the sky and I think it's coming from Nostradamus. He says Mars is very red at this point, very much coming into power. That Mars and the chariot of the sun and the power of fire are working together towards doom at this point. He is saying he may have to put astrological information in this form to make it easier to communicate. His main concern is to make sure it is coming through in a way that is making sense to John in an astrological way. When he puts it in figurative language like this it's much easier to get it through my subconscious since this vessel is acutely aware of her ignorance in this matter. She's concerned about subconsciously influencing it with her knowledge from other areas.

J: *(He had been busily looking up these signs in his Ephemeris.) Mars takes place in the sign of Sagittarius in October of 1997 and the Sun is in its fall in the sign of Libra. Would this be the time that this takes place?*

B: He says that this sounds good.

D: *But by this time the Anti-Christ will have already come into power.*

B: At least in a portion of the world. He says there'll be very much happening at this time. Your concerns are very real and your wildest imaginings about these matters will not be too out-of-place compared to what will be happening. He says it's very important to try to get the bulk of the knowledge together and to spread this knowledge before suppression has a chance to take place.

CENTURY II-29 and V-54 referred to the Anti-Christ's war strategy in his invasion of Europe. After the destruction in Italy he would go up through the mountains to get to France, using "a flying carpet," Nostradamus' word for an airplane. It would be very logical for him to tackle Europe from the south by way of the Mediterranean because he would have the solid backing of the Islamic world. He will have already conquered North Africa and the Middle East. He will set up a regional headquarters in Byzantium (Turkey) to rule that part of the world as he continues his conquest. He will continue to set up these regional outposts in various places. His "bloody rod" (mentioned in both quatrains) represents the harshness of his rule.

CENTURY IV-33

Jupiter joinct plus Venus qu'à la Lune,
Apparoissant de plenitude blanche:
Venus cachée souz la blancheur Neptune
De Mars frappée par la gravée branche.

Jupiter joined more to Venus than to the Moon appearing in a white fullness. Venus hidden under the whiteness of Neptune struck by Mars by the engraved wand.

B: He says this refers to the positions of the planets in regards to the astrological signs. In other words, this is an astrological quatrain. (*Sigh*) I see a picture of him running his fingers through his beard trying to figure a way to put across the concepts.

John was anxious to intervene but I whispered to him to wait until she was through with her interpretation.

B: The influence of Venus, that is, of love and understanding, will be temporarily obscured due to other considerations, particularly the force of Mars, that is, of war. He says the engraved wand represents a symbol of power and weapons. It has to do with an advanced technology that is currently being developed but you are not aware of it. He says he has referred to this technology before. During the time of troubles, at a point when Venus and Jupiter are in Sagittarius—I believe that's what he's trying to tell me—and with Venus being partially obscured by Neptune.—He's having difficulty coming through with this. He says that this pinpoints the time for the onset of the major war that will cause destruction and famine and the plagues that he has mentioned in several other quatrains. He says he's having difficulty putting across the concepts and having me to communicate what he's trying to say, but the young astrologer is welcome to ask questions to try to clarify. Perhaps his questions will help Michel de Notredame think of ways to communicate what he's trying to say.

J: *Okay. In traditional astrology Venus conjunct Jupiter is a beneficial aspect and in Sagittarius it is a sign of religion, philosophy and would open up more spiritual channels and spiritual centers, as I would see it. Neptune, as we describe it in esoteric astrology, is the higher octave of Venus. Meaning that on one side it's the spiritual love of the universe, but*

*on the other side Neptune can be the great sensualist or deceiver or the
great waster of time. So it is with Venus conjuncting with Jupiter in
the sign of philosophy obscured by Neptune taking place now towards
the end of the century in Capricorn, the most materialistic sign. Does
this mean there'll be a ray of hope coming from a more spiritual value system to humankind to prevent this great cataclysm that will be taking place?*

B: He says the ray of hope is there and his purpose for communicating
with these quatrains is to try to at least alter, if not prevent, the worst
aspects of these events from coming up. Whether the events are
altered or not, even if the very worst that can happen happens, there
will still be a great spiritual rebirth throughout the entire world. And
during the time of troubles, people individually will have opportunities
to get in touch with themselves and realize that the materialistic values
were false. After the time of troubles when people start communicating with each other again, they will find out that other people
realize this also. This will cause a great rebirth of philosophy and a
great blending of the best aspects of eastern and western religions. It
will result in a worldwide movement of philosophical thought that is
in accord with what people know and feel to be true. This will bring
about the best aspects of the Age of Aquarius. If people could realize
this ahead of time and hold on to this ray of hope, then they could
alleviate some of the worst aspects of this time of troubles that is
coming. But he fears it may be unlikely that this could happen in any
widespread form, due to the materialistic values held by the majority of
the populace.

CENTURY III-7

*Les fugitifs, feu du ciel sus
les piques.
Conflict prochain des corbeaux
s'esbatans.
De terre on crie aide secours
celiques,
Quand pres des murs seront
les combatans.*

The fugitives, fire from heaven on
to their weapons, the next conflict
will be that of the crows. They
call on earth for help and heavenly
aid when the aggressors draw
near the walls.

B: He says this refers to the various countries asking the more powerful
countries for assistance during this time of the Anti-Christ. Particularly, they will be calling toward countries like the United States who
will still be neutral and not committed to the situation.

D: *What is the meaning of "The next conflict will be that of the crows"?*

B: He says it refers to an aerial battle with unmarked planes. The Anti-
Christ will be trying to take over a part of the world using airplanes.
And there will be other airplanes coming out of the night that will
fight them off. But they will be unmarked so that no one will know

who they belong to. It will be strongly suspected they come from a strong western power who is still officially neutral. (*She was smiling, so it was obvious who he was referring to.*) He says this country who wants to remain neutral and nameless has been famous for doing such things before—providing planes and guns and such to the side they are favorable toward, even though they are officially neutral. He says, not to mention any names, but their initials are U.S.

D: *That's what I figured. Because he said before they would try to remain neutral as long as they could.*

B: He says the United States has been famous for always following this policy, but at the same time helping out every way they can.

During his daring Mediterranean campaign he takes over Monaco and he knows he must get rid of the Prince of Monaco so he can be the official ruler. The reason why Monaco is so important is because of its strategic position in relation to Italy and southern Europe. In CENTURY III-10 he refers to "the great golden one caught in an iron cage" and says this is the successor to Prince Ranier (apparently one of his sons) who will be imprisoned after the takeover.

CENTURY I-37

Un peu devant que le soleil s'excuse,	Shortly before sunset, battle is engaged. A great nation is
Conflict donné grand peuple dubiteux:	uncertain. Overcome, the sea port makes no answer, the
Profliges, port marin ne faict response,	bridge and the grave both in foreign places.
Pont & sepulchre en deux estranges lieux.	

B: He says this quatrain is one with multiple meanings, but one of the meanings does have something to do with what you need to know. This portrays the see-sawing back and forth the United States will go through before getting involved with this conflict with the Anti-Christ. He says "close to sunset" means that in this situation it is known the United States is not at the peak of her powers as she was years before. It's in her sunset, so to speak, so far as her influence and power is concerned. Her star is waning somewhat. There's still some influence and power, but she's not getting as much done as she could have in earlier years. He says "the nation is uncertain" refers to the division of opinion amongst the people of the United States as to whether or not to get involved with this conflict. The seaport being taken refers to the fact that shipping and such will be very dangerous during this time, because the Anti-Christ's "silver fish"—he's referring to submarines—will make the seas very threatening. There are enemy soldiers in the port fouling up shipping. He says a lot of the decisive battles will be battles concerning the taking over of seaports as well.

UPDATE: When this quatrain was translated in 1986 it seemed difficult to imagine where these Middle Eastern countries would obtain their navy from, especially submarines. One possible answer came in 1992 after the breakup of the Soviet Union. U.S. intelligence reports indicated that Iran was buying Russian submarines with the apparent aim of controlling the narrow straits leading into the Persian Gulf. This meant that they could conceivably control all shipping traffic entering the gulf. Iran and other Middle Eastern countries were also buying other weapons, including nuclear ones, and the Soviet nuclear scientists were now looking for jobs with the highest bidder. The unthinkable had now become possible, through extraordinary and unforeseen circumstances.

B: Regarding "the bridge and the grave in a foreign land," he says the word (bridge) also refers to the pope and how he will be in a foreign land. That is to say, he will be looking at things differently than from the church and he will be foreign to the church.

D: *Is this the last pope?*

B: Yes. And he says the grave being in a foreign land refers to one: the fact that many people will be dying far away from home in the course of the conflict. And two: he's trying to point out to both the church people of his day and the church people of the present day, that on the other side of the veil it's very different from what they picture it to be. So it will be very foreign to their concepts. He says this meaning really does not relate to the rest of the quatrain, but he was still trying to get that information across.

Chapter 18

𝕰urope, the 𝕰ternal 𝕭attlefield

D: *He seems a little cross today. Is he feeling all right?*

B: He says it's not a matter of his being cross; it's just that he knows the pressure of time as you do not, and the importance of getting this work through. And he says the extraneous comments gets in the way. He does not intend to sound mean but he says the press of time is becoming ever more urgent, as you would not realize. He is so afraid for our sakes that he is trying to get the information through as much as he can. He has an overview of the situation in general that you have no inkling of.

CENTURY II-84

Entre Campaigne, Sienne, Flora, Tustie,	Between Campania, Sienna, Florence and Tuscany, it will
Six mois neuf jours ne ploura une goutte:	not rain a drop for six months and nine days. A foreign language
L'estrange langue en terre Dalmatie,	will be spoken in Dalmatia, it will overrun the country, devastating
Courira sus: vastant la terre toute.	all the land.

B: He says, as should be fairly apparent, this refers to the time of troubles. The drought refers to the weather changes that will be taking place in relation to the earth changes at the time. The foreign language being spoken and overrunning the land refers to the Anti-Christ's forces taking over Italy and, as before mentioned, Greece, by destroying the cultural centers to help destroy the morale.

D: *Then those city names are just representative of that part of Europe where the drought will occur.*

B: Of Italy. He says, needless to say, it will be very disastrous to the wine industry. He says he is drawing upon an image from this vehicle's brain, and that in future decades one will *not* go to a nice restaurant and ask for a Lafite '98, or what-have-you. It will be a very bad year for wine because of the bad weather.

I found that Dalmatia, which now is a strip of land along the Adriatic Sea, once belonged to the Roman Empire. In Nostradamus' time it belonged to Venice and was surrounded by the Ottoman Empire. This could be a reference to both Italy and Turkey in his type of symbolism.

Campania and Tuscany, in Italy, produce grapes in large quantities, and are famous for their wine making. These are examples of small details being supplied that could not possibly have come from any of the minds of the participants.

CENTURY III-16

Un prince Anglais Mars a son
cœur de ciel,
Voudra poursuivre sa
fortune prospere:
Des deux duelles l'un percera
le fiel,
Hai de lui, bien aimé de sa mere.

An English prince, Mars has his heart in the heavens, will wish to follow his prospering fortune. In two duels, one will pierce him in the gall bladder, hated by him, but well loved by his mother.

B: He says this is an event that will take place close to the beginnings of the war caused by the Anti-Christ. This will precipitate England's involvement with this great war. The English prince, his heart held by Mars high in the heavens, is a young man of the English royal house who is eager to lead the troops into battle. He wants to rescue his friends on the continent; that is, the people that England has diplomatic treaties with. He will be anxious to go. He will be in two major engagements and in one of them he will be defeated. He will be outflanked on the field and he will have to retreat in disgrace. The troops that he was fighting against will spit at him and use his name as a curseword, for he was a good fighter even though he was defeated. His brashly rushing into battle messes up some of the carefully laid plans in the conquest of Europe. And so this man will return to England. However, his mother*land*, England, will be cheering him and will love him all the more for the brave show he made. For trying to help and for carrying the English name and honor bright into battle.

D: *The part, "they will pierce him in the gall bladder," is that what he meant by outflanking him?*

B: Yes. They will outflank him and pierce his forces in the side and hence defeat him.

D: *The translators have interpreted this very literally as a real duel and they said duels don't take place anymore.*

CENTURY II-39

Un an devant le conflict Italique,	A year before the war in Italy,
Germains, Gaulois, Hespaignols	Germans, French and Spanish will
pour le fort:	be for the strong one; the school-
Cherra l'escolle maison	house of the republic will fall,
de republique,	where, except for a few, they will
Ou, hors mis peu, seront	suffocate to death.
soffoque mors.	

B: There will be those in Germany, France, Spain, and Italy, who will be secretly working for the Anti-Christ, helping him to take over Europe. As a result of him taking over Europe and destroying the cultural centers and such, it will affect Europe in such a way that, since they'll be in a state of war, it'll be difficult to continue educating the children because of air raids and such as this. And so the children will have to go without education until the time of troubles are over. Some of them, the ones referred to as suffocating to death, are those with curious minds who need to read and learn because they are of above-average intelligence. They will feel like they are suffocating without the exposure to literature and such they were used to. The phrase, "the schoolhouse will fall," refers to the inability to educate the children due to the war conditions.

John was being given a lot of work to do with dating the astrological quatrains. I remarked once to Nostradamus that he would probably have to come back and ask more questions. It was hard for him to work these out so quickly.

B: He says he understands. One must keep one's inkwell handy and keep it from drying. But sometimes one must stop to replenish the inkwell, so it does take time.—Or, rather the inkhorn.—He says he uses an inkhorn. He realized that the term "inkwell" is what is used in our day but he showed me a picture of a horn used to hold the ink.

D: *(Laugh) Well, in our time we have other writing devices. They're much easier to keep full of ink.*

B: He says he's not interested in that. He can see in the vessel's mind complaints of her running out of ink too often. He says he has the same complaint, that the quill always runs out too fast.

I didn't understand what he meant at the time because nowadays we don't have to worry about our writing implements. This would seem to be only an old-fashioned humorous remark or a contradiction. But later Brenda explained that she does calligraphy and has on occasion complained about the quills running out of ink too fast. Strangely, he apparently picked up this detail from her mind since it fit with his own experiences. It seems that he will associate with what is familiar when he can.

CENTURY I-77

Entre deux mers dressera
promontaire,
Que plus mourra par le mords
du cheval:
Le sien Neptune pliera
voille noire,
Par Calpre & classe aupres
de Rocheval.

A promontory stands between two seas: A man who will die later by the bit of a horse; Neptune unfurls a black sail for his man; the fleet near Gibraltar and Rocheval.

B: He says this refers to the key role that Gibraltar will play in the Mediterranean battle with the Anti-Christ. He says the key man principle in saving Gibraltar from the Anti-Christ's forces and thereby as a result saving the Iberian Peninsula, will later go to his death. He will be killed in an automobile accident. He says he used the phrase, "bit by the horse," because he did not know the concept of automobiles. He says this man is a naval officer but he will die somewhat young. That's why he said Neptune had unfurled a black sail for him.

D: *The mention of Neptune would also refer to him being a navy man.—*
Then the promontory is the Rock of Gibraltar.

B: Yes. And he says that "the fleet near Gibraltar and Rocheval" refers to one of the key strategic places the fleet will need to be in the process of the ongoing sea battles.

D: *They didn't know what Rocheval meant. They thought it was an*
anagram for "rock."

B: He says Rocheval is an anagram for a small obscure port that's not too distant from the Rock of Gibraltar.

CENTURY II-68

De l'aquilon les efforts
seront grands.
Sus l'Occean sera la
porte ouverte:
Le regne en l'isle sera
reintegrand,
Tremblera Londres par
voille descouverte.

In the North great efforts will be made, across the seas the way will be open. The rule on the island will be re-established, London fearful of the fleet when sighted.

B: He says this refers to two events. On the one hand, he says it refers to the way things were between the United States and England during World War II, and how they managed to keep the shipping lanes open between the two countries. And he says it also refers to the time of the Anti-Christ. The Anti-Christ, during his European campaign, will also be attempting to take over Great Britain. Great Britain, being a prime maritime power, can very richly further his forces. He will attempt to take over England but not be entirely successful. So England will be able to reassert herself. Part of the reasons for this will be because there will be the support of the United States behind England, once again.

D: *Does he see that England will be taken over by the Anti-Christ?*

B: He says it's hard to tell clearly what all will be happening because it's a confusing time. The Anti-Christ will attempt to take over once and fail for sure the first time. But he says as best he can tell, the Anti-Christ will succeed in taking over England. And the more stubborn supporters for the underground will flee to Ireland and Scotland. He will not be successful in taking over the *entire* island. It will just be part of England, and he says you'll have kind of like a "rump" United Kingdom.

D: *(I didn't understand that phrase.) A what?*

B: He says you'll understand if you recall your history of World War II, when the Germans took over part of Czechoslovakia. Two-thirds of Czechoslovakia was part of Nazi Germany and the remainder of Czechoslovakia put together a rump government. It was called "rump" Czechoslovakia because is was just a remainder of the country that was still free.

D: *I have never heard that term.*

B: He says you will find it in history books. Thus, they will have a rump United Kingdom. The majority of England will be under the power of the Anti-Christ. But North England, Scotland, and Ireland will not be under his power. Hopefully this event taking place has the possibilities of uniting Ireland. Because if England will be taken over, she will not be able to do anything about Northern Ireland, so Ireland can reunite itself the way it's been wanting to be reunited for centuries.

D: *I can see that Ireland probably would stop their fighting with all this going on.*

B: He says the main reason why Ireland is fighting is because ... the English can be dynamic when they choose to be, but more often they choose to be stuffed shirts instead. And he says the English in your time are being stuffed shirts in regard to Ireland. When England is taken over by the Anti-Christ, they will be in no position to have any say-so as to what goes on in Ireland. And so Ireland will be able to apply its own remedies to its problems, and turn its dynamic energy toward other problems, such as the Anti-Christ. And the Irish spirit, he says, being strong and valiant as it is, and the Scottish stubbornness will play a good ways toward helping the underground movement to survive the worst of the worst days and eventually conquer the Anti-Christ. When all this is over, people who are Scottish and people who are Irish will be proud that they are, because of the role Ireland and Scotland will play.

CENTURY I-89

Tous ceux de Ilerde seront dans la Moselle, *Mettant à mort tous ceux de Loire & Seine:* *Le cours marin viendra pres d'haute velle,* *Quand Espagnols ouvrira toute veine.*	Those of Lerida will be in the Moselle, killing all those from the Loire and Seine. The seaside track will come near the high valley, when the Spanish open every route.

B: He says this refers to part of the role the Spanish will play in the events during the time of the Anti-Christ. They will be a key link in the underground organization to help link the central part of Europe to the outside world after the Anti-Christ's forces have taken over. He says the Spanish will be very open toward helping the underground movement. And the Pyrenees, the mountains between France and Spain, will play an important part in helping people to sneak past the clutches of the Anti-Christ.

D: It says, *"killing all those from the Loire and the Seine."* I know those are two rivers in France.

B: Yes. There will be a lot of bloodshed going on. He says the rivers will run red with blood.—He says once you know the direction the quatrain is supposed to go in, a lot of times it's merely a matter of applying logical progression to the events. Thus, they should be easy for a logical mind to understand.

I did not agree. I think his symbolism is too complex.

In CENTURY II-83 he says when the Anti-Christ is making raids into Europe, the underground fights back. They are referred to as "fog" in the quatrain. He calls them that because they will retreat into the mountain strongholds for protection and come forth very silently, like fog or smoke, when they come forth to fight the enemy. They can also fade away in the same manner. This quatrain also refers to the major trade centers of Europe being brought to ruin, either through direct destruction or through the breakdown of trade.

CENTURY I-98

Le chef qu'aura conduit peuple infiny *Loing de son ciel, de meurs & langue estrange:* *Cinq mil en Crete & Thessalie fini* *Le chef fuyant, sauvé en marine grange.*	The leader who will conduct great numbers of people far from their skies, to foreign customs and language. Five thousand will die in Crete and Thessaly, the leader fleeing in a sea-going supply ship.

B: He says, on the one hand this refers to some events during World War I. But it also refers to events that take place during the time of the Anti-Christ. He's picturing a large group of ships with a lot of fighting men on them, men who can fight either on the land or sea. He calls it a "naval army." I believe he's referring to marines. He says there will be a large force of marines that will try to stave off an attack. Many will be killed in the neighborhood of Crete and Thessaly. But he says they will not succeed. They will have to withdraw, probably to Gibraltar. This is to be expected because the Anti-Christ won't be able to just walk into Europe. There will be a struggle. The Europeans will fight back.

D: *The interpreters said the quatrain translates literally as the leader fleeing in a sea-going "barn," and they have interpreted that as "supply ship."*

B: Yes. He says his fighting ship will be sunk and he will have to transfer his colors to a supply ship because it will be the nearest ship that is still seaworthy and large enough to carry his men. It will be a very fierce battle.

D: *I suppose he described it as "barn" because that was what he saw it as.*

B: Yes. He says he was speaking figuratively. A barn being a place where you store your feed for your horses plus your horses. This ship will have amphibious vessels in it as well as gasoline and such.

CENTURY I-55

Soubs l'opposite climat
Babylonique,
Grand sera de sang effusion:
Que terre & mer, air,
ciel sera inique,
Sectes, faim, regnes,
pestes, confusion.

In the land with a climate opposite to Babylon there will be great shedding of blood. Heaven will seem unjust both on land and sea and in the air. Sects, famine, kingdoms, plagues, confusion.

B: He says the sociological and political effects of the Anti-Christ will be particularly felt in the developed countries which also happen to be northern countries with cooler climates. It will be particularly devastating in the major countries of the northern hemisphere that have cool climates. Babylon had a warm climate. He says it was an agrarian country in the Middle East, when things were still fertile and there was rain. It was very warm and pleasant. Due to the political and sociological upheaval things will be torn and in confusion, and people will not know where to go or whom to follow. It will be a time where many doomsayers will rise up and claim to be prophets, claiming to have revelations and salvation for people. Governments will rise and fall. He says it will be a very confusing time.

CENTURY I-34

L'oiseau de proie volant	The bird of prey flying to the left,
à la semestre,	before battle is joined with the
Avant conflict faict aux	French, he makes preparations.
François pareure:	Some will regard him as good,
L'un bon prendra l'un	others bad or uncertain. The
ambigue sinistre,	weaker party will regard him as a
La partie foible tiendra par	good omen.
bon augure.	

B: He says this once again refers to some of the tactics the Anti-Christ will use. He will ferment rebellion within the countries he's going to take over. He allows the various political splinter groups to believe he supports their cause and their point of view. He lets them think he's going to help them rise to power again, although he doesn't, obviously.

D: *Yes, you said he would be very good at using his golden tongue in making them believe things that weren't true.*

B: By doing this he helps turn the country on itself from within, to weaken it against outside forces.

D: *They relate this to Hitler.*

B: He says he can see where they would get that, but he was mainly talking about the Anti-Christ. He will be following Hitler very closely. He will use guile with everybody. He says, remember your history books. From your point of view it's the past, although it's the future for him. Remember how Hitler talked his way into a lot of concessions that no one else would have dreamed of asking for.

CENTURY I-71

La tour marine trois fois	The marine tower will be captured
prise & reprise,	and retaken three times by
Par Hespagnols, Barbares,	Spaniards, barbarians and
Ligurins:	Ligurians. Marseilles and Aix,
Marseilles & Aix, Arles par	Arles by men of Pisa, devastation,
ceux de Pise,	fire, sword, pillage at Avignon by
Vast, feu, fer, pillé Avignon	the Lurinoco.
des Thurins.	

B: He says this refers to events both during the Spanish Civil War and during World War II and also events that will be coming in the future with the Anti-Christ. He says the marine tower refers to the Rock of Gibraltar.

D: *The translators didn't know what that meant.*

B: He says the Rock of Gibraltar is a very strategic place, and therefore a tower of strength due to its strategic location. Also it belongs to a country that is basically a maritime or a marine power; that is, Great Britain with her navy.

Chapter 19

Experimentation

Nostradamus saw that during the time of troubles the nations would become desperate for any solution to stop the monster. Thus, this also became a time of experimentation. Scientists searched for new and more radical weapons and other methods of war that defied belief. Some of them seem to have stretched man's imagination to the limits.

The first one has its roots in our present time.

CENTURY IX-83

Sol vingt de Taurus si fort terre trembler.	The sun in twenty degrees of Taurus, there will be a great
Le grand theatre rempli ruinera,	earthquake; the great theater
L'air ciel & terre obscurcir & troubler	full up will be ruined. Darkness and trouble in the air, on sky and
Lors l'infidelle Dieu & sainctz voguera.	land, when the infidel calls upon God and the Saints.

B: He says this one has a multiple meaning. Such ones are easy enough to interpret into multiple meanings because of the disasters that happen from time to time in earth's history. He says one of the minor implications of this quatrain has happened in what you would consider the recent past, that is the earthquake in Mexico City (September 1985). But he says that is not the major impetus of the quatrain. This will be an earthquake that will be triggered by a weapon that is currently being developed in secret underground laboratories. He cannot put across the images of how this weapon works, for the concepts are not present in his vocabulary and they're not present in this vehicle's vocabulary either. It apparently will be working on some scientific principle recently discovered that has not really been developed yet. So the concept of it is not generally available to be learned.

D: *Does he have any mental pictures that might help us?*

B: The only thing he's putting across clearly is the operating part of this weapon, the part that actually triggers the earthquake. He's not sure, or rather the concepts are not clear as to whether it is something that is dropped or something that is projected like a laser ray, but whatever the actual operating point of the spear, so to speak, it is airborne. Some extension of the device is carried in a plane and the plane must fly over the area where the earthquake is to be or at least fly over the area where the earthquake must be triggered, regardless of the area the earthquake ends up affecting. But that will not be the entire device. That will simply be like the point of the spear, just the operating part of it. The power behind the weapon and the science behind it will be based in a secret underground laboratory elsewhere. Somehow the power from the underground laboratory will be linked to the airborne device in such a way as to be able to channel it to the desired effect of a triggered earthquake.

Could this possibly be done in some sophisticated way by directing sound waves toward the target?

B: The country that develops this device will be able to hold it as a major threat over the heads of all the major nations. Any nation can be intimidated that has any geological faults in their country that are susceptible to earthquakes. He says it will be very similar to the situation immediately after World War II, of the United States being the only country with nuclear power. This will be a similar advance in weaponry, and the country that develops this will have it to hold over the other countries' heads. He says the concept of it will be so awe-inspiring and frightening, much the way nuclear power was at first to the world, that it will cause everybody, including the infidels, to call upon the saints for protection.

D: *"The great theatre full up will be ruined."*

B: He says due to the development of this weapon and the disintegration of diplomatic relations as a result of this, the United Nations will be dissolved. For this nation will not want to sit down and share this power with the other nations, the way the United States did with nuclear power. Although the United States did it reluctantly, this nation will not even consider the idea. From the concepts he's putting across, one gets the feeling it might be a nation like Russia, or a nation with the power behind it to have secret military research going on in a big way, on a large scale. The attitude this nation will have is that, "The weapon is mine. I'm going to keep it to myself." It's a paranoid nation that will have it and this will cause the disintegration of the United Nations.

D: *"The sun in 20 degrees of Taurus," is that when it's supposed to happen?*

B: He says that refers to when the weapon becomes generally known. It's already in the process of being developed but it's extremely secret. When it becomes more generally known, it will be that date.

D: *The translators think that's when the earthquake will occur.*

B: There will be an earthquake associated with it. That's how people will come to realize there is something fishy going on. For there will start being a lot of earthquakes without the previous buildup of pressure associated with them. He says one side effect of this weapon is that it will create sufficient instability to set off other earthquakes that are apt to go at any time anyway. He's picturing the two major fault systems in the United States. One is particularly unstable. The other one stays stable but then is explosive. The San Andreas and the New Madrid faults. He says the earthquakes triggered by this weapon will cause the San Andreas fault to rumble all the time. The New Madrid fault has always been bad to build up the pressure and then explosively quake. So with the San Andreas fault continually rumbling and vibrating it will set off the New Madrid fault in to a major earthquake. When these earthquakes initially start happening the geologists will think it's by natural causes, but then some of the information will not point to natural causes and they'll begin to suspect something. As more earthquakes happen, through their science they gather more information and confront the scientific world with the evidence they have that these are not natural earthquakes.

During another session I wanted to find out more about this machine and whether it would be related to the Anti-Christ and the time of troubles.

D: *I wanted to ask about the quatrain that dealt with a country that was going to develop an earthquake machine. Also in the same quatrain it said the United Nations would fall apart due to this.*
B: He says he remembers interpreting it.
D: *Does that happen before or during the time of the Anti-Christ?*
B: He says this earthquake device, that this country has for focusing a certain type of energy waves onto certain parts of the earth's crust to trigger earthquakes, is already in the process of being developed. It will be used during the time of the earth changes to create a lot of the earthquakes. This will be basically before the Anti-Christ comes to power. It will contribute to the United Nations falling apart, and that in turn will make things easier for the Anti-Christ. He says this nation that develops this machine will be developing it independently of the Anti-Christ rising to power, but later on when he takes over a certain amount of power he'll be able to start acquiring things like this. Then the Anti-Christ will take over this machine and start using it to his own ends.
D: *That was what was confusing. I thought if someone had a machine that was so powerful, how could the Anti-Christ take that country over.*
B: The Anti-Christ will acquire that machine through guile and trickery, through spies and bribery and all other nefarious means known to man.

CENTURY I-6

L'œil de Ravenne sera destitué,	The eye of Ravenna will be
Quand à ses pieds les ailles	forsaken, when his wings will fail
failliront:	at his feet. The two of Bresse will
Les deux de Bresse auront	have made a constitution for Turin
constitué,	and Vercelli, which the French will
Turin, Derseil que Gaulois	trample underfoot.
fouleront.	

B: He says this refers to some events in World War II, but it also refers to some events to come. There will be some research being done on a more sophisticated sort of radar to make it into a sensing-type device that will provide more in-depth information for the operator. They will be trying to develop this device so it can be used in aircraft. But the first experiments with this will be a failure. Somehow the device will put off the type of sympathetic vibrations to cause the structure of the plane to become weakened and dangerous, due to the dissolving of the bonds between some of the molecules in the metal.

D: *That's what it means by "the eye of Ravenna"? Would that be an anagram for "radar"?*

B: He says it is an anagram for a mythological figure who had great, almost psychic-type powers of knowledge and observation.

In my research I was able to find one mythological figure I think could possibly be the one referred here in symbolism. In Indian lore there is a story about Visnu and the great demon, Ravana. Quoted from *Mythology of All Races,* Volume VI: "At the time the gods were in fear of the demon Ravana, to whom Brahma had granted the gift of invulnerability, and they sought a means of killing him. ... Of individual Raksasas (demons) by far the greatest is Ravana. ... Evil as they are, the demons are formidable fighters. Not only are they numberless, but they are skilled in sorcery and in every magic art, transforming themselves into all manner of shapes, such as those used by Ravana in the abduction of Sita, and spreading universal terror by their appalling roars." This could certainly fit Nostradamus' qualifications as a symbolic figure from mythology, and Ravenna could be an anagram for Ravana.

D: *"When his wings will fail at his feet" has to do with the aircraft?*

B: Yes. He says at this time the scientists will end up temporarily abandoning the research in this project due to diplomatic breakdowns and the threat of war, *etc.*

D: *Will this occur before, during or after the time of the Anti-Christ?*

B: He says it will be occurring at the time of the Anti-Christ but before the Anti-Christ comes to full power. This will be happening in Europe at the time the Anti-Christ is gaining a power base in the Middle East, so the two events won't really be related. But it will be one of the events in Europe that lead up to making it easier for the Anti-Christ to take over Europe.

D: *Do you know if they're doing experimentation on this type of radar at the present time?*

B: He says it's being developed but it's not being experimented on yet.

D: *It would be good if they knew it could be dangerous.*

B: He says there's no way you could warn them about that because they have it as a military secret. They will find out soon enough it is dangerous.

Ravenna was also mentioned in the following quatrain. Could the anagram refer to a place where the laboratories are hidden and where the experimentation is being performed, as well as the demon, Ravana?

Toward the end of inventor Nicola Tesla's life he claimed to be able to create a shield in the upper atmosphere that would destroy any incoming aircraft. The Russians developed a machine (called "gyrotron"), based on Tesla's invention, designed to "sweep the sky of warplanes" by using high-energy microwaves. These high-power microwave weapons would give the operator the same ability to wipe out electronic circuits as a nuclear blast would provide. The main difference is that this new technology is controllable, and can be used without violating nuclear weapons treaties. Tesla described his speed-of-light system as being able to melt aircraft hundreds of miles away. Another quatrain that sounds like the "gyrotron" is CENTURY II-91 on pg. 127. Nostradamus describes secret weapon research done by the Soviets. They develop energy fields that guard their northern approach corridors.

CENTURY II-32

*Laict, sant grenouilles escoudre
  en Dalmatie,
Conflict donné, peste pres
  de Balennes
Cri sera grand par toute
  Esclavonie,
Lors naistra monstre pres
  & dedans Ravenne.*

Milk, blood, frogs will be prepared in Dailmatia: battle engaged, plague near Balennes. A great cry will go up throughout Slavonia, then will a monster be born near Ravenna.

B: He says this quatrain has to do with the uses of nuclear devices during the time of the Anti-Christ. The milk, blood, and frogs being prepared refers to both the instruments of death itself—that is, various atomic weapons—plus the labs nearby where new ones are being developed. He says that last line "then will the monster be born," is about when they will develop this ultimate monstrosity in weapons near Ravenna. This research is already going on in our present. It will come to fruition during the time of troubles.

D: *Does he know what type of a weapon it will be?*

B: He can see what it's like but it's so utterly horrible and fantastic he really doesn't want to describe it. And he's having difficulty connecting the concepts in this vehicle's mind because this vehicle is basically not favorable towards war either.

D: *Then it is not an atomic weapon?*

B: Yes, it is, but it's totally different from any atomic weapon ever invented before.

D: *I won't ask him to describe any more if he's not comfortable with it. But the part about frogs being prepared, how does that relate to this? I can understand the milk and blood, but what is the meaning of the word "frogs"?*

B: That indicates that due to the horrors of warfare, it upsets the ecology to where there are plagues of various creatures and animals across the land, because everything is out of balance.

D: *Can he say which side of the war will be using these weapons?*

B: He says all sides in this upcoming conflict will have their fair share of horrible weapons.

CENTURY II-6

Aupres des portes & dedans deux cités *Seront deux fléaux & oncques n'apperceu un tel:* *Faim, dedans peste, de fer hors gens boutés,* *Crier secours au grand Dieu immortel.*	Near the harbor and in two cities will be two scourges, the like of which have never been seen. Hunger, plague within, people thrown out by the sword will cry for help from the great immortal God.

B: He says this quatrain has a multiple meaning to it. In addition, he assumed the translation is a little bit off. He's saying the word "harbor" does not necessarily mean a harbor in the strict sense of the word, but simply a body of water separating two major cities. One of these cities is London and the other city ... I think he's trying to give me a picture of New York. He says he was referring to a piece of slang in World War II referring to the Atlantic as the "pond." And so these two cities are separated by the pond, even though we're not really speaking of a harbor or a pond, but we're speaking of an ocean. The scourges that hit these two cities will be as a result of some secret research into bacteriological warfare. Some very deadly bug. He wanted me to use the word "bug" because he's not sure if it will be bacteria or viruses, but it will be some sort of disease-causing organisms. It will ultimately be released into the atmosphere in such a way as to affect the population of New York and London. But there will be some mutations in the organisms so they'll affect the two populations in different ways, as there'll be different gene pools involved. Because the organisms are separated from each other they will have some spontaneous mutations and develop in two different directions. It will appear to be two different diseases even though it was caused by the same organism. He says as a result of this plague the service systems within these great metropolises will break down. The people in the surrounding countryside will panic and voluntarily stay away from the city, in effect putting themselves under quarantine. They will refuse to deliver anything to the cities, so that the people within the cities will be starving to death due to lack of food. Not because there's no food to be had, but because no one will deliver it and run the risk of being exposed to the plague. So the services the city provides the people will all disintegrate and fall apart. People will be dying in stacks, he says. People will be looting and raiding stores and such in the city trying to find food and things to eat, and there will be soldiers stabbing them off at bayonet point.

D: *That explains the reference to the sword. They're fighting them off at bayonet point to keep them away from the stores of food?*

B: So they can be distributed. What stores of food are left in the city, the government would want to try to distribute evenly among the population, but members of the population panic and riot to try to get it all for themselves. So they are fought off at bayonet point. And the entire population of both cities calls upon their God for relief from their misery.

D: *Did you say this quatrain also has a double meaning? Because they have another interpretation for it.*

B: He says this is the main meaning we need to be concerned with since it has not happened yet. But out of curiosity he would like to hear their interpretation.

D: *They think it deals with the bombing of Hiroshima and Nagasaki because they were also two harbor cities. That the two scourges were the two bombs and the plague that had never been seen before was the radioactivity. Because the radiation turned the people black, they thought this would be similar to the black plague of Nostradamus' time.*

B: He says it's a good interpretation, but what he was picturing was the devastating result of runaway viruses from bacteriological warfare laboratories.

CENTURY I-46

Tout aupres d'Aux, de Lestoure & Mirande,	Very near Auch, Lectoure and Mirande a great fire will fall from
Grand feu du ciel en trois nuicts tumbera:	the sky for three nights. The cause will appear both stupefying
Cause adviendra bien stupende & mirande,	and marvelous; shortly afterwards there will be an earthquake.
Bien peu aupres la terre tremblera.	

B: He says this quatrain concerns an event that will be initially sparked by man's hand but will basically be a natural disaster. He's using the word "doctors," but I've asked him and he's referring to scientists, those who seek knowledge, research scientists. And he hastens to explain that in his day doctors did both and all kinds.

D: *In our time they are specialized.*

B: Yes, he says they are not Renaissance men. There'll be a group of doctors researching into the powers of the various energy fields of the earth. They'll try to harness these powers and use them for various things including warfare. At the time they finally start doing direct experimentation on the physical world, they will accidentally rupture one of the earth's fields in such a way that a beam of energy will shoot out into space and draw a stream of meteorites toward the earth. This will happen around the North Sea. The meteorites will be drawn toward the earth because of this alteration of the energy fields around the earth. And since they are out there everywhere they will continue to come until the scientists are able to repair the damage. Their rupture in the field throws everything out of balance. Since their instrumentation is still experimental, it is not fine-tuned enough to be able to get things back in good balance. So in the process of trying to repair the damage there is an earthquake soon after when the stress has built up.

D: *Why does he use those three names?*

B: He says those three words were partially reminders to himself as to where he was talking about and partially so there would be some key words in there that will make sense as time unfolds. Since this project will be very dangerous, it will be a secret government project. There will be code words involved and he's using some anagrams of the code names of the project. One of the code names he has anagramized—that's my word I've just made up. To put something into anagrams is to anagramize it, yes?—One of the code words he anagramized into Mirande was a code word having to do with the location of the major installation of this experiment. He says people in general may not ever know the connection of those words with the event; simply because the government will try to keep the whole event under wraps. They won't be able to hide the meteorites repeatedly entering the earth's atmosphere at that one point, but he says it will always be rather puzzling to the people in general as to why it will keep going on.

D: *Then there will be people somewhere who will recognize these code words.*

B: Right. He says there's a possibility some of them may already be recognizable from various government circles. Those code words won't necessarily be translatable into English because it won't necessarily be English-speaking governments that are involved with this.

D: *They have translated this to mean something about meteorites but they're thinking of a natural phenomenon.*

B: He says that to the world at large it will appear as a natural phenomenon. It will be recorded that way in future history texts because the
part the scientists play is such an important secret to the governments
involved that they will not let that knowledge out.

*UPDATE: See the Addendum for more information about the secret
HAARP program and its connection with this quatrain.*

CENTURY X-72

*L'an mil neuf cens nonante
  neuf sept mois,
Du ciel viendra un grand
  Roi deffraieur.
Resusciter le grand Roi
  d'Angolmois.
Avant que Mars regner
  par bonheur.*

In the year 1999, and seven
months from the sky will come the
great King of Terror. He will bring
back to life the great king of the
Mongols. Before and after War
reigns happily.

This is one of the few quatrains where Nostradamus actually gives a date.

B: He says the date is correct. During this time of war there are many
experiments being done and research into things that are normally too
horrible to delve into during times of peace. He says the experiments
have to do with eugenics.

This was an unknown word to me. I assumed it was something
dealing with genetics. I asked him what it meant.

B: He says it is the breeding of people as you would breed animals to
come up with special characteristics.
D: *Is that his word or yours?*
B: It's the word he used. He says it's a long-range type program that has
been going on secretly for several decades or the majority of this
century. During this war they decide to try out some of the products
of this, to see what happens. One experiment they did was to try to
breed back some of the earlier, less civilized, fiercer types of human
beings, still smart but very cunning and strong. He says this is
brought out in time of war and these unfortunate people are used in
fighting to see how much better they do than ordinary soldiers.
They're keeping tabulations on all of this. At this time in the world
there will be wars going on all over and it will be times of great unrest. He
says this 20th century is one of the most war-torn centuries there are.
D: *I believe that. Who are the ones who are doing this experimentation?*
B: (*Pause*) He can't see for sure. Apparently it's some sort of joint effort,
particularly between the major powers. The major powers would
have the money to put into a project like this. Actually, he said, who
would have the *gold* to put into a project like this.

D: *Does he think America is involved in this?*
B: Yes, he does. He thinks it's America, Russia, Japan, and some European countries.
D: *We've never heard of anything like this.*
B: He says it's a very secret project. It's done on a need-to-know basis.
D: *Who does he mean by the King of Terror?*
B: He says the person who is in overall charge of this project is so powerful he's able to affect and to influence policy decisions made in various countries. He's kind of like the power behind the throne and everyone is afraid of him. So he's the real king rather than the leaders. He says there's a possibility you may have heard his name in a different connection, but highly unlikely. This person is very secretive and nobody is aware of the power he wields.

By eugenics I wonder if Nostradamus could be seeing the possibility of genetic manipulation or cloning. This has been successfully done with animals. Scientists have consistently denied it is being performed with humans. Could is possibly be going on in secret? The breeding of a certain type of human that would be programmed for war. Nostradamus seems to insinuate that these people could be used in battle instead of the youth of the world. Could such a human be created by manipulating the genes and then cloning to produce a ready-made army whose only thought and desire would be to kill? Would such creatures be considered human? I could understand what he meant about such experimentation only being carried on during wartime. It would be considered horribly immoral during peacetime to even think of creating such beings in a laboratory.

This could also be referring to what Hitler was doing during World War II when he was trying to create a super race through selective breeding. Maybe this is another case of one quatrain referring to two different yet similar circumstances.

When Brenda read my explanations she did not agree that it referred to cloning. She remembered some of the scenes he was showing her and she thinks he was very clear and positive that it was dealing with human selective breeding. She thought he was referring to a generations-long project first started in the 1930s and continued in extreme secrecy ever since, so that through short generations (teen-aged parents) and selective breeding, a lot of "progress" could have been made in the 70-plus year span. She could be right. After all, she was the one who was viewing the scenes. The selective breeding of people like pedigreed animals is pretty horrible in itself, but I still think there have been such advances in gene manipulation that that could also have a part in this. This could have been so complicated to understand that Nostradamus could form no closer picture to convey to Brenda.

D: *This next quatrain is a strange one because he uses some letters of the Greek alphabet in it. I hope I can pronounce them; I'm not familiar with the Greek letters.*

B: He says do not distress yourself about it. Do the best you can and don't interrupt yourself with apologies. Also, do not be offended if he interrupts with corrections.

CENTURY I-81

D'humain troupeau neuf seront mis à part,	Nine will be set apart from the human flock, separated from
De jugement & conseil separez:	judgment and advice. Their fate
Leur sort sera divisé en depart,	is to be divided as they depart.
Kappa, Theta, Lambda, mors bannis esgarez.	K. Th. L. dead, banished and scattered.

B: He says this quatrain has yet to come to pass and it has a multiple application. On the one hand this refers to the fate of the Catholic Church and on the other hand to an event that will take place close to the end of the time of troubles.

I will omit the reference to the church because I feel it is irrelevant to our story at this point, and it's also repetitive of other similar quatrains dealing with his vision of the future of the church.

B: The other application of this quatrain says that close to the end of the time of troubles there will be a panel of very—he insists on saying—very smart scientists, very developed in their particular fields. They will be brought together as strategists, so to speak, to develop super-weapons in this time of troubles. It's very much like the panel of scientists who developed nuclear weapons during World War II, but he says these will be even worse weapons. The scientists will be isolated, working alone unto themselves and so they will not be aware of the development of the wars or anything of this sort. They will develop these weapons but by the time they are ready the tide of war will have turned and they are no longer on the winning side but on the losing side. As a consequence, their side loses and the winning side finds out who they are. Their fate will be determined according to what part they played in this. Some of them will meet with very horrible deaths. He says each of the Greek letters mentioned here stands for an initial, representing three of these scientists whose fates will be particularly dramatic.

D: *In other quatrains he spoke of scientists experimenting with energy fields, even working on time and things like this that could be used in war. And there was also the one about eugenics.*

B: Yes, these are the ones he was referring to. These scientists will be principally concerned with the eugenics aspect, which will be why the people's reaction to what they have been doing will be so extreme. Although there are many scientists involved, there are nine at the head of the project. This project was initially started in the 1930s, and it has been carried on in secret in various countries through the decades. It will reach its culmination during the time of troubles.

This date (1930s) coincides with Hitler's program dealing with the controlled breeding of a super race. Maybe it wasn't terminated after World War II but has continued and expanded in secret unknown to the rest of the world.

D: *In another quatrain I believe the date we were given was July, 1999.*
B: He says it's up to you to put the quatrains together as to what he has told you. He's just telling you information he sees in this quatrain.
D: *Then these people are the ones that are working behind the scenes unknown to everyone else.*
B: He says he thinks you are making an incorrect connection here. These people, these nine scientists, will be known to the world at large because they will be the ones in charge. Meanwhile, yes, the others behind the scenes have refuge given by sympathetic groups scattered throughout the world. Sympathetic backers, men of wealth and power.
D: *Then these will be scientists we can recognize by these initials (K, T, L)?*
B: Yes. He says when the time comes the initials will be applied to the scientists involved.

In many quatrains Nostradamus referred to the Anti-Christ as the world since at the height of his power he had conquered so much of the world that no one dared defy him. I think the line "The world is near its final period" in CENTURY III-92 means the events mentioned in that quatrain will happen when the Anti-Christ is beginning to wane.

UPDATE: See the Addendum for more information about the science of nanotechnology and its connection with CENTURY X-72 (pp. 246–247) and the above quatrain.

Chapter 20

The Time of Troubles

THERE WERE A LARGE NUMBER OF QUATRAINS we translated that were so general they applied to many wars in the past and could also refer to the time of troubles. Nostradamus explained that wars generally follow a predictable pattern. I'm including the most pertinent here and omitting those that were not specific.

CENTURY I-92

Sons un la paix par tout
  sera clamee
Mais non long temps pillé
  & rebellion:
Par refus ville, terre, &
  mer entamee,
Mors & captifs le tiers
  d un million.
	Under one man peace will be proclaimed everywhere, but not long after will be looting and rebellion. Because of a refusal, town, land and sea will be broached. About a third of a million dead or captured.

B: He says this refers to some of the conditions that will be present during the time of the Anti-Christ. Within the grasp of his realm there will be no fighting simply because he has everyone under his control. But this will not last because people who have had a taste of freedom will only take so much oppression.

D: *A third of a million; that's a lot of people who are going to be dead or captured.*

B: He says there will be very much death. There will be a lot of fighting and a lot of people dying for the cause, whichever side they happen to be on, whichever side they happen to believe in. He says the descriptions from the book of Revelation will fit very closely, about blood being up to horses' harnesses and the rivers flowing with blood and such. There will be much bloodshed. It will be very violent and very traumatic.

CENTURY VI-97

Cinq & quarante degrés ciel
bruslera,
Feu approcher de la grand
cité neufve,
Instant grand flamme esparse
sautera,
Quand on voudra des Normans
faire preuve.

The sky will burn at forty-five degrees, fire approaches the great New City. Immediately a huge, scattered flame leaps up when they want to have proof of the Normans.

B: This is an event that will take place in the war that is to come. He says in this war various diplomatic ties that are currently in effect will not exist then. There will be a different set of diplomatic ties, but one that will still hold true is the friendship between the people of France and the people of America.

D: *That is the Normans?*

B: Yes. He says in this particular event a country on the other side of the conflict will send a bomb towards New York City. It will be spotted in the sky and be watched coming in. I believe he means it will be tracked on radar, but he says watchers will be watching it. The defense system of America will be concentrating on trying to divert or disable the bomb so they will not be able to retaliate against the country (that fired the bomb). As proof of their friendship the French will be asked to retaliate for America which they will do with several bombs and weapons.

D: *What does that line mean, "Immediately a huge scattered flame leaps up"?*

B: That is the various bombs and weapons of the French leaping up and flying toward enemy territory because the response will be immediate. When the American leader uses the hot line outlining the situation and the problem, the French Marshal will immediately contact their armed bases from which planes and self-propelled bombs will leap up on tongues of fire and fly toward the perpetrator of the event.

D: *You said the bomb was approaching and they were watching it. Does it hit New York?*

B: (*Pause*) He's trying to see for sure. He's saying that in this particular war some of the bombs will hit New York and some will be diverted. Sometimes it's difficult to untangle what will happen to which bombs. This particular bomb, he says, will be prematurely detonated along the way so it does not destroy the city. But it will take many human lives by destroying the planes that are flying around it trying to divert it or disable it.

Apparently these will be destroyed by the blast when the bomb is detonated.

D: *Does "45 degrees" refer to the location?*

B: He says that refers to the angle up from the horizon where it will first be spotted so the planes may be scrambled after it.

CENTURY V-98

A quarante huict degré climaterique,
A fin de Cancer si grande seicheresse:
Poisson en mer, fleuve, lac cuit hectique,
Bearn, Bigorre par feu ciel en destresse.

At the forty-eighth degree of the climacteric, the end of Cancer there is a very great drought. Fish in the sea, river and the lake boiled hectic, Bearn and Bigorre in distress from fire in the sky.

I had trouble with the pronunciation of the place names and also the word "climacteric." He corrected me as I read it.

B: He says this event refers to something the Anti-Christ will do. It's not the same event that happened at the Dark Point. (CENTURY II-3, explained in Chapter 14). It's an event further down the line, but connected by a series of events in between.

D: *What about Bearn and Bigorre, are those the names of countries?*

B: Yes, they are place names. He says it's hard to say which countries because the map will be changing so much by that time. Countries as we know them now will not apply in the same way. It will happen on the European continent.

D: *What does he mean by the 48th degree of the climacteric?*

B: He says the circle of constellations can be divided into degrees. Each of these degrees corresponds to certain time periods as well as certain places on the earth.

D: *The translator has interpreted it as meaning a location on the Earth.*

B: Yes, he says it applies to both. He mentioned the 48th degree of the climacteric to point out a place and, in connection with the reference to Cancer, to point out a time as well.

This was one of the first quatrains I took to John to interpret. He was also mystified by the word "climacteric." It is not a term used in modern astrology and he couldn't find it in any astrological dictionaries. He seemed to remember seeing it in some of his books on ancient astrology and this was where he found it. It's defined as an ancient term, meaning the culmination of a major aspect. This is another of the amazing points that were to continue to pop up during this experiment. It adds incredible validity to the translations if a term such as this is used. It couldn't have come from any of our modern-day minds but only from the mind of an astrologer familiar with ancient terminology. Even the translators couldn't associate the term with astrology, only with latitude.

B: All of the countries will be involved with this but Europe will be bearing the brunt of the fighting. He says Europe is the eternal battlefield. The early events that lead up to this will take place during your lifetimes. The events referred to in the first quatrain (CENTURY II-3 which refers to fish cooking in the sea around Negrepont will take place during your lifetime. He says it's going to be a very complicated time.

CENTURY II-40

*Un pres apres non point
longue intervalle
Par mer & terre sera faict
grand tumulte:
Beaucoup plus grande sera
pugne navalle,
Feux, animaux, qui feront
plus d'insulte.*

Shortly afterwards, not a very long interval, a great tumult will be raised by land and sea. The naval battles will be greater than ever. Fires, creatures which will make more tumult.

B: He says this quatrain describes conditions during the time of troubles. There will be great, fantastic naval battles going on, as well as land and air battles. He says the part referring to the naval battles also refers to air battles, because one thing he has found confusing is that navigational terms are used for both navigating on the sea and navigating in the air. So whenever he sees these things symbolically from the future, sometimes he gets conflicting images because they're referring to both although a common phraseology is used.

D: *What does he mean by "fire, creatures, will make more tumult"?*

B: That will be some of the fantastic weapons that are ultra-secret-secret to ultra-restricted right now. When they're brought out for us in war, everyone will be amazed at them.

CENTURY II-60

*La foy Punicque en Orient
rompue
Grand Jud. & Rosne, Loire
& Tag changeront
Quand du mulet la faim
sera repue,
Classe espargie, sang &
corps nageront.*

Faith with Africa broken in the East, Great Jordan, Rosne, Loire & Tagus will change. When the hunger of the mule is sated, the fleet is scattered and bodies swim in blood.

B: This refers to some of the horrible fighting that will be going on. "The fate is broken in the east of Africa," refers to the Middle East and that part of the world. There will be a nuclear confrontation there. That's how the faith will be broken because they will have said in agreement they were not going to use these weapons in warfare. But they turn around and do it anyway. He says he can see very plainly that the major powers of our day keep naval fleets in that area because it is a restless area of the world. The fleets will be scattered in ruins from the violence of the blast. Due to the combination between the radioactive fallout and the effect it has on people and animals and the weather, plus the effect of any volcanoes that may go off, it's going to turn the water of that part of the ocean into a muddy red color. So the bodies of those that have been killed will be floating around in what looks like blood.

D: *What does he mean by, "when the hunger of the mule is sated"?*

B: He is saying you will laugh when you hear this. This will take place when the United States has a Democratic President. He has seen the same pattern that has been observed in your country, that Republican presidents put the country into depressions and Democratic presidents pull it out by getting them involved with a war. He says at this time the United States will have a Democratic President and will get involved with this conflict as a way of trying to stimulate the economy.

D: *I'm not laughing because that would make sense with the mule being a symbol for the Democrats.*

B: He refers to the names of all the rivers because, due to the violence of the nuclear blast and of the earth changes and such, these rivers will change their courses. And the countries that use some of these rivers for boundary lines will have to redraw their boundaries on the maps. He says in that part of the world the water systems will be very messed up.

CENTURY II-74 describes the vast migrations of people across the European continent. Most will be fleeing the places that have been destroyed by the military aggression. There would also be long columns of soldiers moving toward the scene of battle.

CENTURY III-18

Apres la pluie laict assez
  longuette
En plusieurs lieux de Reims
  le ciel touché:
O quel conflict de sang pres
  d'eux s'appreste,
Peres & fils Rois n'oseront
  approcher.

After the rather long milky rain, several places in Reims will be touched by lightning. Oh what a bloody battle is approaching them, fathers and sons' kings will not dare approach.

B: He says this refers to an event during the time when the Anti-Christ is taking over Europe. The long milky rain and the being touched upon by lightning are effects of the use of nuclear weapons in this war. There will be other fantastic weapons used, based upon concepts being presently developed, that you and this vehicle do not presently have any conception of, and they will have devastating results. There will be corpses all over. The times will be very difficult. That is why the very earth will cry out in its pain. He has affected the time line so strongly that the prophets have been able to see him for thousands of years beforehand.

D: *Then it says, "Fathers, sons, kings will not dare approach."*

B: He says this man will be so terrible and so horrible and so powerful that the people who are the rightful rulers of countries will be cowed by fear and will dare not do anything to help stop the ravages of this man. Entire dynasties will be wiped out.

Could this be occurring simultaneously to or after the assassinations of world leaders? If so, this would explain the reluctance of the rulers to defy him.

D: *The translators can understand a rain of blood and things like that, but they do not understand what he means by the rain of milk.*

B: He says he uses the rain of milk to represent the adverse effects these fantastic nuclear weapons will have upon the weather, including such things as radiation rain. These weapons will use a combination of the worst aspects of nuclear weaponry and laser weaponry, and some of the laser weaponry when it's shot down upon the people, will resemble a white substance coming down.

The following quatrain also deals with a rain of milk.

CENTURY III-19

En Luques sant & laict	In Lucca it will come to rain blood
viendra plouvoir,	and milk, shortly before a change
Un peu devant changement	of governor. Great plague and war,
de preteur:	famine and drought will be seen,
Grand peste & guerre, faim	far from where the prince and
& soif fera voir.	ruler dies.
Loing où mourra leur Prince	
recteur.	

D: *The experts think this is related to the previous quatrain.*

B: He says this does indeed refer to the same war. Before this Anti-Christ takes over any place, not just the place he mentions here, he first rains down upon them death and destruction so it will be easier for him to take over. He will travel far from his final resting place in doing this. Some of the events that take place will cause past heinous events to look like child's play in comparison. Another aspect of history moving in spirals is that some of this was partially done by the man named Hitler when he took over Europe. Except he was using rain of blood rather than rain of blood and milk, as he did not have the weaponry described in these quatrains. But he, too, would rain down destruction before taking over a place. One of the things this Anti-Christ will do is to figure out why Hitler failed. That's why he plans on succeeding because he will learn from Hitler's mistakes.

A chilling thought, because Hitler almost succeeded in his reign of terror.

B: He will have access to books not generally available or known to the general reading public. It will be possible for him to obtain secret Nazi documents on Hitler. He will learn his lessons well.

CENTURY I-64

De nuict soleil penseront	At night they will think they have
avoir veu,	seen the sun, when they see the
Quand le pourceau	half pig man: Noise, screams,
demi-homme on verra:	battles seen fought in the skies.
Bruict, chant, bataille, au ciel	The brute beasts will be heard
battre aperceu:	to speak.
Et bestes brutes à parler lon orra.	

B: He says this refers to some future events as well as partially to the present. Each line almost has a different meaning. He will give you the meanings but not necessarily in the order in which the lines are written down. "The brute-beast will be seen to speak." The animals, in effect, will be speaking to humankind and giving them knowledge through research done for the furthering of medical knowledge. He says this will continue to be true. "They will think they have seen the sun at night," refers to the detonation of an atomic-type bomb or laser-type weapon at nighttime. He's not really clear on the description but the weapon produces a huge explosion of light. This will be involved with the war and the results of this weapon, in addition to causing climatic changes, will also produce monstrous birth defects resulting in altered appearances in the children, including some that look almost swinish. Scientists will be frantically researching trying to find a way to alter the effects of this weapon, so far as newborn children are concerned. And when a breakthrough is made it will be from an unexpected source in the animal kingdom.

D: *This refers to that last line again.*

B: Yes, it has a multiple meaning. "Noise, screams, battles seen fought in the skies." He saw that a logical extension of traveling in the skies is being able to fight in the skies. The weapons themselves will make a screaming-type noise as they rush past. It will be very frightening to the people below and very deadly.

D: *The interpreter thought this might have referred to the Second World War.*

B: No. Although a lot of fighting was done in the air in that war, it was basically a ground war. And this war, although there'll be some fighting on the ground for the holding of position, the main decisive battles will be in the air.

D: *The nearest interpretation they could come up with for the pig-like man was the pilots wearing the helmets and the masks for oxygen during*

World War II. They thought that might resemble a pig to Nostradamus.
B: He says that was a logical interpretation, but they're continually forgetting to keep in mind that he tries to put more than one meaning to each line when he can.

This might mean that these lines could also refer to World War II as the interpreters thought, but Nostradamus felt the translation for the future was the most important to relate to us at this time.

CENTURY I-80

De la sixieme claire splendeur celeste, Viendra tonner si fort en la Bourgongne: Puis naistra monstre de treshideuse beste, Mars, Avril, Mai, Juin grand charpin & rongne.	From the sixth bright celestial light it will come to thunder very strongly in Burgundy. Then a monster will be born of a very hideous beast: In March, April, May and June great wounding and worrying.

B: He says the sixth celestial light refers to Jupiter.

This was a surprise because the book mentioned Saturn as the sixth planet.

B: He says he emphasizes the reference to Jupiter by adding the notion of thunder because the day of Thor, which is Thursday, will be the Anti-Christ's day. And Thor is the Nordic equivalent of the Roman Jupiter. He says during those months of the year (March, April, May and June) or rather the astrological signs that represent those months of the year, when Jupiter is traversing these signs as seen from Burgundy, there will be times of great troubles. There will be much bloodshed and warfare and, due to the horrible nature of the weapons, many terrible things will be taking place. What he is showing me looks like the effects of hard radiation.
D: *Radiation burns?*
B: No. Gross deformities caused by parental exposure to radiation. Terrible mutations in nature, in plants and animals as well as the scars on the bosom of the Earth Mother caused by these weapons. He says the Anti-Christ will be the cause of all this. He's the monster behind these monstrosities coming forth.
D: *Then "the monster will be born of a very hideous beast" has a double meaning.*
J: *(He had been looking through his ephemeris.) Jupiter will be in those signs during the years 1997 to 2001?*
B: At this point Michel de Notredame just gestured in a very grandiose manner and said, "Precisely!"
D: *Ah-ha! Isn't it nice to have a friend on this side who can help with*

this?—I have one question here. The translator says that Saturn *is the sixth planet.*

B: He says this is a very natural mistake to make. He has sources to ancient documents that very possibly have disintegrated between his time and what you consider to be the present. He says one of the great lights, due to a war in the heavens, was destroyed. The one which was between Mars and Jupiter is no more. He was counting that one when counting the great lights of heaven so as to throw the Inquisition off the track.

D: *Would this be the one that is the asteroid belt now?*

B: He says this is correct.

D: *That is very clever. I don't think the Inquisition or anybody else would have been able to pick up on that one.*

B: He says he has to be sneaky sometimes.

D: *They thought it was Saturn and that way they were dating the prediction totally wrong.*

B: He says he is curious. What are the dates they came up with?

D: *They said Spring 1918.*

B: He says he's had other visions concerning the World Wars, but this is not one of them.

To me, the following quatrain is a most remarkable example of the workings of Nostradamus' mind and illustrates the methods he used in providing a symbolic description for something he could not understand.

D: *This quatrain has given the translators a great deal of trouble. They all disagree on the translation of one line from French to English. They say the literal translation doesn't make any sense.*

B: He says the literal translation will be all right since the vehicle comprehends English and it will help him to recall what it was that he wrote in the French.

D: *Shall I read it the way they have translated it first?*

B: He says, out of curiosity, yes.

CENTURY II-75

La voix ouie de l'insolite oiseau,
Sur le carron de respiral estage:
Si hault viendra du froment
le boisseau,
Que l'homme de l'homme
fera Antropophage.

The call of the unwanted bird being
heard on the chimney stack;
bushels of wheat will rise so high
that man will devour his fellow man.

The first line is the one that has caused trouble. It has been translated differently in other books. One says: "The sound of a rare bird will be heard on the pipe of the highest story," which doesn't make any more sense than the unwanted bird on the chimney stack. He asked me to read the quatrain again, this time substituting the literal translation for that line.

D: *"The call of the unwanted bird being heard on the pipe of the breathing floor. Bushels of wheat will rise so high that man will devour his fellow man."*

B: He says he's going to use the literal translation because the interpretive translation does not take into account the wondrous thing he has seen in the far future. He says the wording "the pipe of the breathing floor," even though it is awkward, is the closest he could come to what he was seeing of a future device.

D: *Then the "chimney stack" is wrong.*

B: This is true. He says it's a reasonable interpretation given people's average limited outlook. This event will be during a time of war and great unrest. The call of the unwanted bird will be an event where an airplane will be coming in for a landing on the deck of an aircraft carrier—the deck of the aircraft carrier being the breathing floor.

How brilliant! An excellent comparative analogy. A carrier would naturally look like a floor to him if he didn't have a word for it.

B: He called it that because there will be the motion of it moving with the waves, similar to the motion of breathing, plus there being living souls beneath it, as well. This is also another meaning of "breathing floor." He says a plane will be coming in to land but this plane will not belong to that aircraft carrier. It is a very complex situation because in this war the balance of political powers on each side is very complex and delicate. And this plane is from a power that is slightly more closely aligned to the other side, although it's still basically neutral. But to be in contact with this particular nation would have widespread political repercussions so far as this war is concerned. So the people on this aircraft carrier are not really wanting to be in contact with this plane. "The unwanted call on the pipe of the breathing floor," is the plane communicating with them through the radio aerials. He used the term "pipe" because it would be something that would be carrying sound and communication, and this was the closest concept he could find in his language at the time. The plane will want to land on this aircraft carrier because there is an important leader, a general or something of this nature, on the ship. And the plane carries an important emissary, someone who is close to the leader of this country, who needs to deliver important documents and messages. It will be a very complex situation.

D: *Will this emissary be allowed to land?*

B: He says it is difficult to see because the time line splits there and it could go either way. And either way will have repercussions. At this point he's not able to see which time line is likely to predominate, which way the event is likely to go. This is a particular event during this time. The conditions of the wheat are a general condition that lasts during a large span of this war. As a result of this war, normal trade will be disrupted between all the countries. Some countries will have excesses of food, such as bushels of wheat, but the price for them will be so out of proportion no one will be able to buy the wheat. In countries where they cannot get the wheat they will be resorting to cannibalism just to stay alive. And the wheat, meanwhile, will be stored in silos and rotting simply because they cannot get rid of it, cannot get it sold. The price of the wheat is also high in human lives, as they try to get it across to the other countries. It will be very hazardous because shipping will be totally disrupted, so not only will the price be out of proportion but the danger of trying to deliver the wheat will also be out of proportion. Thus, it cannot get to where it is needed for people to eat.

D: *They have interpreted the whole quatrain as meaning a famine which will cause men to become cannibals.*

B: He says if they have interpreted it that way it implies a natural famine from natural causes. But this was not what he was seeing. He was seeing an *enforced* famine caused by the barriers of war, not because of the lack of rain or what-have-you.

D: *They say the unwanted bird on the chimney stack is an owl or another bird of ill omen and it's giving warning that the famine and high prices are coming.*

B: He says that's a reasonable interpretation since the interpreters are not aware of the detailed pictures he sees. He says he sometimes sees a vision that just shows a small incident in a larger happening. He sees everything to the last detail and he writes this down. But it's hard for an outside person to be able to link that up to the larger picture.

This was a perfect example of an obscure and complicated quatrain that would have been impossible to decipher without his help. Once again, it is utterly amazing how clear it becomes when he explains each point. To me, this is proof we are truly in touch with Nostradamus because in such cases only the author would know the true meanings he was trying to get across.

CENTURY I-67

La grande famine que je sens approcher, *Souvent tourner, puis estre universelle:* *Si grand & long qu'un viendra arracher,* *Du bois racine & l'enfant de mamelle.*	The great famine which I sense approaching will often turn (in various areas) then become world wide. It will be so vast and long lasting that (they) will grab roots from the trees and children from the breast.

B: He says this has to do with the climatic changes that take place after the discharge of this terrible device he has already mentioned. He says the phrase "the watered fields shrink" (referring to CENTURY X-70 which was covered in Chapter 15) means that famine will start in scattered areas. Then conditions will continue to get worse and not improve. The famine in the different areas will continue to grow until the areas connect and cover large surfaces of the earth's land masses, so the majority of the world would be suffering. It will affect all the inhabitants of the world because the necessities of food will be so very short and hard to come by. People will get so desperate for food they'll start trying to eat anything, any living tissue for food, including, as he wrote, roots from trees that one ordinarily does not eat. And in some parts of the world, particularly the crowded places such as India, they would be grabbing newborn infants as well.

D: *That sounds awful. It's revolting!*

B: It will be a very grim time.

UPDATE: It was announced in 1992 that southern Africa was in the grip of the worst drought in this century. Meteorologists were warning that it is spreading north to engulf the entire eastern side of the continent. While drought is commonplace in certain regions of Africa, weather and food experts said this year's dry spell is extraordinary for its sweep through food-exporting countries, which normally escape severe drought. Experts exclaimed that this was a major drought from the Cape to Cairo, and all these countries would be importing grains this year. It was declared a serious, serious matter. The failure of rains, accompanied by unseasonably hot temperatures for the planting seasons caused South Africa and Zimbabwe to import vast amounts of grain for the first time in memory. Where would the food come from, now that the former Soviet Union was also making huge demands on the West's free food supply? Is this the beginning of the fulfillment of this horrible quatrain?

D: *It's quite depressing to a lot of people that many of his quatrains deal with tragedy.*

B: He says these events must be lived through if we are to attain the ultimate we'll be working toward. If we survive all these bad events then afterwards we will truly be a pacifist people, a peaceful people. And our philosophy will have changed sufficiently so this part of our path will be different and we will go along a holistic path rather than a technological path.

D: *People say they don't like to read his quatrains because they are very disturbing.*

B: He glares with his eyes and he says, "They're *supposed* to be disturbing. I try to point out to them the very worst of what can happen so maybe they can avoid some of it."

D: *But I guess people don't like to think man is capable of such things.*

B: He says, look at your death count from World War II and tell me man's not capable of *anything.*

D: *They don't like to think our future holds such horror.*

B: He's shaking his head and muttering about the stupidity and shortsightedness of mankind in general.

D: *This is one reason why they hesitate to read his quatrains. They say they would rather not think about such things. You know, the "ostrich with his head in the sand" attitude.*

B: I pictured the analogy for him and he said it is a good analogy. He says he has not heard of ostriches in his lifetime, but I have pictured it.

D: *It means hiding from something that is ...*

B: Without being in perspective, yes. I pictured the analogy for him as the communicator. He sees the picture and he finds it amusing but very true.

D: *People figure if they don't know about something, it won't hurt him, it will go away.*

B: He comments that there is a saying you seem to have, "What you don't know can't hurt you." He says unfortunately that is not true.

D: *It seems that many of these quatrains deal with the Anti-Christ. Nostradamus must have seen a lot about him.*

B: He says this man causes some of the most terrible events in the history of mankind. You will notice he also saw a lot on the French Revolution because it was another crucial and unstable time so far as his country was concerned. These coming events are concerning the whole world and not just his country, so naturally he would see many visions on this.

D: *I wanted to ask something. It seems to me that a lot of these predictions pertain to many different events. I wondered if maybe he was seeing various possibilities that could happen and that they might not all necessarily come true.*

B: He says the main reason why he wanted this communication was to avoid the worst of what he's seen. Some of the so-called "worst-case scenarios" could very easily take place, but with great determination and resolve they could be altered for the better. Unfortunately, at this time the worst things that he has seen would be the easiest events to happen. And he knows he must try his best to help lessen the destruction.

D: *He once said that sometimes he saw a nexus in time and there could be many different paths and therefore many possibilities.*

B: This is correct. He says at this point, since it is such a major nexus, no matter which path we choose it still seems to contain most of these visions. But there are other paths where various amounts of these could be avoided. He says the time of troubles will be a very trying and difficult time. The spirits on the earth at this time are here because they chose to be here, because they knew that any spirit on the earth at this time will be working through large amounts of major karma. He's showing me a picture. He's not giving me words. It's a great karmic wheel divided up into larger sections instead of smaller sections and there are people working off these larger sections as if they were the smaller sections. It's like working off concentrated karma. He says the amount of karma the spirits who live through these times will be able to work off would be the equivalent of ten lifetimes at any other time in earth history.

D: *Is that why he thinks they volunteered to come back at this time?*

B: He says many of them did volunteer, such as your older and more advanced spirits who are needed here to help everybody pull through. There are also some younger spirits here at this time who were just simply feeling adventuresome. However, there are some spirits who are here not necessarily because they wanted to come in their hearts, but because they knew they had to or it would be the end of the line for them, so far as spiritual development goes. So they're not fully volunteers but just enforced volunteers, so to speak, because they knew they had no other choice.

D: *I think those kind of people would be unhappy here.*

B: He says they are, but some of them manage to make the best of the situation and some don't, and that's their choice to make.

Century IV-28

Lors que Venus du Sol	When Venus will be covered by the
sera couvert,	Sun, under the splendor will be a
Soubs l'esplendeur sera	hidden form. Mercury will have
forme occulte:	exposed them to the fire, by a
Mercure au feu les aura	rumor of war will be affronted.
descouvert,	
Par bruit bellique sera	
mis à l'insulte.	

One meaning of this quatrain was covered in Chapter 11, pg. 140.

B: He says the other interpretation has to do with an event dealing with the kind of troubles that are to come near the end of this millennium. In this time of troubles there will be many confusing things taking place. He says in this interpretation the quatrain holds a number of astrological references. He is complaining of my own personal ignorance at this point. He's having difficulty putting across the concepts in a way I can understand them and communicate them to you.

D: *Tell him to do the best he can.*

B: He says he's doing an excellent job, it's my denseness that's in the way. Unfortunately the astrological connotations he's using here are not any good for dating this, but he will try to get to that in a moment. During the time of troubles, at a point when the sun is between the Earth and Venus (and thus from the Earth's point of view, Venus will appear to be hidden by the sun) there will be a visitation from the Watchers, those who have kept an eye on mankind's development. They will approach from the direction of Venus so they too will be temporarily hidden by the sun, but they will be exposed through the powers of Mercury, that is, through the powers of observation and communication. The scientists who are involved with radiotelescopy and its similar disciplines will find an anomaly that will catch their attention.

As they study it they will come to the realization of a strong indication of what they would refer to as a UFO. This is actually the instrument used by the Watchers to observe mankind. As this instrument comes closer to the earth for more observations, the scientists expose the instrument to the fire. In other words, expose it to the light of knowledge. They will find out more about what it is and who the Watchers are when this event takes place. However, as it will be during the time of troubles, this definite proof that there are others out there in the universe will cause great social unrest and panic in some countries that are particularly involved with wars and such. And there will be internal dissension created by fundamentalists whose world view cannot include others in the universe without profoundly shaking their beliefs. He realizes the measurement of Venus being on the other side of the sun from Earth is not too helpful for dating, as this occurs quite often, but he says from his point of view he feels this will take place in either 1997 or 1998.

J: *The sun being covered by Venus. I've always looked at the sun as a symbol of the Great Spirit and Venus as a sense of love, but personal love. Do you feel this could also mean the transformation of more spiritual love among people at that time?*

B: I get the feeling of much pleasure from Michel de Notredame. He says he's very pleased you have picked up on that aspect of it as well. He says the planetary influences upon the Earth will be acting to try to bring about, as you say, more spiritual love among mankind. He says this is another reason why the Watchers choose to come back into contact with mankind at this time, for they are trying to help along mankind's spiritual growth in general, through their gentle prodding, so to speak. And he says you are correct in thinking about the higher aspects of the influences of the planetary bodies involved in this situation.

D: *May I ask, are the Watchers and the Others the same group of people?*

B: Yes, he says, they are the same. He refers to them as the Others because they are *other* than us. They are not us. They are outside. They are others. But he also calls them the Watchers because they have always kept an eye on us and have observed our growth and development. They're looking forward to our reaching the point when we can join their community and help with their grand project in a way that's unique to us.

It was interesting to me that this was almost the same phrasing used to describe these people and their purpose that my subject, Phil, used in my book, *Keepers of the Garden.*

In many other incidents I have encountered the terms "Others" and "Watchers," and they usually refer to extraterrestrials.

Chapter 21

The Cabal

Sans pied ne main dend
aigue & forte,
Par Globe au forte de port
& lainé nay:
Pres du portail desloyal
transporte,
Silene luit, petit grand emmené.

Without either foot or hand, with strong and sharp teeth through the crowd to the fortified harbor and the elder born. Near the gates, treacherous, he crosses over; the moon shines but little, great pillage.

B: He says this is during the time of the Anti-Christ. The moon shining but little refers to the fact that the people involved with this particular situation are out of touch with their psychic and intuitive selves, so the moon shines very little in their lives. The moon represents the celestial body that is in charge of psychic things, so to speak. "At the gate, treachery, they will cross over," refers to the fact that this group will be somewhat like a military junta, but not exactly. (*I didn't understand what she meant.*) He says there is a group of puppeteers or puppet-masters behind the scenes pulling the strings of the figures on stage and changing the scenery as needed. The figures on stage are the political figures in the major world capitals. The scenery changes as you go from capital to capital, but the situation is the same. He says these puppet-masters that are behind the scenes are organized together in a single organization, and they're working for their own ends. But they're very clever in disguising it. They hold positions that appear to be relatively minor, like advisors and under-secretaries and such, but are key positions for their power. And while in the capital itself, close to their employ, they seem to be good, loyal, model citizens working for the same goals as their government is supposed to be working for. But the minute they cross the gates to the outside world all that changes, and they use the information they've gained and pool it together for their organization to work for its *own* ends, rather than being loyal to any one particular government. "Without either foot or hand, with strong and sharp teeth" further describes these people, because they appear not to have any political maneuvering power. They have no foot or hand to push people around with. *But* they have strong, sharp teeth which they have sunk into everything. And they have a firm grip on everything. They are the ones who are really in control. This organization has been in existence for several generations. He says a hint to their existence is to trace the family histories of the banking powers and the money powers in the world. They're very secret and no one knows about them except the families involved. This cabal of leaders has been very slowly but surely building up a worldwide network of power because they want to take over but stay behind the scenes. At first when the Anti-Christ comes along, they feel he's just a new, dynamic, youthful leader from the Middle East they can use to help unite that part of the world and get it under their power. But the Anti-Christ ends up turning the tables on them.

(This refers to the quatrain CENTURY II-18 where the Anti-Christ has them murdered, not realizing they were actually helping him.)

I think it's appropriate to refer to the scandal that occurred during January, February and March 1987, concerning the selling of arms to the Contras in Nicaragua. The insinuations were that the U.S. government was involved. But the Contras claimed the financing was mostly done by a private group of people who have not been able to be traced. Also during this time it was said that huge amounts of money, millions of dollars, which were diverted for this, had simply disappeared. These funds were traced as far as being deposited in certain bank accounts in many different banks all over the world and then just disappeared. The investigators could find no trace or hint of who was involved. This seems to back up Nostradamus' claims of a secret cabal that controls the affairs of the world and keeps wars going for their own ends by supplying weapons, *etc.*

In CENTURY II-89, which was translated in Chapter 10, a secret group of people were mentioned as still being involved in Vietnam. An organization that has kept the war quietly going all these years unknown to the general American public. Could this also refer to the same cabal?

CENTURY II-88

Le circuit du grand faict ruineux,	The completion of the great
Le nom septiesme du cinquiesme	disastrous action, the name of the
sera:	seventh will be that of the fifth.
D'un tiers plus grand l'estrange	Of the third (name) a greater,
belliqueux,	foreign warmonger, Paris and
Mouton, Lutece, Aix ne	Aix will not be kept in Aries.
garantira.	

B: He says this refers to the time of the Anti-Christ. The great disastrous happening being that of the Anti-Christ's successful—or nearly successful—taking over of Europe. The names referred to here are clues to his so-called "cabinet." That's the way people will interpret it on the surface. But it really is an inner clue to the international financiers and bankers that are behind the scenes deciding what will happen, when, and where—the puppeteers.

D: *The cabal we've already covered?*

B: Yes. He says the reference to France and Aix not being kept in Aries means that they will not stay at active war with the Anti-Christ, but things will settle down in such a way to where the Anti-Christ's attention will turn elsewhere. And there in France is where the underground will start flourishing.

D: *Then these names will refer to the people in this secret organization.*

B: Yes. He says when they become known, the way they're listed here in the quatrain will relate to the various familial relationships between them.

D: *You told me before that this group would have something to do with the generations of banking families.*

B: Yes, and other commodity-related families, such as families into gold mines and diamond mines, leather, tins and such as this. The basic colonial barons associated with the European world empires who started their families' fortunes by exploiting the raw materials of the Third World nations. He realizes that to try to trace all that down is a large order, but he says it will become clear in time who all is involved.

D: *It says, "the name of the seventh will be that of the fifth." All that will become clear?*

B: Yes. He says the seventh and the fifth one in line will not only have the same first names, but their family names will be related in such a way that the seventh one will be considered a part of the family of the fifth one; therefore, his name will be that of the fifth. He says it's hard to explain, but it will become clear when the information comes to light.

D: *We've had several quatrains about this secret organization.*

B: But not nearly enough. He says unfortunately he has not been able to penetrate as deeply as he would like into this aspect of the future. He says they have already caused everybody trouble. They manipulate the economy to cause the unemployment rate to rise or fall at their whim. They manipulate the economy to cause inflation to rise or fall at their whim. He says every time you go to the store and have to pay a higher price for a loaf of bread, it's because of them. So they have already affected your life.

That was an interesting idea. You wouldn't think there was anyone behind the scenes powerful enough to do these things, and also to keep wars going for their own purposes.

CENTURY II-18

Nouvelle & pluie subite impeteuse,	News; unexpected and heavy rain will suddenly prevent two armies.
Empechera subit deux exercites:	Stones and fire from the skies will
Pierre ciel, feux faire la mere pierreuse,	make a sea of stones. The death of the seven suddenly by land and sea.
La mort de sept terre & marin subites.	

B: He says this refers to events during the time of the Anti-Christ. Once again, with the earth changes taking place there will be extremes of weather. He says two armies will be lined up ready to go to battle and an extreme weather change, of rain and hail, will take them by surprise. It will prevent them from being able to make contact the way they had planned so they'll turn to an alternative plan and fly planes up above the weather to try to drop bombs on the opposing forces. This is what he means by fire and stones falling from the sky.

D: *What does he mean by "the death of the seven"?*

B: He says there will be a cabal of leaders. They won't be military in the strict sense, but more like financiers and bankers, the powers behind the military pulling the strings. Somehow through the espionage powers of the Anti-Christ they will be discovered and destroyed, which on the one hand would help the Anti-Christ because it will throw the organizations he's opposing into temporary disorder and he can take advantage of this chaos. But on the other hand, it's a little bit shortsighted of him because it's this cabal that has been instigating the warfare that has been going on through the decades and centuries. His destroying them will in effect write the beginning of the end for him because it's the activities of this cabal that have supported what he's trying to do. But now they are removed so the agitation for world war is not there and the natural inclination for world peace will start to assert itself, thereby doing away with the Anti-Christ.

D: *Wasn't he aware of this?*

B: No, if he had known he would have used them instead. All he knew at the time was that they were financing these European forces so they could continue to fight against him.

In several other places in the quatrains there are shadowy secret people mentioned. Do these also have something to do with this mysterious cabal?

In CENTURY V-75 which is translated in Chapter 11, pg. 158, a man in the United States is mentioned.

In CENTURY X-72 translated in Chapter 19, the King of Terror is mentioned in connection with the genetic experiment.

Also in that same chapter another mysterious power group is mentioned in CENTURY I-81. This one is also referring to the genetic experiments.

Could these all be independent references to the same mysterious cabal that really controls the affairs of the world?

Chapter 22

𝕿he 𝕿urning of the 𝕿ide

CENTURY VI-33

Sa main derniere par Alus *sanguinaire* *Ne se pourra par la mer* *guarantir:* *Entre deux fleuves craindre main* *militaire,* *Le noir l'ireux le fera repentir.*	His hand finally through the bloody Alus, he will be unable to protect himself by sea. Between two rivers he will fear the military hand, the black and angry one will make him repent of it.

B: He says this refers to the downfall of the Anti-Christ's supreme commander. He will make a major failure of judgment on the field so the bulk of his forces are captured or killed. The battle involved will be an extremely strategic one. The black and angry one refers to the Anti-Christ and his reaction to the situation.

D: *They say that word "Alus" is an unsolved mystery. Is it an anagram?*

B: He says this refers to the misuse of some technology that has not yet been developed. When this supreme commander makes this major judgmental error, part of that error is the misuse of this technology in such a way as to cause his downfall.

D: *They thought he might have been trying to give us the name of the third Anti-Christ in an anagram*

B: No, this is not so. He says this is somewhat related to the other quatrain about his choosing this supreme commander.

CENTURY VI-21

Quant ceux du polle artiq *unis ensemble,* *En Orient grand effrayeur* *& crainte:* *Esleu nouveau, soustenu* *le grand tremble,* *Rhodes, Bisance de sang* *Barbare taincte.*	When those of the Northern pole are united together in the East will be great fear and dread. A new man elected, supported by the great one who trembles, both Rhodes and Byzantium will be stained with Barbarian blood.

B: As long as things look totally hopeless, the Anti-Christ will seem all powerful and all conquering. But this is when his star is falling and his power is beginning to give way in certain crucial places. This refers to when those of the northern pole—that is the United States, Canada and Russia particularly, and later on, northern Europe—manage to unite together. Even though the Anti-Christ has taken over all of Asia, after a certain amount of time he's not able to control Russia. Russia breaks free and unites with those countries that have not yet been conquered. This union, particularly of the United States, Canada and Russia, strikes fear into the heart of the Anti-Christ because he can see the beginning of the end where he might fail at this point. So he chooses another field commander to continue the campaign, but this effort will fail. Rhodes and Byzantium, being major regional headquarters, will see some of the bloodiest fighting. The northern pole alliance in their effort to break down his chain of command, communication and such, to help crumble his power, will try to wrest the rest of the world from his grasp.

D: *They interpret this quatrain as an alliance with U.S. and Russia, but they think it is at the beginning of a war.*

B: He says it will be the turning-point in this grand conflict where it will seem, for the first time, that maybe the good guys will come out on top after all.

CENTURY VIII-17

Les bien aisez subit seront desmis	Those at ease will suddenly be cast
Par les trois freres le monde mis	down, the world put into trouble by
en trouble,	three brothers; their enemies will
Cité marine saisiront ennemis,	seize the marine city, hunger, fire,
Faim, feu, sang, peste & de tous	blood, plague, all evils doubled.
maux le double.	

B: At one point the victories will be coming so often and so fast they become complacent. They start taking their victories for granted and they become overconfident. As a result they start losing their battles so they begin to see that their power is not forever. He says the hunger, fire and plagues and such all doubled refers to the fact that the Anti-Christ will not hesitate to use bacteriological warfare as well as conventional warfare. The normal effect of these things will be much worse than usual since the causative organisms will have been developed to be much more lethal. He says at this point the Anti-Christ will be at the peak of his power and will have taken over a good part of the world, so he's becoming complacent. The three brothers who will make the world tremble refers to the alliance between North America, northern Europe and Russia. ("The alliance of the pole" referred to in CENTURY VI-21. See pp. 270.) He used the term they would cause the world to tremble because this alliance will trouble the Anti-Christ. And at this point, in effect, he *is* the world because he has taken over so much of it.

D: *They are interpreting those three brothers as the Kennedy brothers.*

B: He says the Kennedy brothers, even though they were involved with politics, have not done anything to discombobulate the world. They just do a good job of getting themselves killed off. Just because there happen to be three brothers who are politically famous does not mean the quatrain refers to them.

D: *I guess they take it very literally when he says "brothers." At another time you mentioned two brothers and they thought you were speaking of the Kennedy brothers then also. But in that case it was America and England. So now I see that when he says "brothers" he sometimes means an alliance.*

B: Many times, yes.

Three brothers were also referred to in CENTURY VIII-46 which was interpreted in Chapter 15. "When Mars will take up his horrible throne, the Cock and the Eagle, France and the three brothers."

B: Once again he refers to the hope of the world, as he calls it, the alliance between North America, northern Europe and Russia. And this is where his patriotism is peeking forth. He says France will also be allied with them in spirit, if not actual physical alliance. France will be weakened from the Anti-Christ's degradations to where she may not necessarily be much help, but she will be allied with them in her thoughts and her heart.

It seemed it would be inevitable that another major figure would arise in the world during this time of terror to confront the Anti-Christ. So far no one had been prophesied until we came to this quatrain and we were introduced to a man who would become a main character in our strange scenario.

D: *This quatrain has a very strange name in the beginning. It might be hard for me to pronounce. It is "Ogmios" in English and "Logmion" in the French. Does he know the word?*

CENTURY V-80

Logmion grande Bisance approchera,	Ogmios will approach great Byzantium, the barbarian league
Chasse sera la barbarique ligne:	will be driven out. Of the two laws
Des deux loix l'une l'estinique lachera,	the pagan one will fail, barbarian and freeman in perpetual struggle.
Barbare & franche en perpetuelle brigue.	

B: He says he knows the name you're trying to say. He says this particular quatrain has a multiple meaning, partly allegorical or figurative, and partly in preparation or warning. It mainly refers to the outcome of the time of troubles, the eventual downfall of the Anti-Christ. He says the crux of the struggle will be in that gray area of the continent where you're really not sure if it's Asia or Europe. It will seem very questionable as far as the outcome is concerned for quite some time. Because the entire time the Anti-Christ is in power he'll be trying to attain more power and there will be constant struggle between his forces, whom Michel de Notredame refers to as barbarian, and the people who are still free from his tyrannical rule. He referred to his law as being pagan since it's against the central source of spiritual power, regardless of what name you wish to apply to this source. It's mainly a matter of semantics anyway. He says those who struggle against the central spiritual force are automatically doomed to fail sooner or later because they're working against the fabric of the entire universe. It's just a matter of how far they go before they fail and what effects they have on the lives around them.

D: *Is it just wanting more and more power that will cause the failure?*

B: He says that is usually the ultimate downfall of many tyrants. Since he's power hungry his sub-commanders will also be power hungry and his empire will fragment about him. As a result, the political map of the world will change. He says the geographical map will look much the same and the continents will still be shaped the same, but the lines you draw on them to divide them into countries will be different afterward, as a result of this time of troubles.

D: *What does he mean by the word, "Ogmios"?*

B: He's referring to the classics. He says, go back and reread your classics if you want the answer to that one. The education in your time period is generally neglectful in this area and he's trying to get you to broaden your mind.

D: *I'm willing to do my research.*

J: *To me, Ogmios means a great leader or a great hero.*

B: Correct.

J: *Does this mean there will be a great leader to combat the Anti-Christ?*

B: He says, yes, there will be. Any time a great tyrant rises up it's a matter of cosmic balance that a great hero rise up to balance this. This will help bring the tyrant down and reestablish the balance of the universe in a way that is harmonious to the central source of the spiritual.

D: *Will this be a leader of another country?*

B: No, not of another *country*. A leader will rise up who will be generally acclaimed and acknowledged by *many* countries that are not under the rule of the Anti-Christ, but that are struggling against the Anti-Christ. This leader will probably rise from the underground movement. There are always one or more underground movements to help combat tyrants from within. In one of the countries he conquers they will have a very tightly organized underground movement. And this leader will arise from this organization. He says when the conflict is coming to an end and "Ogmios," the great leader from the forces of good, confronts the Anti-Christ, it will be in that area of Eurasia close to Constantinople. As he said, in that area where you're kind of in Europe but kind of in Asia too. He says this leader will originally come from somewhere in central Europe. This man is very well prepared spiritually to take on this task, for his opponent will be very powerful with negative spiritual forces around him. And Ogmios will need to be well girded for battle, on all planes.

J: *Will he be of a religious or scientific bent?*

B: He will be of the people. He is a man who will have worked up through the ranks, so to speak. He started out from a simple background and what he attained, he did by working for it honestly. He has some technical training. The main skill he relies upon is his practicality. He's able to see to the root of matters. He's an old soul and he has his priorities straight. He knows what's important and what isn't for the final outcome. And he is one of the ones that will help pave the way for the great genius who will come after the Anti-Christ. For this man realizes he's not the one to lead the world to ultimate peace. But he is the one to help bring down the one who would destroy the world so as to leave room for the one who will guide the world to ultimate peace.

Research revealed that Ogmios is the Celtic equivalent of Hercules. Quoted from *Mythology of All Races,* Volume 3: "A Gaulish god Ogmios is represented as an old man, bald-headed and with wrinkled and sunburnt skin, yet possessing the attributes of Hercules. He draws a multitude by beautiful chains of gold and amber attached to their ears, and they follow him with joy. The other end of the chains is fixed to his tongue, and he turns to his captives a smiling countenance. This native god of eloquence was regarded as Hercules because he had accomplished his feats through eloquence; he was old, for speech shows itself best in old age; the chains indicated the bond between the orator's tongue and the ears of enraptured listeners." The Celts believed eloquence was more powerful than physical strength.

This might be a fitting description. If the Anti-Christ has such a golden tongue he's able to conquer countries without a fight, then his opponent would have to be similarly gifted. Eloquence would be a main requirement. How else would Ogmios be able to gain followers?

When Brenda laid down the Tarot cards for three of the hooded figures seated around the pearl table, there was one more left to be interpreted. This was the hand for Ogmios, the Nemesis of the Anti-Christ.

B: (*She laid out the cards.*) Starting out with the upright Fool which is partially obscuring an upright Ace of Batons, the next card is an upright Knight of Cups which is partially obscured by an upright Judgment. Then a fully exposed upright Wheel of Fortune and finally a fully exposed upright Sun.

D: (Laugh) *I just got an inspiration when you said the Fool. He would have to be a fool to go against the Anti-Christ.*

B: (*Laugh*) The eternal optimist.

J: I don't look at the Fool that way. (*The card shows a man ready to step off the edge of a cliff.*) Here we see two paths, and it's up to us to make sure we take the right one. Because if we take the wrong path it's curtains.

D: *You could fall off that cliff.*

J: Yes, and we have to have faith and trust our inner spiritual being. The Ace of Batons represents the birth of new enterprises. There's a flowering wand, and I always look at batons and wands as flowering cuttings, as from a plant. You put them in the right medium and they flourish. Here it shows that if you put this person in the right medium, he will truly flourish and grow into the oak of great strength.

D: *Then he will take the right path if the Ace of Batons is lying over the Fool.*

J: The Knight of Cups is a card which represents a romantic or an idealist. Someone always trying to see the best in other people. It's a good card. I like the Knight of Cups. The only thing they have to do is to really bestir themselves. They have to be pushed. The next card is upright Judgment. This represents an awakening, a change of consciousness, a new spiritual feeling. He will have to feel this way if he's going to go up against the Anti-Christ.

B: It's partially obscuring the Knight of Cups.

J: Well, the Knight of Cups represents that by trusting one's spiritual values and goals one can achieve anything they want. And the Sun blesses it all. The Sun is a wonderful card to have in a reading because it represents leaving the past behind, remembering the good things of the past but being really excited about the beautiful new life one leads in the future. And then the upright Wheel of Fortune represents that it's fated. I always look at the Wheel of Fortune as fate. When I see Major Arcana cards in a reading, I always say these works are not so much caused by the individual himself, but by fate or karma. His reading looks good. He will have to bestir himself. It won't be easy. He's probably right at that Knight of Cups stage in his life now.

B: I think it's interesting that of all the cards I've laid out tonight, this is the only hand where the cards are all upright. The others had a lot of inverted cards.

Again, all this is quite amazing. There was no way anyone could have put all of this together off the top of their head and had it fit so perfectly.

CENTURY V-24

Le regne & lois souz Venus eslevé,	The kingdom and law raised under Venus, Saturn will dominate
Saturne aura sus Jupiter empire:	Jupiter. Law and empire raised
La loi & regne par le Soleil levé,	by the Sun, will endure the worst
Par Saturnins endurera le pire.	through those of Saturn.

B: He says this refers to the organization run by the one he has referred to as "Ogmios." This organization will survive through the worst of the troubled times and serve as a basis of future governments after the Anti-Christ has been put down. He says the glory and the positive nature of the sun will be behind Ogmios and help him go through the worst. Ogmios is a man of great stature. He will be a gruff kind of very direct person. This man makes a good friend but he says you wouldn't want him as your enemy. That's why he makes such a good adversary for the Anti-Christ. He will be an upstanding man of strong principles and morals. The principles are his own and not influenced by ecclesiastica. That's why he's the one to bring about the downfall of the Anti-Christ, for this man is a leader and will have an organization under him to help with his quest. But he says he won't want to have a ring in his nose.

CENTURY II-85

Le vieux plain barbe soubs le statut severe,	Under the severe authority of the old man with the flowing beard, at
A Lyon faict dessus l'Aigle Celtique:	Lyon it is put above the Celtic Eagle. The small great one perseveres too
Le petit grand trop autre persevere,	far; noise of weapons in the sky, the Ligurian sea is red.
Bruit d'arme au ciel: mer rouge Ligustique.	

B: He says the small great one refers to Ogmios because he's small, in that his forces will be small and his resources will be small. He'll be part of the underground and will be scraping together what he can. But he's the great one because he will go on to victory and eventually overcome the Anti-Christ.

D: *Who is "the old man with the flowing beard"?*

B: He says the old man with the flowing beard placed above the Celtic eagle represents the distortion of values that will come to a head during this time. The old man with the flowing beard is a symbol representing distorted religion. Religion that's basically, as you put it, fundamentalist. It's like a stern old man holding a thick oaken stick over his followers, to make sure they don't step out of line. And the Celtic eagle represents honor, valor, and loyalty to one's country, things of this nature. One of the major troubles of this time will be those caused by people with distorted world views, the followers of the various fundamentalist religions, not just Christian religions, but Muslim as well.

D: *I hope we eventually get to a quatrain that says what happens between Ogmios and the Anti-Christ.*

B: He says it will be a long, gradual, hard thing.

D: *You mean the battle or what?*

B: The war.

D: *But somewhere in these quatrains is the climax of what really happens between the two?*

B: He says, what makes you think the two will ever personally meet?

D: *I was assuming.*

B: He says assumptions are dangerous.

D: *We call Ogmios the Nemesis of the Anti-Christ. Would that be correct?*

B: Close enough.

CENTURY IX-73

Dans Foix entrez Roi ceiulee Turban,	The king enters Foix wearing a blue turban, he will reign for less than
Et regnera moins revolu Saturne,	a revolution of Saturn; the king
Roi Turban blanc Bisance cœur ban,	with the white turban, his heart banished to Byzantium, Sun,
Sol, Mars, Mercure pres de la hurne.	Mars and Mercury near Aquarius.

B: He says the Anti-Christ will take over Europe and begin to take over the world with the idea of establishing some sort of dynasty. This person, due to his cultural background, is very conscious of the influence of families rather than the influence of certain individuals. That a family which is powerfully placed can have a major effect on the flow of history. As he likes the game of power and he's obsessed with power, to him, one of the ultimate power plays is to be able to manipulate power across a long span of time through the influence of his familial line. However, this is not to be, for he will be overthrown by Ogmios and then the great genius will come to balance the forces, the energies, and to heal the Earth.

D: *Which one is the Anti-Christ, the blue turban or the white turban?*

B: Blue. The white turban refers to the great genius.

D: *It says the one with the blue turban will reign for less than a revolution of Saturn.*

B: He says that is very clear, why are you puzzled? He just got through explaining that the Anti-Christ is wanting to establish a rule of power for a long span of time but it will not last nearly so long as what he's wishing. It will be very temporary. He says it's like building a fire with grass—it burns up very quickly.

D: *Well, they say that 29.5 years would be the revolution of Saturn.*

B: This is true.

D: *I think in another quatrain he mentioned that the Anti-Christ's war would last for 27 years.* (CENTURY VIII-77, Chapter 14, pp. 192.)

B: He says this man will have an effect on the history of earth and will be in the limelight, so to speak, for less than this period of time. And not for the long period of time he's aiming for.

D: *Then those astrological signs will be able to give us the dates?*

B: He says if one has the charts for the following millennium that will give you an idea of when the conflict will finally end and the establishment of a new world order will begin, so the great genius may come to the fore.

Another indication of the length of time the Anti-Christ would reign, so to speak, was given in CENTURY II-10.

B: The very evil century (mentioned in the quatrain) is the time that's coming, and includes the time leading up to it. The whole 20th century in particular, but especially since World War II, has not been particularly peaceful. So he's referring to it as evil. And the time since World War II to the end of the time of troubles will almost encompass a century itself.

I believe this means that since World War II took place in the late 1930s and early 1940s, that the end of the time of troubles would occur in the 2030s or 2040s, more or less.

B: He's emphasizing again the importance of getting these quatrains translated. He says they *must* be translated. The information *must* be present in this time line even if it's only present in manuscript form. As long as it's present in some sort of form, it's very important. He's not able to be more clear about that at this time.

Chapter 23

𝔄ftermath of the 𝔗hird 𝔚ar

CENTURY II-44

*L'aigle pousée entour de
    pavillions,
Par autres oiseaux d'entour
    sera chassée:
Quand bruit des cymbees,
    tubes & sonaillons,
Rendront le sens de la dame
    insensée*

The eagle driven back around the
tents will be chased by other birds
around him. When the sound of
cymbals, trumpets and bells will
restore sense to the senseless
woman.

B: He says this refers to some of the defeats the United States will suffer
while fighting against the Anti-Christ. He says it also refers to the
deterioration of the political situation inside the United States, before
and during the time of troubles. But after the time of troubles are over,
people are celebrating their victory and their freedom. This celebration will reawaken in the United States the concept that is embodied
by the Statue of Liberty. The concept of liberty and rights and such
which have been dead because of the situation of war and the Anti-
Christ. They will come back alive; people will have their rights again
and things will be better than they were before.

CENTURY VI-24

*Mars & le sceptre se trouvera
    conjoinct,
Dessoubz Cancer calamiteuse
    guerre:
Un peu apres sera nouveau
    Roi oingt,
Qui par long temps pacifiera
    la terre.*

Mars and the sceptre will be in
conjunction, a calamitous war
under Cancer. A short time
afterwards a new king will be
anointed who will bring peace to
the earth for a long time.

B: He says he is using some of these astrological signs here as allegory rather than specific indications of time periods. Mars and the scepter in conjunction refer to a leader—he's thinking an American president—who is particularly hungry for war. The sign Cancer applies in several ways to how the events wrap themselves around to be ripe for war. He says someone under a strong Cancer influence will be the pivotal point in causing these events to fall into place for war. One of the leaders will have a strong Cancer influence in his horoscope.

D: *The American leader?*

B: No, not necessarily. Some of the major *happenings* in this war will take place while the sun rules in the house of Cancer. He says that after this war takes place the people will be tired of war and will elect another president. A new king will be anointed who wants peace and will work for it. And there will be peace for some period of time afterwards. There is a way of relating the planets and the houses of the planets to the other constellations that are not necessarily zodiacal constellations. He says if you want to narrow down a time period, look for a conjunction of Mars with a favorable relationship to Cassiopeia and with Mercury in favorable aspect to Gemini and Cancer. He says this may help the astrologer or it may be confusing to him. But he must keep an open and flexible mind and be willing to experiment. He must follow his inner voice and if he comes up with an idea that seems preposterous, try it out anyway.

Cassiopeia is not one of the zodiacal constellations. It is located near Polaris, the North Star. It sounded as though Nostradamus was giving John a test to see if he would be able to use his intuition to decipher the strange meanings of the symbols in the quatrains. Maybe he thought if John would be able to understand this, then he would be the one to work with me. Of course it all made no sense to me.

D: *They translated the scepter as meaning Jupiter and said Mars and Jupiter would be in conjunction and they came up with a date from that.*

B: What date did they find?

D: *They said it would be at the end of Cancer which would be about the 21st of June, 2002.*

B: (*Pause*) He says that may be close. It will still be during the strength of the American union. The strength of the American union will wane in the future, but this will be before that time.

Later when I took this quatrain to John to decipher he said he understood the reference to Cassiopeia. The following is his interpretation:

Cassiopeia is a prominent circumpolar constellation as seen from the middle latitudes on Earth. To the ancients, Cassiopeia represented a queen on her throne. In astrological terms it lies near the first degrees of the sign Taurus. Its meanings are: sorrows in love, outwardly serious but fun-loving, mystical preferences, positive negativity, fame through the help of superiors, and last (but maybe important to the quatrain) demonic powers. When in conjunction with Mars it represents an in-born ability to rise to influence. Determined but unforeseen adversaries could dislodge this rise. Legal difficulties and possible self-destruction are indicated since Cassiopeia lies opposite the Celestial North Pole from Ursa Major which might also be figured in Nostradamus' prediction. Ursa Major's main star, Tsieh-Kung, influences as a keen, resourceful, conservative, studious and fearful mind. Maybe these describe the natures of the participants of the quatrain. Mars is in conjunction with Cassiopeia at least once every 2 to 3 years. To be in good aspect with Gemini and Cancer it would have to be in the first 3 degrees of Taurus. This would form a semi-sextile to planets in Gemini and sextiles to planets in Cancer. Mars and Jupiter might not have to be conjuncting in Cancer. Instead, Mars and Jupiter could be in the first degree of Taurus conjuncting Cassiopeia and making sextiles or beneficial contact with planets in Cancer and Gemini. Mars and Jupiter will be in conjunction in Taurus from March 24, 2000 to April 16, 2000. Could this be the times Nostradamus was referring to?

CENTURY IV-29

Le Sol caché eclipse par Mercure,
Ne sera mis que pour le ciel
second:
De Vulcan Hermes sera faicte
pasture,
Sol sera veu pur, rutilant
& blond.

The hidden Sun eclipsed by Mercury will be placed only second in the heavens. Hermes will be made the food of Vulcan, the Sun will be seen pure, shining and golden.

B: He says in this quatrain he was using the sun and Mercury/Hermes and Vulcan as symbols of higher aspects to try to illustrate the grand design that is emanating from the center of the wheel during the time of troubles and the time of healing afterwards. I used the term "the center of the wheel" because of the illustration he's trying to show me which I will explain in a minute. He uses the sun to represent the overall power of the universe from which everything came. He's using Mercury to represent the materialistic aspects of technology. He's using Hermes, in relation with Mercury, to also represent modern technology as applied to communication. And he's using Vulcan, meaning the one who deals with fire, to represent warfare in this case, or those that deal with the weapons of warfare and thereby deal with fire. He used that phrase, "the hidden sun," to represent the fact that the world has gotten out of touch with their source. People are not aware of the source from which they sprang and thereby they search for fulfillment and happiness in other areas and do not succeed. They think it's found in modern technology. Thereby he stated the "sun being eclipsed by Mercury." He says it's held only second, meaning what they hold first would be personal pleasure and happiness. And they're trying to find happiness through technology, thereby separating themselves from the central source of the universe. But during the time of troubles the horrors of war and bloodshed—the powers of Vulcan, in other worlds—will cause them to realize that technology does not contain the answer to happiness which he stated by Mercury being consumed by Vulcan. By the end of this time of troubles when the time of healing comes, people will be brought back to the source. The will realize from whence they sprang and where they are going. This is when the time of healing will take place. People will become more mature spiritually and be able to heal themselves and heal the world, going much further in preparing to join the community of the Watchers.

D: *What was the symbology of the picture of the wheel?*

B: The picture that he showed me, is like a wheel with a central hub and the spokes radiating outward. I'm not sure but it seems that the hub of the wheel represents the source from which everything has come and the spokes radiating outward indicate the channels of power. Each space between the spokes appears different. You know on the physical plane when one looks between the spokes of a wheel one sees whatever background is behind the wheel, but on this wheel the background is different between every pair of spokes. It appears to represent the various influences the different aspects have upon the situation and the various possible outcomes as the result of the stronger or lesser influences of these different powers.

D: *I can see the difficulty you would have translating a concept like that. It sounds very complicated.*

B: It's confusing to me. And I'm not sure what the rim of the wheel represents in this symbolism.

J: It sounds almost like a picture of a horoscope wheel. The sun would represent, like you said, the source. But with each one of the houses representing a different department or area of life. Maybe this is a reflection of something similar in the spiritual or the higher levels.

B: I feel you could be correct. What you say feels right. Michel de Notredame is nodding. He says that concept is correct. It's a matter of applying the concept of the horoscope wheel or whatever it's called to the higher planes, the spiritual side of the situation that is coming up.

CENTURY II-87

Apres viendra des extremes contreés,
Prince Germain, dessus de throsne doré:
La servitude & eaux rencontrées,
La dame serve, son temps plus n'adore.

Afterwards there will come from a distant country a German prince upon the golden throne. Servitude met from over the seas. The lady subordinated, in the time no longer adored.

B: He says this refers to two different events. One is an event that took
place approximately 350, 400 years ago. The other interpretation of
this quatrain is a statement on society in general, including his time
and your time. He says "the lady no longer adored" refers to the fact
that the female aspect of deity has been neglected, reviled and ignored.
And when the time of peace comes after the Anti-Christ, this lack will
be made up. For in early days the female aspect of the deity was
worshipped. The masculine aspect was also worshipped, but as being
subordinate to the female aspect of deity. Then the patriarchal era
came into being and the masculine aspect of deity came to be
worshipped, with the female aspect of deity totally ignored, reviled and
pushed down. What society will need to come to terms with and be
able to handle is that deity is both male and female, neither male nor
female. They need to be able to deal with all these aspects of deity in
a balanced way, in order to develop a more balanced universal view.

D: *I thought that in his time it was a masculine deity with the dominance
of the Catholic church. But he is referring to the way it all started out?*

B: He says to unstop your ears. If you will listen to what he says, he says
that in his time and in your time too it's a masculine deity. But he says
that in *early* times, in ancient history, it was a female deity. He says
he's appalled at the lack of your education, but perhaps the research
you do in relation to this book will help make up for the lack. He's
surprised the classics are not covered in the educational system. He
deems it to be a great loss.

D: *Well, it has been 1500 years ... I'm sorry, 400 years since his time.*

B: He says that, yes, it's been 1500 years or more from the ancient times
to your time, but just a generation before you the classics were covered
in education, then came to be neglected following World War I. He
says it's a great loss to western civilization as a whole.

This seemed to be a constant bone of contention between Nostradamus and myself and was to continue throughout my work with him.
He couldn't understand the neglect of our schools to teach these things,
for in his time period it was considered the mark of a higher education. He
had no way of knowing how much the focus has shifted away from what
is truly "ancient" history.

This may also explain the translators' problems in understanding his
quatrains. We are all looking at them with our modern frame of mind and
education; thus we cannot see the subtleties of his schooling that definitely
colored the symbolism he incorporated into his puzzles.

CENTURY I-29

Quand la poisson terrestre	When the fish that travels over
& aquatique,	both land and sea is cast up on
Par forte vague au gravier	to the shore by a great wave, its
sera mis:	shape foreign, smooth and frightful.
Sa forme estrange sauve	From the sea the enemies soon
& horrifique,	reach the walls.
Par mer aux mure bien tost	
les ennemis.	

B: He says the interpretation of this quatrain may not be taken seriously by many who see it. The fish that flies over land and sea—he says what he finds in this vessel's mind that fits what he was seeing is that concept known as UFOs. After the time of conflict there will be much closer contact with the powers behind these vessels. One of them will be heading for an undersea base they have established, will malfunction and be cast up on the shore.

D: *Do they have bases under the sea?*

B: He said that's what he said. On the seafloor.

D: *"From the sea the enemies soon reach the walls." Does he refer to the people in the UFOs as being the enemy?*

B: Yes, the people will perceive them that way because they are frightened.

D: *But they're not really an enemy, are they?*

B: Some are and some are not.

D: *You've talked to me before about the Others and the Watchers. Is this another type?*

B: He says there's more than one group of Watchers out there. Some mean well for mankind and some have more selfish motives in mind.

CENTURY II-19

Nouveau venus lieu basti	Newcomers will build a place
sans defence.	without defenses, occupying a
Occuper la place par lors	place inhabitable until then.
inhabitable:	Meadows, houses, fields, towns
Pres, maisons, champs,	will be taken with pleasure.
villes prendre à plaisance,	Famine, plague, war, extensive
Faim, Peste, guerre arpen	arable land.
long labourable.	

B: This refers to an event he calls a "green" revolution. He says after the Anti-Christ, people will want to turn to peace. They will want to turn back to the earth, get in touch with the basics of life, and there'll be new life-styles being developed and explored. He says there was a hint of this in the American social revolution of the early 1970s. People will be developing extended families for support because it will take a larger group of people than just the nuclear family to build new communities, new places. And they will build so everyone can be very much in contact with the earth. They will be very ecology conscious. They will be doing all they can to help heal the earth and to bring in the new age that will be coming after the Anti-Christ. They will be reclaiming land and making it good for crops. Land that has been either wasted, misused, or not able to be used for all these many years. And since everyone is turning toward peace, the building of defenses is not necessary.

D: *One thing that confuses me. The last line says, "Famine, plague, war, extensive arable land." Does that refer to the war that's already past?*

B: Yes. And "extensive arable land" refers to the rebuilding they will be doing. They will be tearing down cities to make more room for farming. He says it will be the reversal of the trend of the 20th century which was putting farm land under concrete for cities. In the 21st century the trend will be in the other direction, the tearing down of cities to expose more growing land back to the sunlight.

D: *I was thinking maybe it meant they would be warring among themselves over the land.*

B: No, because so many will have been killed during the time of the Anti-Christ there won't be as much population on the Earth. There'll be enough land to go around. People will be so tired of war that when they come to a place where they're short of land, instead of fighting over what land there is, they create more land—so that all can have plenty.

The first line of the quatrain seemed to contradict this interpretation. "Newcomers will build a place without defenses, occupying a place *inhabitable* until then." But I believe this is an innocent error of translation or perhaps a printer's mistake. I consulted a French dictionary and found that "inhabitable" in the original translates to "uninhabitable" in English. The interesting thing is that I read the English translation to Brenda, but Nostradamus ignored the error because he knew the correct meaning of what he was seeing. Another example that we are actually in touch with the author of these prophecies.

Chapter 24

Ⲧⲏⲉ Ⓖreat Ⓖenius

CENTURY IV-31

La Lune au plain de nuict sur le haut mont,	The moon, in the middle of the night over the high mountain, the
Le nouveau sophe d'un seul cerveau l'a veu:	young wise man alone with his brain has seen it. Invited by his
Par ses disciples estre immortel semond,	disciples to become immortal, his eyes to the south, his hands
Yeux au midi, en seins mains, corps au feu.	on his breast, his body in the fire.

B: He's going to explain this in prose which means the explanation of the lines will not necessarily be in the same order as they were written down. He says in the future there will be this man, who will be one of the highest, most developed geniuses ever to appear in our present history of man. He says this gentle man made the decision to use his genius to help rather than to hurt mankind, so he is always inventing and envisioning things that will help man. Since he's such a genius there are many people who study under him to try to comprehend the great fount of ideas that come forth from him. One of the things he envisions to help alleviate the miseries of mankind on earth is self-contained, self-supporting space stations. They will be like space colonies and will be large enough to be seen from the Earth as small moons. He envisions this to help relieve the poverty, crowding and things of that nature that could be alleviated if there were more space and cheap energy resources available for mankind in general. These stations he visualizes will be practical to build. He envisions them in such a way that the technology of the time would easily be able to handle building them. And the way he presents the ideas they are attractive to the politicians as well as to the scientists, so he's successful in getting these things done. As a corollary to this development, another thing he envisions is a way of transplanting some of his genius and knowledge into a type of organic computer so it will still be there to serve mankind after his body has aged and died. He develops it to thc highest point possible to transfer his genius, or rather duplicate his genius and his knowledge, so he still has it but it's also in this organic computer. That is the meaning of the lines "his eyes pointing southward, his hands on top the breast, his body in the fire." For part of the process of doing this he must be engulfed by a particular piece of medical machinery that sends energy along all of his nerve passages to stimulate the brain in such a way as to be able to project the essential parts of the psyche that are needed for this organic computer. And it will feel like the body is on fire.

D: *That's a very strange translation. Has he shown you any mental pictures of what this organic computer would look like?*

B: I can't see anything. I don't think we have the concepts yet. The only clear idea that comes through is that this organic computer will be essential in the running of the space colonies. Somehow it will help them to function to their highest degree, but I can't get any pictures of what it looks like.

D: *I guess I automatically think if something is organic it has to be nurtured and fed and ...*

B: Yes, the building blocks of this computer have to be grown and developed in the laboratory. You know of the child's experiment where crystals are made to grow in filaments inside of a sealed glass— it's something similar to this but using certain types of liquids with certain chemical building blocks in them, causing this computer to grow and develop along certain biological formations. Almost like chains of protein, but done in such a way so it can be integrated into certain computer circuits.

D: *I was thinking if something was organic it could die, so to speak.*

B: This is true. However, the way this is developed through this man's genius, it is self-renewing like the cells of your body. Some of the organic parts will eventually wear out and get old. But meanwhile it will have replicated itself, so there will be organic parts sloughing off from this device but there won't be any loss of knowledge because it will be continually self-renewing. He says applications of this computer will be applied wider and wider to where it would totally alter the technology of mankind.

UPDATE: When this quatrain was translated in 1986 the idea of an organic computer was totally beyond my comprehension. However, a discovery in 1991 put the concept within the realm of plausibility. The problem with traditional computer chips, the microscopic devices that make computers work, is that there is a limit to how small they can be made. A group of researchers at Syracuse University reported they are now able to store and retrieve information from a tiny block made of the protein "bacteriorhydapsin." This is a substance derived from a bacteria found in salt marshes. They say that six small cubes of this material, each a mere one-centimeter to side, could store the entire Library of Congress.

It will probably be many years before the computer industry will be able to put this discovery to use, but it definitely is organic if it is derived from bacteria. This could be the substance, or something similar and equally fantastic, used in the computers during the time of the Great Genius.

D: *This apparently will be something that will happen in the far future.*

B: He envisions the 21st century, perhaps the 22nd. He says even though it seems very fantastic to us, it will not be as far in the future as one would think. Because of this man's genius he will speed up the process immensely in developing things that seem very fantastic to us now. It was very easy for him to spot this man along the nexus of time paths because he creates such a large ultimate effect. He's at a nexus of time lines, but anything he does will affect the various futures the Earth could travel along. So he was a prominent light—that's the way he's describing it—he was a prominent light on the landscape of time. He says he's a very knowledgeable person, and he decided to apply his remarkability through science rather than through philosophy, so he could help mankind materially rather than just mentally. He says this man is one of the major forces that will help the Earth recover from the scars of war it will have gone through. He will help heal the Earth so mankind in general can be whole and happy and living well again. He will appear after the Anti-Christ. This man will be able to see how the Earth is scarred and how it could be healed, and he decides to apply his life to that. He's the main antidote to the Anti-Christ.

D: *That's good because the Anti-Christ sounded so final. This shows that we do have some hope for the future.*

B: He says, yes, the universe has to keep things balanced. You can't tip the scales all the way one way without them swinging back the other way. And this man, due to the nature of his genius, causes the scales to swing back toward a good phenomenon happening. He will apply himself in such a way that things will balance and even out and be better all the way around.

D: *The scales pulled one way toward the very evil man and now can come back toward the very good. I'm glad to hear that. It was very depressing.*

B: He says if they went toward the very evil man and just stayed there they would be out of balance and it would tear apart this part of the fabric of the universe. So it cannot be. He's chuckling at this point. He's saying, "See, I'm not always a doomsayer."

D: *Yes, I did accuse him of that, didn't I? (Laugh) Well, this gives me a little bit of hope that maybe all of his quatrains won't be gloom and doom.*

B: He said so much about the gloom and doom because he has no worry about mankind surviving the good times. It's a matter of whether or not they're going to survive the gloom and doom. And he tries to warn people of it so they'll be braced to survive it. Then they'll be around to enjoy the good times afterward.

CENTURY I-56

Vous verrez tost & tard taire
grand change,
Horreurs extremes, &
vindications:
Que si la lune conduicte
par son ange,
Le ciel s'approche des
inclinations.

Sooner and later you will see great changes made, dreadful horrors and vengeances. For as the moon is thus led by its angel the heavens draw near to the Balance.

B: He says this relates to the earlier refrain about the man who is a genius. He has already mentioned that after the horrors of the Anti-Christ and such the scales will have to swing back the other way to balance things out. The "moon drawing near led by its angel," is the space colonies developed by this genius. The way its computers are organized and developed into organic computers are guided by him and led by him, the inventor of this and the head of the research in this. Through his efforts things will be balanced out again and brought back to normal.

D: *Then many times when he refers to a moon he is referring to these space colonies.*

B: He says with the concepts he had in his own mind and the words he knew, that was the only word he could come up with. Communicating with you like this through this vessel's mind with its more advanced technological concepts, he can see it was space colonies and space stations that he was seeing.

D: *In the first part it says "great changes, dreadful horrors and vengeances." Those will come before?*

B: Yes, he says the great changes and the horrors and vengeances will be from the Anti-Christ and from the rise and fall of the governments, the sects and such.

When I was working with Elena, Nostradamus said one way I could be sure I was really in communication with him again would be to perform a test, so to speak. To have him interpret a quatrain through someone else that he had already interpreted through Elena. He said if he interpreted it in similar words—it did not have to be word for word, but close enough that it had the same meaning—then I would know I was really in touch with him again.

I really did not need proof. He had already supplied me with more than enough information and similarities that I knew it could not be coincidence. But I knew that for the sake of my readers and any skeptics I probably should perform the test. I had purposely hesitated until we had worked on this material for several weeks and had translated over 60 quatrains. I suppose the human side of me kept putting it off. What if the interpretations did not match? Maybe my faith in this project would be shaken. The evidence was, in my eyes, overpowering. But what if he couldn't pass the test? Would it throw a shadow over the whole experiment? I knew I would have to take the chance. I finally decided it was time to walk out on thin ice and ask for an interpretation of a quatrain that Elena had previously interpreted through Dyonisus. I picked the first one she had found on her own, the one about the hidden Biblical discoveries. Of course Brenda knew nothing about what I intended to do. When she was in trance I humbly explained the situation to Nostradamus.

D: *I hope he doesn't resent this. I'm going to perform a test. Is he aware of when I was working with the other woman before she moved away?*

B: Yes. He says that it was a most strange and wondrous communication through one of his foreign students, the Greek one.

D: *Yes. And it was difficult because the student didn't seem to understand a lot of what he was communicating to me.*

B: He's shaking his head at this point and says, "Those Greeks can be stubborn and sometimes it gets in the way."

D: *(Laugh) Before the other woman left, Nostradamus gave me some instructions and this was one of them. He told me to perform a test, so to speak, if I found another vehicle. So I don't want him to be insulted.*

B: He says, no, it's necessary to present these truths to prove that this is a true and clear communication and not a hoax. It's important this information be brought through, and that it be accepted as authentic. If it's not, then all of this is for nothing.

D: *That's true. To me there have been too many so-called "coincidences." The way the whole thing has fit together so well between the two different vehicles, I cannot see it as a hoax. But it worries me too. I believe in it so much I'm afraid that maybe it will be proved wrong if I perform a test.*

B: He says that would be a great jolt to your belief system.

D: *There was a quatrain that Elena interpreted through Dyonisus and at that time Nostradamus said he would give me more information on it later. He told me that if I would bring up this quatrain again and if he said the same things—similar, but not in the exact same words—I would know I was actually in touch with him.*

B: He says, yes, this is true. The words will be similar but he will be able to expand more using the broad vocabulary available through this vehicle. He says, please continue.

D: *During that time she was told to meditate and try to understand the translations, then he would correct them. The instructions have changed since then.*

B: He gave different instructions to fit the different vehicles.

D: *Yes. Now I am doing it instead. I wonder, should I read her interpretation? At the time he said it was not totally accurate and he expanded upon it.*

B: He says for the purpose of this test, it might be better if you just read the translation in the book and then have him expound upon it as he has done with the others. That way people cannot say the vehicle heard what the other person had to say about it. And for you to see the parallels, so if indeed they do fit together, it will prove that it's a true communication.

D: *All right. Then I'm willing to take the test too, if you know what I mean. This quatrain was worded differently in the book that she had.*

CENTURY VII-14

Faux esposer viendra topographie,
Seront les cruches des monuments ouvertes:
Pulluler secte saincte philosophie,
Pour blanches, noirs, & pour antiques verts.

He will come to expose the false topography, the urns of tombs will be opened. Sect and holy philosophy to thrive, black for white and the new for the old.

I took a deep breath and crossed my fingers, hoping he would pass the test he had imposed upon himself.

B: He says this is another quatrain that has more than one interpretation since it refers to more than one event. One interpretation refers to the man who will rise as an antidote to the Anti-Christ. This genius that has been mentioned before. The phrase "he will expose the false topography" means he will show that the way things are looked upon, they have a false appearance. That the philosophies and sciences have been built upon mistaken premises, thereby building a mistaken picture of the universe. What he discovers and what he develops will help people come closer to the true appearance of the universe, of how it really is, in relation to the life force that permeates everything. He says a lot of this knowledge will affect the philosophies in religions, but it will also help explain discoveries of old documents that had been shunted aside due to people's way of looking at things. He says various documents, such as those found in some of the tombs of Egypt and at Qumran, and various other documents that will be found are examples of this. They will be linked together in a cohesive manner to explain earlier versions of major religions that will seem totally topsy-turvy to the way they've been interpreted through the years, thereby appearing to be black for white. He says the new interpretations of these, based on the new understanding of old writings that had been obscure before, will make so much more sense to people it will replace the old way, the narrow-minded way, of looking at things. He says this will cause a sweeping change in the world, particularly in matters of religion and philosophy. Simply because this discovery that is initially pictured as being a discovery in science will be more metaphysical than is first realized. And it will make clear the connections between the physical universe and the metaphysical universe as dealt with by religions. He says a minor event this quatrain refers to as well, is an event that has already taken place. In the early 19th century there was a man who came into possession of some Egyptian documents of ancient times that were discovered in some tombs. And this man had a trace of psychic ability. Through this he gave an interpretation of these documents that was partially correct and partially incorrect. But he used this interpretation of these documents in the founding of a new Christian sect. Some of the beliefs of this sect disagreed with the prevailing beliefs at the time and made the followers of this sect very suspect. For they seemed to be looking at some things backwards from what the theologians at the time assumed they should be, based upon the Bible, since these followers were also going by the information obtained from these Egyptian documents. He simply mentioned this as a minor event that this quatrain also described. History moves in spirals.

Weeks later it occurred to me who he might have been speaking of. I believe he was seeing Joseph Smith and the beginnings of the Mormon church in the 1800s. That sect is supposedly based upon the discovery of ancient writings.

B: But the major event he thought was important to the well-being of mankind was the one he expounded upon the most—the first event that has not yet taken place from your time point of view, this genius, the antidote to the Anti-Christ. The developments he does and the effects it will have upon the world and the population in general will be those foretold by people envisioning the Age of Aquarius. He says as a result of this, world-wide peace will be imminent. People will be able to free their inner selves and open themselves up to the higher powers and the higher levels of the universe. In effect, it will make every person a philosopher as they will be open to these things, whereas before only philosophers were. As a result, the sects and religions that embrace these newly-discovered true principles will be very widespread as people will want to get together and share their experiences in exploring these upper regions.

He says he wanted to make sure it was clear that he was not meaning to imply the genius will discover the documents himself. The documents will have been discovered by others. But through the discoveries this man makes regarding the basic structure of the universe and the nature of God, he is able to make sense of a lot of things that did not make sense before. And things will come together as a whole.

I think it was most remarkable that out of all the quatrains in the book, he also associated this one with the discovery of ancient documents. Even though the wording was different, I think it was so close in subject matter I could say he had passed the test.

B: He says *you* are to be the one to judge whether the interpretation is close enough to be deemed a true communication. When using two different vehicles, each vehicle contains their own perceptions of the world and their own concepts regarding communication and philosophy. So some of the concepts may be worded differently or may seem only similar instead of alike. But he says that part of the test was for *you* to judge whether it was a true communication, and he will accept what you decide.

D: *We also had a third party involved with Dyonisus. Through the other woman, he said the quatrain dealt with a discovery of something similar to the Dead Sea Scrolls. They were discovered about 40 years ago and have revolutionized people's thinking due to the philosophy they contained. Dyonisus said it would be a discovery of something new that had to do with the Bible or along that line.*

B: He says when you relisten to your device, you will find that he did mention Egyptian documents and documents at Qumran and others that have not yet been discovered, also similar ones in the Middle East.

D: *Dyonisus said he was particularly thinking of ones that would be discovered before too long. He was going to tell me where they would be discovered and draw a map of the location, but then he decided other people might use this for monetary gain.*

B: Yes, he says this must be prevented. Even though he's using this communication to clarify quatrains, sometimes some secretiveness is still necessary in the delicate areas.

D: *Dyonisus did not give as much detail or as clear of a communication because of the time period he was speaking from. Those were our stumbling beginnings. Through this vehicle we are getting a much clearer communication and a lot more detail than we were before.*

B: He said that he is glad for that.

D: *But both interpretations do deal with the discoveries of ancient documents. So as far as the test is concerned, I think it's pretty close.*

B: He says he leaves it to you. He says he knows he is truly who he is, and he knows the line of communication has been set up. But the test was mainly set up to reassure you, and also for any naysayers and critics you may run across in your work.

D: *And there will be many.*

B: He says, yes, there will be.

CENTURY III-2

Le divin verbe donrra à la substance,	The divine word will give to the substance (that which) contains
Comprins ciel, terre, or occult au laict mystique:	heaven and earth, occult gold in the mystic deed. Body, soul and
Corps, ame esprit ayant toute puissance	spirit are all powerful. Everything is beneath his feet, as at the seat
Tant soubs ses pieds comme au siege Celique.	of heaven.

D: *This one they have listed as an "alchemistic" quatrain.*

B: He is familiar with the word. He says the phrase "alchemistic" qua-train is accurate because this quatrain refers once again to the genius that will be the savior of mankind after the Anti-Christ has ravaged and gone. What seems to be fantastic claims of alchemy will become realistic and possible because of the discoveries this genius makes and the concepts he perceives. The new philosophy engendered by this man's discoveries will encourage the development of mental powers and anything will seem possible because there will be a greater unity of mind, soul, body, and emotions than there ever was before. So people will be able to manipulate the basic forces of the universe in a way that will seem utterly fantastic to those not involved with the occult. He says that up to that time such manipulations were per-formed by people closely involved with occultic and psychic things that deal with these forces anyhow, even though they do not fully understand what they are dealing with. But in this future time under-standing will be there as well which will make the dealings a lot more effective. Thus, many amazing and wondrous things will be done in an every-day sort of way.

D: *I think when I read the translator's interpretation he may get angry again.*

B: I have warned him. He says he is braced.

D: *She says: "Alchemistic quatrain. Although many commentators dismiss this verse, I think it is a rare and important description of Nostradamus' beliefs and experiences. The 'divine word which takes on substance' is either Nostradamus literally calling forth the spirit who inspires him to prophecy, or an incantation which gives him divine powers. 'The occult gold and the mystic deed.' He feels his body to be possessed of great powers, and possibly the last line indicates that during his prophetic sessions he felt disembodied. That his soul was outside his body looking down on himself, at the foot of the heavenly seat. This is a common trance-like experience. Alternately, Nostra-damus could mean that the spirit of inspiration came down to him and is as much present beneath his feet and therefore under his control, as it is at its heavenly source."*

B: He says this person is a very mixed-up person. Some aspects of what she says are totally ridiculous, but one or two phrases are viable. He says, for example, right now, even as he speaks, his spirit is separate from his body but he's not looking down upon himself. Even though it's a ridiculous interpretation, he can see where she would get this. But that's the way it goes sometimes. It is such interpretations that made this project necessary.

CENTURY III-94

De cinq cent ans plus compte l'on tiendra	For five hundred years more they will take notice of him who was
Celui qu'estoit l'adornement de son temps:	the ornament of his age. Then suddenly a great revelation will
Puis à un coup grand clarté donra,	be made which will make people of that (same) century well pleased.
Que par ce siecle les rendra tres contens.	

B: He says this has a double meaning. The major meaning he was wanting people to know is that the man being referred to here is the genius that has been previously mentioned. What he discovers and what he establishes will make positive and sweeping changes for mankind in general, and it will stand. Through the succeeding centuries people will grow up and live under the light of his discoveries and continue to develop themselves. Then, after the allotted time has passed, another discovery will be made that will be just as awe-inspiring and sweeping as the genius' discovery. It will intermesh so well people will be able to burst free from all physical bounds and there will be no limit to their positive development. He says that is the major interpretation of this quatrain. Once again, showing how history will move in spirals, there was another man in the past, Leonardo da Vinci, that was considered a bright light of his time and well regarded in succeeding centuries. Some of the things this genius will discover will bring to light even more the greatness that was Leonardo da Vinci. He says it is most interesting how it all interrelates in this manner.

D: *They say that Leonardo da Vinci did invent many things that were ahead of his time.*

B: He says all of the most interesting and amazing of Leonardo da Vinci's discoveries and inventions had to be hidden or destroyed because of the Inquisition and the ignorance of the people around him.

D: *Oh, he was having the same problem. We do have a lot of his papers and his notes that have come down to us.*

B: He says there are a lot of them that have been locked away in the Vatican Library.

D: *Does he know why they were considered controversial?*

B: He says they weren't merely controversial, they were downright heretical.

D: *What subjects did he deal with?*

B: Every subject conceivable. He says that's the way Leonardo da Vinci was. He could conceive everything. Due to da Vinci's writing about his own discoveries and making logical extrapolation based upon his inventions and discoveries, he was able to explain some of the happenings in the Bible as being due to man's technology and not due to miracles of God. And this was considered to be very heretical. It was lessening the glory of God. They didn't care for his interpretation of various prophets of the Old Testament such as Elijah and Ezekiel and some of the things written by Isaiah. Theirs were the more fantastical things that people had not been able to interpret. They just lumped it under the general category as being the glory of God. Leonardo would expound upon and show reasons why it was referring to things man could do, rather than just being the glory of God.

This may have been another reason for Nostradamus being so obscure in his writings. He has already seen what happened when someone wrote about these things and were not discreet about it. He already had an example of the consequences of writing things down in plain language.

D: *Did they take these papers after da Vinci's death or while he was alive?*

B: Both.

D: *We have a lot of them that describe some of his inventions and different books on anatomy that he wrote and things like that. It sounds like he was also a great philosopher.*

B: Oh, yes.

D: *But it has been so many years you would think the Vatican would release some of these documents.*

B: The Vatican would still not want to release a lot of them. But the majority of them are tucked away and gathering dust and mostly have been forgotten.

D: *That's probably what happened to a lot of things down through history. I like to read him the interpreter's translations from time to time because I like to see what he says.*

B: Besides jumping up and down and pulling on his beard.

D: *(Laugh) They have interpreted this quatrain as referring to Nostradamus. That he is this great man. They say "almost every interpreter of Nostradamus' quatrains have used this one as a guarantee of the inspired nature of their works." They claim this gives them the authority, so to speak, to interpret.*

B: He says that is a misuse of this quatrain. If you wanted to apply it in that manner then it would be particularly applicable to *this* case since this is a never-before used channel of communication with him. That should please other studiers of Nostradamus in your time period. But he says this is not what he had in mind.

D: *I wondered about that. He has never spoken like this to anyone else? Then maybe it will impress upon people the importance of our translations of these quatrains if it's never been done before.*

CENTURY IX-65

Dedans le coing de luna viendra
rendre,
Ou sera prins & mis en terre
estrange,
Les fruitz immeurs seront à la
grand esclandre
Grand vitupere à l'un grande
louange.

He will come to take himself to the corner of Luna, where he will be taken and placed on foreign land. The unripe fruit will be the subject of great scandal, great blame, to the other great praise.

B: He says this refers to when the time of trouble is over, the space program is once again taken up and space exploration seriously considered. This has to do with the establishment of L-five colonies of space stations. (*I didn't understand.*) L-five, L dash numeral five (*L-5*). Space stations for the attempt of manufacturing things in space for durability and particularly for the possible establishment of a scientific base, perhaps on Mars. He says at this time a communication and scientific base will have already been established on the moon. This is somewhat in the future when decent funding has been provided for such a grand endeavor. He says the commander of the lunar base will be kind of the head supervisor of the project since he's out there and in that part of the world. (*We all laughed at that remark. He obviously intended it as a joke.*) He's there on site to keep an eye on things and will get overanxious about the schedules and the deadlines, and start pressing the construction workers to get this particular solar power generator station finished ahead of time for an inspection by an important person from earth. They manage to get it done in time but only at the expense of the quality of construction, making it dangerous. One person will be brave enough to risk his career and step forward to expose what is going on. He will be proven correct and will be praised because he was brave to do it. However, this lunar superintendent will have great blame because the unripe fruit is the station that was not completed correctly. It will be his fault and there will be a large scandal and a lot of political shiftings will occur because of various people being asked to resign from their posts, etc.

D: Then where it says, "*he will be taken and placed on foreign land,*" that means the base on Mars. (Someone handed me a note.) *You were talking about the solar power station. Are they going to use crystals or crystal power in any way with this?*

B: The solar power is sent first to the space stations. Their major reason for existing will be to collect solar power and solar energy and transmit it to the Earth as a form of clean, practically free energy that people can use to live and grow without doing atrocious things to the Earth in the process. He says the technology will be very developed. There may be some crystals involved, but the solar cells you're familiar with

with today will be considered obsolete at that time. There will be new ways of collecting the solar energy and transmitting it to where it is needed.

D: *Will this happen during the time of the genius?*

B: Yes, the genius will have such a profound impact on the development of mankind he will be almost deified. He will have great respect and honor.

D: *John was wanting a date for the genius. I was thinking you said maybe the 21st or maybe the 22nd century. Is that right?*

B: No, that's incorrect on your part. He says the genius will come the second generation after the Anti-Christ, in the mid-21st century. If you will observe your history, the development of our civilization and the development of technology has been increasing and happening at an ever faster rate. Like going up a pyramid. The higher up the pyramid you go, the faster things and new inventions come. And this trend will continue. Things will be changing so much that technology will be in a constant state of flux. He says you seem to think this is far in the future, and you forget you're at the end of the 20th century now. You will be living in the 21st century. It's not that far off. He says that of the people in this room of child-bearing age, the time of the genius will come in the time of their grandchildren.

D: *That will give us a rough idea of a time sequence.*

They did interpret this as having something to do with space because of the mention of Luna, but they were thinking of a space race between America and Russia.

B: They're being egocentric again, he says. He doesn't like how they keep trying to put bindings and limitations on what he sees. The main thing that upsets him is that he has gotten the impression they assume he sees only for France and not for the world. He says, "Do you not think I am concerned for the whole world? France is not the only place on Earth with people." He did a rude gesture and made a rude noise at this point. He says, "They're blockheads. We must try to understand."

UPDATE: Refer to the Addendum for more information about the science of nanotechnology and its possible connection between the Great Genius and his organic computer.

Chapter 25

⚡hc ꝼar ꝼuture

Le corps sans ame plus n'estre en sacrifice.	The body without a soul no longer at the sacrifice. At the day of death it
Jour de la mort mis en nativité:	is brought to rebirth. The divine
L'esprit divin fera l'ame felice,	spirit will make the soul rejoice
Voyant le verbe en son eternité.	seeing the eternity of the word.

B: He says this is referring to a set of circumstances far in the future. The 20th century is working its way toward this, and it's in sight but there's a way to go. One thing he was envisioning was the great advances in medicine. He says in your time, the first glimmerings of this can be seen in how the surgeon in the operating chamber can bring people back who are clinically dead. They have brought them back to life to where they can live for years afterward. He says medicine will continue to develop so man will seemingly live forever, for he says the body is too wondrously made to die so quickly. He's referring to the average life spans in his time. And he saw a time in the future where people who had died could be brought back to life in many wondrous ways, either by breathing the spirit back into the body before it had begun to corrupt or by making a new body like the old and breathing the spirit back in. He says there are many wondrous things he had seen in regards to this technology. Before this is developed, there will be a breakthrough in science that will upset all the theoretical phases of all the sciences, and man will finally touch God, so to speak. The spiritual core of the universe that relates all things together through the force of life will finally be discovered, and the central source of this is the divine spirit. He says when this source discovered, it will be possible to breathe life back into bodies us g some of this life spirit that permeates everything.

D: *That would have to be a long time in the future.*

B: Yes. But he says it would be easier for an average person in your time to conceive of that, than it would be for a person in *his* time.

D: *I can see it would be utterly impossible for people in his time to under-stand. We have made many advances that make it seem like it could be possible. I thought when I first read this quatrain it had something to do with the death of the world.*

B: He says not in this case. However, the discovery of this central spirit, this life force, will be such a sweeping change to everything that it will almost seem like a rebirth of the world. He says everything having to do with the way man thinks, his philosophy, his medicine, his science, everything will be totally changed and turned upside down. What was once considered impossible will be possible. And he says many wondrous things will occur. It is impossible to describe it all.

D: *The translator thinks this quatrain refers to Nostradamus' religious beliefs.*

B: He says that's not a bad guess for someone not knowing what they are doing with it. This discovery will affect philosophy as well and there will be a sweeping change. So, in a way, the results of this will affect everybody's religious beliefs and he can see why the interpreter would get a religious feel from it.

D: *She writes, "If there is any occult meaning in this quatrain, it is very deliberately hidden."*

B: He says, "Of course! What does 'occult' mean?!"

D: *(Laugh) They couldn't have begun to get this interpretation out of it.*

CENTURY I-69

La grand montaigne ronde
  de sept stades,
Apres paix, guerre, faim,
  innondation:
Roulera loin abismant
  grands contrades,
Mesmes antiques, & grand
  fondation.

The great mountain, seven stadia round, after peace, war, famine, flooding. It will spread far, drowning great countries, even antiquities and their mighty foundations.

B: He says he was speaking allegorically here and very symbolically. The mountain he speaks of will be the development of a new philosophy that will be more compatible with the reality of the higher planes and life here on Earth as well. This mountain and this philosophy will have seven basic concepts that appear simple on the surface but are actually very deep. The "seven stadia round" are symbolic of the seven basic principles of this philosophy from which all the other more advanced thought will grow. The way Earth will be ready for this philosophy is that after a period of peace the people become lax and not caring about the higher aspects of things because they have everything easy. After going through a period of war and famine and hardships and such—which turn minds toward higher things, thinking there must be something better than what is here—they will be ready to accept this philosophy. It will absolve the contradictions that people have to deal with now in their philosophy. This new way of thinking will spread across the Earth and people will find it acceptable. So as a consequence it will overturn the older, established religions. And hence it will have sociological effects and will affect the laws of the country too, since the laws are based on religious and social principles. He says this philosophy will have its roots in the thinking patterns of the Age of Aquarius.

D: *The translators said "it will spread far drowning great countries" referred to a great flood.—I've noticed several of his quatrains refer to religions and philosophies and things along that line.*

B: He says the way religions and philosophies develop affect mankind in general, so it shows up whenever he's looking into the future. That's a very important part of life and the world.

D: *This next quatrain contains an anagram they have interpreted. I may have to read you the original word in French because they have changed the letters around.*

B: He says first try it with the interpretation and then he will probably ask for the original word in French. But he says to continue.

CENTURY II-22

Le camp Ascap d'Europe partira,	The aimless army will depart from
S'adjoignant proche de l'isle	Europe and join up close to the
submergée:	submerged island. The NATO fleet
D'Arton classe phalange pliera,	folds up its standard, the navel
Nombril du monde plus grand	of the world in place of a
voix subrogée.	greater voice.

D: *The word NATO is what they have made from his anagram.*

B: He says, "And what is the anagram?"

D: *In the French it's ARTON, and they have changed it to NATO.*

B: He says to read it again and substitute NATO with ARTON. (*I did so.*) He says this is a combination of several things, as usual. In the future, after the calamitous events at the end of the 20th century, the present organization and alliances among the various countries, particularly the western countries, will dissolve and new alliances will be formed. After the old alliances have dissolved and while the new alliances are in the process of forming, the people who were involved with the peace-keeping underneath the system of the old alliances will be at loose ends, so to speak. He says there is a secret naval base, or intelligence base, that has been constructed on the American continental shelf underneath the ocean so it would be secret. The heads of staff will be meeting there to decide what actions to take in regards to the new alliances being formed. The idea of having this intelligence base under the sea will stem from the legends about Atlantis. He says, kind of in parentheses, he also threw in that bit about the submerged island as a hint to the fact that one day in the future there will be discoveries of submerged remains of this great civilization that gave rise to the legend of Atlantis.

D: *That was what I thought he might be inferring to, so we're on the right track.*

B: Yes. He says he had multiple meanings in this quatrain. That's why that line refers to Atlantis in an indirect way. He says the interpretation of ARTON to NATO is essentially correct in general meaning but not in details. By the time this happens NATO will not be known by that name any longer, but will be a similar organization that developed from NATO. When this dissolves and new alliances are formed, it will be in reaction to and as a result of the stress of war these countries will have gone through. He says that line "the navel of the world in place of a greater voice" means that at the time when this is taking place, the military scientists—and by this phrase he does not mean those who study the art of making war, but those doing research for the military—will discover a new ... force. For example, there is magnetism, gravity and electricity, forces like that. He says they'll discover a new force, and this will give supporting evidence to some of the Eastern philosophies about the nature of the universe. As a result, those countries in that part of the world, particularly India, will turn inward to contemplate this discovery so they may rise in greater glory rather than turning outward and staying in communication with the whole network of nations. He says it's not really a discovery but a realization. The evidence of this force has been in front of us and has always been there but the facts have been misinterpreted and have been associated wrongly.

D: *I suppose they find other uses for it?*

B: Yes, for the facts that are there. Fact number one is linked to something totally different. Fact number two is linked to something else. And fact number three is just considered a statistical aberration, for example. Then suddenly some genius will have an idea and link these three supposedly unrelated facts together, working through this to discover there's another force involved with the workings of the universe. This force will explain many things from Eastern-type traditions, such as teleportation and various wondrous happenings such as that.

D: *Could he tell me any more about the finding of evidence of Atlantis?*

B: He says it truly did exist, but not in the form popularly supposed. Many picture it as being a Greek civilization of some sort with colonnaded temples and such. He says in truth it was not like this at all. One thing about Atlantis that scientists will have to realize is that they used stone the way the 20th century uses metal. They had ways of working stone, of making it malleable like clay and then letting it harden again to stone. They worked with forces and energies that could be conducted through stone the way electricity is conducted through metal. He says it was a civilization based on a totally different concept of the world. Hence, when the archæologists find it, it will be difficult for them to understand what they do find.

D: *Do you know where they will find this evidence or these remains?*

B: I'll ask him.—He says there'll be remains found in various parts of the world because the civilization of Atlantis was a world-wide civilization. There have been a few small crumbs of evidence found already, but scientists have not put two and two together, so to speak. There's a major city of that civilization on the American eastern continental shelf. And there is one where the Sea of Japan now is. There is another major center under the ice of Antarctica. There are evidences of this civilization in Central and South America. And he says there are others in various places. Some of these evidences have been found and some have not. He says that some of the megalithic structures about the world are related to this civilization as well, particularly structures with mathematical preciseness about them such as the ones in Great Britain. He says it was a most wondrous civilization and when the scientists finally figure out about it, when they start discovering these ruins and everything, it will revise their picture of prehistory.

D: *We have the idea it was located on a submerged island somewhere out in the middle of the Atlantic.*

B: He says at one time part of it was on an island simply because of the levels of the ocean water. It's now part of a continental shelf because the waters of the ocean rose sufficiently to cover up this island. But that was not the center of the civilization nor was it the only place where that civilization existed. There were all these other places, and they were in communication with one another for they were one civilization.

D: *Has he gotten this information on Atlantis from reading or from his visions?*

B: He says he has seen it through the mirror and through another device he has. He's showing me a picture of it. It's like a curved piece of metal, like a very shallow metal bowl with a tripod balanced over it. And from the tripod is suspended a crystal. But I don't know how it's worked or operated.

Maybe this had something to do with the focusing of the flame through the crystals she mentioned before. Maybe somehow it reflected the light down onto the surface of the bowl. Any reflective surface could be used as a focal point for gazing and concentration.

D: *We have been told Atlantis perished in a great catastrophe. Does he know what happened?*

B: He says he can describe some of the events but he's not sure of the cause. He can give us his suspicions if we wish to hear unfounded facts.

D: *That's okay, because it's always been a mystery and people theorize about it anyway.*

B: He says mankind had become very advanced. Their civilization was advanced in the direction they had grown. It didn't have the wondrous machines your civilization does, simply because this civilization had developed in a different direction. Man relied more on the PSI part of the abilities of the mind to accomplish things rather than relying on the nimbleness of fingers to do it. Consequently, civilization had a totally different pattern, and with this use their abilities became quite common. When the civilization seemed to be at the point of really flowering and coming into its own fulfillment—he's not sure if some extraterrestrial civilization intervened or if a natural accident simply happened. He says if a natural accident happened, it seems like the Earth and the solar system somehow went through a cluster of asteroids and such. But if it was not an accident but by design, then some extraterrestrial civilization gathered together these asteroids and such, and the Earth passed through them. And these huge chunks of rock racing through the atmosphere and hitting the ground messed up the climate and caused shock waves. Quite a few of them landed on some of the cities and destroyed them totally. It happened in such a way that mankind lost every vestige of civilization he ever had and had to start from scratch again. He says some evidences of these huge pieces of rock that struck the Earth can be seen. These rocks, even though some of them were irregularly shaped, have left behind basically round impact points. He's saying you can easily see this by getting a good map drawn by a mapman with a steady hand. You'll notice there are some bodies of water that are basically round. He says the Sea of Japan, the Caribbean Sea, the Gulf of Mexico and others throughout the world mark some of the places where these huge rocks struck the Earth and the ocean waters came flooding in, destroying the survivors.

D: *That's a very interesting theory. One of the theories people have in our time is that they had some kind of mysterious power and they misused it.*

B: He says they didn't misuse it. They did have a mysterious power but they had become so advanced with it that he gets these strong feelings they were a threat to someone else, not through belligerence, but just through being advanced.

D: *It's one of the theories that, being men, they went too far and misused the power for the wrong reasons, creating some kind of an accident. But there are many theories. That's really all we have.*

B: Yes. He says one day some of the secrets will be found out but it will take a while. That which puzzles mankind keeps his attention the longest. At this point he kind of chuckles. He says, "Two examples are Atlantis and myself."

D: (Laugh) *Very true. I really believe his quatrains would not have survived into our time if he had made them simple.*

B: He agrees with you.

D: *He kept mankind wondering all these years about what he was trying to say. I really believe if he had written them down in plain English they would have been destroyed.*

B: (*Pretended aggravation.*) He says, "In plain *French,* if you please."

D: *(Laugh) All right. If he had written them down in plain language, I believe they would have been destroyed a long time ago. They would not have survived as a puzzle.*

B: He says they would have been destroyed at his death. He says that regardless of whether he dies naturally or is killed by the Inquisition, all of his writings would be burned right there on the spot if they were able to understand them.

CENTURY IV-25

Corps sublimes sans fin	The heavenly bodies endlessly
à l'œil visibles:	visible to the eye come to cloud
Obnubiler viendront par	(the intellect) for their own reasons.
ses raisons:	The body, together with the
Corps, front comprins,	forehead, senses and head all
sens chief & invisibles.	invisible, as the sacred prayers
Diminuant les sacrees oraisons.	diminish.

D: *They have no explanation for this one. They don't understand it at all. They put it down as an occult quatrain. Occult usually means ...*

B: (*Interrupted*) Hidden. He says this has a multiple meaning. It has a metaphysical meaning as well as a physical meaning. The metaphysical meaning is that mankind in general will start to develop themselves spiritually. The knowledge they need for this development has been in front of them all along but they haven't seen it. And when they start to realize what is there, it will confound them. He says the other interpretation of this is that at one point in the far future there will be interstellar space travel. "The heavenly bodies endlessly visible" refers to the stars which just keep going on and on. And these ships they'll be traveling in will be controlled by emanations of the mind and PSI power, rather than by mechanical manipulations.

D: *That would explain the last part too, "Senses and head all invisible."*
   He might be interested in what the translators say in their interpretation. "The prayers of the last line are the invocations to the spirits made by Nostradamus. As they finish, he is possessed."

B: He snorted with disgust at this remark and said, "Tear it up and throw it away."

D: *They think this is describing his "sensation of bodilessness that he experiences when he is in a predictive trance when his mind and intellect are used by the heavenly beings for their own purposes."*

B: I'm finding out he has a sense of humor, for at this point he momentarily imitated the physical reactions of an epileptic during a seizure. (*She began jerking her arms and legs in imitation of what she was seeing.*)

D: *He means the kicking?*

B: The quivering. He's being humorous. And when he stopped that, he remarked, "That never happens when I'm doing this. I am not possessed."

D: *Oh, he thinks that's what people look like when they're possessed?*

B: Well, he says that people who are epileptic are people who are possessed, so far as they know in his time. He's shaking his head and says it's time for him to go if such ridiculousness is to be borne. He says he's never possessed. He knows exactly what he's doing at all times. He says it's a good thing he was able to get in touch with us to set things straight.

So Nostradamus was not totally enlightened. There were still some things he didn't know about. He apparently accepted this explanation from the church or from the medical knowledge of his day that when someone had seizures they were possessed by evil spirits.

CENTURY I-17

Par quarante ans l'Iris n'apparoistra,
Par quarante ans tous les jours sera veu:
La terre aride en siccité croistra,
Et grans deluges quand sera aperceu.

For forty years the rainbow will not be seen. For forty years it will be seen every day. The dry Earth will grow more parched, and there will be great floods when it is seen.

B: He says this has to do with some of the troubles the Earth will have to go through. This is not related to the Anti-Christ but to future troubles in the far future. He says, yes, there will be a lot of floods and droughts at the time of the Anti-Christ, but this particular quatrain is another example of the scales swinging one way and then another. This is when there are troubles for the Earth again, when the rainbow does not appear for 40 years. He says this will cause a 40-year drought. The only way people will survive will be by melting the ice from the poles or by extracting pure water from the sea. That's the only way they'll get water for growing the crops and such. Then in an attempt to balance this out, the scales will swing in the other direction and there is a rainbow every day, causing copious rains and a lot of floods. The time element is not necessarily 40 years, however. He was using that as a concept for 40 cycles. He says he was speaking of larger cycles. The main thing this is indicating is that somehow mankind will do something to cause the environment of the Earth to get out of balance, out of kilter, so as to trigger an ice age. The sort where the water is being captured in the ice at the poles so there's no water for rain for a period of time. Then it will swing the other way when the ice age ends and there's too much water everywhere. Because the poles will be melting at a copious rate and there will be a lot of rain and floods and the sea levels will rise again. He says this is a natural part of the history of Earth. It happened in the past and it will happen again in the future. And once again, as it was the last time, this ice age will cause this civilization to fall. It will crase all traces of this civilization so that another civilization will have to rise afterward, the way it did this time. He says this seems to be a natural cycle in the age of Earth.

D: *Could these cycles be longer or shorter than 40 years?*

B: He says definitely longer. When he's looking across the far reaches of time, sometimes it's difficult to pinpoint the exact number of years, but you can tell general cycles. For example, in this case he says it will probably be 4000 years one way and 4000 years the other way. It's cycles of millenniums.

D: *When I read this I thought maybe he was referring to a tilt or shift in the axis of the Earth.*

B: He says this is also involved. You are correct. Mankind will have been walking along the edge of this cliff, because some aspect of their technology will be endangering the delicate balance of the ecosystem. And the shift of the axis will destroy that balance sufficiently to trigger this ice age.

D: *This quatrain is definitely gloom and doom but it will be a long time before it comes to pass.*

B: He says it's a natural cycle. Do not be alarmed by it, for mankind has survived such cycles before.

D: *But the problem is that mankind always has to start over again.*

B: He says they wouldn't necessarily have to start over again if there was a way of preserving the knowledge. But usually people's concerns get narrowed down to just surviving. They don't worry about preserving the knowledge.

D: *Well, maybe that great genius he spoke of will have something to do with this.*

B: He says that's a possibility, although the two events are far removed in time. He says we'll just have to wait and see.

CENTURY II-95

Les lieux peuplez seront inhabitables:	The populated lands will become uninhabitable, great disagreement
Pour champs avoir grand division:	in order to obtain lands. Kingdoms given to men incapable of prudence.
Regnes livrez à prudents incapables,	Then for the great brothers, death and dissension.
Lors les grands freres mort & dissention.	

B: This is one of those events that does not have to take place. It can be prevented. He says in previous quatrains we have translated, he has referred to an event where man overcomes the balance of the Earth and causes great changes in the climate and the seasons, causing much hardship and famine. As a result of this, many lands that are now major agricultural lands producing a lot of grain and food for much of the world will be frozen and will not grow food any longer. And the people who live there, who have grown food there will leave these lands like rats leaving a sinking ship. They will be running to lands that can still be lived in and can still grow food. There'll be a lot of dissension and fighting as the lands get more crowded and each tries to push the other out. He says as a result of the panic there'll be several stupid decisions made. The "kingdoms" refer to areas of power rather than areas of land. And people who are given responsibility in certain areas will make poor decisions that will escalate into major disasters, as a result of not thinking clearly under pressure caused by this horrendous change of climate. The two brothers that will experience dissension and destruction refer to the United States and the United Kingdom.

The United States and England have been referred to as brothers in several other quatrains.

D: *They have translated this as referring to the Kennedy brothers.*
B: He says there are other quatrains that refer to the Kennedy brothers. That is not one.

CENTURY X-74

Au revolu du grand nombre septiesme	The year of the great seventh number accomplished, it will appear
Apparoistra au temps Jeux d'Hecatombe,	at the time of the games of slaughter, not far from the age of the
Non esloigné du grand eage milliesme	great millennium when the dead will come out of their graves.
Que les entres sortiront de leur tombe.	

B: He says this refers to when the end of the world is approaching. He says the entire age of the world could be divided into seven great portions. The first six of these have been experienced and fulfilled, and we're in the seventh portion now. He says the seventh portion of these ages has to do with man and his doings. At the end of this age will be the end of the age of mankind, after this seventh age is accomplished. Although the Earth will continue to exist for a few ages after that, man will have served his purpose and accomplished what he needed to do here on Earth. He will be elsewhere instead, and the wheel of karma will no longer send men to Earth but to other locations.

This sounded very similar to what Phil said would happen in the future of man in my book *The Keepers of the Garden*.

D: *But this is not going to happen soon, is it?*

B: He says, no. When writing quatrains on karmic matters, one has to take into effect the great wheel of the universe and the slowness with which it moves. So far as the universe is concerned it might appear that it's going to happen soon. But that's only in relation to the great age of the universe. When it comes to the brief spans of man's lives, it will seem to be far in the future.

D: *That's a relief. What does he mean by, "It will appear at the time of the games of slaughter"?*

B: He says that between now and then, civilization will have fallen down and been rebuilt several times. Some of the traditions and conventions of the former civilizations will survive and be passed down, but each time this happens they will be perverted a little bit more. He says the games of slaughter of that time stem directly from the Olympic games of your time. This regular meeting every four years of all the nations to perform these sports events will gradually—through the succession of civilizations with intervening periods of savagery—be perverted into something resembling the gladiatorial games of ancient Rome. He says it's just simply another natural example of the circle of time. The games started out in athletic form in ancient Greece, became perverted to violence in Rome, and then when the games were reinstated it was of sports orientation again. But once more in the far future they will become perverted into violence and bloodshed.

D: *Maybe I'm beginning to think a little bit like him because I picked up on the connection with the gladiatorial games. And by "the dead will come out of their graves" he's referring to the transfer of their souls elsewhere from this planet.*

CENTURY I-48

Vingt ans du regne de la lune passez,	When twenty years of the Moon's reign have passed another will take
Sept mil and autre tiendra sa monarchie:	up his reign for seven thousand years. When the exhausted Sun
Quand le soleil prendra ses jours lassez,	takes up his cycle then my prophecy and threats will
Lors accomplit & mine ma prophetie.	be accomplished.

B: He says he wrote this quatrain in response to a question put to him once. It had been noticed his prophecies were coming to pass and someone remarked, "You've written so many of them and you're still writing more. How long will it take for all of these to come to pass?" So he wrote this quatrain in reply, pointing out to them that the number of years into the future he was seeing had no limit. He could see, he says, not to the end of time but to the end of Earth.

D: *Is that what he meant by the exhausted sun? That would mean whenever the sun gave out?*

B: He says whenever that happens Earth will long since be dead. But he did see the sun give one last burst of energy in a grand explosion and then die down to nothing. This part of the quatrain has to do with the fact that he could see to the end of Earth's time when the sun explodes and totally incinerates the planet. He says, however, that is extremely far off in the future and has no bearing on your time whatsoever.

D: *But does he mean that all this would happen within seven thousand years, or does that have another meaning?*

B: He says the lines about the "twenty years of the moon's reign and then another will take up the reign for seven thousand years" he put in this quatrain because of the Inquisition. That points out that if we are able to survive these wars he saw ... He's trying to avert these wars because he saw many visions of what could come to pass if we didn't kill ourselves making war first. One of the things he saw was an extensive and peaceful space expansion and exploration program, people expanding and living out in strange environments, being prosperous and growing. He says there will be a base established on the moon. It will be a major center of communication and scientific research. During this time this base's major purpose will be for developing—he's calling them "freestanding space stations," meaning independent of everything and everybody else. I think he's meaning self-sufficient, so I am substituting that more modern term.

D: *Did he call them space stations or is that your interpretation?*

B: Well, he didn't call them anything, he pictured them. They have various shapes: some are cylindrical, some are conical and some spherical. All of them have large solar sails attached to provide them with the energy they need. He says the moon base will be developing and building these space stations. After a period of time of doing this, the major impetus of growth will move to the space stations. That's where the main central work for the trade and the industries will be, so the moon will not have such a major place in the scheme of things anymore. It will remain the nexus of communications but the scientific research and the industry and such will move out to the space stations. And Earth will enter a major period of prosperity and growth because there will be room to grow and enough for everybody. Things will be basically peaceful if Earth manages to avoid certain bad decisions that could lead to war, and if Earth updates her civil laws so there won't be so much grass-roots unrest. He says this period of space exploration and living ... he chuckles and says it's much like the speculative literature this communicator likes to read (science fiction). This period will last for a very long time, very easily seven thousand years, if not more. He says once again he had to combine two prophecies into one quatrain.

D: *They have interpreted this as having to do with the date of the publication of his quatrains and the completion of his prophecies. They thought he meant it would be seven thousand years until the end of the world. The translator says: "It was a commonly-held theory in the Middle Ages that the world would come to an end in the beginning of the seventh millennium. This information originated from the* Book of Enoch *which was general reading in the first and second centuries but was removed by the church from the holy Scriptures." Does he have any comment on that?*

B: He kind of quirks his eyebrow at this point and says that is a reasonable assumption. But he says, "The tool that I use is not always reasonable." And at this point he gives me a picture of that mirror.

Chapter 26

The End and The Beginning

(O)CCASIONALLY THERE WERE TIMES when Nostradamus would stop the sessions if he sensed that the vehicle (Brenda) was not feeling up to par. He was very protective of her and as a doctor often advised her of ways to help herself. A few times he stopped the session to try healing her by directing energy to various parts of her body. He said that was difficult to do because of the time distance involved, but he often succeeded in easing any discomfort long enough for us to complete a session. Because she displayed no physical symptoms as I monitored her, I had no way of knowing anything was wrong until she awakened and described what was bothering her.

Nostradamus said several times that the project was urgent and he was deeply worried about getting the information through to us in time because to him it seemed that the events were dangerously close. We reached the point where he was zipping through 30 quatrains at breakneck speed during an hour session. We had the distinct impression he was trying to cram in as much as he could and leaving only when he absolutely had to. He said it was possible to push all the information through at once, but he did not want to burn out the vehicle. He knew that good vehicles were hard to find and he didn't consider the project urgent enough to harm her. He wanted to take care of her so he was insured the information got through, even though it was taking longer than he had anticipated. Of course, Brenda was glad he was so concerned about her welfare. He felt comfortable working through her because her education provided a good vocabulary structure and a broad base for grasping concepts, but he warned us that circumstances beyond our control might interrupt the project. I could not anticipate any reasons for probable delay but then I had not anticipated anything that had to do with this project.

When Nostradamus wrote his quatrains they could easily fit into a large book, especially as they did not include interpretations. I became aware that the amount of information coming through could not possibly be contained in one book. He agreed that the prose explanations he was giving greatly lengthened the quatrains. But he said it was up to me to make decisions on how to put it together, as long as the important parts dealing with our present and immediate future were not left out. He was pleased that the field of communication was clearer in our time period, with a lot more material being printed and distributed because of the higher literary rate but he was disturbed that the process of getting a book printed was more complicated. He had not taken these things into consideration when he had ordered me to get this into print as quickly as possible. In his time it had been much easier because there were not that many books or people who had the ability to write them. However, he was confident the books would be printed in time because he could foresee this. I greatly needed his reassurance in my moments of doubt.

D: *I've been wondering why he chose me to be the one to do this. Did I have any kind of an association with him in a past life?*

B: He says the reason why he chose you was not because of any past karmic associations. Of the various people that he could see in future times that had this sort of connection with this plane in regards to the various pathways of time and the various dimensions of time and the way they interact, you were the most strategically located. Others are also located well but he knew he had best condense his communication to one person, if possible, or through one person, if possible. Thus, he could concentrate his energy on putting the information through, rather than having to disperse his energy by trying to establish communication. He says the way you're located you're involved with this work plus you are in contact with souls with the type of mentality that could handle the information and communicate it clearly so it will be exposed to the world for others to learn.

D: *In the beginning he really surprised me when I was speaking to his student, Dyonisus, and he came through.*

B: Yes. He says that due to the nature of your work, this was necessary to establish primary contact with you. He knew you would never have known that this vehicle could be used in this sort of communication unless he had contact with you through the established channels you were accustomed to.

D: *It seemed to be such a strange way of doing it that the odds were against it succeeding.*

B: He says only if you are rational about it. If you can rely on your intuition and see the pathways of time as he can see them, he says it's working out just right, just the way he had seen that it would work out.

D: *Did he ever try to contact people in other time periods and get these messages through to them? The idea occurred to me that maybe he had contacted someone in every time period where he saw something happening.*

B: He says this is the major contact for this planet. He has contacted other people in future time periods, not because this has failed, but because these other people in these other time periods are on other planets. He wanted to try to disperse the information to these people who also have knowledge of his writings, to help clarify the information there too. He says he had been in contact with the Others, and they were interested in his writings and his visions, because he would see things for them too. And he would send them quatrains we don't know of here, for they don't have to do with this world but with their planet instead.

D: *Then he wasn't just concerned with our world.*

I know when this information comes out there will be many imitators and many people who will say they also are in contact with Nostradamus. But he said he was not contacting through anyone else?

B: This is correct. He says that to contact through several channels would disperse his energies so the communication would not be as clear and there would be conflicting results. He only desired one clear channel to communicate through. Initially he was trying in similar directions to establish a channel. But once this channel was established, he abandoned the other efforts because they were superfluous.

D: *Knowing human nature, other people will come forth and say they are also in contact with him.*

B: There will be others who will come forth and say, "Oh, but this is what Nostradamus has revealed to me." And he says these people are acting on their own delusions, and most of them will be religious fanatics of various sorts.

D: *I believe we have more than enough proof already that we are truly in contact with him.*

B: He says there's no such thing as sufficient proof when you're dealing with a true skeptic. He says the books will be published. He really doesn't care if the skeptics believe or not because his main desire is to get those who are open-minded to thinking about the events coming to pass and having a different way of looking at them. He says one or more of these thinkers will be in a position to do something about it. And some of the decisions they make will be colored by what they have read in your book. He says this will be sufficient to alter the events toward favorable outcomes.

This was easily the most amazing case I had ever conducted. If it had not been for the tape recordings and the witnesses, it would be difficult for even me to believe. On the surface, to any rational person, every angle of it was absolutely impossible. I fully expect that I and my subjects will be accused of perpetrating a gigantic hoax. But even if that were possible, it could never explain the information that came forth. I will leave it to the skeptics to argue that away. To me, it still seems unbelievable that all of this happened in only a few short months. When I began working with Elena I didn't even know what a quatrain was. Although I'm a writer I'm not a poet and have had no experience in that field. And the only definition I knew for the word "century" was the traditional one. How then, can common logic explain how we have become, within a few months, apparent experts on the writings of Nostradamus? How were we able to untangle and explain logically the puzzles that have perplexed mankind for 400 years? No, it's quite obvious this did not occur because of any superior intellect on the part of Brenda, Elena, or myself. Something else was at work here, some outside agency. This is the only explanation that makes any sense. Somehow, through methods known only to the great master himself, Nostradamus was able to see that he had disguised his quatrians so perfectly to protect them from the fires of the Inquisition that he had also made them completely indecipherable to future generations, those same generations that he had hoped to warn. He apparently decided to attempt to reach someone living in the time period where he saw the most tumult, someone living in a time where the people would be more enlightened and willing to accept his predictions. He hoped that if he could get the true visions across to us maybe it would not be too late to prevent them from happening. He must have been very heartsick to see that people of the future could not understand what he was trying so desperately to tell them. He risked his life to write these down for posterity, and he spent years laboring over them. He could have just shrugged his shoulders and said, "Well, at least I tried. I've done my best. If they don't understand, then it is their fault. Let them suffer the consequences."

Now that I have come to show Nostradamus' personality, I know that his love for mankind would not allow him to do that. Just seeing the future was no longer enough. He felt he must *speak* to the future. I wonder how long he sat searching his magic mirror, groping for some way to make contact? I wonder how many plans and possibilities went through his mind until he hit upon the one that was successful? I do know that I would not have been chosen and I would never have been contacted if I had not already been working with time and space using regressive hypnosis. I can see now that Elena was the bridge. The odds were enormous against my finding someone who had been one of his students in a past life. Could he see this future connection of his student, Dyonisus, through his mirror? Was he able by some method to contact Elena's guide, Andy, to help us in setting this whole thing up? Did he hope that my curiosity would be sparked and I would feel compelled to continue and search until I found another connection?

Many questions, the answers to which will probably never be known. I do know that I was only an instrument in this remarkable adventure. I believe beyond a doubt that Nostradamus himself initiated this project. From July 1986 to February 1987 we translated over 300 of the quatrains. It is almost impossible to believe that so much was accomplished in so short a time. I have only included some of the quatrains in this book because of the length. I deliberately chose the ones that experts have said are unexplainable and those that they think pertain to the future. It is amazing what wisdom is contained in this small cross section. I believe he has much, much more to tell man in those remaining quatrains. Thus I intend to remain with this project until they are all translated and the wonder of Nostradamus is at last revealed to the world.

I recommend Erika Cheetham's book as a cross reference because of her translation and her explanation of obscure and foreign words (*i.e.,* Latin, Greek and Old French) that are interspersed among the quatrains.

As Brenda once said, "He has made his obeisances and left." But he has not gone for good. In the sequels to this book he will continue to dazzle us with his remarkable foresight. Will he succeed in warning us? Is there still time to change our future? Can we afford to take the chance that he is wrong? Will mankind listen? I pray that we will. For the things that Nostradamus foresaw for our world are too horrible to ignore. And, after all, it's the only world we have.

THE END OF VOLUME ONE.

Addendum

(Added in 1996

to cover all three volumes.)

Addendum

Volume I of *Conversations with Nostradamus* was first printed in 1989, and Volume II followed in 1990. When the books were reprinted in 1992 it was noted that some of the prophecies had already come into fruition. It was then decided to revise the two books by adding updates of events; this created the revised editions. Volume III was first printed in 1992. The books became a living and evolving entity requiring updating each time the books went into reprint. It is becoming nearly impossible to keep the books updated. I receive phone calls and letters from my readers who say they are reading the books and simultaneously watching the described events happen on television. The information is current to our time period.

This is the fourth printing of Volume I in 1996, and there has been so much new information coming forth that it was decided to add this addendum rather than revise the entire trilogy. I hope it will not be confusing to those who have only read Volume I, because I will refer to new information pertaining to all three volumes. With the explosion of the Internet communications many of my readers have assembled details that would have been impossible if I had relied on my own research. I am grateful for their assistance and for the many magazine and newspaper articles that were forwarded to me. Their diligence makes the job of research much easier for me.

Century II-60 (Vol. 1, pg. 253) appears to have been fulfilled with the election of President Bill Clinton in 1992. The quatrain predicted that the United States would have a Democratic President during the Time of Troubles. When this explanation was given in the late 1980s I thought it was doubtful because President George Bush seemed to be firmly entrenched in Washington. But to many people's surprise Clinton was elected. All during his first term I waited for the rest of the prophecy to come true—that he would lead the United States into a conflict to stimulate the economy. In another quatrain Nostradamus said that the year 1995 would be a turning point, a decision-making year. He said that during that year the world would decide whether it would start down the path that leads to the Third World War or continue along the path we were presently taking (the least harmful path). It bothered me that toward the end of 1995 President Clinton committed our troops to the conflict in Bosnia. This was a fulfillment of the quatrain and also went against other Nostradamus warnings. He had given us the scenario of events that would lead up to the Third World War. One of these was that we would go to war in the gray area of Europe after a succession of small wars in the Middle East. He called it the "gray" area because he said you don't know if you're in Europe or in Asia, and he mentioned Macedonia, and Albania because he didn't have a name for Yugoslavia in his time. In Volume III he said we should not get involved in this area, because if the sectors broke apart it would make the country more vulnerable to takeover. I get the impression from the prophecies that our involvement in that area of the world will escalate and we will have great difficulty removing our troops.

NOSTRADAMUS INSISTED that we must stop the underground explosions of nuclear weapons (Volume I). It was hoped that his warning had been needed when the United States stopped their testing. A temporary national moratorium on nuclear tests took effect in 1992. In 1993 President Clinton considered resuming underground nuclear testing in Nevada, because some experts wanted to enhance the safety and reliability of existing weapons. The United States wisely decided to discontinue the testing, but other countries (such as China, North Korea, and France) were not so cooperative.

The threat was reawakened when France insisted on firing eight tests near a Pacific island during 1995 and early 1996. The entire world was horrified and there was much protest, even in France. The objections were totally ignored as France conducted test after test, insisting that there would be no harm done. Of course they were wrong, and it became gradually clear that Nostradamus knew what he was warning about when he said that the shock waves from the explosions would reverberate through the tectonic plates of the Earth. Within a few days of each test severe earthquakes and volcanic eruptions occurred. It should have been obvious to anyone that it was not coincidence. They were directly tied to the explosions. Within two days after a test in October 1995 an earthquake struck Japan, then Indonesia, then a volcano in New Zealand erupted. All of this occurred within one day and seemed to follow a pattern of progression around the Pacific rim. After another test an earthquake in Mexico and a volcanic eruption in Nicaragua occurred within the same day. Following a test during the Thanksgiving holidays in November 1995 there was an earthquake in Egypt strong enough to produce cracks in Chephren, the second largest of the three great pyramids.

It appeared that the French President reluctantly realized the truth in early 1996. He met with President Clinton in Washington and they agreed to do no more testing. France stopped after six of the proposed eight detonations. Did they stop in time, or has irreparable damage already been done? During the summer of 1996 America was leading the growing global consensus for a treaty to ban nuclear weapons testing. But they were having trouble gaining the cooperation of two of the other powers: China and India (who has nuclear potential but does not yet have a nuclear arsenal). India bluntly refused to participate, complaining that the treaty favors the five declared nuclear powers: Britain, France, Russia, China and the United States. China is helping India's adversary Pakistan attain nuclear capabilities and missile factories. It is believed Pakistan will have these capabilities within two years. No wonder India is concerned. The treaty bans only test explosions of nuclear weapons, making it difficult for less advanced nations (such as India) to develop nuclear technology. Existing nuclear powers are allowed to continue refining their own weapons with computers and other technology. The United States recently announced plans for a supercomputer capable of simulating nuclear explosions. The treaty, as it is written, would force India to give up an important defense option. India wants the nuclear powers to commit themselves to getting rid of their nuclear arsenals over time. [On August 22, 1996, India vetoed the test ban proposal in Geneva, Switzerland. However, the U.S. and other countries are still committed to the test ban and the years of work they have done. In spite of the objections the U.N. overwhelmingly endorsed the global treaty in Sept. 1996.] The U.S. said that Iran is as little as 10 years away from becoming a nuclear power itself. Russian assistance to Iran on developing civilian nuclear reactors eventually will help Iran develop nuclear weapons.

During July 1996, just 11 hours before international negotiators sat down to push through the global nuclear weapons test ban, China detonated what it said would be its final nuclear test explosion, believed to be China's 45th. China objected to the treaty because it wants to make it more difficult to order inspections if a nation is believed to have conducted a test.

Also during the summer of 1996 two accidents at a Ukrainian nuclear power station killed a worker and released radiation. During 16 weeks in 1996 each of Ukraine's five nuclear plants suffered a mishap in which radiation leaked or a reactor was shut down. The accidents underscored international fears over the safety of Ukraine's Soviet-built, cash-strapped nuclear plants. Ukraine's nuclear plants are so cash-starved that they can barely buy fuel. Routine maintenance and safety upgrades are postponed. Even small mishaps at nuclear plants are politically sensitive because of official Soviet efforts 10 years ago to conceal the explosion of a reactor at Chernobyl that resulted in the world's worst nuclear disaster. [It was Sweden who told the world of the mishap.]

Western nations have pressed Ukraine to shut down the Chernobyl plant. Two new reactors are to be finished within two years to compensate for the shutdown. The U.S. and its closest allies have promised more than $3 billion to complete the plants and streamline Ukraine's energy sector; but Ukrainian officials have complained that the money is being released too slowly.

In 1995 it was announced that the new nuclear plant in Japan would be built directly over an active earthquake fault [as is the one north of San Diego]. Japan said it realized the danger, but stated there was no other place to build it.

In a July 1996 newspaper article investigative journalist, Dale Van Atta, added another aspect to the continuing nuclear nightmare. He said at a lecture that the threat of a nuclear attack on U.S. soil is as real as ever. He saw it as being inevitable, and said it could occur within the next 10 years, and possibly five, with New York as the possible target. His information was based on U.S. intelligence sources. He said the number-one threat is still Russia because of the thousands of nuclear bombs remaining in the vast nation, many of which are unsecured. He said Russians are so poor that they will be willing to sell the weapons and other high-grade uranium to guarantee hard currency for the future.

☆ ☆ ☆

𝐀 LARGE VOLUME of the new information I received concerned the discovery of two new comets: Hyakutake and Hale-Bopp. In many quatrains Nostradamus mentioned comets in various symbolism, and these were directly connected to events that would occur during the Time of Troubles.

CENTURY II-46 (Vol. I, pg. 54): "In the sky will be seen a fire dragging a trail of sparks. (Quatrain refers to famine in Africa.)

CENTURY II-62 (Vol. I, pg. 124): "... when the comet will pass." (Concerning Time of Troubles, especially referring to Mabus [Sadam Hussein].) In the Fall of 1996 he reared his head again, so this prophecy is still in the process of coming true.

CENTURY IV-67 (Vol. I, pg. 173): "... a long meteor." (The *dry* quatrain. Great geological troubles. Earthquakes and volcanoes affect weather. A very bright, easily-seen comet, previously unknown.)

CENTURY II-15 (Vol. I, pg. 198): "A bearded star." (A major comet clearly visible in the sky of the Northern Hemisphere. Signs leading up to the assassination of the present pope.)

CENTURY II-96 (Vol. I, pg. 223): "A burning torch will be seen in the sky at night." (Events before the Anti-Christ comes to full power.)

CENTURY VI-6 (Vol. III, pg. 163): "A bearded star." (Events associated with the succession of the last popes. Also refers to the rise of the Anti-Christ.)

At the time of originally writing the books the main comet that was expected to be in our skies during this time was Haley's Comet. Yet in some of the quatrains Nostradamus described a new comet that the scientists did not know about. This definitely fit the qualifications of the

Hyakutake and Hale-Bopp Comets. They were unknown until recently discovered in 1995 and 1996, and correspond with other astrological signs mentioned in the quatrains.

Goro Adachi's information from the Internet:
CENTURY VI-97 (Vol. I, pg. 251): "At 45 degrees the sky will burn."

At the time of perihelion (closest to the sun—April 1997), Comet Hale-Bopp's angular distance (elongation) in the sky from the Sun will be about 45 degrees. And it will be located in the northern sky at declination +45 degrees (which means the comet will be right above geographic latitude (45 degrees). It will make its closest approach to the Earth on March 23, 1997.

Some of the places located on latitude 45 degrees: Lyon, France; Belgrade, Serbia (and the whole former Yugoslavia region); Tuzla, Bosnia. On longitude 45 degrees: Baghdad, Iraq. France's nuclear testing started with the discovery of Hale-Bopp. NATO/US entered the Bosnian civil war with U.S. headquarters at the city of Tuzla. The connection with Iraq and Saddam Hussein is obvious.

Comet Hale-Bopp has an orbit of over 3000 years. The orbit is a very long, stretched-out ellipse. This comment about the elliptical orbit sounded very much like Nostradamus' reference to a new star that would be discovered. In Volume Two (pp. 112 and 113), he revealed that: "We will discover two more planets, and they will cause tremendous excitement. The two planets are a part of another solar system that had a binary star (two stars, or two suns). There were two stars which exploded, and these planets were thrown into our orbit. Our solar system and that solar system are overlapping now. Uranus, Neptune, Pluto and these two new planets were previously part of this other solar system. They are not in an exact orbit but are drawn to the sun, like Pluto. They have a wider degree of arc. The binary star was an older system and it exploded and burnt itself out."

Also in my book *Jesus and the Essenes* the Essenes knew about another star. They had a model of the solar system that was in perpetual motion. The model contained *ten* planets, and the one that is unknown to us had a stretched-out, elliptical orbit.

These two separate references in my books probably refer to actual planets rather than comets, yet it is interesting that in both cases an elliptical orbit is mentioned.

Goro Adachi found some astounding additional information in CENTURY IV-67 (Vol. I, pg. 173) that greatly added to the work in this book.

"In the year that Saturn and Mars are equally fiery, the air is very dry, a long meteor. From hidden fires a great place burns with heat, little rain, a hot wind, wars and raids."

"The year that Saturn and Mars are equally fiery." Goro thought that line might mean Saturn and Mars would both be in the same fire sign. He found that during the 1996–98 timeframe Saturn would stay in Aries through the period, and Mars would be in Aries twice, presenting two windows: Mars in Aries: April 7–May 3, 1996 and March 5–April 15, 1998.

In the transcription Brenda said: "When Saturn is in a fire sign and at the time the Sun moves into a fire sign, there will be a comet. This will be a very bright, easily seen comet. But it will be perhaps previously unknown. This coincides with the time of great geological troubles."

Interestingly, Brenda doesn't mention Mars but instead refers to the position of the Sun. Incredibly, the mention of the Sun (which is not mentioned in the quatrain) makes it clear that the comet is Hale-Bopp. Hale-Bopp was discovered on July 23, 1995 and the Sun was in Leo (a fire sign) from July 24–August 24, 1995. Also Hale-Bopp's perihelion is around March 30, 1997 when the Sun is in Aries (a fire sign) from March 21–April 21, 1997.

When Goro put this information on the Internet a reader told him that "Saturne & Mars esgaux combuste" is an ancient astrological term which actually means burning or "conjoined with the sun." It becomes increasingly obvious that this information could not have come from Brenda since she had no knowledge of astrology. The reference to the position of the Sun had to come directly from Nostradamus. We can see that the information was actually consistent with the original French quatrain.

Later when Comet Hyakutake was discovered Goro was asked how this would affect the prophecies. He concludes that it does not disprove but rather adds to the validity of the information. The quatrains mentioning comets during the Time of Troubles could refer to both of these, since Nostradamus considered comets as omens, "harbingers of doom." In January 1996 Hyakutake was discovered and came very close to the Earth on March 25, 1996. It was bright in the sky during March to May. Perihelion (closest to the sun) was on May 1. Hyakutake's declination was at +45 degrees on April 6 (Aries, fire sign), and its elongation was 45 degrees on April 7. Coincidence? Goro found that both comets (Hyakutake and Hale-Bopp) fit CENTURY IV-67 perfectly, and he could be accurate considering the depth that Nostradamus applied to his quatrains. They often refer to more than one event, and he was an absolute genius at cramping an incredible amount of information into the deceptive four lines of a quatrain. Goro thinks the significance of all this astrological and astronomical confirmation is that it is trying to tell us: IT IS TIME! Nineteen ninety-six is the "official" beginning of the fulfillment of many of the prophecies predicted for the Time of Troubles.

Goro also had interesting additional information regarding CENTURY V-92. "After the SEE has been held 17 years, five will change within the same period of time. Then one will be elected at the same time who will not be too agreeable to the Romans."

During my work with Nostradamus we interpreted all of the known quatrains, but there were far too many to be included in the books (even though there were three volumes). I was told to concentrate on the events occurring in the next 20 years (from 1989). During the process of elimination only about half of our interpretations were included in the books. Many of those excluded dealt with the past, and many were repetitive or did not add any new information to the scenario I was trying to show. I am often asked whether there will be a fourth book containing the quatrains that were excluded. I do not think so, because I did not consider them to contain very much additional information. I believe such a fourth volume would be anticlimatic.

CENTURY V-92 was one of these that did not make it into the final editions. I remembered the quatrain and after seeing Goros reference on the Internet, I searched through the hundreds of pages of transcript to locate it. It was interpreted by Brenda in July 1989 according to my records. This part of the transcript was short, so I will include it here so it can be compared with Goro Adachi's conclusions. It is interesting to note the similarity, because no one else has seen our interpretation until now.

B: He says this quatrain is in the process of coming to pass. It refers to the elections of popes to the head of the Roman Catholic Church. He says we are in the process of going through the five that will be elected in the same amount of time—the middle part of the quatrain.

D: *You mean the others were in the past?*

B: Yes. He says the first line refers to a pope who was pope for 17 years, a rather lengthy period of time. Then the next line says five will be elected in the same period of time. He says that means in the *following* 17 years there will be five popes. Then one will be elected that will not be agreeable to the Romans. He says that refers to the pope that comes after those five. He will be very unpopular.

D: *That is the last pope?* (Yes.) *That will be one reason why he will be unpopular, I guess. He is the last pope of the Catholic Church.*

One of the reasons I did not include this quatrain in the books was because I thought the same information was covered already. Another reason was because I couldn't seem to make the number sequence come out correctly in my research. Goro Adachi seems to have been able to do what I could not, even though he has never seen our interpretation.

Goro's finding from the Internet: Pope John Paul II has held the Holy See for 17 years as of October 17, 1995. If the above quatrain referred to JPII he should not be still alive. It doesn't seem to apply to him if you consider the second line "five popes will follow in sequence," because Nostradamus indicated in several quatrains that there would only be two popes following the present one. This is also verified by the predictions of St. Malachy (see Vol. II). Goro found that there was a pope who held the See for exactly 17 years: Pius XI (February 1922–February 1939). The five popes that followed him were: Pius XII, John XXIII, Paul VI, John-Paul I, and our present, John-Paul II.

Goro makes only one small error concerning the last line, and this is debatable, because his interpretation would also fit. He wants to change the wording from, "Then one will be elected at the same time..." to "Then one will be elected of the same duration." According to my French dictionary "temps" can be translated as "time" or "duration," so this would make sense. By this he meant that both popes (Pius XI and JPII) would serve for the same length of time, and that JPII would be different from other popes. "One who will not be too conformable to the Romans," meaning that JPII was the first non-Italian pope since Adrian VI (1522–1523).

In our interpretation Nostradamus was referring to the last pope, the Pope of the Anti-Christ, who would be disagreeable to Italy because of the damage he will do to the Catholic Church. I think it is possible that Goro's interpretation is also acceptable. I have worked with Nostradamus for so long that I have learned the way he thinks. Goro seems to be the first person who has corresponded with me that is able to get inside the mind of Nostradamus in the same manner, and appreciate the genius of the great man.

Through his deductions Goro has come up with two places (Lyons, France and Belgrade, Yugoslavia) as possible assassination sites for the present pope. I have received information from one of my readers about Astro-cartography. This is a complicated astrological process where the horoscope is placed over a map of the world, and many determinations can be made, including the place of death. The resulting chart looks very much like a biorhythm chart. The reader demonstrated how such a chart depicted correctly that President John F. Kennedy would die in Dallas and Martin Luther King, Jr. would die in Memphis. According to the present pope's astrocartography chart he will die in *Belgrade*. This information was given to me in 1991, and since that time the pope has not been allowed to enter Yugoslavia. Maybe this is why the assassination has not occurred yet. Maybe history can be changed and this prediction can be averted if he stays out of that country.

Century v-15 (Vol. III, pg. 161): "The current pope travels back and forth to various spots on Earth to visit sections of the Catholic Church. This places him in danger because he can't be protected as well, but they can't do anything about it because the pope insists. Nostradamus says he sees that someone will assassinate the pope in a place where there has been unrest." Does this also refer to Belgrade, because there has been no comparable unrest in France?

At the time of writing these books I could not understand what purpose the assassination of a religious leader would serve. But now in the late 1990s it is obvious that it fits in with terrorism. Nostradamus said that there would be an increase in terrorism during the Time of Troubles because one way to fight a war is to demoralize the enemy. The logic would be to strike at what the country holds dear—their cultural and religious heritage. Terrorists attempt to create fear by fighting from the shadows. Nostradamus also said that during the Time of Troubles assassinations of world leaders would increase. It would become so common that no one would think anything of it. That prediction has certainly materialized.

CENTURY IV-67 continues: This quatrain mentions droughts. Nostradamus called it his "dry quatrain." In 1996 the Great Plains/Wheat Belt (the central part of the U.S.), where the majority of the country's wheat is planted, was hit by a MAJOR drought. It was probably the worst one in half a century. Some experts were calling the conditions the worst since the dust bowl days of the 1930s. Wheat supplies dropped to the lowest level in half a century, and the corn supplies reached a 20-year low. The drought even affected the cattle industry (including dairy cattle). Pastureland was too dry for cattle to graze and high grain prices left many ranchers unable to afford cattle feed. From Kansas south to Texas, one of the worst droughts on record pushed thousands of farmers on the Great Plains to the edge of financial ruin and spurred panic selling of cattle in some areas. It was said that it was the first time farmers sold pregnant cattle for slaughter. This was expected to have effects on dairy products as well as meat.

CENTURY III-42 (Vol. III, pg. 170) seems to refer to the same "dry quatrain." "This represents worldwide famine. I see a lot of farms, vineyards, and orchards, but everything is bleached dry. The fields appear to be burnt by the sun." When asked when this would occur, Nostradamus replied, "Soon enough in your lifetime." And he indicated it would be before the Anti-Christ comes to power, and he will use this as one of his tools.

For more detailed information of Goro Adachi's findings, contact him on the Internet (E-mail address: <adachi@cris.com>). His web site is www:

http://www.concentric.net/~adachi/prophecy/prophecy.html

☆   ☆   ☆

I was in for some very strange surprises when I began lecturing on the Nostradamus material in the early 1990s. When I wrote the first two books I had done no research into the complicated scientific concepts. I was like a blank sheet of paper with no preconceived notions. I was also told not to censor any of the material, but to present it exactly as it was given. This was difficult to do because of the extremely serious nature of some of it. There were many instances when I wanted to change it or tone it down, for fear of getting into trouble with authorities or experts. Instead I obediently obeyed and presented the material in the manner it was given to me, with myself only acting as the objective reporter taking no credit for its content.

At some of my first lectures people in the audience began educating me to the similarity of some of the material to other written sources. This did not confuse me, but rather filled me with a sense of awe that Nostradamus' visions could indeed be based on fact if others recognized its implications. Further, I was filled with the horrific possibility that the predictions might be close to fulfillment if my readers and listeners could recognize and identify elements that were strange and unknown to me.

After discussing (Chapter 19, Vol. 1) on experimental weaponry at one lecture, I was approached by a man in the hallway who told me, "Your information about secret weapons is not science fiction. I know because I am working on it." This announcement sent shivers through me. Was Nostradamus correct when he said that much of the weaponry was already invented and being worked on in secret laboratories? Was he correct when he said much of what he saw was already completed and being hidden by our government? During World War II the experiment on the atomic bomb was the best kept secret in the world. If a project of such death-dealing properties could be kept secret, how many other futuristic concepts with each greater destructive possibilities are also being worked on?

In Volume One we discussed earthquake machines, weather control machines and time-altering experiments. My readers and listeners asked if I was familiar with the work of Nikola Tesla. At the time I knew he was a famous scientist who was ahead of his time in the 1920s and 30s. His miraculous inventions had been considered nonsense and were not pursued. It was said that Russia displayed more interest in his concepts than the United States, and that they continued his experiments. (See CENTURY I-6, Vol. I, pg. 241 and CENTURY II-91, Vol. I, pg. 127 for quatrains dealing with Russian inventions that sound like Tesla technology.) It was also said that when Tesla died in 1943 the FBI searched his apartment, and his most important research papers disappeared. With this idea in mind it might be possible that the machines Nostradamus saw could have been an extension of Tesla's original concept. Tesla did invent the AC (alternating current) that is used in electrical systems. It was his more radical ideas that disturbed investors of his time. He claimed to have discovered a way to provide free electricity to the entire world without the use of wires. Of course, the money-hungry profiteers would never agree to sponsor such an invention, and the idea was buried. Tesla also demonstrated an earthquake machine utilizing vibrations. All of this sounds too similar to what Nostradamus saw to be coincidence.

Information began to come to light in 1996 about the HAARP project in Alaska which appeared to take the original Tesla technologies to the ultimate and most disastrous. Such Star Wars scalar technology is right out of the Tesla days. The patents say that the work of Nikola Tesla in the early 1990s formed the basis of the research for HAARP.

HAARP: *High-frequency Active Auroral Research Program*
The HAARP system is a tool, a radio frequency transmitter and broadcasting system of immense power. When completed it is expected to produce beams of at least 10 billion watts, and later 100 billion watts of generated power is hoped for. The military described their excitement about the possibility of "seizing" control of the ionosphere and bending it into the shape which serves their purposes. Their first target is the electrojet—a river of electricity that flows thousands of miles through the sky and down into the polar icecap. Through this project the electrojet will become a vibrating artificial antenna for sending electromagnetic radiation raining down on the Earth. The machine could also allow Earth-penetrating tomography ("X-raying" the Earth) over most of the northern hemisphere. Such a capability would permit the detection and precise location of tunnels, and other underground shelters.

Manipulation of trapped electrons and ions above the earth can interfere with, or cause complete disruption of guidance systems employed by even the most sophisticated airplanes and missiles. The ability to transmit electromagnetic waves of varying frequencies over very wide areas can interfere with all modes of communication, land, sea and air, at the same time.

Environmentalists are concerned about the effect this would have on animals and humans in the area of the earth-probing. It would interfere with wildlife migration patterns, because they rely on an undisturbed energy field to find their routes. The frequency used in this experiment is the same at which the human brain operates. The impact on people as a nonlethal weapon has not escaped attention, and has already been experimented with. Nonlethal technologies are now referred to as "disabling systems." As a nonlethal weapon it could cause confusion in enemy troops or simply put them to sleep.

Experts say one of the jobs of the Army would be to reshape American values so they would accept new weapons. The idea is to indoctrinate by being taught to *believe*, rather than being given all of the facts so a person could *think* about the issues and make reasoned decisions. It can be better stated as: "propaganda-versus-persuasion by reason."

HAARP spokesmen described it as pure scientific research on the aurora borealis (Northern Lights) and research on the ionosphere's ability to affect communications. The military said there would be no more magnetic disturbances than what occurs naturally, for instance solar storms. Although it was funded by the U.S. Air Force and Navy, they said it was not a weapons system. That HAARP could be used for better submarine communication, would replace over-the-horizon radar system, and could wipe out communications over an extremely large area, while keeping operator-controlled communications systems working. Through its earth-penetrating tomography it could provide a tool for geophysical probing to find oil, gas and mineral deposits over a large geographical area. It could be used to detect incoming low-level planes and cruise missiles.

On the surface it looks like a harmless research project. In broader perspective it resembles the secret Manhattan Project which produced the atomic bomb. At that time, during World War II, this was the best-kept secret in history. Congress didn't even know what they were funding, because the money was funneled through various channels that were difficult to keep track of. This is still going on and is called "black budget" projects. I did a lot of research into the development of the atomic bomb. This is covered in more detail in my book *A Soul Remembers Hiroshima*. In the 1940s secrets were easier to keep because our minds were directed and focused on the war, and we were only told what we needed to know through newspapers, radio and movie newsreels. Now with computers, TV, radio and the Internet, knowledge can be distributed almost instantaneously. No wonder the government is trying to regulate the Internet.

The HAARP program funding was temporarily frozen in 1995 by the United States Senate. Yet the project moved forward, funded from *unknown sources*.

My information about this formidable experiment comes mainly from the book, *Angels Don't Play This HAARP,* by Jeanne Manning and Dr. Nick Begich. Published in 1995 by Earthpulse Press, P.O. Box 201393, Anchorage, Alaska 99520. It is extremely well researched and documented with extensive footnotes relating to source material.

None of this information is included here purely to frighten anyone. It is in all of our interests to know the capabilities that can be used against us. It doesn't mean they will be, but knowing about it is the first line of defense.

HAARP is a series of antennæ array located at Gakona, Alaska, where there are fewer than two people per square mile. It is a perfect place for secret experiments. VLF (very low frequency) and ELF (extremely low frequency) electromagnetic waves are generated and sent to the antennæ array. ELF can have positive or negative effects, depending on the intent of the operator. They can heal or destroy.

The HAARP project will cover 33 acres and eventually they plan to have 360 antennas 72 feet in height. It is expected to be completed and in full operation by 2002. The plan is to begin experimenting in early 1997 by heating or exciting 30-mile-wide holes directly above the experiment, rather like a giant microwave oven. The large array of antennæ would beam a billion watts of electromagnetic power—at radio frequencies—up through the atmosphere. It would be the biggest "zapper" in the world! They will punch a hole and measure the results, punch another hole, *etc.* They expect it will take about three months for each hole to close, and the data will tell them how to focus the eventual virtual mirror. HAARP will dump enormous amounts of energy into the upper atmosphere, and they don't know what will happen. With experiments on this scale, irreparable damage could be done in a short time.

When completed HAARP will be the biggest "heater" in the world, more powerful than anything in existence. The effects are unknown once the energy is released beyond certain thresholds. The HAARP has been called the Skybuster or the Super Heater. With this system no satellites are needed to beam the generated energy into the sky. The high-frequency signals developed are designed to ionize the energy in the upper atmosphere, which consists primarily of nitrogen. This ingenious development bypasses the need for satellites by using the antennæ on the ground. At very high altitudes the effects would multiply if a high enough power level was used. It is a principle that small input can create a large output. The effects are created by resonance instead of direct zapping.

Research facilities associated with HAARP are located in Arecibo, Puerto Rico and Fairbanks, Alaska. Other installations are at Tromso, Norway; Moscow, Nizhny Novgorod and Apatity in Russia; Kharkov, Ukraine and Dushanbe, Tadzhikistan. None of these existing systems, however, have the combination of frequency capability and beam steering agility required to perform the experiments planned for HAARP. But HAARP is part of a global cooperative effort that includes USSR, Canada, Japan, Greenland, Norway, Finland, New Zealand and others. Other transmitter sites are located in Greenland, South Pacific, Japan and Europe. Experiments can be run with all these other transmitters working together; thus a much larger effect could be created.

Scientists studied the sensitivities of living cells and nervous systems, and said it doesn't take *strong* magnetic fields to make a difference. Fluctuations of very weak fields can dramatically affect the cellular level of life.

The stratosphere and ionosphere are protective barriers around the Earth that keep harmful cosmic rays from reaching the surface. These are already in a delicate and fragile condition partially due to past experiments. Dr. Daniel Winter says that "Certain features of the magnetic grid keep an atmosphere nestled around a planet. Mars lost her atmosphere and we are losing ours. The Earth's orbital pole is doing radical excursions out of tilt—with the lunar orbit destabilizing—and the ability to hold atmosphere and ozone is weakening, particularly at the poles. The planet is very sensitive to bouncing such power in and out of the atmosphere. HAARP stands to slice a huge tear in the fractal of magnetic Alaska. Earth will feel this change in charge, as a tearing wound that will not heal."

Top scientists say HAARP will not burn "holes" in the ionosphere. That is a dangerous understatement of what HAARP's giant gigawatt beam will do. Because of Earth's axial spin a burst lasting more than a few minutes will slice through the ionosphere like a microwave knife. This will not produce a "hole," but a long tear—an incision.

One of Nostradamus' prophecies definitely sounds like the HAARP project. In CENTURY I-46 (Vol. I, pg. 244): "This quatrain concerns an event that will be initially sparked by man's hand but will basically be a natural disaster. There'll be a group of doctors (scientists) researching into the powers of the various energy fields of the Earth. They'll try to harness these powers and use them for various things including warfare. At the time they finally start doing direct experimentation on the physical world, they will accidentally rupture one of the Earth's fields in such a way that a beam of energy will shoot out into space and draw a stream of meteorites toward the Earth. This will happen around the North Sea. The meteorites will be drawn toward the Earth because of this alteration of the energy fields around the Earth. And since they are out there everywhere they will continue to come until the scientists are able to repair the damage. Their rupture in the field throws everything out of balance. Since their instrumentation is still experimental, it is not fine-tuned enough to be able to get things back in good balance. So in the process of trying to repair the damage there is an earthquake soon after when the stress is built up. Since this project will be very dangerous, it will be a secret government project. To the world at large it will appear as a natural phenomenon. It will be recorded that way in future history texts because the part the scientists play is such an important secret to the governments involved that they will not let that knowledge out."

In the quatrain it says the disturbance (tear) in the atmosphere occurs around the North Sea. This could be where one of the transmitters are located. Or it could be where it bounced down toward the Earth, because the beams would be deflected back, plus the tearing effect could occur over another area than intended.

In CENTURY I-22 (Vol. I, pg. 166): This quatrain describes a weather manipulation machine similar to the HAARP program. "Mankind will have developed some devices to moderate the weather and be able to have some say as to how the weather will be. The machines that are in charge of these computations and calculations will become too clever for their own good. Consequently, through the fault of their programming, which will not be spotted until too late, they will accidentally cause the weather to misfunction so as to cause a great deal of damage through unseasonable ice and hail. The men running this will not realize that if one tries to force the weather to do one thing for too long that the natural pattern will finally overcome the interference and perhaps cause some unseasonable weather in the process of trying to get things back in balance again. As a result, these computers, while trying to overcome the natural forces that are trying to get things back in balance, will blow a fuse, so to speak, and become damaged beyond use."

Again in CENTURY X-70 (Vol. I, pg. 196): One of the multiple meanings of this quatrain refers to "a type of atomic device, not exactly a bomb, that when set off will do something to the planetary climate. It will displace an air mass that will upset the balance of hot and cold so that a greenhouse effect will get out of balance and run to the extreme and do drastic things to the climate, which in turn will affect agriculture."

Also CENTURY X-71 (Vol. I, pg. 198) refers to the same device: "The earth and air freezing is another effect of the atomic device that will throw everything out of kilter. All manner of solutions will be tried to counteract what happened but they will not be successful, in spite of the fair words of the governments to their peoples to try to keep them from panicking."

Machines such as HAARP could also have an effect on winds and effect an atmospheric mass such as that associated with El Niño. El Niño is a periodic change in ocean currents which have altered weather patterns in the past. In CENTURY IV-15 (Vol. II, pp. 235–237), it is explained how the manipulation of El Niño can effect the weather of the world.

Could the term "secret fires" in CENTURY IV-67 (Vol. I, pg. 173) be referring to HAARP or some other secret military weapon? Some kind of dangerous device hidden from the general public?

Earth and the life forms on it vibrate and resonate in harmony. Radiant energy from the sun and materials and vibrations of the Earth support life. Man-made sources are already disturbing the harmony. Investigators noted that most recent technologies have been aimed at shielding people from nature—to "conquer" and control her, while designing ever more dangerous weapons systems with which to more efficiently strip all life from the planet. The writers of *Angels Don't Play This HAARP* say the inventors of the HAARP project are suicidal in their disregard for the consequences to our entire planet.

Deliberate ionospheric disturbances could resonate with the materials in the Earth and trigger an earthquake. Nostradamus described an earthquake machine with similar properties in CENTURY IX-83 (Vol. I, pp. 238–240). A March 1993 newspaper article revealed the reality and existence of such an incredible machine. An abbreviated quote: "There is the presence of strategic military installations in Georgian territory (Soviet Union), such as the tectonic laboratory at Eshera near the Abkhazian capital of Sukhumi. Georgia's President Shevardnadze says that this establishment is involved in experiments to set off earthquakes in a directed manner in order 'to keep under control the whole Near East region.'" This information came to light after these regions pulled away from the Soviet Union. They feared the Soviets would not let them go because of these strategic weapons, and might try to gain these lands back.

Another theory is that one can literally do genetic engineering with HAARP by using the frequency to resonate with the DNA and thereby open and close it. The annihilation of particles (from the particle accelerator) releases a pattern that controls the way the DNA will reassemble itself. Genetic programming suggests something far beyond the prospect of biological warfare. It also includes the possibility of scrambling or rearranging our DNA. One scientist said that if this system were beamed at the entire population, it would genetically destroy the human race.

Another frightening aspect of HAARP is its ability to scramble the human brain by interfering with its normal functioning. By altering these frequencies with ELF waves the personality or mood of people can be changed. They can also be put into a deep sleep. It is being called the biggest brain-entrainment device ever conceived. In the right hands it could be of great benefit to mankind if used to heal mental and nerve disorders, and curing drug and alcohol dependencies, among other things. But the critics of HAARP are worried about the negative affects of mind manipulation that these waves could have on large groups of people (even entire populations), especially since the device can be remotely activated from a long distance and be virtually undetectable. The military could alter what people thought and, at the same time, know what they thought. All of this sounds like science fiction, but it is definitely possible and is *scientific fact.*

Nostradamus foresaw a similar weapon in CENTURY II-2 (Vol. I, pg. 167). In this quatrain Nostradamus describes a new type of weapon that will be developed. "A type of radio wave that at certain frequencies and intensities can be lethal. It can cause intense pain in the nerve endings and destroy certain portions of the brain." This sounds like HAARP frequencies that manipulate brain functions.

Paul Schaefer says, "Unless we desire the death of our planet, we must end the production of unstable particles. A first priority to prevent this disaster would be to shut down all nuclear power plants and end the testing of atomic weapons, electronic warfare and Star Wars." These are all things that Nostradamus warned us about.

In the book, *Angels Don't Play This HAARP,* the scientists kept talking about the spirit of the world and trying to bend it or change it to benefit their needs. This sounds very similar to Nostradamus' prediction that the Anti-Christ would attempt to control the very spirit of the world (Volume II). Does the AC gain control of this machinery? There are some located in areas he would have access to (Ukraine, for example). The earthquake machine is mentioned in Volume I, and it was said that the AC would gain control of it. Is this the same machine?

The term "charged particle rain" was mentioned in the literature about HAARP. Could this electronic rain of streams of particles be the white rain seen by Nostradamus (CENTURIES III-18, III-19, Vol. I, pp. 254, 255). These two quatrains have references to milky rain: "The long milky rain and being touched by lightning are effects of the use of nuclear weapons in this war. There will be other fantastic weapons used, based upon concepts being presently developed (1986), that you and this vehicle do not presently have any conception of, and they will have devastating results. He uses the rain of milk to represent the adverse effects these fantastic nuclear weapons will have upon the weather, including such things as radiation rain. The weapons will use a combination of the worst aspects of nuclear weaponry and laser weaponry, and some of the laser weaponry when it's shot down upon the people, will resemble a white substance coming down."

THIS IS *not* the first time scientists have experimented without knowing the outcome of their actions. When they developed the atomic bomb they really did not know the effects it would have on the atmosphere when it was detonated. One theory was that it could have ignited all of the hydrogen atoms in a chain reaction, and could have destroyed the world. In Volume II Nostradamus said this actually did occur on another time line. It was a highly dangerous situation at that time in the 1940s but the scientists' main concern was developing a bomb and discovering the results of an experiment that had gone too far to stop. The same thing is happening again with HAARP. The experimenters admit they do not know what the outcome might be if they pump unprecedented levels of radio-frequency power up through the upper atmosphere to heat parts of the unpredictable ionosphere.

[The following information is taken, in part, from the *American Legion Magazine*, October 1995, article entitled "St. George Is Expendable"]

In the past the U.S. government destroyed the lives of thousands of Americans with its secret atomic testing programs in the Southwest and the Pacific.

Officially, the atomic bomb has only been used twice as a weapon against human beings. The first case was Hiroshima on August 6, 1945 and Nagasaki on August 9, 1945. But history does not take into account the 250,000 GIs involved in the testing following World War II, or the tens of thousands of civilians living in small communities in the surrounding area of the Nevada test site, who were exposed to the radioactive fallout of nearly two decades of open-air atomic testing.

The military also experimented on civilians in hospitals without their knowledge. Under the guise of conducting medical treatments the people were exposed to large doses of radiation to monitor the effects it had on their bodies. Some of these studies have only recently been released (or exposed).

Innocently, the military did not realize the effects the open air radiation would have on people because nothing was known at the time of the deadly long-range effects of such testing. But they, as scientists, were determined to find out. Thus many of their experiments were done in secret to avoid public outcry.

In 1946 the federal government moved the entire population of Bikini Atoll in Micronesia (167 natives) to another island so the military could perform atomic tests. In all, 23 bombs were detonated at Bikini, and an additional 43 at nearby Eniwetok. The resulting contamination has rendered the Atoll uninhabitable for all time. The natives were never allowed to return. Over 42,000 servicemen and scientists participated, and they were unaware of the danger they exposed themselves to. Then, to add to the radiation fallout, Russia began their own atomic testing in 1949.

During this time the military decided to start testing on American soil in 1951, and insisted on telling surrounding residents that there was no danger. Over a twelve-year period 126 atomic bombs were detonated above the Nevada test site, in spite of warnings from top scientists. In March 1953 the tests averaged one atomic detonation a week for three months. (See *American Ground Zero: The Secret Nuclear War* by Carole Gallagher and *The Myths of August* by Stewart Udall.) Residents of neighboring towns were given no warnings, or assured that there was no danger. From the beginning of the Nevada test site program GIs were drafted into the nuclear tests to serve as observers and participants—or, as some would later say, guinea pigs.

The small town of St. George, Utah, was one place that was unknowingly affected during a dozen years of above-ground atomic testing which began in 1951. The town lies 100 miles east of the Nevada test site, and was often in the direct path of the dust clouds spewed into the sky by the blasts. In a study presented in 1979 it was found that the cancer rate in St. George is 143 percent higher than the state norm. For childhood leukemia alone, the southern Utah's death rate was 250 percent greater than the state average, and it is thought that these figures may be conservative.

One test in particular demonstrates the negligence that marked the testing program. On March 1, 1954, a 15-megaton hydrogen bomb, code name *Bravo*, was detonated on the Bikini island of Nam. Seven hundred fifty times more powerful than the bomb dropped on Hiroshima, the blast vaporized much of Nam and two smaller islands. Fallout rained across 7,000 square miles of the Pacific and fell on islands as far away as 300 miles.

In 1958 Dr. Edward Teller, known as the "Father of the H-bomb," traveled to Alaska with a proposal to blast a chunk of coastline off the map. He wanted to prove that nuclear explosions could be a tool for geographical engineering (Project Chariot). Their plan was to explode six thermonuclear bombs underground at Cape Thompson, Alaska, to dig a harbor. The philosophy was that if it was successful the procedure could be used to create a new Panama or Suez Canal. In this case, they were met by extreme opposition from Eskimos living within 30 miles of ground zero. Three brave scientists who spoke out against the experiment lost their jobs and were blackballed. But at least between the opposition of the Eskimos and the scientists the experiment did not occur. The scientists were then able to move their experiments to Nevada where objections were not presented by the populace, and the damage was not disclosed by the government until decades later.

Also in 1958, the same year that the Van Allen radiation belts were discovered, the U.S. Navy exploded three nuclear bombs into the belt (Project Argus). The White House advisor said the Defense Department was studying ways to manipulate changes of "earth and sky, and so affect the weather" by using "an electronic beam to ionize or deionize the atmosphere over a given area." The Van Allen belts are zones of charged particles trapped in Earth's magnetic field 2000 plus miles above the Earth. The ionosphere extends to 620 miles.

A series of weather changes began in 1960 which many scientists directly related to atmospheric nuclear testing. By shooting these devices off before they had enough information to know it would create problems they changed the wind patterns for years. During 1961-62 Soviets and the USA blasted many explosives into the atmosphere. Three hundred megatons of nuclear devices depleted the ozone layer about 4 percent. This was the beginning of the depletion. Later spacecraft launches also affected the ozone layer and ionosphere. Climatologists couldn't look ahead and see that droughts, floods and abnormal temperatures would continue beyond that decade. During that time national governments were already able to manipulate weather for military purposes, and this has continued into the 1990s.

During the Vietnam War the U.S. Department of Defense used rainmaking, lightning and hurricane manipulation methods in Project Skyfire and Project Stormfury. The military studied both lasers and chemicals that could damage the ozone layer over an enemy. They looked for ways to cause earthquakes, as well as detect them, in Project Prime Argus. As Nostradamus said, many things are done during time of war that would never be allowed in peacetime because it would horrify the people.

In 1966 world-recognized scientist Gordon MacDonald described the use of weather manipulation, climate modification, polar icecap melting or destabilization, ozone-depletion techniques, earthquake engineering, ocean-wave control and brainwave manipulation using the planet's energy fields. He also said that these types of weapons would be developed and, when used, would be virtually undetectable by their victims. (Source: *Unless Peace Comes,* Chapter: "How to Wreck the Environment.")

In the 1970s the Soviet Union wanted to change the climate to make Russia a more comfortable place to live. Proposals included removal of the Arctic ice pack, damming of the Bering Strait and rerouting Siberian rivers. Many countries in the world thought that with atomic power at their disposal they could finally recreate the living conditions of the world to suit themselves, without thinking of the long-range consequences.

After congressional hearings in the late 1970s, open-air testing was stopped, but underground testing continued.

The research of the nonprofit Institute for Advanced Studies revealed (through earth-monitoring with sensitive instruments) a connection between underground nuclear tests and earthquakes. Nostradamus warned us about this in Volume I and insisted the nuclear testing must be stopped because we were not aware of the consequences on the entire planet. The shockwaves reverberated throughout the tectonic plates, and affected areas of the world far removed from the original test sites.

The HAARP super heating effect of the ELF waves on the mirror that would be created above the Earth could cause acceleration of the melting of the icecaps. The sea levels could easily raise by 150 feet, and would devastate the entire civilized world. Such an invention could easily cause the effects that Nostradamus saw in Volumes II and III, when we produced maps showing the meager amount of land that would remain after such a catastrophe. Also could such a device cause a significant change in a planet's electrical circuit or electrical field? Could scientists unwittingly short-circuit the Earth, causing a wobble that could melt the icecaps and create the map scenario in Volume II? Many experts have assumed it would take an axis shift to produce such a major melting, but if this experiment was successful HAARP could produce the same devastating effects.

Before men detonated underground nuclear tests or did anything else that was massively invasive to the state of balance of Earth's systems, we were already on an unstable planet. Judging by the increase in the geomagnetic "noise" (disturbances in the earth's magnetic field) heard on Earth, some scientists speculate that the sun may be approaching a time of change. Whether or not the sun goes through a time of spectacular hot flashes in the near future and throws even more particles at Earth, the fact is that Earth is being affected right now. The fact that the Earth is getting hotter was reported in the New York *Times* in 1991. The article said that Arctic ice had decreased by 2 percent in only a nine-year period.

It has recently been discovered that there are active volcanoes beneath the ice cover of Antarctica, and the temperature of the water beneath the continent is now the same as that of the Mediterranean.

This information was obtained from a reader who found it on Prodigy interactive personal service (an internet service) and dated March 2, 1993. The article is entitled "Fire in Antarctic's Belly."

More than 1100 dormant or active volcanoes were discovered clustered on the ocean floor near Easter Island in the Pacific. And now volcanic activity is reported—with ominous overtones—in Antarctica. Pockmarks in the West Antarctic ice sheet suggest volcanoes lie deep below. Scientists have concluded that a mountain with the mineral characteristics of volcanic rock rises 650 meters above the bedrock of Antarctica, which itself is buried below some 2000 kilometers of ice. The data indicates the peak is much like the cone shape of Japan's Mount Fuji. It is believed to be a recently active volcano. If it becomes active again, the implications are worrisome and potentially disastrous. It is not likely that the volcano could erupt and blow the ice sheet sky high over the Southern Hemisphere. The real concern is that the volcano and others like it that are believed to have produced the circular depressions in the ice sheet will provide enough melt to the sheet's base to lubricate the slide of the sheet toward the sea. The collapse of the West Antarctic ice sheet and its movement into the surrounding ocean would generate a global sea level rise of nearly 20 feet, the geophysicists estimate. That would have enormous consequences on low-lying shorefronts all around the world.

I have also received mail that tells me that the glaciers in Sweden are melting at an unprecedented rate. In appears that the planet is already warming. We do not need reckless experiments on the weather to speed it up.

HAARP has been described as one of the most dangerous weapon systems since the development of thermonuclear weapons. Maybe this was why Nostradamus remarked about the United States and Russia phasing out nuclear weapons. He said it didn't matter, they had invented something much deadlier. The powers did not need nuclear weapons any longer; they are outdated.

☆ ☆ ☆

IN 1995 we had a record number of hurricanes. So many that we ran out of names in alphabetical order. The scientists explained it by saying that the ocean waters were unusually warm, and this aided the development of more hurricanes of greater force. The first hurricane in 1996 was way ahead of schedule. The season normally begins in late August or September. This season began in July. (See also hurricane prediction from CENTURY VIII-16 (Vol. III, pp. 142–143.)

☆ ☆ ☆

Computers and the World Wide Web

In Volume II (Chapter 14): "666, The Secret of the Number of the Beast," deals with the coming technology involving computers. Such sophisticated development was unheard of in 1987 when this information came through. We were taking the first fledgling steps. Computers were just beginning to become popular on the market, and had not yet been put to widespread uses that developed in the 1990s. I wrote my first five books on a typewriter, so I was exhilarated with the purchase of my first computer in 1986. I only used it for its word-processing capability. Even at its snail's pace it was easier than using the typewriter—except when it decided to play games with me and destroy a day's work in a keystroke. In such cases I had visions of my words floating around somewhere in limbo, never to be recaptured. Later models were more reliable, yet I never envisioned it as more than a glorified typewriter. So Nostradamus' predictions concerning computers seemed like science fiction in the late 1980s.

From page 132: "The Anti-Christ will have great communication systems at his disposal because I see him talking into computers, and it's his voice that's activating the computer."

Page 134: "Through his communication networks he will have access to the files of all people: birth data, financial information, and things of this nature. So it will be doubly hard to oppose him when he controls the world banking industry and the world economic credit." I asked about the significance of 666 in the book of Revelation in the Bible. "He's showing me columns and columns of numbers and more numbers. It looks like information that is usually stored in computers. And this number, 666, might be the Anti-Christ's personal code number that he enters into the different world systems, because he establishes a world system of communications and a computer network."

At the time this information came through it seems impossible for a computer system to connect the entire world. I thought it was definitely a futuristic idea, and I mused that it might happen in a hundred years, if it happened at all. How mistaken I was. How could anyone in the late 1980s conceive the idea of a world wide web becoming reality in only *ten* years. And it is definitely a reality that all our birth data, financial records, and other information concerning our lives are now part of a vast computer network. If we could not believe such a possibility a short ten years ago, what other predictions are coming into fruition at an inconceivably fast pace?

The computer predictions continue from page 135: "He will have already set up a computer network that will leave countries vulnerable. He will be able to destroy their economic base by having access to information. Nostradamus is showing me a picture of a globe with a lot of threads surrounding it (world wide web). He says, 'He will have the master key to it all and will bring nations down to the ground by cutting off their communication with the rest of the world.' He will even invent a computer that will function from a psychic brain level. A person will be able to turn it on by mentally commanding it, rather than even speaking to it." Voice-activated computers are being developed in 1996 and could be on the market soon. A computer using the frequency of our brain is now conceivable, and could be the next advancement in computer technology.

Nostradamus indicated in Volume II that the Anti-Christ would be considered a world savior in the beginning. He would be seen as benefiting mankind with his wondrous inventions. But he saw the dark side emerging once the computer networks had been established. "The countries of the world will experience a lot of prosperity by using his system. Financial considerations will be given to them if they become part of his system, and if they do not 'play ball,' they will be cut out and suffer as a result. When the mantle of complete evil takes over he will start exterminating the people he feels are useless to his system. When he changes, he will try to wipe out people who have no economic benefit for his world scheme. He will wipe out groups of people. Just as Hitler tried to exterminate the Jews, he'll try to exterminate people that he feels are not worthy to live on this planet: the sick, the poor, the enfeebled, and people who have no value in his eyes. Using his network, he will instigate mass euthanasia. There will be no escape because everything will be on file.

"For example, if one's son was retarded, or if one's mother was too old and unproductive, or if one's sister was mentally or emotionally unbalanced, they would all be slated for extermination. Everything is crippled because he controls the communications network. As a result, he knows what is going on everywhere. We've become a computerized society at that point and everyone will have a certain number that will be stored in this main computer. (In America, our social security number?) This number will be indelibly tattooed on your hand, forearm or forehead, depending on what level of his system you belong to. The people in the upper echelon of his system will have this engraved on their forehead so they can walk in any place. The number will be automatically read, to bid them to enter. For most of us it will be indelibly engraved on our hand. This will be done with a laser and will be painless. It will not look like a birthmark or a defect but will be invisible unless scanned by optical equipment. This way we will be able to go shopping, buy food, and enter certain places that are necessary to our work or career."

This concept of everyone having a number is also predicted in the book of Revelation in the Bible (Rev. 13:11–18). This sounded futuristic, but it is also becoming reality in our lifetime now. In my travels all over the world I am finding experiments along these lines have already begun. I also receive corroborating information from my readers, in the form of newspaper and magazine articles. In America all of our other identifying numbers (military service IDs, driver license, *etc.*) are being replaced by our social security number, to facilitate record keeping by only having one number. This is also occurring in other countries. Some are instituting cards to be used that would have all personal data encoded in a computer strip (such as Smart Cards and the new medical cards in the U.S.).

In some European countries a computer chip is placed under the skin of the hand. When they buy anything at a store they only have to pass their hand over the scanner, and the money is automatically transferred from their bank account. No cash money exchanges hands, and the necessity of writing checks is eliminated. In some countries (Australia for one) it has been proposed to permanently identify (by computer chips or some other method) all newborn babies. Some of these proposals are meeting opposition, but the arguments are that we are becoming a computerized world society and these advancements will make things easier and faster. They will make identification more verifiable, and will eliminate crime.

Singapore has already become a completely computerized country. It is said that they can know the whereabouts of any citizen at any moment. Because Singapore is a small country [though densely populated], it would be the guinea pig, and results could be easily monitored and studied. It was felt they could try the experiment there first before applying the concept elsewhere. It sounds to me as though the era of "Big Brother" is arriving, and at a speed we thought inconceivable a few years ago.

In another quatrain Nostradamus refers to the Cabal (Vol. 1, Chapter 21) as having a significant part in this computer network, and actually helping the Anti-Christ in the beginning.

In CENTURY V-23 (Vol. II, pp. 253–254): "These men control the whole world situation right now in your time. They are very, very powerful. They are very well hidden, but they control most of the economy of both the known world and the third world. They manipulate different agencies of the U.S. government and other countries, because they have the power to do so. They're going to create problems, not because they want money—they have all the money they could wish for. He's showing me _tons_ of gold. They [the Cabal] want power and control. These men are the leaders of the world, but you don't know of them. You don't even know their names. The media doesn't know of them. They're kept clandestine, but they have great influence, especially on the presidents and leaders of the different world governments. In fact they're trying to manipulate the government of the Soviet Union to bring another leader into the net. They control part of the media and can do anything they want. Their power is enormous. He's showing me a picture of the globe with lines on it that he has drawn, and everything is tied together (world wide web?). These men are the movers and shakers of the world. He shows me that they are shaking the world."

☆ ☆ ☆

Nanotechnology

NANOTECHNOLOGY: a new science that allows researchers to manipulate individual atoms. Nanotechnology is also based on the concept of tiny, self-replicating robots.

The term Nanotechnology has been used to describe a number of sciences that deal with dimensions of less than 1.000 nanometers. The underlying principle of nanotechnology is its promised ability to rearrange the atoms in a given substance or object to create a new substance or object. Rearrange the atoms in lead, for example, and you actually would get gold. This sounds like the ancient science of alchemy, and Nostradamus said that alchemy was actively practiced in his day and was the forerunner of modern chemistry. He also said that during the time of the Great Genius (Vol. I, Chapter 24) the fantastic claims of alchemy will become realistic and possible.

In our interpretation many of the quatrains described concepts so complicated and advanced that there were no words for them, either in Nostradamus' time or ours in the late 1980s. Now with the many advances in computer technology there are finally words and names to describe the indescribable. One of these concepts is the science of nanotechnology. It is now said that the reduction of computer chip size has reached its limitations. The only way to go smaller is to resort to the cellular level. "Nano" means "very tiny," so we are looking at a science that can produce machines or robots so small they can only be seen on the microscopic level. This science has opened a entirely new world of possibilities. Extremely tiny machines or robots could be injected into the human body and be able to travel through the blood system for a variety of purposes.

The computers have verified that it will also be possible to reproduce or replicate portions of the human body by duplicating the DNA information in a person's cells. From the medical viewpoint it would be an astounding breakthrough to be able to duplicate and replace amputated limbs and diseased organs of the body. This could be what Nostradamus referred to in CENTURY II-13 (Vol. I, pg. 299) when he spoke of doctors and scientists replacing or creating an entirely new body when the old one had become too diseased to continue. He saw the human body being perfected to the point that it would never die. Of course, this could be a blessing or a curse. In my work with aliens, especially in *Legacy from the Stars*, I discovered that they use methods similar to this. They do not have to die until they are ready to. I had heard of cloning, where the body would be duplicated by growing from a cellular level in the same manner that a baby is formed, except that this would be an exact duplicate of the original. In the science of nanotechnology cloning would be too slow. With the help of computers the body could be quickly replicated when the genetic DNA code of the cell is read.

This sounds like a tremendous medical miracle, but knowing human nature it is obvious that certain people would discover ways to use this method for war. In this case it sounds like quatrain CENTURY X-72, the famous 1999 quatrain (Vol. I, pg. 246). Nostradamus said he saw the development of armies through eugenics to produce men without morals, virtually killing machines. This nanotechnology method would indeed be faster than the cloning or genetic manipulation that I thought he was referring to.

Also with this method the development of an organic computer, such as Nostradamus saw the Great Genius using, would be totally possible. He said (CENTURY IV-31, Vol. I, pg. 288) it would be "self-renewing like the cells of your body. Some of the organic parts will eventually wear out and get old. But meanwhile it will have replicated itself, so there will be organic parts sloughing off from this device but there won't be any loss of knowledge because it will be continually self-renewing. Applications of this computer will be applied wider and wider to where it would totally alter the technology of mankind." Scientists say that the microscopic robot cells would be able to duplicate themselves.

Experts say it would also be possible to duplicate a person's intellect and place it into one of these machines. All of this will be possible since everything is energy, and thought processes can be stored and duplicated as energy. In quatrain CENTURY IV-31 Nostradamus says that the Great Genius perfects this new technology, invents the organic computer, and then "as a corollary to this development he envisions a way of transplanting some of his genius and knowledge into this computer, so it will still be there to serve mankind after his body has aged and died. He develops it to the highest point possible to transfer his genius, or rather *duplicate* his genius and his knowledge, so he still has it but it's also in this organic computer." The rest of the explanation of this quatrain described the process used.

All of these concepts sounded like science fiction in the late 1980s when we were receiving this information. But now a short ten years later it is not only within the realm of possibility, it is being actively worked on by scientists all over the world. The possibilities of nanotechnology are increasing daily and are mind-boggling. There are several laboratories all over the world, including three in California, working on this, so it is fast becoming our future and our reality.

(From the New York Times, *April 11, 1995: "A Vat of DNA may Become Fast Computer of the future.")*

Theorists hope to tap the vast computing powers they see in the memory and processing of nature's genetic machinery. One new proposal is for a memory bank containing more than a pound of DNA molecules suspended in about 1,000 quarts of fluid, in a tank about a yard square. Such a bank would be more capacious than all the memories of all the computers ever made. The reason is that chemical reactions occur very fast and in parallel, so that if the DNA molecules are synthesized with a chemical structure that represents numerical information, a vast amount of number-crunching is done as the reaction proceeds.

Although the field of biological computing is still in its infancy, computer scientists are likening today's first wobbly steps to the early development of electronic computers. Scientists have commented: "The floodgates have started to open. I have never seen a field move so fast. A door has opened to a whole new toy shop."

A DNA computing system would bear no resemblance to a conventional computer, raising the question of what a computer is. Scientists have said, "It's quite exciting. It's a completely new way to think about computing. Our minds are prejudiced to think about computing in terms of computers we build ourselves. But it's important to free our minds to think about how computing might occur naturally." That means that DNA might not be the only new type of computer. "There might be a lot of computers out there, and I suspect there are."

Note: This brings up the concept that our entire bodies are computers, in the way they operate. [It might be said that computers thus far are a reflection of *us*.] And our entire body could conceivably be used as a computer. (Hooked up to wires or machines?) It also goes along with the idea that we are parts of the body of God, and are transmitting information (experiences, emotions, *etc.*) to Him, as suggested in my other books. This also sounds similar to the UFO and alien communications that we are transmitting information to their data banks. Maybe they don't really need the implants after all. Maybe much of the information is transmitted by our energy, especially if the aliens are among the more "advanced" beings. They did say they could tune in to our specific vibrations, and that everyone's vibration or frequency was different from everyone else's and quickly identifiable to them. This also goes along with the idea of Nostradamus tuning in on my frequency, and the way he knew when I brought someone new to him. He did not recognize their vibration until he realized that I was behind them. He probably didn't know how he was doing it. He was just more sensitive to individual vibrations than the average person.

The advantages of DNA computers would be that they are a billion times as energy efficient as conventional computers. And they use just a trillionth of the space to store information. By exploiting the extraordinary efficiency and speed of biological reactions molecular computers can perform more than a trillion operations per second, which makes them a thousand times as fast as the fastest computer.

But, more important, computer scientists describe DNA computers as "massively parallel," meaning that with billions or trillions of DNA molecules undergoing the chemical reactions, it would be possible to do more operations at once than all the computers in the world working together could ever accomplish. One of the simplest ways to use DNA might be as a memory system. Dr. Baum said, "You can store vast quantities of information in a test tube." A DNA memory could hold more words than all the computer memories ever made.

It would not be difficult to envision this as one computer running all the systems of the world—a so-called "brain" of the world. In time of peace this would be wonderful, but in time of war it would be horrific. Who would control the use of the "brain," what government? And where would it be located that it would be safe from takeover by hostile forces? On what continent? Or would it be safer on a space station orbiting the Earth? Whoever controls the "brain" controls the world. Fortunately, Nostradamus saw this advancement occurring after the Time of Troubles when we have entered the 1000 years of peace. The other scenario would be too horrible to imagine. I wonder whether or not the scientists have considered these possibilities as they take their first "baby steps" into the world of the future.

One scientist warned that there would be drawbacks. He said, "As time goes by, your DNA computer may start to dissolve. DNA gets damaged as it waits around in solutions and the manipulations of DNA are prone to error." This was precisely the question I asked Nostradamus. I thought if something was organic, or living matter, it would have cells and parts that would die. He indicated that this type of organic computer would be able to duplicate and repair itself. This concept is so new to the scientists they have not yet considered this possibility, that cells can duplicate themselves and thus keep the computer living indefinitely, under the right circumstances. No wonder Nostradamus couldn't show Brenda what this machine would look like. The concepts were not existing in anyone's mind in 1986, and were therefore indescribable by anyone.

Apparently Nostradamus saw that the Great Genius would be the deciding factor to tie all the ingredients together and create the working model. At least Nostradamus saw this great man using these concepts for good. I hope that the negative applications that he saw before the end of the Time of Troubles do not come to pass, and we can proceed peacefully and easily into the time of the Great Genius and the millennia.

☆   ☆   ☆

New Material Since Completion of
Interpretation of Quatrains in 1989.

At my lectures all over the world I am often asked if I have communicated with Nostradamus since the completion of the work on the quatrains in 1989. People want to know if there are any new predictions. When the work was completed I moved on to other projects and wrote other books. I consider Nostradamus a living person and I was told not to bother him with trivial pursuits. In Volume II we were told that my visits with him take up more time than I thought. In what appeared to me to be a one or two hour session was actually for Nostradamus four to six hours, or most of his day. When we journey through time to contact him apparently different laws of physics are at work. Space is not only affected, but also our concept of time is no longer valid. This has also been shown to be true in my work with aliens. They repeatedly say that time is an illusion. It was created by man, but in reality it does not exist. Thus I do not have sessions to contact Nostradamus unless it is for an important reason, such as to ask about current world affairs.

During all these years since I first began my work with Nostradamus, I have tried to protect the identity and privacy of my subjects. I have done this at their request so their lives would not be disrupted by the notoriety and skepticism that often accompanies such a project as this. I have been approached by some TV shows that wanted to sensationalize the material in my books. They mostly wanted to try to discredit the information with their choice of skeptics. I am not interested in this type of program since they could conceivably destroy 17 years of my work in one show, and they would not even look back, but continue on to the next victim that would further their ratings. So I have been selective of the programs I have appeared on. I have been fortunate to appear on many that have handled the material in the proper way: NBC's *Ancient Prophecies* I and II, CBS's *Mysteries of the Ancient World,* A&E's *Biography* series, Sci-Fi's *Mysteries, Magic and Miracles,* and CNN's *Showbiz.* The BBC in London, *Current Affair* in Australia, TVE in Spain and CNN in Bulgaria have also been considerate of the material. Anyone in our field of psychic research who appears on a show takes a risk because you are ultimately in the hands of the producer, director and editor. The information can be twisted to appear in any number of ways, some of which may not be beneficial. You never know until the show airs how you will be treated.

In June 1994 I agreed to an interview by *Encounters* for a show on prophecy being shown on the FOX network. They requested to film live regressions where the subjects would contact Nostradamus. Normally I would have refused, but they seemed to be genuine in their promise that the subjects would not be exploited, and would be treated with dignity and respect. I asked around for volunteers and Brenda and Phil (Vol. III and *Keepers of the Garden*) finally agreed to do the show on the promise that they would not be made to look like "sideshow freaks."

On June 18, 1994 the director, Denny Gordon, flew into Fayetteville, Arkansas (the nearest city), and had a TV crew travel from Little Rock. We met at the Hilton Hotel in Fayetteville. I had not had any sessions with either Phil or Brenda for several years, and they had never met each other before this date. Each of them were to arrive at different times so they would not hear each other's session. I arrived first and they filmed my interview. In all, the entire day's work lasted for approximately five hours. It is not uncommon to film several hours of material and have only 5, 10 or 15 minutes appear on a show. They like to have a lot of material to choose from.

Phil was the next to arrive and they filmed an interview as Denny asked him questions about the contact we had made with Nostradamus and how he felt about it. He became emotional several times because he felt very personal about the relationship we had established between Nostradamus and himself.

After his interview the crew prepared the room for the session by having a cot brought up to the room. They thought it would be easier than setting up the cameras in the bedroom of this two-room suite. While the arrangements were being made Denny took me into the other room and gave me a list of questions she thought would be appropriate. I was appalled by their simplicity. She wanted me to ask Nostradamus why he had decided to put the prophecies into code and other simple questions. I told her I had asked all of these questions when we first began to work. I felt it was an insult to ask them again. I suggested asking questions about current world affairs. I didn't think we should bother the man unless we wanted to know something important.

I told Denny some of the questions I thought we should ask each subject. She was surprised. "Oh, you mean, cut right to the chase," she said, and I agreed. She thought this would make for a more interesting interview. I was especially interested in the current situation involving North Korea and the possibility of nuclear confrontation. Also a comet was due to hit Jupiter and people thought this would have an adverse effect on our own planet, maybe even disastrous consequences. These were the type of things I wanted to discuss, and I would ask the same questions to Brenda when she arrived for her interview in the afternoon.

Phil settled onto the cot with cameras and lights all around him. He was apprehensive, because we had not worked for several years and he worried that the keyword might not be still effective. I knew this would not be the case. When given the keyword it worked as quickly as it always had in the past. The same was also true of Brenda; it worked beautifully, as though there had been no lapse in working.

During the session Denny operated a hand-held camera and moved around the cot to get different angles. One time she even climbed up onto a chest of drawers to film looking down on him. All of this commotion around me was distracting, to say the least. Even though they were quiet, the movement was distracting. It did not bother Phil at all, even though the lights were quite bright. When he entered his deep trance state he became oblivious to anything going on around him, and focused entirely on his journey through time and space to locate Nostradamus.

When he made the contact it was interesting that Nostradamus knew something was unusual about the session. He was aware there were others in the room, and their energies were disturbing to him. After some concentration he was able to ignore these influences and communicate. As they filmed, I operated my tape recorder. The following parts of the transcripts will be condensed to focus on important elements.

I explained to Nostradamus that this session was different because we were using a method that would get the information out to a wider audience.

P: He says that the effort is not so much to the people in the room as to the people in the world. The message is taking root and growing. It will have a life of its own beyond those in this room. He says that he has not seen you in some time, but had anticipated your return as you seem never to be out of questions.

D: *(I laughed.) That's true. But I thought we had finished our work so I haven't been coming for quite a while.*

P: He says, not so. That your work has hardly begun, and that you will soon find yourself in *his* shoes, in the breath of the inquisitors.

D: *(Chuckle) Does he think that?*

P: He says he *sees* this. He doesn't *think* it. He says that he's glad he's on this side of the mirror. However, he says he does feel pity somewhat for those who would think to trifle with this endeavor. For they are calling upon themselves the wrath of the destiny of this planet. And so will soon find that their brash callousness and presumptions will be answered in short order by the events which they will call upon themselves. He says this is a mirroring of the time point at which he is, and is simply a repetition of that which he has experienced. It is your work which is mirroring his work. And so you will find, to your disgust, many of the same elements at work in your time frame that are at work in his. However, no effort will succeed, as this is again the destiny of this planet for the work to succeed. He says it didn't work in his time, and it won't work in yours.

I then prepared to ask him the questions, and he impatiently told me to get on with it.

D: *There's been a lot of talk lately about the country of North Korea. Is he able to perceive where that country is?*
P: Yes. He's representing this as a snake in symbology.
D: *The country of North Korea is causing a lot of problems now because the governments of the world think they have atomic power and it may be a threat. What can he say about that?*
P: He says the head of the snake—and here I'm reading the symbology—is severed. That is to say, the leader of this country will be removed, and the effort will appear to be successful. But this work will continue in other quarters outside of the country, however, collaborating *with* this country. He is saying the leader will be removed from office.

I was thinking that didn't seem possible because the President had been in office forever. He was firmly entrenched as leader of North Korea. I didn't see how it could happen. Later when Phil awakened he said he saw the leader dying, but that it was not a natural death. It would be a deliberate assassination to remove a leader that was becoming a threat to the overall plan.

D: *Does North Korea have atomic power?*
P: He says that is relative, depending on how you wish to define it. They have the ability to use it, however he says, in the way you are speaking, not so. At least not in the manner yet. He says from his perspective, the ability to project is not there. The warheads themselves are there, however, there is not at this time a launch vehicle.
D: *Are they a threat to the United States or the rest of the world?*
P: He says there is no need to ask such a question, for the answer is self-apparent.
D: *Could he see the possibility of going into some kind of conflict over this situation?*
P: He is showing an alignment of Venus and Mars. And says this is a marker of the time when the decision to destroy these weapons will be made. There will be a preemptive strike against those facilities which house these weapons when the two planets are aligned. That is to say, the warheads and the materials and machines for making them.
D: *I'm not an astrologer. How do you see it in the mirror?*
P: In a straight line between them.
D: *Then if we do this preemptive strike to destroy the weapons, will this lead to something more dangerous, or will that be the end of it?*
P: He says that is merely the end of one small chapter in an overall

much larger picture. That there is a proliferation which would be the cutting off of the head of one of the snakes of the hydra.

My second question dealt with Yugoslavia, or the "gray area" of Europe as Nostradamus has called it. He called it the "gray area" because you don't know if you're in Europe or Asia. In several quatrains he mentioned Macedonia and Albania, because he didn't have a name for Yugoslavia in his time. I wanted to know if the United States would be having problems with that area in the year 1994.

P: There will be an earthquake which will divide the boundaries. He says it is difficult to overlay his view of the world with our own. The boundaries are as of the sand and the wind. However, to pinpoint the area, there will be an earthquake followed by a black rain in that area in late summer, in August. He cannot see the time any better than that.

D: *But will the United States become involved in actual war, conflict, in that area?*

P: He says that has already occurred. And wonders how you know it not.

D: *You mean our people actually fighting in those areas in 1994?*

P: That is accurate.

D: *As far as we know we have not become actively involved.*

P: He says that is not the case. That there has been subversion in many areas since ... I'm seeing a picture of George Bush.

D: *Then you mean we are actually involved but the people don't know it?*

P: Yes. He says the boundaries will shift again, and they will continue to shift. The lines are not drawn permanently. The boundaries could be drawn in sand and be as permanent.

D: *Will anybody be a winner?*

P: No, not in what you would define as a winner. That is to say, peace in a peaceful state. There will be war in that area for many years yet.

D: *Will the public ever know that we are actively involved?*

P: Yes. He says that the evidence has already been presented, yet many have not recognized it for what it is. However, there will be a gradual realization that this has been going on for some time.

D: *Then it will eventually be made public?*

P: It will *become* public, not *made* public.

I then asked him about the situation in Haiti, where our troops had been sent in 1994. Our involvement in that country had been predicted in Century II-78 (Vol. II, pg. 37).

P: He says he sees this as the unwanted bastard child of democracy.

D: *That's interesting terminology. Will the United States be involved in any conflict there?*

P: He says he assumes you refer to more than that which you already have. And so will anticipate that you mean more than you have said. He says the answer then would be that there will be less rather than more of involvement, in the short term. He does not see a conflict. What he sees is a massive rescue effort. He says the island is in no position to fight. It's too broken, too poor. The conditions there will be bad because some petty men in power are trying to keep their grasp on power. They are doomed to failure from the start because of their methods. He shows me they're being pulled down off their pedestals by the people themselves. But that will cause much pain and bloodshed for them. And they will need help afterwards healing. What needs to happen is for everyone to band together and try to help them, and try to set things straight again. Because the people want nothing but to be able to live in peace. But he says this would be an insignificant event compared to that which is to be in other areas.

D: *Then it's more or less being blown out of proportion.*

P: Only to say there will be more pressing problems elsewhere which make it seem insignificant by comparison. For instance, areas in Europe, the Common Market countries which will collapse, financially speaking. There will be a collapse of the European Common Market.

D: *Can you give us any idea of a time frame?*

P: There are many influences on this event which would either preclude or include it and other events as well. There are at this time many unresolved issues which could prevent it, or perhaps worsen it. It is at this time a juncture in the time line, which is too fine to distinguish the outcome. However, there will be comets falling which will denote the onset of this event. This would be a display of many, many falling stars during the Time of Troubles. Such that the night sky will be as bright as day. He says this is the signal that the rumblings from beneath the ground will increase. That is to say, figuratively and literally. This would be an omen, not a cause.

I then asked him if his predictions about the coming Anti-Christ and the Third World War were still on target, or had we managed to forestall them or slow them down. He said there was at this point no change. The events were still formulating, but that the focused efforts of the people of the world could still lessen the impact.

After this short session Brenda arrived and the whole thing began again. Phil had never met her. He stayed for a while to watch the interview.

A few weeks after this session the President of North Korea died of a reported heart attack. This seemed natural because he was in his 80s. He was succeeded by his son who had never been taught anything about running the government. He seemed to be an ineffective wimp, exactly the type of puppet the Cabal would want to have in power in that country. The situation in North Korea had reached a crisis point, and seemed to be on the verge of exploding. We were at a crossroads and were about to attempt to destroy the nuclear weapons in North Korea, and dangerous confrontation seemed inevitable. The death of the President avoided this. Later it was found that the North Koreans did have nuclear weapons, but had not yet developed the delivery systems, just as Nostradamus had said. The new leadership has proved to be so ineffective that in the Fall of 1996 North Korea was said to be on the brink of famine.

A week after this session I was in the Dallas airport on my way to another lecture when I noticed the cover of *Time Magazine* on the newsstand. It read, "North Korea, the Headless Beast," exactly fitting Nostradamus' description of the loss of one of the snakes of the hydra.

I knew the hydra as a microscopic organism that we studied in biology. It had many arms similar to an octopus. But I found the hydra is also a creature from Greek mythology—a serpent with nine heads. Every time one head was severed, two new heads immediately appeared. The monster was eventually destroyed by Hercules.

The symbolism is clear and completely in line with Nostradamus' use of Greek mythology to code his predictions. The many arms of the hydra are joined to one body, symbolizing many parts being controlled by a central part. Signifying again that North Korea is only one of the puppets. A puppet which, in this case, had been cut off from the central, but which would be replaced by another: the regrowing of the head. Also, I wondered about the reference of its being killed by Hercules. Could this refer to Ogmios, the Celtic Hercules, who would eventually overthrow the Anti-Christ?

After her interview with Denny, Brenda laid down on the cot and we began our session. Denny wanted me to ask a few of her questions in addition to the ones I had asked Phil. I was trying to repeat the same questions so we could compare their answers. This was also the reason for not having them present for each other's interview. Brenda would have no knowledge of what Phil had said.

I used my induction technique and the keyword worked beautifully even though it had been several years since I had worked with Brenda. She, like Phil, became oblivious of the cameramen and the bright lights surrounding her as she slipped into the familiar deep trance state. She had no trouble locating Nostradamus, and he was aware that time had passed in our world since our last contact through Brenda.

B: I am speaking with Michel de Notredame. He is glad to see me. He says that as part of his talent he has a sense of the multiple layers of time. And he knows that in our time stream some time has passed since I've done this. And he's expressing pleasure with me being here to communicate.

D: *You can tell him that since we completed the interpretation of all of the quatrains that have come down to us, they have been printed in three books, and they are available now in our time period.*

B: He's nodding his head with satisfaction. He says he knew it would happen. And he says it's very good that this information is out. It needed to be. He was doing this to warn us, and to perhaps give us a chance to try to change.

I agreed to ask a few of Denny's basic questions, and I asked Nostradamus if he would mind repeating information that had already been covered.

B: He says he understands. It's like teaching a class. And when you have a new class of new students you have to go back over the same material again to get them caught up with the students who have already been there.

D: *That's true. We do know that the quatrains he wrote are in a form of code. Can he explain to people why he did this?*

B: Yes. He says you have to understand that in his time period in Europe it was a very unsettled time. A lot of economic turmoil because of the plague and people dying with diseases that no one could do anything about. And then there were the political turmoil of all the different princes and dukes and royalty wanting power for themselves. And there were also the priests, and the representatives of the church, who also wanted to wield power for themselves as well, for the sake of making the whole world be part of the church. So consequently, with all this turmoil, everyone had to conform to what was deemed acceptable. And if you tried to do other things the authorities would not like it, because it would upset their applecart, so to speak. Particularly the church authorities. And he's telling me that his talent was there as far back as he can remember. And he felt that it was a gift from God. He says there really wasn't any special talents in his family that he knew of. He thinks it may have been a particular gift given to a key individual at a particular time as it is needed. He says perhaps they agree to it before they come. At any rate, it was there. And he felt it was his duty to bring forth the information he was getting, regardless of what the authorities said. But at the same time it wouldn't do any good if he was killed right away, or imprisoned. So he put them in code so the information would be there, but they wouldn't be able to use it as direct evidence in court because they really couldn't prove anything if they decided to persecute him for it. He's saying that he wrote down what he saw. He was very truthful with that. He said it would endanger his soul to lie about what he sees in his visions. And he's saying that there are things that are going to come to pass, and there are things that have a strong likelihood of coming to pass, but the people have a chance of changing the situation, if they would but try. If people say that some of his predictions are wrong, he's not saying that he's perfect—he's human. But he says to the best of his ability he wrote down what he saw. If some of the things he has seen do not come to pass, perhaps the people were able to change the situation where they could avoid what he had seen. Also remember too, he says, that each of his quatrains has multiple applications. It's like a spiral; time and history moves in a spiral. Things work around and a similar situation comes up, but it's later on and it's a little bit different. And although one may see a situation that seems to fit a quatrain, and say, "Oh, but it didn't happen. It didn't work. The quatrain's wrong." He is saying that may not necessarily be the correct application of the quatrain. Wait until the situation comes around again a century or so down the road, and then see what happens. The visions come all the time, and having to put these things in code slows down the process somewhat. He says it's very frustrating to have to do this. And so whenever he saw a series of visions that seemed similar to each other, he would try to condense them down into one quatrain, so as to at least have the information there in some form. He says that had the situation been different at his end he would have expanded further, and perhaps written additional quatrains to cover the different situations. But that was not to be.

D: *There are many scholars in our time who think he had a message encoded in his numbering system of the centuries. What does he have to say about that?*

We had covered this in Volume One, Chapter 8 and he joked about it rather than give a direct answer. This may add additional information.

B: He says that the way he first set them down—he said he did end up going back and rearranging them to put them into a better order. If the numbers have been retained that he used, then that is part of the overall picture. He says using things like astrological congruences and numerology and various other encoding devices, that he did do this with the numbers. He says that he salutes the scholars for picking up on this. He said it was one of the things he was doing to try to slip past the Inquisition.

D: *The scholars want to know, should we pay closer attention to any clues that are hidden in the numbering arrangement?*

B: He says that would be wise. And he says you can get a sense of what kind of system he was using with the numbering, by how some of the numberings are used in the quatrains themselves. He says it's the same basic framework. Of course, it all depends on whether they are using the same numbering that he used in his day. He hopes that the numbering has been retained. He says it may be wise to trace the history of the various editions of his quatrains to make sure no editorial changes have crept in.

In Volume Three we discovered that some changes had definitely crept in when we found several quatrains that had been changed, and some that he said he did not write. Most of these discrepancies were in the Tenth Century of quatrains.

I then decided to ask some of the same questions I had asked Phil. I told him I was speaking to him from the year 1994.

B: He has a comment to make. He has tugged at his beard a bit. He said, "1994. I remember some of the quatrains I've written about that time period. I'd be willing to bet you've been having some earthquakes." (I agreed.) He says it would be wise to track the pattern of the earthquakes. Where they're occurring and when and what strength, because there is an overall pattern involved.

D: *Can he be more specific? What does he mean by a pattern?*

B: He says it's something that can be observed regarding some of his quatrains. The energies that have been generated by industry and war and such things have been disharmonious to the natural energy of the Earth, and have caused an imbalance. Consequently, as things develop in the social, economic and political spheres, there will be echoes of this in the natural world.

I asked if he was familiar with the country of North Korea.

B: He says that as a man in his time frame he is not familiar with that country. But he knows from his gift that it is an Asian country.

D: *In 1994 they are saying they have the possibility of nuclear armament. Could he see anything about that?*

B: He can try to look. (Pause) He can't get a good sense of it. He says it's like a veil or a cloudy curtain that's in the way. He feels that there may be some troubles coming up because the picture he's showing me, it's like looking down on the Earth from a high vantage point through a screen of smoke. And at various spots on the map there is a bright flash coming forth. He says he's showing me bright flashes in the Middle East, but he cannot say what the source of them are.

D: *They're afraid there might be military confrontation or warfare with the country of North Korea and the United States or the rest of the world.*

B: He feels that if one were to keep in mind the custom of the land, and try to deal accordingly, that the leader of North Korea is more bluster than anything. He feels that the major place to be cautioned about is the Middle East, for he keeps focusing on the Middle East.

I then asked him about the "gray area" of Europe, the area he had called Macedonia and Albania. I asked if he could see what was happening there in 1994.

B: He sees brother against brother. What he sees would make you weep. He says the Earth weeps. The children of the Earth should not be against each other so.

D: *Is the United States going to be involved there in the conflict?*

B: He says many people are going to be involved, particularly Europe and the United States, to try to fix the situation. And what is unfortunate is that the fixing is more like a bandage rather than a cure. They're trying to fix the outside without going to the hearts of the people. The fixing must need to be in the hearts of the people, and not just with keeping guns away from them.

Denny spoke softly to me. She wanted to know if there was anything he would like to say to the people of the United States, especially about the condition of the world in general.

B: He asks, "What aspect in particular?" There are many things happening that he has seen. There is political. There is physical. There is economic. And there are things having to do with the church. What aspect?

D: *The physical conditions. Let's try that one first.*

B: He says that things are out of balance. The energies are not in harmony, and there must be a balancing soon. The Earth cannot stand this stress much longer. He says, in general, the whole planet is in distress. She cries out. And something will have to give to help things get back into balance. He says the things that will be happening will be affecting the majority of people all over, either directly or indirectly. And he says that the weather will continue to be strange. There will be strange phenomena seen in the sky. And the ground will shake. And the ocean will rise up.

D: *What kind of strange phenomena in the sky?*

B: Flashes of light. Streaks of light. The stars ... he shows me the stars whirling around, like one is on a merry-go-round watching the stars. He says the Earth will have to ... he uses the simile of "shrugging her shoulders," to get everything settled back down and straight again.

D: *What does that refer to, in his symbolism?*

B: He says he has seen through his gift, and he is aware that your scientists know that when the Earth spins around it's not an even spin, that she wobbles around a bit as she spins. He says it's like a spinning top. It will spin almost straight for a while, and then it will do a couple of stronger flips, and then straighten up and spin evenly again after getting balanced. He says it's like being at the fair and watching the tightrope walkers. They are walking evenly, and then they start to get off balance and they have to weave around to get their balance back.

D: *What effect would that have on the Earth?*

B: He says there will be strong winds and earthquakes and storms. And he says the people of Earth will cry out in their calamity. He says that particularly people in areas that are unstable will need to be careful, because when this starts the ground will slip. And he says there's going to be physical changes to the Earth. He knows in many of his quatrains he has said that if one tried one could avoid some of these changes, regarding the political and social changes. But regarding these changes to the Earth, he's not sure what one would do to avoid them. He says it may be too late because of the disharmony caused by wars and what humans are doing to the Earth.

D: *Does he mean this one is a larger situation?*

B: It's more like an accumulative effect. Once it gets to a certain point the amount of energy it takes to undo what has been done is so much greater than letting it go ahead and work itself out. He says at this point the best one could do is continue to work for the light, and put out as much positive energy as you can. To try to lessen the effects as much as possible.

D: *One more question I want to ask you about. Is he aware of the planet Jupiter?*

B: Yes! One of the great lights in the sky.

D: *Yes. In our time, 1994, they're talking about the possibility of a large comet hitting the planet Jupiter. And they're wondering, if it does happen, will this effect Earth in any way?*

B: He says there will be effects on the Earth, because everything is connected to everything else. Physically the effects will be very subtle, at least at first. There may be some long-range effects, but not any immediate life-threatening effects or anything like that. He says the main effect it will have on Earth is regarding the higher levels of energy. He says that since everything is connected to everything else through the different levels of energy, the collision will effect everyone through the higher vibration of these energies that are put out by Jupiter. Since the planetary configurations affect people anyway, people would be wise to be aware of how Jupiter affects their horoscopes. So that they would be prepared for this calamitous event, because it will load calamitous things happening in that area of their horoscope chart.

D: *I think the people in our time are worried if it's going to affect our weather in any way, or physical Earth conditions.*

B: The effect would be similar to having some bad sunspots. The Earth has been through much worse things in the past regarding the sun and the sunspots and survived.

D: *Does he have anything to say about the economy of the U.S. or the world in general, in this year or the next year?*

B: Regarding the economy. He says that although things may appear to be all right on the surface, they're still basically unstable underneath. The premise on which the economy is based is an unsound premise. And he says it is an unsound structure. The main thing is to pray that nothing momentous or calamitous happens in regards to world events, because it would have the possibility of having a large effect on the economy. He's saying the world has become too dependent on "imaginary money." And he says, since everything's being done with futures, with possibilities—and one never knows what's going to come in the future for sure—instead of dealing with solid money, that it is like building a house on sand.

I then asked my last question about whether the predictions of the third Anti-Christ and the possibility of the Third World War were still on target, or if we had managed to change this probability.

B: The change is not widespread enough yet to be able to affect the whole world. Although things are changing, like in Europe and the United States and some other countries, the parts of the world that would be most apt to spark the trouble are the areas of the world that have changed the least. But the rest of the world needs to direct positive thoughts and positive energy. Energy for growth and change and harmony, particularly in the Middle East in general, so that it would help diffuse the negative energies building up there.

I was then getting ready to close the session when Nostradamus stopped me.

B: He says he has one more thing to add about the Middle East. He says there will be an incident regarding some sort of contamination or pollution in the Indian Ocean. And in order to keep it contained they will have to block in or to destroy the Suez Canal so that it will not spread to the Mediterranean. He says in that area of the world there will be something wrong with the ocean water and they will try to keep it contained. They will want to keep it from spreading. And he says they may have to do away with the Canal.

D: *Can he see what kind of contamination this would be?*

B: The picture that he shows is of the water changing color. He says that due to a substance in the water, or perhaps some microorganism—he does not call it this. He's showing me the picture. He had no name for it. That due to some imbalance in the water, or perhaps some radiation, or both, it becomes unbalanced and out of control. It starts multiplying rapidly and killing off the fish and plants. They must try to do something to contain it, and keep it from spreading. Apparently where it starts will be in a part of the ocean that does not have major currents, just minor ones. And they feel they will have a chance to get it under control before it gets into the major currents, because they are afraid if that happens it will be spread throughout the Earth's oceans.

D: *It starts in the Indian Ocean, you said.*
B: It's at the corner of the Indian Ocean by Arabia.
D: *And this will happen when? In our time period now?*
B: He says that it will happen soon, within the next three years or so.
D: *So that's another kind of catastrophe we will have to watch for.*

After these sessions Denny left immediately for the airport to catch her plane back to Hollywood, and the rest of the crew gathered their equipment and returned to Little Rock.

Two weeks after this session the President of North Korea died from an apparent heart attack. I called FOX studio and talked with the producer I had worked with. I told her that it appeared that the prediction had come true, but that Phil had the feeling it was not a natural death, but an assassination. She said that several psychics had also called the studio with the same impressions. I said that our information was certainly validated, because the film that was shot in Fayetteville was dated.

This interview was supposed to be shown a few months after the filming on FOX's *Encounters*. A portion of it was shown in a preview, but the interviews were omitted from the show at the last minute. I was told it was to be used later, but as far as I know it has never been shown on *Encounters*. Since 1994 I have been called to do other interviews for that network, and I asked them what happened to the film. No one seems to know, but this is understandable because their staff changes often and one person is assigned to work on one show and may know nothing about what another person is doing. It still may be shown someday, because it contained information that validates Nostradamus' ability to see the future.

IT SHOULD BE OBVIOUS that it will be impossible to keep these books updated. They are an evolving entity and continue to change as verifying information continues to come to light. It should be increasingly obvious that we are in the Time of Troubles, as seen by Nostradamus, and it is up to us to see if the worse-case scenario will continue to unfold. Those who are familiar with this material will be able to see if the subtle and seemingly small influences will affect the larger picture. I will continue to collect information from my research and my readers, and more will be added at each reprint of the trilogy. If readers already have the older editions of this book (Volume One), this addendum may be purchased separately. Contact the publisher for details.

UPDATES ON THE PROPHECIES - 1999 to 2001

In Volume III quatrain #III-48 Nostradamus referred to the beginning of the AIDS disease, and also predicted the time of its decline. "He says 15 years will elapse between the first case until a cure is found. By that time it will be comparable to the plague of his time. It will wipe out a lot of people." In 1997, due to advances in medical treatments, AIDS dropped from the top ten causes of death. It had been *15* years since the start of the disease, and in 1997 there was a 47% decline in AIDS-related deaths.

Weather changes were increasingly in the news, especially the admission (finally) that the world is warming. Nine of the hottest years in history have occurred in the last 11 years. 1998 was declared the warmest year in 500 years. The ocean waters are heating up all over the world. The temperature of the Pacific Ocean along the California coast has risen two degrees. That does not sound like much, but it is causing the death of many sea species. Creatures normally found only in the warmer southern waters are being seen in the northern waters for the first time.

The perma-frost is melting in Alaska, causing the tundra to turn into swamp where trees and plants cannot grow. It was reported that of the 27 glaciers in Europe in 1980 only 13 exist today, and they are fast receding. Three miles of ice has melted in Antarctica. As a result penguins in that area are not producing and are dying. Their main food (krill) lives in ice, and they have to swim farther to find it. These changes demonstrate that all species are interconnected all over the earth, and the demise or affliction of one affects all the rest.

Other weather changes were becoming more severe. In 1999 tornadoes were striking large cities for the first time on record. An extremely rare tornado hit Salt Lake City, and another hit Oklahoma City. That one had the highest winds ever recorded. The tornado was one mile wide, and stayed on the ground for a half hour wreaking a great deal of havoc. The extremely unusual in weather phenomenon is becoming the norm.

In September 1999 "Floyd", the largest hurricane in U.S. history hit the entire East Coast, fulfilling Nostradamus prophecy in Volume III, quatrain #VIII-16. Preparations for the coming storm caused the largest peacetime evacuation in U.S. history. Winds over 150 mph created rains up to 20" that devastated some areas, most notably North Carolina and Virginia.

In his prediction Nostradamus said that the storm would hit and cause damage to the NASA facilities at Cape Canaveral in Florida. "He says perhaps if they know far enough ahead of time they will be braced with protective measures in preparation for it." Amazingly it did not cause much damage when it went through that area. The authorities said all the space shuttles were put underground, and damage was less than expected because during the past two years buildings had been strengthened, and precautions taken against hurricanes. Maybe someone in authority finally listened to his warning. The hurricane was massive and struck the *entire* East Coast. There was less damage from winds because it moved so quickly up the coast. The worst was from the torrential rains. He said, "The waters will flood everything. The hurricane will go into the history books because it will be so large and ferocious. It will be the largest of this century." That was a very apt prediction because the storm struck at the close of the century.

My readers are a great help by supplying information that I could never find through research. A woman from Estonia sent an interesting correlation to quatrain #IV-11 in Volume II. The quatrain predicted the rise of the Tsar and the Russian aristocracy and its putdown by the Communist Party. One of the main symbols in the quatrain was the "twelve red ones" referring to the soldiers. My correspondent wrote, "Maybe I can help with the quatrain. There is a most famous Russian poem known by everybody in Russia, **TWELVE** by Alexander Block. It is about twelve red soldiers that symbolize the tragedy of the Russian revolution which killed all the aristocracy, and together with the aristocracy the entire Russian culture. Later it did lead to the death of the country. It is more than obvious that none of you have ever heard about the greatest Russian aristocratic poet Alexander Block, or about his symbolic poem **TWELVE**."

India's development of an atomic bomb in 1998 was predicted in Volume III, Page 141. Yet throughout the entire year of 1998 the only thing that consumed the news was the affair between President Bill Clinton and Monica Lewinsky. There seemed to be nothing else happening in the world as everyone focused on the testimonies and the trial. A prediction by Nostradamus in Volume III #VIII-14 seemed amazingly accurate. Part of the quatrain reads: The offense of the adulterer will become known, which will occur to his great dishonor. From the interpretation: "This seems to refer to a government figure. My first impression was the President of the United States being caught doing something unethical."

The latest news leading toward organic computers (as seen by Nostradamus in Volume I). In July 1999 the research on "quantum" computers that could be a billion times faster than Pentium III was announced. The headline read: "Beyond the PC: Atomic QC." Because the size of microchips has reached its limit, scientists have been searching for a way to process more information with smaller components. This has led to the development of the DNA computer described in the addendum. The new quantum computers will use atoms instead of chips, thus taking the science into new realms that challenge the imagination. This concept has been proven to work and the U.S. government is setting up a laboratory at Los Alamos to perfect it. "Quantum computing's starting point came when physicists realized that atoms are naturally tiny little calculators. 'Nature knows how to compute,' says MIT's Neil Gershenfeld (one of the inventors)." Closely mimicking science fiction the article stated: "Around 2030 or so, the computer on your desk might be filled with liquid instead of transistors and chips. It would employ quantum mechanics, which quickly gets into things such as teleportation and alternate universes and is, by all accounts, the weirdest stuff known to man. Quantum computing looks like an attractive option, because of its potential power and because the supply of raw material is more endless than silicon. It's the biggest untapped resource in the universe." Anyone who has read my books about UFOs and aliens knows this is the type of thing I have been writing about for twenty years. It is finally coming out of the realm of supposed "fiction" into workable reality. The incredible inventions seen by Nostradamus no longer seem impossible as we move into the millennium.

The most incredible prediction in 2000 was the fulfillment of the "hung jury election" (Volume I, #VII-41) It is so accurate that it needs no further explanation.

The saddest fulfillment of the predictions occurred on September 11, 2001, and I believe it signals the beginning of the most horrible quatrains referring to the beginning of the Third World War. Century #X-6, Volume III refers explicitly to the bombing of the Pentagon. Century #VI-97, Volume I refers to the bombing of New York, and also indicates more horror and terror to come, in the form of biological explosions. An almost humorous quatrain in worthy of mention (Volume III, #X-41) about the use of fund-raising concerts during this time period. The largest to date was the "Tribute to Heroes" broadcast September 21, 2001 on 27 networks.

I do not know if further updates will be added, unless it is something extraordinary. My readers will find incredible accuracy in all three volumes. The future is truly upon us, and sadly it appears that we are in the midst of the Time of Troubles and the entry into the Third World War. We can only do what Nostradamus suggested and use the power of our minds to neutralize or lessen the effects.

Index

A complete index for all three volumes of *Conversations with Nostradamus* will appear at the end of Volume Three.

A complete index and quatrain index for all three volumes of
Conversations with Nostradamus *appear at the end of Volume Three.*

Quatrain Index

A *complete index for the quatrains in all three volumes of* Conversations with Nostradamus *will appear at the end of Volume Three.*

About the Author

$\mathcal{D}$OLORES CANNON was born in 1931 in St. Louis, Missouri. She was educated and lived in Missouri until her marriage in 1951 to a career Navy man. She spent the next 20 years traveling all over the world as a typical Navy wife and raised her family.

In 1968 she had her first exposure to reincarnation via regressive hypnosis when her husband, an amateur hypnotist, stumbled across the past life of a woman he was working with who had a weight problem. At that time the "past life" subject was unorthodox and very few people were experimenting in the field. It sparked her interest, but had to be put aside as the demands of family life took precedence.

Photo by Richard Quick.

In 1970 her husband was discharged as a disabled veteran, and they retired to the hills of Arkansas. She then started her writing career and began selling her articles to various magazines and newspapers. When her children began lives of their own, her interest in regressive hypnosis and reincarnation was reawakened. She studied the various hypnosis methods and thus developed her own unique technique which enabled her to gain the most efficient release of information from her subjects. Since 1979 she has regressed and cataloged information gained from hundreds of volunteers. She calls herself a regressionist and a psychic researcher who records "lost" knowledge. The *Conversations with Nostradamus* trilogy are her first published books. *Jesus and the Essenes* has been published by Gateway Books in England. She has written eight other books (to be published) about her most interesting cases.

Dolores Cannon has four children and twelve grandchildren who demand that she be solidly balanced between the "real" world of her family and the "unseen" world of her work. If you wish to correspond with Dolores Cannon about her work, you may write to her at the following address. Please enclose a self-addressed stamped envelope for her reply.

Dolores Cannon, P.O. Box 754
Huntsville, AR 72740-0754

Books by Dolores Cannon

Conversations with Nostradamus, Volume I
Conversations with Nostradamus, Volume II
Conversations with Nostradamus, Volume III
Between Death and Life
Jesus and the Essenes
Keepers of the Garden
A Soul Remembers Hiroshima
The Legend of Starcrash
They Walked with Jesus
Legacy from the Stars

Conversations with Nostradamus is available
in abridged form on audio tape cassette.

For more information about any
of the above titles, write to:

OZARK
MOUNTAIN
PUBLISHERS

P.O. Box 754
Huntsville, AR 72740-0754

Wholesale Inquiries Welcome